Galloping at Everything

GALLOPING AT EVERYTHING

THE BRITISH CAVALRY IN THE PENINSULAR WAR AND AT WATERLOO, 1808–15

A Reappraisal

by

Ian Fletcher

SPELLMOUNT

Dedicated to the memory
of Jack Slade and William Erskine,
two madmen on horseback

British Library Cataloguing in Publication Data:
A catalogue record for this book is available
from the British Library

Copyright © Ian Fletcher 1999, 2008
ISBN 978 1 86227 419 8

This paperback edition first published
in the UK in 2008 by
Spellmount Limited
Cirencester Road, Chalford
Stroud, Gloucestershire. GL6 8PE
www.spellmount.com

Spellmount Limited is an imprint of NPI Media Group

1 3 5 7 9 8 6 4 2

The right of Ian Fletcher to be identified
as the author of this work has been asserted by him
in accordance with the Copyright, Designs
and Patents Act 1988

Typesetting and origination by NPI Media Group
Printed in Great Britain

Contents

List of Maps

List of Plates

1. Arthur Wellesley, 1st Duke of Wellington.
2. William Carr Beresford. Noted for his reorganisation of the Portuguese army in the Peninsula, he was, nevertheless, less than able on occasion, notably at Albuera. He was also one of the central figures of the fight at Campo Mayor.
3. John Gaspard le Marchant. One of the most influential soldiers of his day, he was killed at Salamanca, 22 July 1812.
4. Henry, Lord Paget, one of the great cavalry commanders. His affair with Wellington's sister-in-law barred him from serving with Wellington's army in the Peninsula, although as Lord Uxbridge, he commanded the Allied cavalry at Waterloo with great skill.
5. Stapleton Cotton, later Lord Combermere. He possessed none of Paget's flair and dash but proved Wellington's most reliable cavalry commander.
6. John 'Black Jack' Slade. Generally considered to be one of the more inept cavalry commanders in the Peninsula, he was responsible for the debacle at Maguilla.
7. Robert Ballard Long, an underrated cavalry commander and one of the central figures of the fight at Campo Mayor.
8. Trumpet Major William Wheldon, 13th Light Dragoons, one of the great Peninsular War cavalry regiments. Wheldon was Lord Hill's orderly trumpeter during the later stages of the Peninsular War. He is seen here wearing his Waterloo medal.
9. Colonel Taylor, 20th Light Dragoons, killed in action at Vimeiro, 21 August 1808.
10. Sir Hussey Vivian. He served with distinction in the Peninsula and at Waterloo.
11. Loftus Otway, who commanded the Portuguese squadrons during the fight at Campo Mayor.
12. Colonel Peter Hawker, 14th Light Dragoons. He fought at Oporto and was wounded at Talavera.

13. Lt Col Henry Webster, 9th Light Dragoons. A good depiction of a Peninsular War cavalry commander, complete with Marmaluke sabre.
14. Private, 1st (Royal) Dragoons, one of the most distinguished of Peninsular and Waterloo cavalry regiments. This picture shows the uniform worn at Waterloo.
15. An unknown officer of the King's Dragoon Guards, 1812.
16. Officer, 6th Inniskilling Dragoons, *c.* 1811. The regiment saw no service in the Peninsula but this is a good depiction of the sort of uniform worn by heavy dragoons in Portugal and Spain with their unusual watering cap.
17. A private of the 7th Hussars on patrol in the Peninsula.
18. A fine study of a 15th Hussar, *c.* 1810.
19. Paget's hussars charge at Sahagun, 21 December 1808.
20. They repeat the exercise at Benavente eight days later. Both actions were fought during the ill-fated Corunna campaign of Sir John Moore.
21. 10th Hussars on patrol during the Corunna campaign.
22. The same regiment skirmishing, also during the Corunna campaign.
23. The 23rd Light Dragoons come to grief in the dry watercourse at Talavera, 29 July 1809.
24. Corporal Logan kills Colonel Chamourin of the 26th Dragoons at Campo Mayor, 25 March 1811. Logan is depicted wearing the later 1812 pattern uniform.
25. The battlefield of Campo Mayor, as seen from just outside the town. The 13th Light Dragoons charged over the hills to the left of the picture, whilst Beresford halted the heavy dragoons by the side of the road in the foreground.
26. The bridge at Usagre, where Lumley's heavy dragoons 'chastised' their French opponents.
27. The scene of the fight at Villar de Puerco, 11 July 1810. Gouache and his infantry formed square in this field successfully to repulse attacks by British light dragoons.
28. Light dragoons gathering intelligence in the Peninsula. A fine illustration of the sort of work which occupied them for a great deal of their time on campaign.
29. A superb study of a light dragoon on patrol in the Peninsula. This very accurate painting is a wonderful depiction of a cavalryman on active service.
30. The scene of the fight at Villagarcia. Le Marchant and the 5th Dragoon Guards charged out of the olive groves away to the right of this photo before engaging the French across the plain.
31. Maguilla, showing the broken ground and river in front of the village where Slade was brought up by Lallemand's reserves.

Introduction

It is the afternoon of 18 June 1815 and the place is the bloody, muddy field of Waterloo. A massive infantry attack has just been launched by over 15,000 French troops of D'Erlon's I Corps against the left centre of Wellington's Anglo-Dutch army. Napoleon's Grand Battery of over seventy guns has done its job of softening up the Allied infantry and now it is all up to the French infantry, struggling gamely but resolutely up the slopes towards their objective. As they get to within thirty paces of the Allied infantry they halt and open fire, driving back their adversaries, slowly but steadily, until they themselves are brought to a standstill by veteran British infantry, thrust forward by their divisional commander, Sir Thomas Picton, himself a veteran of countless actions in the Iberian Peninsula. Deep within the dense French columns the sense of exhilaration turns to impatience, then to anxiety and then...panic and bewilderment. French troops are falling everywhere, and falling fast. Those at the head of the column are literally cut down where they stand whilst at the rear of the column the men begin to stream away like sand through an hour glass. But it is not the firepower of the British line that has inflicted such pain and panic on the French. No, it is something equally powerful and just as destructive – a full-blooded charge by 2,000 heavy British cavalry. These two brigades, the Household Brigade and the Union Brigade, will wreak so much havoc upon D'Erlon's corps – some 2,000 killed and wounded, 3,000 prisoners and two Imperial eagles are among the haul – that, for the remainder of the afternoon, Napoleon will never again attack in any serious fashion against that part of Wellington's main line. And yet up on the ridge of Mont St Jean the Commander-in-Chief of the Anglo-Dutch army, the Duke of Wellington, watches with a mixture not of joy and satisfaction but of horror, frustration and probably an overwhelming sense of *déja vu*. True, he is mightily relieved at having seen off the first real French infantry attack to be thrown against him, but it is one which has left him seriously bereft of cavalry for the remainder of the day as a result of the heavy casualties inflicted upon the Household and Union Brigades during their successful charge.

It must have seemed to Wellington like a return to the bad old days in Spain and Portugal when it appeared to be almost impossible for his cavalry to achieve anything substantial without subsequently pressing the self-destruct button and undoing all of their previous good work, a malaise which set in from the very outset of the war in the Peninsula. Indeed, at Vimeiro on 21 August 1808, his first major battle was marked by a cavalry charge by the 20th Light Dragoons which saw the regiment lose its commander in a rash gallop into enemy lines in pursuit of beaten infantry. It was a trend that was to continue on and off through the war, which lasted from 1808 to 1814, and which has left the British cavalry with a reputation of being 'mere brainless gallopers'.

But is this the true picture, and should we not search for the reasons that this reputation, undeserved in my opinion, was acquired? I certainly think so, for I believe the poor reputation of the British cavalry in the Peninsula is a false one, based upon a handful of very high-profile misadventures, such as Vimeiro, Talavera and Maguilla, for each of which there at least twice the number of shining successes, some major and some minor – which often get overlooked. Indeed, even these misadventures can in part be explained and, upon further examination, be seen in their true light, as we shall discover when we look at Campo Mayor, for example, to see what really happened. Furthermore, there is much day-to-day operational work, such as patrols, intelligence gathering, escort work and foraging, at which British cavalry excelled. True, there were occasions when piquets were taken prisoner or when units were beaten in small combats, but that is the business of war and it is a very fortunate commander who finds himself at the head of an army which never tastes the flavour of misfortune or mishap. Wellington's British cavalry proved more than adept at piquet work, at the gathering and transmission of intelligence, on forage and escort duties and on the field of battle where they forced their much vaunted and supposedly superior opponents to run on dozens of occasions. In fact, on the field of combat, there is hardly a single instance of a British cavalry unit being punished in the same manner that they themselves punished the French. No, not even Maguilla – the 'unluckiest combat of the war' according to Oman. We shall also discover how the performance of the cavalry, as compared to the British infantry, suffered as a result of their very low numbers, of a lack of good cavalry campaigning country and from the lack of a decent overall and consistent cavalry commander. We shall also see how the majority of the successes achieved by British cavalry in the Peninsula were won when Wellington himself was not present, the conclusion being that his mistrust of his cavalry was great enough for him to rely heavily on his wonderful British and Portuguese infantry.

Although this book is a reappraisal of the performance and reputation of the British cavalry, it is also a reappraisal of historians such as Sir

Charles Oman, whose treatment of the cavalry has generally been followed, sometimes blindly, by successive historians. Oman's conclusions, which I think are often erroneous, have been very influential over the years and, appearing as they did in his momentous work, *History of the Peninsular War*, it is little wonder that they have rarely been challenged. And yet they frequently differ enormously from the conclusions of Oman's great contemporary, Sir John Fortescue, whose own magnum opus, *The History of the British Army*, often takes third place behind the works of Oman and Napier, author of the third, very influential work, *The War in the Peninsula*. Fortescue and Oman differed on many occasions, particularly in their treatment of the British cavalry, but the former's verdict on such important episodes such as Campo Mayor, for example, is invariably overlooked. As a result, Oman's has generally been the version followed by historians who have not really bothered to investigate the episode properly for themselves. Hence, Oman's conclusion, incorrect in my view, and his damning verdict on the British cavalry have been perpetuated. Indeed, Rory Muir, author of the recent *Tactics and Experience of Battle in the Age of Napoleon*, actually goes so far as to state that Campo Mayor was a famous defeat for the British cavalry, which is a quite incredible statement but is typical of historians who fail to see beyond the Oman view.

It should be said from the outset that this book is devoted entirely to the study of Wellington's British cavalry and not that of his German allies, the superb and ever-reliable King's German Legion who were not, however, without their own faults. These worthies emerged from the campaign in the Peninsula with a reputation second-to-none. Indeed, the difference between the British and their KGL comrades can best be summed up by that most astute of observers, John Kincaid, of the 95th Rifles, It was Kincaid, who spent many a month working at the outposts with both British and KGL cavalry, who said, 'If we saw a British dragoon at any time approaching in full speed, it excited no great curiosity among us, but whenever we saw one of the first hussars [KGL] coming on at the gallop it was high time to gird on our swords and bundle up.' The KGL had their low points as well as their highs but this is not their story, nor is it the story of either the Portuguese or Spanish cavalry which fell under Wellington's command.

The writing of this book has involved several individuals whom I would like to thank. Timothy Edwards, Richard Old and David Chantler (not to be confused with the eminent historian, as is often the case!) all loaned me items from their own very extensive collections of Peninsular and Waterloo literature, for which I am extremely grateful. David, in fact, was a great help, offering opinions and views on a variety of cavalry related subjects in addition to the actual structuring of the book at a stage when things were slacking off. David was also a companion, along with Richard Old, John Seabrook, Hugh Macdonald-Buchanan and John

Strecker – who can claim a relative in the 9th Light Dragoons who, we believe, was at Arroyo dos Molinos during Hill's raid in October 1811 – on several trips to the Peninsula and to Waterloo, following the fortunes of Wellington's cavalry. There is nothing like actually seeing the ground in order get a wider appreciation of the problems faced by the cavalry and our travels took us to all of the locations featured in this book, including several hours up and down the motorway in search of the battlefield of Venta del Pozo whilst Maguilla was likewise a difficult fight to follow, particularly as there are no maps – as far as I am aware – of these actions. The majority of the battlefields are, however, both well documented and in good condition and picking our way through the olive groves above Villagarcia and Campo Mayor, or walking across the fields at Salamanca, Sahagun and Morales, certainly brought us closer to Le Marchant, Long, Cotton, Paget and comrades. I must also thank David Grant for reading the manuscript and for running his red pen through it. My good friend, Philip Haythornthwaite, was also kind enough to supply both pictures and some contemporary newspaper cuttings from his vast collection, for which I thank him.[*] Sir Charles Oman's piece on the organisation of the army, which was printed in his *Wellington's Army 1809–1814*, was most useful and I thank Lionel Leventhal, of Greenhill Books, who reprinted the work in 1986, for allowing me to reproduce the cavalry element of it. The staff of Las Haras in Tarbes, France, were also very helpful during two visits in 1999. The farm was set up by Napoleon in 1806 to produce horses for his light cavalry, and the staff were most helpful in answering questions relating to the breeding, care and feeding of horses, in addition to showing me examples of early saddles. Sue Fletcher (no relation!), of HM Collection, Windsor, was kind enough to seek out the wonderful Dighton painting of Sergeant Charles Ewart, taking the 'eagle' of the 45th Regiment at Waterloo, and I thank Her Majesty the Queen for giving me her gracious permission to use it on the cover of this book.

Finally, I must thank my long-suffering publisher, Jamie Wilson, for his support and his patience in waiting for the manuscript to be delivered. I am sure there were times when he must have thought that, far from galloping at everything, the project was, in fact, limping to nowhere. Thanks.

Ian Fletcher
Rochester

---

[*] Brian Ambler very kindly loaned me the Hartley Mss.

PART ONE
The British Cavalry

CHAPTER I

Officers and Men

If the tough topographical nature of the Iberian Peninsula had a major impact on the performance of Wellington's cavalry by way of the strict limitations imposed upon it, then the lack of an outstanding and consistent cavalry commander was as keenly felt. Indeed, it ranks as one of the main and most obvious reasons behind the inconsistency of the British cavalry.

Wellington's senior cavalry commander in the Peninsula was Stapleton Cotton, later Lord Combermere, who had seen service in the Netherlands, South Africa and India.[1] By no means brilliant, Cotton, who was born in 1773, was by far the most consistent cavalry commander, a man who commanded Wellington's cavalry from June 1810 until the end of the war, save for a spell of leave in 1811, and from July to October 1812 following his wounding at the Battle of Salamanca. In fact, Cotton returned to England again in December 1812 and did not return to the Peninsula until 25 June 1813. Cotton's traits were reliability and obedience to Wellington, rather than brilliance and genius. He was a man to be trusted in most situations and can best be described as a good team player, qualities which, in Wellington's army, were of great importance. The drawback to this was that he lacked the brilliance of either Paget or Le Marchant, and as a consequence the cavalry was not able to continue in the pattern set by the former at Sahagun and Benavente. Indeed, it was rather like the situation in the Light Division under Robert Craufurd and, after his death, Charles Alten. Craufurd was a brilliant but controversial leader who led his division to many a great deed. He was, however, a man who was prone to errors of judgement and over enthusiasm, something which often drove Wellington to despair. The situation changed dramatically after Craufurd's death when Alten was placed in command. Here, Wellington had a divisional commander upon whom he could rely, a man who would not risk his division or take chances no matter what the circumstances. The down side to this was that the Light Division would never again shine as gloriously as it did under Craufurd and, although it achieved many further glories, particularly in southern France, the division was never quite the same after Craufurd's death. Similarly, Cotton lacked the brilliance of Henry, Lord Paget, whose flair and dash in the true style of a hussar was sadly missed after his departure from the Peninsula in 1809. However, Cotton was Wellington's type of commander, someone who adhered strictly to his orders and rarely strayed from them. Hence, when Napoleon escaped from Elba to spark off the Waterloo campaign, it was Cotton whom Wellington requested to command the cavalry. The Duke of York overruled Wellington, however, and so Cotton missed out.

It is quite ironic that two of the finest cavalry commanders the British Army possessed were present in the Peninsula for a frustratingly short time. The two commanders in question are Paget and John Gaspard Le Marchant, two soldiers who have attained almost legendary status in the history of the British Army in the Peninsula. They had vastly different reasons for their premature departure from the Peninsular War, Paget being *persona non grata* with the army after eloping with Wellington's sister-in-law, whilst Le Marchant met a hero's death at the Battle of Salamanca in July 1812. Although Le Marchant served only as commander of the Heavy Brigade – command of the cavalry as a whole resting with Stapleton Cotton – there is little doubt that his influence, ingenuity and knowledge of cavalry in general would have had a tremendous effect on the British cavalry in the Peninsula.

When the British Army arrived in the Peninsula in 1808 there were so few cavalry – just 240 – that an overall cavalry commander was not required. However, when Sir John Moore assumed command of the army the cavalry, consisting of the 7th, 10th, 15th and 18th Hussars and the 3rd Light Dragoons KGL, was placed under the command of Henry, Lord Paget.[2] Born in 1768, Paget was Colonel of the 7th Hussars, a rank he had held since 1797 when the regiment was still a light dragoon regiment. He had seen action in the Netherlands in 1794–5 and in the Helder campaign of 1799, although there was little scope for the sort of cavalry action which he craved. However, it was the years 1797 and 1798 that were perhaps of greater importance when he strove to introduce much needed improvements throughout the cavalry. It is quite a coincidence that he was helped enormously in this work by Le Marchant, who was serving in the same regiment, and of whom we shall speak later. Paget's reforms did not stop with the organisation of the cavalry but extended to the tools of their trade. The Paget Cavalry Carbine was standard issue for light cavalry during the Napoleonic Wars and was a carbine which Paget himself had designed with Henry Nock, the celebrated gunmaker. Paget commanded the British cavalry during the Corunna campaign and led them to two notable triumphs, at Benavente and Sahagun. It will always remain one of the great 'what ifs' of our military history when we consider what Paget might have achieved had he been allowed to return to the Peninsula. Unfortunately, his relationship with Wellington's sister-in-law made this impossible, although he did serve during the Waterloo campaign in 1815. Even here, however, Paget's abilities have been called into question. Indeed, commenting on his performance during the Waterloo campaign, Michael Glover wrote, 'The short campaign showed how fortunate it was that he had never commanded the cavalry in the Peninsula.'[3] A little harsh, perhaps, although Paget, then Lord Uxbridge, did admit to making mistakes at Waterloo. We shall evaluate his performance in the chapter on the campaign, later in this book.

The second – and potentially greatest – cavalry commander in Wellington's army, was John Gaspard Le Marchant, a comrade of Lord Paget's and, like him, a great innovator and a man who brought about some of the most significant changes in the British cavalry of the late 18th and early 19th centuries.[4] Le Marchant was born in 1766 and had served in the Flanders campaign of 1793–4. It was as a result of many observations made during this campaign that Le Marchant set to work to put right some of the ills afflicting the British Army – and the cavalry in particular – at the end of the 18th century. These included the introduction of the famous sword drill for use throughout the cavalry, along with a new light cavalry sabre to go with it. We know he also submitted a design for a new heavy cavalry sword but this was never taken up and, instead, a sword based upon an Austrian model was introduced. But perhaps his most significant and lasting plan was for a military college for officers which, in 1799, was finally set up at High Wycombe and which was the forerunner of the Royal Military Academy at Sandhurst. Le Marchant did not arrive in the Peninsula until 1811, but whilst he was busy in England between 1808 and his arrival in the theatre of war, he could console himself that his drill and his light cavalry sabre were working to great advantage in combats throughout Spain and Portugal. It is a great pity that Le Marchant's spell of duty lasted such a short time but at least he demonstrated, in two very successful actions, what he could achieve at the head of his cavalry, first at Villagarcia and then, on 22 July 1812, at the Battle of Salamanca, where his heavy cavalry destroyed eight French infantry battalions in the greatest demonstration of the power of heavy cavalry the war had seen.

Any analysis of Cotton, Paget and Le Marchant will invariably suggest the same conclusion, that they were all very good at their job, as their respective services demonstrate. Indeed, the sight of Cotton and Paget serving together at Waterloo would have been truly wonderful and, in fact, it might have actually happened had not Wellington's request for Cotton been denied. The realms of fantasy could be extended even further by imagining the sight of all three of these great soldiers – had Le Marchant lived long enough – fighting side by side at Waterloo. One wonders just what they would have accomplished together. But it was not to be. The respective achievements of Cotton, Paget and Le Marchant are not in doubt, but much of the real interest in Wellington's cavalry lies with other British cavalry commanders, and in particular two whose exploits put the cavalry firmly under the spotlight and who led the cavalry at the two most infamous incidents of the war, Campo Mayor and Maguilla.

The first of these was Robert Ballard Long, who commanded the cavalry at the fight at Campo Mayor on 25 March 1811.[5] Long attracted much criticism in the Peninsula, and still does today, mainly because of his part in the affair, something which we will put right later in this book. But, of course, one had to see much service in order to attract such attention and Long, to his credit, did in the Peninsula, particularly in the south during 1811 and 1812. Although Long commanded his brigade and, for that matter, Beresford's entire cavalry, for long periods, during which it turned in a thoroughly workmanlike performance, it is Campo Mayor that has been a slur on his reputation ever since, with all but a few historians holding him responsible. Hopefully, that will change. Born in 1771, Long was highly regarded by his men, particularly for his training methods and matters relating to the internal discipline of the 15th Hussars immediately prior to the Peninsular War. He enrolled in the Royal Military College, where Le Marchant was one of its directors, and in 1803 became Lieutenant Colonel of the 2nd Dragoon Guards in Ireland during a difficult two-year period. William Tale, of the 15th Hussars, recalled many anecdotes concerning Long when the latter was in command of the regiment – then still the 15th Light Dragoons – all of which paint a very positive portrait of Long as 'kind and persuasive... highly accomplished gentleman and thorough-bred soldier.'[6] Tale went on to write, 'The untiring energy of Colonel Long was no less effective in accomplishing other reforms inseparable from the formation of the fully-instructed hussar – whether as regards the barrack-room, the stable, the menage, the drill, and the ultimatum – the field, on all which points his instructions were inimitable.'[7] Perhaps Tale's most important judgement was reserved for last. 'The creditable and efficient manner in which the regiment made the Peninsular campaign, was not slightly attributable to the excellent instructions of Colonel Long.'[8] The fact that Long was much liked by his men can be borne out by the fact that they called him 'Bobby Long.'[9] Long's greatest failing was his inability to resist complaining. He appears to have got into arguments with virtually all of those around him, save for Rowland Hill, with whom it seems to have been impossible to fall out. The dispute between Long and Beresford that followed the fall-out over the Campo Mayor business continued long after the war had ended and even after Long's death.

Cotton, Le Marchant, Paget and Long were the most prominent cavalry commanders in the Peninsula but there were other very reliable cavalry-men, such as William Lumley, essentially an infantry officer, and George Anson. There were also those who proved to be very disappointing, such as William Erskine and, somewhat famously, Jack Slade. Erskine was gen-erally regarded as being mad and in fact committed suicide in Lisbon in

April 1813 by throwing himself out of a window. It is somewhat surprising, therefore, that when Wellington appointed Erskine as head of Beresford's cavalry in southern Spain in April 1811, he declared Erskine the best choice. 'You will find him more intelligent and useful than anybody you have. He is very blind, which is against him at the cavalry, but very cautious.'[10] Given the fact that the despatch was written just a month after Long's action at Campo Mayor, it is not surprising that 'cautious' was a quality Wellington warmed to, despite the fact that Erskine was considered almost blind. What an indictment of British cavalry commanders! Erskine needed little time to demonstrate his many failings. He had already bodged the operation at Sabugal on 3 April 1811, and during the coming year would again show his ineptitude at Almaraz and during the escape of the garrison of Almeida. In fact, by July 1812 things had become so bad that Wellington was moved to write, 'It would likewise be necessary to supersede Sir William Erskine, upon whose sanity, I am sorry to say, much reliance cannot be placed. He deprived us of many of the advantages which would have resulted from Sir Rowland Hill's expedition to the Tagus in May, and it is impossible to trust to his judgement in any critical case.'[11]

Slade, on the other hand, whilst not being mad (although one of his sobriquet's was 'Mad Jack'), proved to be a most controversial cavalry commander. He is universally criticised both by historians and by his contemporaries. Slade first came to prominence for his eccentric behaviour during the Corunna campaign of 1808–9. At Sahagun, the arrival of the 10th Hussars was delayed, fortunately not crucially, owing to his now-infamous 'Blood and Slaughter!' speech. He appears to have been a man who, if he could, would avoid action and even basic staff work. He 'let no possible opportunity of inaction pass him – pretending not to comprehend orders, which the events passing before him would have made comprehensible to a trumpeter – complaining that his hands were tied, and letting the opportunity slip – a curse to the cause, and a disgrace to the service.'[12] He was even censured by the Adjutant General for forgetting to submit returns in spite of repeated requests. The most serious mistake committed by Slade was almost certainly the erosion of morale throughout his brigade between 1811 and 1812 which manifested itself, this time crucially, at Maguilla, an episode which we shall examine in a later chapter. The lack of confidence in his leadership was the most damning side of his service in the Peninsula and yet he served in Wellington's army from 1809 until mid-1813. Have historians been harder on the man than is really deserved? After all, it is difficult to imagine any officer displaying the sort of ineptitude universally attributed to Slade surviving for so long in such a successful army. Was there more to Slade's abilities as a cavalry commander than we actually give him credit for? I suspect not and, in fact, it probably says more about Wellington's inability to rid himself of inept officers.

By the end of the Peninsular War the British cavalry could count in its number some very efficient cavalry officers with a vast amount of experience between them. Among them were Colquhoun Grant, not to be confused with Wellington's head of intelligence, Sir Hussey Vivian, Sir John Vandeleur, Sir William Ponsonby and Lord Edward Somerset. These cavalry officers had all served with distinction in the Peninsula, although they experienced contrasting fortunes at Waterloo. There were others, regimental commanders and officers, too numerous to name, who served throughout the Peninsular War where the learning curve had at times been very steep. The cumulative result, however, was a vital contribution to the Allied victory in the Peninsula and at Waterloo.

One of the alleged great failings of the British military system of the late 18th and early 19th century, and indeed throughout its history, has been the purchase system, whereby rich officers were allowed to purchase for themselves a higher rank, regardless of experience. It was a system which caused scores of officers much grief, officers who, despite having a wealth of experience, lacked the necessary funds to obtain further steps in promotion. For example, the early career of Robert Craufurd, to name just one famous and gifted officer, was stunted because of the system. Lacking sufficient funds, Craufurd was forced to suffer the 'conspiracy of mediocrity' as less gifted but wealthier officers, 'uneducated fops', were promoted over his head. The system is frequently condemned for denying good officers promotion whilst allowing idiots to prosper but this is not always the case and, as an example, we may cite possibly the greatest soldier Britain has ever produced, Wellington himself, whose career prospered as a result of the purchase system. It is a subject which demands much closer analysis, more than can be allowed in this book, but there are a few points which concern us that should be addressed here.

The main attack on the purchase system has been that it allowed inexperienced and unqualified men to attain positions of high command. Hence, whilst the French Army enjoyed command by officers who generally gained promotion through their ability, Britain's army boasted fewer generals of equal ability. One notable historian has written, 'while the general standard of the British officer corps was well below that of the French, a minority of officers was so good as to be able to carry the rest at least under a general of Wellington's calibre.'[13] Given the success of Wellington's army, it is somewhat difficult to reconcile the above statement with fact. Indeed, this 'minority' must have been very good to have carried the rest of the army with it to victory. The statement, whilst heading in the right direction, is ultimately lost in a tide of hard fact. Wellington's army, though admittedly containing many uneducated officers, did, nevertheless, contain a very high proportion of first-rate regimental officers who, whilst not achieving great fame, went about their business effectively, gaining experience as they did so, to provide Wellington with the nuts and bolts of an outstanding military machine, one whose performance at the Battle of the Nivelle in November 1813, prompted Wellington to write afterwards, 'it is probably the most complete machine for its numbers now existing in Europe.'[14] High praise for an army allegedly consisting of many inept officers carried along by a few of high calibre. Ultimately, I would suggest that too much is made of the defects and merits of the purchase system. Also, there is too little evidence to show that officers who 'bought their way up' were, in fact, unfit for service. Michael Glover, in his *Wellington's Army in the Peninsula, 1808–1814*, has shown that by far the greater percentage of promotions by purchase occurred in the cavalry, the average number between 1810 and 1813 being 45.1% as against 17.7% in the infantry.[15] The inference that the cavalry therefore contained a potentially greater number of officers unfit for command is not made, although we do find another historian citing this as a reason for the ineptitude of Wellington's cavalry. Indeed, in quoting Glover's figures, we find him writing, 'the figures are most revealing and, perhaps, best explain why the infantry was more reliable in battle than the cavalry. With a purchase rate over two and one-half times greater than the infantry, the cavalry was led by men with far less professional experience than their infantry counterparts; and when one considers that almost two-thirds of the officers entered the service with absolutely no military training, it is not surprising that the cavalry often went astray.'[16] Again, there is no evidence to suggest that officers who bought their way up were inept. Also, the overwhelming proportion of purchases in the cavalry between 1810 and 1813 were within the lower ranks, with just 7% being from major to lieutenant colonel. Given that it was officers of these ranks who commanded the cavalry the theory that the cavalry were led by officers unqualified to command is flawed.

Another popular myth concerns the status of cavalry officers. Despite requiring considerable funds to maintain their position in the regiment, the majority of cavalry officers were not members of the aristocracy. A similar myth surrounds the three regiments of Foot Guards, for although over a third of all the titled officers in the British Army were to be found in the Foot Guards, the majority of them were from the landed gentry or were the sons of professionals, merchants and tradesmen.[17] A similar situation was to be found in the cavalry. At Waterloo, the entire British cavalry corps could boast just one peer, thirteen sons of peers, seventeen sons of baronets, two knights, one son of a knight, one Italian prince, one Hanoverian baron, and one son of a German countess.[18] This is hardly what one might term an aristocratic assembly. The overwhelming majority of cavalry officers came from the classes named above, such as the landed gentry or professional classes.

There is little doubt that many cavalry officers lacked any knowledge whatsoever of the basic principles of command and control, but was this a failing of the purchase system or simply a flaw in the methods of training? It is clear that many officers came to the command of cavalry regiments without any knowledge of their craft but not all of these arrived in the Peninsula. Sadly, there were some notorious cases involving hapless idiots who did serve in Spain, like Major Camac, of the 1st Life Guards. After having arrived in the Peninsula in late 1812, Camac was exposed as a thoroughly inept officer, unable to get his regiment to perform the simplest of manoeuvres. Shortly after the regiment's arrival at Lisbon in December 1812, Major General Rebow asked Camac to change front to the rear by inwards wheel-about-wheel of half-squadrons upon the centre. Apparently, Camac, unable to even begin the movement, rode about in front of the regiment, totally confused, his ignorance apparent to all. After being shown the correct manner to perform it, Camac attempted to perform the manoeuvre himself on the beach but only succeeded in getting his men to wheel out into the sea.[19] Curiously enough, when Colonel Gordon was requested by Rebow to inspect the regiments of Life Guards he could find no fault. 'The men and horses appeared to me in very good condition generally, and perfectly equipped for the field, and that in the military appearance of the regiments no fault could be found. The officer of the 1st Regiment under Major Camac offered no difficulty.'[20] When he inspected the 2nd Life Guards, however, it was a different story. 'Lieutenant-Colonel Barton of the 2nd Regiment was full of difficulties... as relating wholly and solely to the interior economy of the respective troops; and this officer appeared to me not only to be wholly uninformed of the most common duties of regimental service, but to be wanting in those exertions which your Lordship has a right to demand from every officer serving under you... I hear he has resigned, as well as some of his officers; and I hope it may be so.'[21] As further proof of Barton's ineptitude, Gordon went on to point out that the regiment had left England without several staff officers including the Veterinary Surgeon and Paymaster. Fortunately, officers like Camac and Barton were few and far between and even those with similarly scant experience learned in time to undergo basic manoeuvres although, as we shall see, some of the most important tasks, such as patrol and piquet work, had to be learned 'on the job' as there were no regulations relating to these most important tasks in the current regulation manuals.

The other ranks came from all walks of life. The impression that most recruits for the cavalry entered the army with some experience of horses is a false one. In fact, their backgrounds were not dissimilar to the infantry as were their motives for joining. Debt, bad masters, unemployment, the quest for perceived glory, regular food and wages; these were the usual reasons for joining His Majesty's army. Men had enlisted in the army for years, and would continue to do so for the same reasons. The men who joined to fight under Marlborough at Blenheim and Ramillies did so for much the same reason that their descendants would do in 1914. The prospect of having a number of men, plus a system, looking to their welfare was a great incentive to those faced with unemployment, and there was never a shortage of volunteers prepared to accept the King's shilling. The men of 1914 may have been more enlightened than their redcoated ancestors but their reasoning was, nevertheless, the same. Indeed, the suggestion that the men of 1914 enlisted to thrash the 'Hun' is now considered to be something of a myth. Unemployment was equally high in 1914 but the army's system was even more highly developed with a much larger number of support troops to look after the well-being of the fighting man at the front. King George's men were no different, save for the fact that once they had enlisted it was normally for a term of what amounted to life, with nothing but a painful death on the battlefield to terminate one's service. But the incentive of a most handsome bounty was too tempting to resist for many a poverty-stricken man. Indeed, £23 17s 6d bounty, payable in 1812, was a fair fortune for the average farm worker or labourer.[22]

Pay was also an incentive to join the army. A sergeant could expect to receive 2s 2d per day, a corporal 1s 7 ½per day and a private 1s 3d per day. Of course, pay was never really regular on campaign and was often as much as three months in arrears. But for all its hardships the army represented a far better option than that at home, and recruits were rarely in short supply. It should also be remembered that British Army recruits were volunteers. Naturally, there were deserters but the problem was never a very serious one, unlike in other armies. Indeed, the Portuguese troops, conscripts, were often brought to the front in irons to stop them deserting.[23]

The officers and men of the British cavalry regiments served their king and their country well throughout the Peninsular and Waterloo campaigns. They may have lacked the finesse and training of their French counterparts but there is no escaping the fact that, after some tough knocks in the field, they graduated from virtual beginners in 1808 to experienced veterans by 1815. As we shall see the occasions when French cavalry got the better of their British counterparts in fair, stand-up fights, are very few indeed and it is only the handful of misadventures that has tarnished their reputation between 1808 and 1815. The full story of these actions will be recalled in the second part of this book.

Notes

1 The full story of Cotton's career can be found in *Memoirs and Correspondence of Field Marshal Viscount Combermere* (London, 1866), two volumes, by Mary, Countess Combermere and Capt. W. W. Knollys.
2 The classic account of Henry, Lord Paget is *One Leg: The Life and Letters of Henry William Paget, First Marquess of Anglesey* (London, 1961), written by the Marquess of Anglesey.
3 Michael Glover, *Wellington's Army in the Peninsula, 1808–1814* (Newton Abbot,

1977), 228.

4　See Denis Le Marchant, *Memoirs of the late Major General Le Marchant* (London, 1841).

5　Robert Ballard Long's letters were edited by T.H. McGuffie and published as *Peninsular Cavalry General* (1811–13); *The Correspondence of Lieutenant-General Robert Ballard Long* (London, 1951).

6　William Tale, *Jottings from My Sabretasche* (London, 1847), 22–3.

7　Ibid. 36–7.

8　Ibid. 38.

9　Ibid. 42.

10　Wellington to Beresford, 24 April 1811, *The Despatches of Field Marshal the Duke of Wellington during his various campaigns* (London, 1838), VII: 503.

11　Wellington to Lord Bathurst, 9 July 1812, *Despatches*, IX: 277.

12　Hercules Pakenham, quoted in Glover, *Wellington's Army in the Peninsula*, 227.

13　Correlli Barnett, *Britain and Her Army, 1509–1970* (London, 1970), 238.

14　Wellington to Lord Bathurst, 17 November 1813, *Despatches*, XI: 306.

15　Glover, *Wellington's Army in the Peninsula*, 83.

16　Ed Coss, 'The Misadventures of Wellington's Cavalry from the Peninsula to Waterloo', *A.F. W. C. Journal*, X, No.1, April 1988, 21.

17　The term 'tradesmen' should not be confused with the current meaning of the word. In the 19th century a tradesman might be a doctor, banker or lawyer. For more on the social standing of the Foot Guards see Ian Fletcher, *Gentlemen's Sons: The Foot Guards in the Peninsula and at Waterloo, 1808–1815* (Tunbridge Wells, 1992), 10–20.

18　Philip Haythornthwaite, *British Cavalryman, 1792–1815* (London, 1994), 7.

19　George James Sulivan, *The Peninsular War Memoirs of Lieutenant George James Sulivan, 1st Regiment of Life Guards*, 1812–14, MSS, Private Collection.

20　*Supplementary Despatches*, Gordon to Wellington, 25 December 1812, VII, 504.

21　Ibid. 504.

22　Glover, *Wellington's Army in tile Peninsula*, 27.

23　On 25 July 1811 John Mills of the Coldstream Guards, wrote, 'The conscripts for the Portuguese army I see are brought in in irons, and are forwarded from jail to jail till they arrive at their regiments. Above a thousand have deserted lately. One regiment that was 1,200 strong is now 500.' Ian Fletcher (Ed), *For King and Country: The Letters and Diaries of John Mills, Coldstream Guards, 1811–14* (Staplehurst, 1995), 52.

CHAPTER II

Horses and Forage

'The Peninsula is the grave of horses,' wrote Wellington in early 1812. 'I am very badly off for horses, having lost some, worn others out, and others being useless... and I have lost 14 upon a Stud generally of 10 in three years.'[1] How many he was to lose during the remaining years of the war in the Peninsula is not known, but considering the lengths of marches during the retreat from Burgos, the advance to Vittoria and the 1814 campaign in France, it is likely that he lost many more by the end of the war. The rugged terrain over which much of the war in the Peninsula was fought had a detrimental effect on the performance of the British cavalry inasmuch as there was not really any great room for manoeuvre on a large scale. Furthermore, it took its toll upon the horses themselves in terms of what might be called sheer 'wear and tear'. Indeed, a combination of hot weather, bad roads and a shortage of forage made life very hard for the horses of all combatant nations. However, I have found no evidence to suggest that the poor condition of the horses had a detrimental effect on affairs on the battlefield, and it is the performance of the British cavalry on the field of battle upon which successive historians have based their conclusions.

The strength of the British cavalry arm was very low in comparison with the infantry, whilst the terrain did not lend itself to cavalry operations on a large scale, other than in certain areas which can be said to be 'peripheral'; in the south, for example. The lack of an overall, experienced cavalry commander did not help either. All of these are major factors in the performance and subsequent reputation of the British cavalry in the Peninsula but the often poor condition of cavalry horses is not, in my view, such a major factor, because when it came to the field of battle they rarely let their masters down. Take Maguilla and Campo Mayor, for example, two shining instances of flawed analysis over the years. Both of these episodes involved long gallops both in advance and retreat, and yet on neither occasion was the condition of the horses called into question. At Campo Mayor the horses of the 13th Light Dragoons were more than a match over a distance of some ten miles for those of the French

26th Dragoons who had suffered from their sojourn in Portugal. And at Maguilla, a long, wild gallop over a similar distance in the heat of a southern Spanish summer appears to have had little effect on the horses during the actual chase, although they were understandably exhausted at the end of it. The reasons for the British cavalry's misadventures at those actions which have drawn criticism, such as Talavera, Villar de Puerco and, indeed, Maguilla and even Waterloo, have little to do with the poor condition of the horses. It is true that a larger number of cavalry would certainly have been a bonus for Wellington but this may have been cancelled out to an extent, owing to the unsuitable terrain which did not allow for effective cavalry operations anyway. Nevertheless, in such duties as piquet and patrol work it certainly would have been an advantage for Wellington to have been able to put greater numbers into the field. And whilst this is not a comparison with the French cavalry, it is worth noting that, compared with the condition of the French horses, particularly during the period following Masséna's retreat from Portugal, Wellington's cavalry had a distinct advantage over their more numerous French counterparts.

The problem of procuring sufficiently good horses for the British cavalry regiments in the Peninsula surfaced fairly quickly. In fact, as early as the first month of the war, in August 1808, Wellesley's cavalry, at least what few he had, having sailed to Portugal with the intention of procuring local horses, discovered that this plan was flawed from the start. The local horses were just not up to the job. The British Army in South America during the abortive Buenos Ayres expeditions of 1806 and 1807 had run up against a similar problem when they had attempted to purchase horses locally.[2]

British cavalry horses had, in the 18th century, tended to be of the heavier charger type, suitable for dragoons whose main task was perceived to be the charge. However, the advent of the light cavalryman, and in particular the hussar, called for a lighter type of horse. The result was the speedier carriage horse or light hunter, suitable for the sort of work which Wellington's cavalry would be employed upon in the Peninsula for most of the time, e.g. patrol work, reconnaissance, intelligence gathering.[3] The emphasis on the charge may not have been lessened too much in the eyes of the heavy cavalry but there was certainly a realisation amongst the cavalry that heavy dragoon horses were not what was required for most of the time and that the days of the great charger type horses were numbered. Indeed, when Wellington's army moved into the Pyrenees and the southern France campaign areas, the heavy cavalry were sent to the rear, leaving only certain light cavalry regiments with the main army, cavalrymen who were suitably mounted on lighter horses which could carry out the sort of tasks listed above. Heavy cavalry horses generally stood around 15 hands, with light cavalry horses being slightly smaller. In fact, an inspection of the 2nd (Royal North British) Dragoons in 1813 showed that of the regiment's 708 horses, 57 were 16 hands, 256 15 ½ hands, 340 15 hands and 55 14 ½ hands.[4] We are indebted to none other than Wellington himself for a good description of the sort of horses he considered most suitable for the Peninsula. In a letter to the Earl of Bathurst, dated 14 April 1813, he complained about the lack of good horses coming from England.

I acknowledge that I am one of those who are incredulous respecting the difficulties of procuring horses in England for the service of the cavalry and artillery of this army. One thousand horses for the cavalry in this winter and spring would have given the army the service of three, if not four, regiments of cavalry, from which I have been obliged, by orders from the Horse Guards, to draft their horses, very much against their inclination. We are now so deficient in horses for the artillery, that I shall, as usual, take the field with an equipment of artillery far inferior to that of the enemy, and to what I intended to take with me; and we shall have no spare horses whatever.

Surely horses of five and six years old cannot be wanting in England; and, if it is possible to collect in three months in France between 30,000 and 40,000 horses for the remount of the French cavalry and artillery, it cannot be impossible to collect in Great Britain and Ireland one twentieth of the number for the supply of this army. It is very possible that the persons usually employed to supply horses, and the ordinary means, and perhaps even the ordinary price, are not sufficient to procure a large supply at the moment; but England must be much altered if there is any deficiency of horses.

I think the question of price is deserving of some attention. The sum of 25 guineas is paid for a dragoon horse, but he is rising three years old, and is not fit for work, and much less for service, for a year and a half or two years. In estimating his cost to the public at five years old, the age at which we prefer them here, it is not unreasonable to add to the sum about half as much more; if that be true, would there be anything unreasonably extravagant in giving £40 or 40 guineas for five or six year old horses or mares for the regiments on service, and £45 or 45 guineas for horses for the artillery abroad? If it is not thought expedient to do this, there remains then only to draft the five and six year old horses from the regiments on the home establishment, and to make a great effort to replace them in the regiments by purchases of two or three year olds at the usual price. But if this is done, care must be taken that the regiments on the home service do not send us out their old and worn out horses, as they did upon a former occasion, of which there is one instance of the whole remount of one regiment dying in consequence of one day's work.[5]

This last reference is, no doubt, to the sixty-one horses which were sent out to the 14th Light Dragoons in July 1809, having first been rejected as unfit for service with the Irish Commissariat Corps. Lord only knows why these horses were deemed to be fit enough for the rigours of the campaign in the Peninsula when they were not able to stand up to the workload in Ireland. Little wonder, therefore, that the draft proved totally useless. In fact, the 14th Light Dragoons, one of the most distinguished of Peninsular War cavalry regiments, have left us a record of the turnover in horses between 1809 and 1814. It makes interesting reading. In 1809, 720 horses travelled to the Peninsula with the regiment. 664 remounts followed over the years whilst a further 381 were received from other units, 63 were taken from the French and 14 drafted from the Spaniards. A total of 1,842 horses passed through the regiment in the Peninsula, therefore, with a very low number, 278, actually returning home to England at the end of the war, some 1,564 having fallen along the way.[6] Ironically enough, at an inspection of the 14th on 21 July 1814, just four days after the regiment had landed at Dover, the Duke of York was moved to comment 'They appear as if they had never been on service.'[7] Another regiment that saw a great deal of service in the Peninsula was the 13th Light Dragoons, a regiment which, between February 1810 and its return to England in July 1814, got through no fewer than 1,009 horses, an average of almost 250 a year.[8]

As regards the colour of these horses it is worth mentioning that in the 18th century virtually all cavalry horses were black, but by the beginning of the Peninsular War regiments were allowed to employ horses of other colours although some, notably the Household regiments, retained the use of black horses only. The 1st (Royal) Dragoons and 3rd Dragoons were also mounted on black horses but only until 1811. However, I would suggest that, like uniform regulations, which were quickly ignored out of necessity, if a horse was lost and no other black horse available, then it is certain that cavalrymen would have mounted whatever colour horse was at hand. After all, in battle it mattered little what colour a horse was so long as it could gallop in and out of action. It was the same with the 2nd (Royal North British) Dragoons, or Scots Greys, who rode grey horses. It is highly unlikely that any trooper of this particular regiment would have passed up the opportunity to mount a different coloured horse at Waterloo once Jacquinot's lancers set about the regiment after their charge up to Napoleon's Grand Battery. Light cavalry regiments were mounted on horses of various colours.

One notable difference between British and French horses was that the former were 'nag-tailed' or 'docked'. This had the effect of making British horses recognisable at distance or in half-light and, in fact, when the army introduced the 1812-pattern uniforms, with the British light cavalry adopting the French-style bell-topped shako, the length of the horse's tail was often the only distinguishing mark between the two sides' cavalry.

Care of the horses was of the utmost importance. The lack of good forage was a bad enough problem but it was absolutely criminal for any cavalryman to lose his horse simply through neglect. The business began on board the transports carrying the regiment and its horses overseas. The journey to Lisbon might only take around eleven days which, compared with longer journeys to India, Egypt or even South America, might not seem too bad. However, the passage across the Bay of Biscay often proved a real trial for horses whilst even calmer passages proved equally arduous, with the horses cooped up aboard ship with little or no ventilation. It was recommended that horses not be embarked until the last moment and if possible the horses were to be stabled within a few miles of the port of embarkation in order to be taken aboard immediately prior to sailing. If this was not possible, it was recommended that the horses not be embarked until not more than two hours prior to sailing. Once on board, the horses were placed in slings in stalls, with one stall left unoccupied in case of illness or sickness. During the first night aboard the horses were to be fed a 'mash with some nitre', whilst during the voyage bran should make up a large part of their daily ration, with care being taken that they were not either over fed or over heated. Each cavalryman was to wash down the fetlocks and hooves of his horse every hour, with particular attention being paid to the horse's face, eyes and nostrils. Ventilation was very important and the hold must be well ventilated, which was usually done by wind-sails, the ends of which were to be shifted to different parts of the hold. If, due to bad weather, the hold was kept closed for some time, the cavalrymen were advised to wash down the stalls with vinegar and water and to sponge the horse's nostrils with the same. Once the ship reached its designated port, the horses were disembarked, upon which 'a cooling regimen as to food and gentle exercise' was the best means of restoring them to good health and preparing them for service.[9]

'The object of good grooming is the maintenance of the horse in bodily fitness for the work man requires of him.'[10] So wrote Lieutenant Colonel Fytzwygram, of the 15th Hussars, in 1862. Although nearly half a century had passed since the end of the Napoleonic Wars, these words were no less true of cavalry in Wellington's day. Whether or not the cavalrymen in Wellington's army appreciated the necessity of constant grooming of their horses is not clear. It was certainly recognised in the Victorian period. However, one small insight into the philosophy of the Peninsular cavalryman was given by the Household regiments which arrived in Portugal towards the end of 1812. The squadrons of the Horse Guards and Life Guards quickly discarded their combs and brushes as surplus equipment, the consequence being that the coats of their horses deteriorated very rapidly. The cavalrymen obviously did not realise that in order to clean the horse's skin properly the skin must be groomed with a good, stiff brush, stimulating the oil glands. The friction of the brush brings more blood to the surface and, naturally, to the skin, and from this increase of blood on the surface arises increased activity of the oil glands and in turn, an increased secretion of oil. In this way the horse maintains a glossy coat. However, if a horse is not brushed properly, dirt tends to collect on the surface of the skin and this obstructs the sweat and oil ducts. The sweat glands gradually become choked and it is not long before disease takes hold. Exercise has the same effect, bringing more blood to the surface and increased activity in the sweat and oil glands. However, it was important that the horse was brushed immediately after exercise otherwise the sweat, if allowed to dry, would choke the glands and thus be to the detriment of the horse's health. There were many other procedures to be adopted although brushing was probably the most obvious one to ensure a glossy coat.

The cavalry regiments in Wellington's army each had a veterinary surgeon and we are fortunate that John Shipp, Veterinary Surgeon to the 11th Light Dragoons and then the 23rd Light Dragoons, has left us an account of his experiences in the Peninsula and at Waterloo. Shipp was obviously an intelligent man and his observations are very acute. In fact, he went on to write *Cases in Farriery, in which the Diseases of Horses are treated on the principles of the Veterinary School of Medicine.* In the book, Shipp wrote extensively on the causes and treatment of various conditions, much of his research being carried out at first hand in the Peninsula.[11] One major problem for Wellington's cavalry was a lack of horse shoes. Indeed, it is a problem dealt with by Shipp who complained that when he first joined the 11th Light Dragoons, many of the horses were lame from corns. William Verner, of the 7th Hussars, claimed that of the 580 horses of his regiment lost during the Corunna campaign the majority were lost owing to a lack of shoes. Such was the confusion during the campaign that supplies of horse shoes, which were present somewhere along the line, were nevertheless lost and as a result hundreds of horses either fell by the wayside or were shot by their former owners when they boarded the ships waiting to take them back to England. As a result of this, each man was henceforth ordered to carry a spare set of shoes and sufficient nails with him on campaign.[12] John Shipp claimed that the average weight for the shoes used by the horses of the 11th Light Dragoons was fifteen and a half ounces, 'which weight I find best for the general run of hunters.'[13]

The care and maintenance of the cavalry arm of Wellington's army was not made easy by the rugged nature of the Peninsular terrain and the poor condition of most of the roads. Nor was it made any easier by the frequent lack of forage. As with many aspects of the campaign, Wellington benefited from having the Royal Navy at his disposal, by which means he was able to import supplies directly from Britain. However, this represented only a small percentage of the forage which the horses were fed, the overwhelming proportion being procured by the Commissariat Department or by the regiments themselves in the field. The official regulations stated that the ration was to consist of fourteen pounds of hay or straw and twelve pounds of oats or ten pounds of Indian corn.[14] The proviso was that three days' corn was to be always issued and carried. However, when supplies were scarce this ration had, naturally, to be reduced. Therefore, we find a General Order dated 31 January 1810 which states that owing to the shortage of straw the ration was to be reduced from fourteen to ten pounds. These, of course, were what might be termed 'regulation rations' but in reality the situation was often far worse and many horses were lost through starvation and from disease caused through a lack of forage. Often, horses would resort to eating grass and in doing so would swallow small stones and, unfortunately, die.

Some idea of the amount of forage required to keep the army going can be gauged by a statement from Sir John Bisset, who for a period was Commissary-General in the Peninsula. Bisset's calculations were based upon a regiment of cavalry, typically comprising six troops, and with a total strength of 407 all ranks.[15] The horses and mules attached to the regiment numbered 478. The regulation allowance of wood fuel alone would therefore be 1,586lbs. With a strength of 407, the regiment would require 407 lbs of biscuit and a further 407 lbs of meat, these amounts being the daily regulation ration. In addition, there was 400 rations of spirit or wine, carried in two 200lbs casks. In order to feed the horses and 'mules, 4,780lbs of corn (478 rations at 10lbs per ration) and a further 5,786lbs of hay or straw had to be carried (478 rations at 12lbs per ration), as well as the 1,586lbs of fuel. Therefore, the total weight in fuel and rations to be carried by this single regiment of cavalry amounted to no less than 11,123lbs, and this was just a single day's weight. As three days' rations were normally carried, the actual amount to be carried was, in fact, 33,369lbs. Now, as each commissariat mule could carry only 200lbs, it required 167 mules to carry the three days' supply, although Bisset advised taking a further 111 mules, which was two-thirds again. This gives a total of 278 mules, just to carry the supplies which, along with the 478 horses and mules belonging to the regiment, makes a grand total of 756 animals to 407 men of the regiment, a ratio of nearly two to one.

Bisset went on to extend the calculation to a brigade of cavalry, comprising three regiments.[16] Based upon three regiments, totalling 1,221 all ranks, with a troop of Horse artillery, staff and commissariat staff (1,430 all ranks), Bisset calculated the number of horses and mules at 1,658. The fuel required amounted to 5,770lbs, the ration of biscuit to 1,430lbs, the meat ration 1,430lbs, being live oxen, a further 1,400 rations of wine or spirits, weighing in at 700lbs, 1,658 rations of corn weighing in at 16,580lbs, and a further 1,658 rations of hay or straw, weighing in at 19,896lbs. All this amounted to 38,606lbs, for a single day's ration, and 115,818lbs for three days. The total number of commissariat mules required to transport this amount numbered 579 (at 200lbs per mule) and with an additional two-thirds of 386 mules came to a grand total of 965 commissariat mules. This, together with the 1,658 horses and mules of the brigade of cavalry, totals no fewer than 2,623 animals which is again a ratio of animals to brigade strength

35

of almost two to one. Given the above numbers we can well imagine just how much forage was needed to keep Wellington's army on the move and just how many mules were required to carry it. In fact, Bisset gives a grand total of no fewer than 8,815 commissariat mules as being present with the army in June 1812, whilst the number of horses and baggage mules with the army numbered a further 16,165, a grand total of 24,980.[17] The total number of officers and men in Wellington's infantry, cavalry and artillery numbered 53,300, which reverses the ratio between men and animals to around two to one. Little wonder, therefore, that it is very difficult for us today to imagine what an army on the march actually looked like.

Much has been made of the difference between the manner in which the cavalrymen of the King's German Legion and the British cavalry looked after their horses. The former are universally regarded as being far better at the job. August Schaumann made some very astute observations in his wonderful memoir, *On the Road with Wellington. In it, he writes:*

> The English cavalry soldier looks upon his horse as a machine, as an incubus, which is the cause of all his exertions and punishments. He ill-treats it. And even when forage lies within his reach, he will not, of his own accord, lift a finger to get it. The commissary must procure everything, and actually hold the food to his own and his horse's mouth. Even the officers do not give a commissary the smallest help, and grumble when they have to hand him over a few men even as a protective escort. From the colonel downwards, all they can do is to find fault with the forage, and every day they repeat the remark: 'I shall report it.'
>
> How different things are in the German cavalry regiments of the legion! Every officer and man tries to help. 'Provided you pay,' they exclaim to the commissary, 'we will see that it is procured.' Whereas all the English cavalry regiments were going to pot, the German were distinguished from the first to the last moment of the campaign by their fine efficient horses and men. Nevertheless, I must do justice to the 14th and 16th English Dragoons, by admitting that they were an exception to the rule, that they at least acknowledged the efforts I made, and that their active, useful, courageous and skilful officers, eagerly supported me, even in the matter of detailing parties for foraging.[18]

Schaumann also recalled the bad habit that British cavalrymen developed of selling their forage in order to buy drink. He was concerned by the fact that the British cavalry horses were looking very thin, despite having a good amount of forage. The answer came from an unlikely source, as he later recalled.

> One day, however, when I was talking to the Jiuz de Fora of my trouble, he smiled and said, 'If your horses grow thin it means that the people in my

district grow all the fatter, and surely that is a good thing!' Very much aston-
ished, I begged him to interpret these cryptic words. 'Well,' he said, 'this is
how it happens. Hardly have the dragoons drawn their corn than hundreds
of old women appear on the scene with bottles of brandy or wine concealed
in their aprons, with which they bargain with the men for the return of the
corn. Your horses have hardly any corn, although they have probably had
heaps of straw and grass.'

Apparently, Schaumann galloped off to inform General Payne, the cavalry
commander at the time, of this practice, whereupon the furious general
issued a General Order detailing officers to superintend the feeding of
horses and not to leave until the last grain of corn had been eaten by
the horses. Any dragoons who were discovered to have subsequently
disobeyed the order were flogged. The upshot was that, 'the horses grew
fatter, and the poor townsfolk thinner.'[19]

Nevertheless, despite Schaumann's criticisms of the British dragoons
and their care of their horses, the French evidently regarded English
horses as superior to their own. Indeed, captured despatches showed that
officers in France were sending requests to their comrades in Spain for
'fine English officers' chargers.'[20] It is hardly surprising, therefore, that
the French were overjoyed when they captured the entire piquet of the
11th Light Dragoons, under Captain Lutyens, in June 1811, on the banks
of the Guadiana river, an episode dealt with in another chapter. 'As both
regiments had only just arrived from England [the action involved the
2nd Hussars KGL as well], and were beautifully equipped in the matter of
horses, saddlery and arms, etc., the joy of the French over their magnificent
capture may well be imagined. The finest horses among this lot (worth at
least fifty golden louis apiece) were acquired by the French generals, while
the others went to the leading cavalry officers of the French army. Lord
Wellington is said to have been terribly put out by this event.'[21]

The business of procuring forage was one of those day-to-day, but very
necessary, tasks which consumed so much of the cavalryman's time on
campaign. It was also a task that was often fraught with danger, particularly in southern France in 1814, when enemy patrols were liable to
stumble across any given British unit whilst at foraging.[22] William Tale,
of the 15th Hussars, was involved in more than a few such incidents of
forage patrols being surprised or attacked by French cavalry. In fact, Tale
has left some good accounts of various foraging expeditions in the valleys
around Macaye. When forage became scarce in the winter of 1814, patrols
were sent out to forage wherever they could. Tale later wrote:

> For about a fortnight, the fertile valleys of Macaye and Mendionde supplied
> us with excellent hay. These resources now became completely exhausted,
> and ceased to supply a bent; and as our limits were bounded by a line of

demarcation tacitly submitted to by the belligerents, a substitute for the said herbage was sought for and found out, and the green and young tops and sprouts of gorse, gathered in abundance in the neighbourhood, formed an excellent and invaluable substitute for provender for our cattle for about a month. The process of gathering, chopping, and bruising (for the two latter of which tools were provided) imposed no little toil upon the hussar; but the task was cheerfully submitted to, and he was amply compensated for his labour, by the preservation of his horse in service condition, if not from almost starvation. The gorse, after being minced and bruised, was mixed with the yellow corn – that is, when we could get the latter to blend with.[23]

The forage, once collected, was gathered in large nets which the cavalry-men hung over their saddles. Tale also makes a very useful observation on the cavalry of the King's German Legion who, as I have already stated, are regarded as being superior to the British cavalry in many aspects of their art, and particularly in the care and maintenance of their horses. Tale wrote:

Some German hussars quitted the town on our entering it, and I imagine it had been their quarters. I really envied the well-fed, sleek, and clean appearance of man and horse, particularly the latter. The Germans have ever sustained the reputation of taking great care of their cattle, to which I willingly subscribe; but I do not go to the length of some writers in according to them such a vast super-excellence over the English dragoon. That the German was not mindful of his own little comforts, one horseman was able to bear testimony, by the ample supply of culinary vessels dangling about him.

The opinion I am about to enumerate is purely, and solely my own, and if wrong I alone am accountable for it; but, for the life of me, I could not help thinking that the force in question [the KGL] were permitted a little more latitude than we were ourselves in the matters of *meum and teum*; that their peccadilloes on that score, if not openly sanctioned, were winked at; that what would be denounced as plunder if done by us would be ascribed in their case as a little harmless liberty allowable on campaigning. The foregoing allusions apply solely to the feeding department; and a rush for the fellow, say I, that would not plunder for his horse where all fair means had failed.[24]

If things were bad enough for the cavalry, they could be far more serious for the local farmers who saw their harvest carried off by both the Allied and French armies, often with little prospect of payment. Indeed, if the French carried off the harvest there was virtually no chance whatsoever that the farmer would receive any recompense, whereas at least Wellington had developed a system by which farmers were paid. Corporal Andrew Hartley, of the Royal Horse Guards, wrote in his journal in 1814:

We generally forage for our horses on the road. We dismount in a field of barley, oats or wheat (if neither of the two former is to be procured), pointed out by the Commissary, and without further ceremony take as much as we can carry. We have seldom the trouble of cutting it. I think the poor farmer often loses his year's labour as the Commissaries never pay on the spot, but give Bill on the Commissary General payable perhaps in half a year, or perhaps not at all.[25]

It should not be forgotten that, apart from the horses of the cavalry, forage also had to be produced to feed the thousands of mules which accompanied the army, the horses of the artillery and Commissariat and, of course, the hundreds of horses belonging to staff and infantry officers.[26]

So, to return to the opening lines of this chapter, the Peninsula was, in Wellington's own words, 'the grave of horses'. Of this there is little doubt, as the casualty rate amongst the horses of the 13th and 14th Light Dragoons alone bears out. However, I would also return to my own point, that the poor condition of British cavalry horses was not a major factor in the overall performance in the Peninsula, nor was it at Waterloo. It was a problem for the cavalry of both sides although it appears to have been far more serious for the French, particularly after the harrowing period during and after the retreat from the Lines of Torres Vedras. The problem of obtaining sufficient forage was far greater for the French, whose armies were much larger and their supply lines longer, unlike the British cavalry who at least could be assisted by direct imports via Lisbon or, later on, from Passages. In fact, it is generally accepted that many British horses, particularly those belonging to Wellington's intelligence officers, or 'exploring officers' as they are often called, were so much better than the French horses that the latter, whenever they spotted these exploring officers lurking around the edges of the French camps, often ignored them, accepting the fact that, mounted on their own inferior horses they would not have a chance of catching them.

The main problem for the cavalry lay in maintaining a strong cavalry force in the field. Bad roads and poor forage made this impossible, but these are not reasons why the British cavalry has received a bad press over the years. Nor can the failure of the British cavalry be put down to the poor condition of the horses, for if this was a major factor we would be reading of incidents where British cavalry had been taken by the French simply because they had run out of steam. But this did not happen. At Talavera and Vimeiro, for example, the heavy losses were sustained in action in the midst of enemy cavalry. Even at Maguilla, where Slade's cavalry galloped for miles in pursuit of and in retreat from enemy cavalry, losses were not due to horses simply giving up. At this latter action British dragoons were overcome in the pursuit but there is little evidence to suggest that this was due to the poor condition of the horses, otherwise the whole force would have been taken. After all, such a long gallop in such heat would surely have taken its toll on them. Large numbers of British cavalry in the Peninsula would certainly have been an advantage to Wellington, although given the rugged nature of the Peninsular terrain it is doubtful whether he could have found room to employ a very large cavalry force anyway. As proof of this we may consider the Vittoria campaign of 1813 for, just when Wellington's cavalry was at its greatest strength, the Pyrenees loomed up, forcing him to leave his heavy cavalry behind at Logrono whilst he advanced into the mountains without them. Indeed, the Peninsular terrain was almost certainly a far greater factor in the performance of the British cavalry than was the condition of their horses. For that reason, we must examine the topography of the Iberian Peninsula, southern France and, indeed, the Low Countries in a separate chapter.

Notes

1 Elizabeth Longford, *The Years of the Sword* (London, 1969), 268.

2 *The Trial at Large of Lieut. Gen. Whitelocke, late commander of the Forces in South America* (London, 1808).

3 The standard work on British army horses is Major G. Tylden's *Horses and Saddlery: An account of the animals used by the British and Commonwealth Armies from the Seventeenth Century to the Present Day with a description of their Equipment* (London, 1965).

4 Bryan Fosten, *Wellington's Heavy Cavalry* (London,1982), 21.

5 Wellington to Earl Bathurst, 14 April 1813, *The Despatches of Field Marshal the Duke of Wellington during his various campaigns* (London, 2832), X: 295–96.

6 Col. H. B. Hamilton, *Historical Record of the 14th (King's) Hussars* (London, 1901), 158.

7 Ibid. 158.

8 C. R. B. Barratt, *History of the 13th Hussars* (London, 1911), I: 262.

9 *General Order*, Horse Guards, 6 December 1813.

10 Lt. Col. Fytzwygram, *Lectures on Horses and Stabling* (London, 1862), 35.

11 John Shipp, *Cases in Farriery, in which the Diseases of Horses are treated on the principles of the Veterinary School of Medicine* (Leeds, 1808). Shipp's own experiences are told in Ernest Gray's *The Trumpet of Glory: The Military career of John Shipp, first veterinary surgeon to join the British Army* (London, 1985).

12 Ruth Verner (Ed), 'Reminiscences of William Verner, 7th Hussars', *Journal of the Society for Army Historical Research, Special Publication No.8* (London, 1965), 15–6.

13 Gray, *The Trumpet of Glory*, 22.

14 General Order, *Coimbra*, 30 May 1809.

15 Com. Gen. Sir John Bisset, *Memoranda and Observations regarding The Duties of the Commissariat on Field Service Abroad* (London, 1846), 38–9.

16 Ibid. 39–40.

17 Ibid. 37.
18 Anthony Ludovici (Ed), *On the Road with Wellington; The Diary of a war commissary in the Peninsular Campaigns,* by August Ludolf Friedrich Schaumann (London, 1924), 219.
19 Ibid. 218–9.
20 Ibid. 83.
21 Ibid. 311.
22 One notorious incident involved the 10th Hussars who were surprised by an enemy unit on 9 January 1814 at Macaye. The proceedings of the subsequent court martial of the commanding officer, Colonel Quentin, were published in 1814 and includes a wealth of detail relating to the incident and forage work in general. See *The Trial of Colonel Quentin, of the Tenth or Prince of Wales's Own Regiment of Hussars* (London, 1814).
23 William Tale, *Jottings from my Sabretasche* (London, 1847), 189–90.
24 Ibid. 201–2.
25 Corporal Andrew Hartley, MSS Journal.
26 For a very interesting and entertaining chapter on horses and forage see Anthony Brett-James' wonderful book, *Life in Wellington's Army* (London, 1972).

CHAPTER III

Organisation, Tactics and Training

British cavalry regiments in the Peninsular and Waterloo campaigns were organised into squadrons, which was the basic tactical unit, and each of these squadrons comprised two troops. The organisation of cavalry regiments had changed regularly over the years between 1794 and 1808. For example, at the outset of the Revolutionary Wars, the old six-troop establishment was increased to nine, but at the turn of the century this had been increased to ten troops, two of which formed the depot squadron whilst the other eight troops, formed into four squadrons, took the field. In 1811 this was increased to ten active service troops, with two more still forming the depot squadron, whilst the light cavalry regiments were increased again in 1813 to twelve troops. The 7th Hussars, for example, took the field in the Peninsula in 1813 with ten troops, leaving two at home as the service depot.[1] These were the regulation establishments but what was actually put into practice differed enormously. The Household Cavalry regiments, the 1st and 2nd Life Guards and Royal Horse Guards, sent only two squadrons each to the Peninsula in late 1812, and repeated the exercise at Waterloo. The British cavalry regiments in the Peninsula and at Waterloo were always well below strength, as were the infantry regiments. In theory, each regiment, with a troop strength of around sixty to seventy men, ought to have fielded no fewer than 450 to 500 men, assuming six troops present. However, this was rarely the case and of the seven British cavalry regiments at Salamanca, for example, not one could muster 400 all ranks. Indeed, the 16th Light Dragoons numbered just 273, with the 11th Light Dragoons fielding the strongest regiment at 391.[2]

From regimental organisation we move on to the higher level of organisation, at brigade and divisional level. The Appendix in this book demonstrates how the organisation of Wellington's cavalry altered over the years, beginning with the extremely weak force with which he began the Peninsular War in 1808, and continuing through the Vittoria campaign and on to Waterloo, by which time the British cavalry had grown into a very strong force. The cavalry regiments were usually brigaded with two to each brigade, although sometimes three were brigaded together. The 13th

Light Dragoons, in fact, often found themselves unattached. Although the regiments were frequently moved about between brigades it was rare for different types of cavalry to be brigaded together. Generally, the light cavalry regiments were kept separate from heavy cavalry, although Slade's brigade in 1810 and 1811 consisted of the 1st (Royal) Dragoons and the 13th and 14th Light Dragoons, the latter two being replaced by the 12th Light Dragoons in 1811. But this was unusual. By mid-1811 Wellington's cavalry was strong enough for it to be split into two divisions, the 1st Cavalry Division, under Cotton, consisting of two brigades plus Madden's Portuguese, and the 2nd Cavalry Division, under Erskine, comprising two brigades also. On 21 April 1813 the two divisions were amalgamated to form one cavalry division under Cotton.[3] Things were rather more complicated at Waterloo with so many more Allied regiments joining the British regiments, but the various brigades still formed one single cavalry division under the command of Lord Uxbridge, formerly Lord Paget.

Cavalry tactics in the Peninsular War were based upon the *Instructions and Regulations for the Formations and Movements of the Cavalry*, which was printed for the War Office in 1796. The manual was written by David Dundas as part of his attempts to produce a uniform system of training for the cavalry. It was divided into several useful sections covering the movements by which the regiments changed position and formation, movements in open column, counter march, close column, echelon, and movements in line, each section being broken down into several more sub-sections. The usual method for cavalry when marching in column was in ranks of threes, hence the oft-quoted command, 'threes about!' In spite of its defects, it makes for very good and thorough reading and was required reading for all cavalry officers.[4] The manual was the product of observations made by Dundas in northern Germany and Flanders in 1794 and 1795, whilst the Prussian systems and the work carried out by General Sir James Stewart Dertham proved of equal inspiration.[5] The drill of the British cavalry in the late 18th century was 'in as hopeless a state of chaos as that of the infantry and with consequences yet more depressing,'[6] and it was Dundas's hope that his manual would bring about a single common system of training and for this he can be congratulated. However, the implementation of his system was quite another matter. Indeed, for the vast majority of cavalry officers much of the *Instructions and Regulations* was ignored as they focused heavily on what they considered to be the single most important thing in a cavalryman's life – the charge.

The charge; it was to be the scourge of British cavalry over the coming years, particularly in the Peninsula, whilst the Waterloo campaign saw further outstanding examples of what cavalry officers considered to be the pinnacle of their careers. Even light cavalry regiments, whose main function was certainly not the charge, engaged in them, and they were usually effective. Much of the obsession with charging dates back to 16 July 1760 and the Battle of Emsdorf, where the 15th Light Dragoons made a spectacularly successful charge against French infantry and completely routed them.[7] From then on, cavalry regiments set about trying to repeat the achievement, which the 15th Light Dragoons did again at Villers-en-Cauchies in 1794. As a result, Emsdorf and the charge became permanently fixed in the minds of British cavalry officers who sought to emulate the feat wherever they could do so. The cavalry charge was considered of equal importance in Napoleon's army and had been demonstrated with great effectiveness at battles such as Marengo, Austerlitz and Eylau, but if it was uppermost in the minds of Napoleon's cavalry officers it was certainly not the only thing to which they gave their attention, unlike British cavalry officers, who thought of little else. Consequently, all movements in training and, indeed, in the field, were executed at great speed with the emphasis firmly upon shock. This was all very well but it was done at the expense of everything else, such as control, and, sadly, the greatest errors committed by the British cavalry in the Peninsula were usually associated with a lack of control. An even greater example occurred at Waterloo, which we shall also deal with later.

The great charge of the British heavy cavalry at Waterloo appears to have driven Wellington to distraction after he had experienced similar incidents of what he perceived to be the misadventures of his cavalry during the Peninsular War. Proof of this can be gauged by the fact that he was moved to write a memorandum on the manner of executing cavalry charges. In the memorandum, addressed to General Officers commanding Brigades of Cavalry, Wellington set out very detailed and precise instructions on how cavalry charges should be made, with a great emphasis being placed upon the need for keeping a reserve in hand at about 450 yards from the main attacking line. In fact, the very first sentence runs, 'It is so desirable that a reserve should be kept in all cases in which the cavalry is employed to charge, that it appears to be a matter of necessity; and the officers and troops should be accustomed to form and conduct this reserve in exercise.'[8] This reserve, Wellington stated, had two purposes; the first, 'to improve and complete the success of the charge; secondly, to protect the retreat of the troops retiring, supposing those who charge are unsuccessful, or possibly to acquire success after their failure.' As we shall see, it was this vital reserve that was missing at several incidents in the Peninsula and at Waterloo, a reserve which almost certainly would have spared the blushes of the British cavalry at Maguilla, Talavera and, indeed, Waterloo itself. 'The proportion of the body of cavalry to be kept in reserve must depend upon the nature of the ground and of the body of troops to be attacked. It should be not less than half of the body formed for the operation, nor should it exceed two-thirds. It follows, therefore, that every body of cavalry should be formed in two or three lines. The second line should be in line, the third might be in columns of such a size as that they could readily be formed into line.'[9]

It was all good sound advice, but unfortunately it came a few years too late, for there was never again to be an opportunity for Wellington to put his instructions to the test. The benefit of hindsight is wonderful, of course, and Wellington's instructions were, as I have said, based upon his personal experiences in the field. However, it is surprising that his cavalry commanders frequently failed to employ such tactics themselves, though the need for a reserve must surely have been apparent to them. There are, perhaps, two possibilities, the first being that, with the British cavalry below strength for much of the Peninsular War, officers employed all or most of their cavalry in the main attacking line in order to give it the necessary power. Hence, there were no other troops available to form a reserve. The second, and most likely reason, is that some cavalry commanders, obsessed with charging, simply failed to recognise the importance of having a reserve. There were, of course, vastly differing circumstances to each of the actions, successful or otherwise, involving the British cavalry between 1808 and 1815 and for that reason the above explanations do not always ring true. But I do feel that they are not too wide of the mark.

It was the obsession with the charge and with speed of movement that proved so detrimental to the British cavalry between 1808 and 1815. William Tomkinson, of the 16th Light Dragoons, wrote, 'We do every thing so quickly that it is impossible men can understand what they are about.'[10] And he was right, for far too many officers considered the charge to be the only thing of importance. The spirit of the fox hunt was certainly alive and well throughout the regiments of King George's army. As regards the charge itself, there were three ways in which it could be performed. The first, and most common method, was the charge in line. In fact, each line of cavalry charging actually formed in two lines, or rather two ranks, one close behind the other. The 1796 manual gives three and a half feet as the distance between the two lines, 'sufficient for the wheeling of ranks.'[11] Squadron commanders rode in front of their squadrons, which were formed of two troops, with the trumpeters beside them in order to sound the all-important orders whenever required. The second method of charging was in echelon, which involved staggered sections of the regiment charging, right in front, with the other sections coming up at distances between 100 and 200 yards, so as to hit the enemy formation at successive points, one after the other. It was not so easy to execute such an attack but it could be quite devastating if done properly.

Another method of executing the charge was by attack in echiquer, a kind of checkerboard formation, part line, and part echelon, whereby if four small formations charged, for example, the first and third (counting from the right) hit the enemy line at the same time, albeit at different points, with the second and fourth formations hitting it soon afterwards. The charge in line was the most common formation employed by the British cavalry in the Peninsula, with Salamanca being the most devastating example. The trick was, of course, to be able to halt a charge once it had been delivered. Its results had to be assessed and the next and best course of action decided upon before it could be continued. Decisions had to be made quickly which, in the heat of battle, was not always easy. If troops were not rallied quickly they might fall prey to enemy cavalry, whilst scattered parties of cavalry were useless to any officer in need of larger bodies of troops with which to follow up successful attacks or to cover retreats. It was a dangerous business and was one which was fraught with many more problems than those associated with infantry, whose formations were slow-moving and, as a result, far easier to control. The result was, therefore, that unless cavalry officers kept a tight rein on their men, cavalry charges were frequently in danger of degenerating into mob-like fox chases, to which Wellington referred in his infamous 'galloping at everything' outburst.

In fact, many of the most damning criticisms of the British cavalry came from their commander-in-chief, Wellington, who was never short of a few words on the subject. Indeed, some of his most famous quotes concern the cavalry. Writing in March 1813, he said, 'Our cavalry is the most delicate instrument in our whole machine. Well managed, it can perform wonders, and will always be of use, but it is easily put out of order in the field. None of our officers are accustomed to the manoeuvres of large bodies of cavalry; and if any serious accident were to happen to a large body, such as a full brigade of cavalry, while we should be forward in the plains, we are gone, and with us our political system, our allies, &c. &c.'[12]

'Our cavalry never gained a battle yet. When the infantry have beaten the French, then the cavalry, if they can act, make the whole complete, and do wonders; but they never yet beat the French themselves.'[13] Wellington's views did not change even with the passing of the years. Writing in 1826, he again returned to the failings of his cavalry and to the lack of control displayed by its officers. 'I considered our cavalry so inferior to the French from want of order, although I consider one squadron a match for two French squadrons, that I should not have liked to see four British squadrons against four French; and, as the numbers increased, and order of course became more necessary, I was more unwilling to risk our cavalry without having a great superiority of numbers... Mine would gallop, but could not preserve their order, and therefore I could not use them till our admirable infantry had moved the French cavalry from their ground.'[14] This was a little unfair to the cavalry but it did strike at the heart of the problem, the lack of control exerted by the officers over the men. However, he did recognise that, in a stand-up fight, British cavalry, even outnumbered, were more than a match for the French.

The emphasis on speed and the charge, coupled with a lack of control by officers, were bad enough, but when one adds an apparent lack of horsemanship, we have a very potent recipe for disaster. Even the horses themselves were cited as a reason for some of the failings of the British cavalry. Writing in the *Royal Military Chronicle* in October 1811, a British officer, writing under the name of 'Eques.', made some interesting observations regarding English horses. 'It is notorious that in every charge the British horses run away with their riders; and that, after the first effort has been made, it is a work of much time and difficulty to bring them again into regular line.'[15] The problem arose from several causes, he declared:

> ...partly from the peculiar breed of our native horse; partly from his ill breaking; and partly through his unskilful riding. The English horse has a greater tendency to throw his weight upon his shoulders, and to move his fore feet nearer the surface of the ground, than any race of continental horses that have fallen under my observation. The foreign cavalry have usually a disposition to poise themselves upon their haunches, and to lift their fore feet high in the air. They are consequently lighter in hand, and less liable to fall forward; but, then, what they gain in safety, they lose in velocity; for whatever movement is made by the leg perpendicularly is so much lost for horizontal progression. Our Englander, therefore, excels them in swiftness in all his paces, without so much shew and flutter he performs his work more quickly, and with less bodily labour. His impulse forward is indeed prodigious; and it has been truly said, that the lightest British cavalry is not only far more active than any French body of horse, but is, in the charge, infinitely more powerful and weighty than the heaviest squadrons of the enemy.
>
> The difficulty of restraining the English horse, after his powers have been called into full action, arises, therefore, partly from physical causes, which cannot be readily remedied. But something may be remedied by education. The old discipline of the menage might correct the over-preponderance of the English horse towards his shoulder; and although I would not have him dressed like the barb to turn upon the pivot, nor, while standing in the stable, would I have his hind legs tied to the manger; yet I would wish him to be more obedient to the rein, and so sensible of the curb, as to be readily recovered from full speed within the space of thirty to fifty yards. Our troop horse should be more carefully broken, and better thrown upon his haunches; and, with the horse, the rider should be more pertinaciously drilled than is habitual in our cavalry regiments.[16]

The lack of horsemanship can be traced in part to the lack of proper regimental riding schools. Indeed, there appears to have been very little emphasis placed on horsemanship and on such aspects as jumping, for example. Our anonymous correspondent, quoted above, went on to add, 'It has surprised me to observe how much this essential part of an officer's education is neglected. In our royal military colleges equitation does not enter into a course of instruction. A cadet at Woolwich may have completed his studies, and may have received his commission for the artillery or engineers, without having ever mounted a horse in his life; and this will appear the more extraordinary when it is known, that there is a royal riding school at Woolwich expressly instituted for the use of the regiment.'[17]

He may have been referring to officers of artillery and engineers but riding schools were by no means uniform in the cavalry. Most cavalry regiments were sent to Woodbridge in Suffolk, where Lord Paget, assisted at times by Le Marchant, trained cadres of officers and men who then went back to train their own regiments. In fact, Paget made an immense contribution to the training of British cavalry through his methods at Woodbridge and in some ways Woodbridge was for the cavalry what Shorncliffe was for the light infantry. Often, whole regiments went to Woodbridge, or to Maidstone, another large cavalry depot. Overall, the system was not ideal but it worked well enough for British cavalry regiments to be able to take the field in Portugal and Spain in relatively good order, and with the passing of time officers and men gained greater experience, becoming very accomplished riders, accomplished enough to be able to see off the French in scores of actions, as we shall discover later in this book.

With the emphasis firmly on the charge, attention to matters such as routine work of patrol and outposts duties was neglected. Indeed, the reader will find no references to these most vital tasks in the 1796 manual. The only manuals of any real value relating to the duties of light cavalry had been published almost twenty years earlier. Captain Robert Hinde's *Discipline of Light Horse*, and Thomas Simes' *Military Guide for Young Officers* gave ample advice on the employment of light cavalry and their duties as regards patrols, escort duties, skirmishing and piquet work. Sadly, these works were not improved upon by Dundas in his 1796 manual. As John Pimlott pointed out in his book on the British light cavalry, the greatest disadvantage of the 1796 manual was that it made no distinction between heavy and light cavalry. 'As many of these units existed specifically for, or had strong traditions in, the charge, the new regulations naturally stressed that tactic above all others, and the relatively small section which dealt with skirmishing and dismounted drill was easily ignored by light dragoon commanders.'[18] This was the crux of the problem. Even heavy cavalry had to train to skirmish, and whilst the manual could effectively be termed a heavy cavalry manual, there was little in it relating to this vital function, whilst light cavalry duties were ignored altogether. Hence, the mania for the charge was perpetuated by light cavalry commanders to the detriment of their real duties.

Proof of the shortcomings of Dundas's manual can perhaps be found in the performance of the light cavalry in the Peninsula. Instances of successful – and unsuccessful – charges by them are rife. Sahagun, Benavente, Villar de Puerco, Campo Mayor, Talavera; the list is fairly substantial. All are proof of the light cavalry's implementation of Dundas's manual, with its emphasis on the charge. However, as regards the real duties of light cavalry the story is much different. The manuals of Hinde and Simes were all that light cavalry officers could draw on for advice, although further attempts, both official and unofficial, were made over the years leading up to and during the Peninsular War to introduce a system of light cavalry drill. The consequence was that much of their knowledge had to be gained in the field, as demonstrated in the chapter on patrol and piquet work in this book. Fortunately, and perhaps ironically, they proved more adept at what might be called their 'self-taught' duties than the duties set out in Dundas's manual which might be termed 'heavy cavalry work,' i.e. the charge.

The introduction of a uniform system of cavalry drill by Dundas in 1796 coincided with another important manual, John Gaspard Le Marchant's *Rules and Regulations for the Sword Exercise of the Cavalry*, published in the same year. Le Marchant had observed at first hand the ineffectiveness of the cavalry sabres used by the British cavalry in Flanders in 1793–4. The long, unwieldy heavy cavalry sword, with its ornate guard and grip, would not have looked out of place on the battlefield of Culloden, whilst the old 1788-pattern light cavalry sabre, though more effective than its heavy cavalry cousin, was still considered to be too long and weak. The result was that Le Marchant submitted two designs for new sabres, the result of much thought and testing. Sadly, only one of his designs was accepted, being the new 1796-pattern light cavalry sabre, the new pattern for the heavy cavalry sword being based upon the existing Austrian heavy cavalry sword. The coming years would see the 1796-pattern light cavalry sabre become one of the most successful light cavalry sabres the British Army has ever had, and its powers demonstrated upon numerous battlefields from Sahagun and Benavente right up until Waterloo. The heavy cavalry sword, on the other hand, proved to be less effective, if more feared. In the hands of a trained heavy cavalryman it was a deadly weapon, capable of inflicting terrible wounds. The story behind the development and introduction of these two swords can be found in the chapter on weapons in this book.

New cavalry swords demanded a new drill and so Le Marchant's manual was published.[19] The importance and usefulness of the manual cannot be overstated, for I believe it was at the core of many a British cavalry victory in the Peninsula. The advantages enjoyed by the British cavalry in being mounted upon better horses than their enemy was certainly significant, but the fact that they also had a very scientific and effective sword drill was equally so. Indeed, the famous six cuts devised by Le Marchant were so popular that even small boys could be seen on the streets up and down the country, going through their paces with sticks. The manual covered all aspects of sword drill, from parry and guard to attack, and cavalry troopers would spend long periods going through the drill. A circle was painted upon a wall to simulate the face of an enemy and, standing about four feet away from it, the trooper would proceed to go through the six cuts as well as other movements. It was all about wrist action, and troopers were forbidden to bend their elbows unless cutting at dismounted enemy cavalry or infantry, or when practising certain parrying moves. The irony is that one of, if not the most famous sabre cut of the Peninsular War, delivered by Corporal Logan of the 13th Light Dragoons, which split open the skull of Colonel Chamorin, of the 26th Dragoons at Campo Mayor, was not one of the six cuts! In fact, Logan's cut, straight down through Chamorin's skull, exposing the brain apparently, is not in the manual, although, unfortunately for the French colonel, it still proved very effective.

The disadvantage of Le Marchant's manual matched that of Dundas's drill manual. It made no distinction between light and heavy cavalry. Indeed, whereas Dundas's manual ignored light cavalry duties, Le Marchant's sword drill appears to have been designed with light cavalry only in mind, with particular reference being made to the use of the sabre in close-quarter combat, the sort in which light cavalry might find themselves engaged whilst on patrol or out skirmishing. However, it did present to the cavalry a uniform system of sword drill which, along with Dundas's manual, ensured that the British cavalry at the beginning of the 19th century now had a solid foundation upon which to base their training. Furthermore, Le Marchant's manual also included a section on the control of the horse.[20] He had devised a very clever piece of equipment, consisting of a ring, five inches in diameter, with an opening or inner circle of four inches diameter. The ring was suspended on a hook which hung from a metal arm attached to a pulley. Le Marchant's drill involved a cavalry trooper riding at the ring at speed, from a distance which varied between fifty and seventy yards, whilst giving point at it (i.e. aiming the sword at it). The idea was to thrust the point of the sword through the ring which drew upon the pulley. The rider then had to bring his horse to a halt before the pulley stopped and yanked him back. The rider was, of course, required to keep control of his horse all the time. It was called 'running the ring' and was a very effective way of training troopers in both sword drill and horsemanship at the same time.

Through the unstinting efforts of men like Dundas, Le Marchant and Paget the British cavalry was able to take the field in the Peninsula in a fit state to take on the much-vaunted French cavalry. Although the business of patrol, skirmish and piquet work would prove a steep learning curve it would, nevertheless, be negotiated and by the time Wellington's cavalry marched through France to the Channel ports in July 1814 it was a force to be reckoned with. The manuals were not perfect and the drill at times deficient, but if, as Wellington said, Waterloo was won on the playing fields of Eton, then an equally important contribution was made years before on the training fields of Woodbridge.

Notes

1 There is much good information to be found in Bryan Fosten's *Wellington's Heavy Cavalry* (London, 1982), Philip Haytbornthwaite's *British Cavalryman 1792–1815* (London, 1994), and H. C. B. Rogers' *Wellington's Army* (London, 1979). At times, the information in one book contradicts that in another but, together, they provide good background information on the cavalry, its organisation, uniforms and weapons, etc.

2 These Salamanca figures are from Appendix X in Sir Charles Oman's *History of the Peninsular War* (Oxford, 1902), V: 595.

3 See Sir Charles Oman's *Wellington's Army, 1809–14* (London, 1913), 343–73.

4 *Instructions and Regulations for the Formations and Movements of the Cavalry* (London, 1796). An entry at the beginning of the manual reads, 'His Royal Highness is pleased to direct further, that every Officer of Cavalry shall be provided with a Copy of these Regulations, and the Commanding Officers of Corps are to take Care that this Order be duly observed.'

5 See Richard Glover's *Peninsular Preparation: The Reform of the British Army, 1795–1809* (Cambridge, 1988), 135.

6 Ibid. 135.

7 At Sahagun, on 21 December 1808, the 15th Hussars went into action crying, 'Emsdorf and victory!'

8 Instructions of Field Marshal the Duke of Wellington to the General Officers commanding Brigades of Cavalry in the Army of Occupation, published in Gurwood's *The General Orders of Field Marshal the Duke of Wellington in Portugal, Spain and France, from 1809 to 1814, in the Low Countries and France, in 1815, and In France, Army of Occupation, from 1816 to 1818* (London, 1837), 480–2.

9 Ibid. 480.

10 *Waterloo Campaign, 1809–1815* (London, 1895), 135.

11 *Instructions and Regulations*, 3.

12 Wellington to Cooke, 16 March 1813, *Supplementary Despatches, Correspondence and Memoranda of Field Marshal the Duke of Wellington* (London, 1860), VII: 587.

13 Sir George Larpent (Ed), *The Private Journal of F. Seymour Larpent, Judge- Advocate General attached to the Headquarters of Lord Wellington during the Peninsular War, from 1812 to its close* (London,1853), I: 306

14 Sir Herbert Maxwell, *The Life of Wellington, The Restoration of the Martial Power of Great Britain* (London, 1899), II: 138–9.

15 'British Cavalry,' in *The Royal Military Chronicle*, October 1811, 489.

16 Ibid. 489.

17 Ibid. 490.

18 John Pimlott, *British Light Cavalry* (London, 1977), 10.

19 John Gaspard Le Marchant, *Rules and Regulations for the Sword Exercise of the Cavalry* (London, 1796). Ironically, the illustrations in the book show a cavalryman using the old 1788 light cavalry sabre.

20 Ibid. 69–72.

CHAPTER IV

Cavalry Weapons

The weapons used by the British cavalry, particularly the heavy cavalry swords, have come in for some criticism over the years, but they appear to have had no real damaging effect on the performance of the cavalry. True, Wellington's cavalrymen probably would have sent more Frenchmen to the grave rather than the hospitals had they proved more effective, but I do not consider this to have had any real bearing on their performance in the way that terrain, numbers and command and control did. Nevertheless, as with cavalry organisation, it will not go amiss to take a look at the sort of weapons wielded on active service by both the light and heavy cavalry.[1]

British cavalry in the Peninsular and Waterloo campaigns were armed with two regulation swords, the light cavalry sabre and the heavy cavalry sword, both dating from 1796. The two versions were vastly different with the light cavalry sabre drawing high praise and the heavy cavalry sword attracting nothing but derision. When the Napoleonic Wars broke out the British cavalry were armed with 1788-pattern swords. The heavy cavalry sword was a straight bladed sword with a 39-inch blade, pointed at the tip, and a hilt of half-basket of steel bars. The sword was 47 inches long overall and weighed 3lbs. The design was copied from the sword used by the 6th Inniskilling Dragoons. Apparently, all heavy cavalry regiments, save for the Household Troops, were issued with the sword. The light cavalry version was six inches shorter overall than the heavy cavalry version and weighed three ounces less. The blade was curved with an iron single-bar stirrup hilt. Compared to the later 1796-pattern light cavalry sabre the 1788-pattern sword feels much longer and less manoeuvrable, although it is a well balanced weapon.

When the Duke of York embarked upon his campaign in Holland in 1793 one of his officers, Major John Gaspard Le Marchant, noted that hardly any two British cavalry regiments were armed with the same sword. It is evident, therefore, that the standardisation laid down in 1788 had yet to take grip, even five years on. He also made pertinent observations about the quality of the swords, adding that the most popular sword used by the troopers was a most cumbersome weapon indeed and that it was prone to shatter upon the first blow from an enemy's sword. He also noted that many of the wounds inflicted upon British cavalry were, in fact, self inflicted, usually as a result of a lack of proper training. The campaign did not pass without the British cavalry achieving some measure of success, however, but it was the observations made by Le Marchant that had, perhaps, the more lasting effect.

Le Marchant came to the conclusion that both heavy and light cavalry should be equipped with the same sword, a curved sabre for slashing and cutting. His design was submitted to the Board of Cavalry General Officers in 1796 but was only adopted in part, for the Board decided to continue the practice of issuing different swords to heavy and light cavalry. Le Marchant's design for the light cavalry sabre was accepted and adopted as per the General Order of 27 June 1796. It had a much more pronounced curve than the old 1788 version, measuring 33 inches, with an iron stirrup knuckle bow and leather grip. Officers' sabres were often very ornate compared to the simpler design issued to troopers. The sabre was carried in a steel or iron scabbard with suspension rings for use with a waistbelt. Some officers' sabres had leather scabbards. The broad tip of the blade – it was wider towards the tip than at the hilt – was to draw complaints from French officers after they saw the effects that the sabre had upon their men.

The sabre was to see widespread use in the Peninsula right from the outset. On the retreat to Corunna Lord Paget's hussars made light work of French hussars at Sahagun and Benavente, whilst the terrible cutting power of the Light Cavalry sabre was demonstrated at Campo Mayor, in March 1811, when Corporal Logan, of the 13th Light Dragoons, slew the colonel of the French 26th Dragoons with a cut that 'nearly cleft his skull asunder, it cut in as deep as the nose through the brain.'[2] Creditable actions were fought later on at Usagre and Villagarcia involving light cavalry. At this latter action, at Villagarcia on 11 April 1812, often referred to mistakenly by some historians as Bienvenida, Cotton's cavalry won a victory over the French after which Captain William Bragge, of the 3rd Dragoons, was moved to observe that, 'It is worthy of remark that scarcely one Frenchman died of his wounds, although dreadfully chopped, whereas 12 English Dragoons were killed on the spot and others dangerously wounded by thrusts. If our men had used their swords so, three times the number of French would have been killed.'[3] Here, Bragge is making direct reference to both the heavy cavalry sword and the method of its use. George Farmer, of the 11th Light Dragoons, also made some pertinent observations regarding the British use of the sabre. Farmer was taken prisoner, along with Lutyens' piquet of the same regiment, whilst on duty on the Guadiana river in 1811. He later wrote:

> The wounds inflicted in this trifling affair were all very ghastly. Being inflicted
> entirely with the sword, and falling, at least among the French, chiefly upon

the head and face, the appearance presented by these mangled wretches was hideous; neither were we, though in almost every instance pierced through, one whit more presentable. It is worthy of remark, that the French cavalry, in nine cases out of ten, make use of the point, whereas we strike with the edge, which is, in my humble opinion, far more effective. But, however this may be, of one fact I am quite sure, that as far as appearances can be said to operate in rendering men timid, or the reverse, the wounded among the French were much more revolting than the wounded among ourselves.[4]

The 1796-pattern Heavy Cavalry sword was not of Le Marchant's design and was based squarely on the 1775 Austrian cavalry sword. It had a 35-inch long straight blade, with both edges sharpened for the 12 inches near the tip. It had a single knuckle-bow and a disc-shaped guard pierced with holes. Officers' versions had an ornate hilt compared with the troopers' simple design. One notable feature of the blade was its hatchet point which made it difficult to thrust home and, indeed, by the time of the Waterloo campaign in 1815, troopers of the Royal Dragoons at least were told to sharpen their swords on both sides to achieve a spear point which was much more suitable for the thrust. It was a tremendously fearsome weapon and yet was extremely cumbersome. Bragge's reference to the method of the sword's use brings us to a subject for which there is no room for discussion in this book. Suffice to say that one school advocated the thrust whilst the other thought the cut to be the only way of using the sword. It is quite ironic that Le Marchant, the designer of the Light Cavalry sabre, died in his first major action, at Salamanca on 22 July 1812, armed with his sabre and yet leading the Heavy Brigade which did such devastating work in destroying eight French battalions.[5]

Today the 1796-pattern Heavy Cavalry sword is a much sought-after beast, due partly to the romance attached to the sword in the wake of the Scots Greys' famous charge at Waterloo on 18 June 1815. During the charge Sergeant Ewart captured the 'Eagle' of the French 45th Regiment of the Line. During the fight, Ewart slayed a lancer, an infantryman and the eagle bearer, all of whom perished by way of cuts, rather than thrusts. It is also interesting to note that by killing the enemy lancer Ewart proved that in spite of their nine-foot lances they were not invincible by any means. Ewart's own sword survives today and is one of the original hatchet-pointed swords, not one with a spear point.[6]

Heavy cavalry officers also carried a dress sword, dating from 1796, which consisted of a straight blade, often very ornately decorated, with a gilt pommel, knuckle bow and boat shells and a silver wire grip. This was carried in a black leather scabbard with brass mounts. Dress sword knots were crimson and gold. The Household Cavalry carried the 1796-pattern heavy cavalry sword although officers carried a straight-bladed, basket hilted sword, with a brass scabbard.

At the beginning of the Napoleonic Wars British heavy dragoons were armed with the very cumbersome heavy dragoon carbine, with a barrel which measured all of 42 inches. Imagine having to load and fire this from horseback. In 1796, however, the Board of General Officers approved the issue of a new heavy cavalry carbine with a much shorter 26-inch barrel. Its overall length was 41 inches and it weighed about 8lbs. The bayonet was 15 inches long and weighed a further 13 ounces. Calibre was .75. The following year, many of the carbines were issued with Henry Nock's 'screwless lock', a device by which the trigger mechanism was hidden behind the locking plate. The carbine was attached to the rider's shoulder belt byway of a side bar which was affixed to the stock and which clipped on to the belt by way of a spring clip.

Light cavalry regiments were issued with the famous Paget carbine, the standard light cavalry carbine in the British army of the Peninsular and Waterloo campaigns. It featured a barrel 16 inches long, had an overall length of 31 1/2 inches and had a calibre of 0.66. Innovations included a swivel ramrod and bolted lock, a sort of 'safety catch' which proved most useful for cavalrymen on piquet duty.

In 1803 the 10th Prince of Wales's Light Dragoons were issued with the Baker Cavalry Rifle with a 20-inch barrel and an overall length of 35 inches. Calibre was 0.625. Like the infantry version of the rifle, the barrel was browned, and it had a rear sight and a small compartment for keeping cleaning tools. The carbine also sported a swivel ramrod to prevent its loss in action. A sling bar was fitted to the left side of the carbine which, by way of a spring clip, was attached to the shoulder belt of the cavalryman. A variation of the Baker Cavalry Rifle was introduced around 1813 with a pistol grip stock instead of the usual scroll guard. Dimensions were roughly the same as in the standard Baker Cavalry Rifle, a 35 ½ length overall with a barrel length of 20 ¼ inches. The calibre was 0.625.

The short barrels of both the Elliot Carbine, the Paget Carbine and the Baker Cavalry Rifles did little for the weapons' accuracy but like the Baker rifle, their short, neat forms tuck comfortably into the shoulder and feel just right. The men who used the carbine had different views, however, and thought them pretty useless. But they did prove their worth on occasion. Private Levi Grisdale, of the 10th Hussars, captured the French general, Lefevre-Desnouettes, at Benavente on 29 December 1808 after first sending a shot from his carbine across the Frenchman's cheek. Whether it was the Paget carbine is difficult to say as it had only been introduced that year. It is quite possible that Grisdale was using the Elliott carbine.

In addition to the cavalry carbines both heavy and light dragoons and hussars were armed with pistols. These varied from the Heavy Dragoon pistol, with a 12-inch barrel, to the Light Dragoon model, which sported a 10-inch barrel. As with the muskets, large numbers of pistols were purchased from the arsenals of the East India Company. One of the more attractive pistols was the New Land Pattern pistol which, like the Paget Carbine, had a swivel ramrod to prevent its loss in action. We know that, like infantry officers who took their own private sporting guns with them to the Peninsula, cavalry officers too were wont to take their own pistols with them. As such, a wide variety of non-regulation pistols were used on active service, many with superb levels of craftsmanship.

Notes

1 The standard work on British army swords is Brian Robson's *Swords of the British Army; The Regulation Patterns 1788 to 1914* (London, 1996).
2 *The Courier*, 20 April 1811. Kindly supplied by Philip Haythornthwaite.
3 S.A.C. Cassels (Ed), *Peninsular Portrait, 1811–1814: The Letters of Captain William Bragge, Third (King's Own) Dragoons* (London, 1963), 49.
4 George Gleig, *The Light Dragoon* (London, 1844), 100–1.
5 See chapter 7 in Part 2, 'Mixed Fortunes: From Salamanca to Burgos and Back.'
6 There are numerous examples of the 1796-pattern heavy cavalry sword in Portugal in museums at Obidos and Busaco, all of which have spear points. Whether these were modified during or after the Peninsular War is not clear but it is possible that the Portuguese cavalry ground down the blades to make spear points. Also, just because we have no written evidence to show that spear points were used by British regiments in the Peninsula, it does not mean that the practice did not happen.

CHAPTER V

Piquet and Patrol Work

The bulk of this book concerns itself with the performance of the British cavalry on the field of battle. However, battles in the Peninsula were few and far between, with just over twenty in the six years of the war. Smaller actions and skirmishes were much more frequent but even these accounted for just a fraction of the time spent by the British cavalry during the campaign. We must ask ourselves, therefore, what they were doing for the rest of the time. Well, like their brethren in the infantry, they were mightily bored for most of the time although they did at least have a good deal more routine work to undertake which alleviated the boredom to an extent. Such work included the gathering of intelligence, patrol work, foraging and escort duties and, of course, piquet work.

The British cavalry did not have an entirely happy time when performing some of these tasks and, indeed, have drawn much criticism over the years from historians who have often accused them of being unable to perform basic operations. This accusation is not entirely without foundation although, like the analysis of their performance on the battlefield, the British cavalry's reputation for piquet work has also suffered as a result of two high-profile misadventures. The overwhelming mass of operational work was carried out without a hitch. Furthermore, unlike the analysis of successful actions, which are very easy to identify, it is difficult to quantify the success of outpost and piquet operations in the Peninsula; misadventures at the outposts are identifiable by their very nature and by the consequences for those troops for whom the piquets should have been providing valuable cover. If piquets are surprised and taken the particular episodes are easy to identify. The obvious extension to this is to assume that all other piquet operations were successful by the mere fact that nothing untoward ever occurred. If this is the case, and it is, admittedly, a very crude exercise and assumption, it would appear that the British cavalry piquets and outposts were, in fact, very efficiently and effectively organised. The truth is probably to be found in between the two, with some very serious incidents, such as the capture of Captain Lutyens' piquet of the 11th Light Dragoons on the Guadiana in June 1811. These are matched by months of lengthy, uninterrupted but unremarkable work which, by its sheer ordinary and routine nature, goes unrecorded.

The vital business of intelligence gathering was usually the remit of Wellington's so-called 'exploring officers' – men like Grant, Waters and Cocks, all of whom spent long periods behind enemy lines or on the fringes of French encampments, counting enemy numbers, talking to the local people and clergy and liaising with the Portuguese or Spanish guerrillas. The stories of Colquhoun Grant in particular are so entertaining and fascinating, not to mention enlightening, that they fill a book on their own.[1] Waters, too, is the subject of many a Peninsular tale, but the most important work relating to the period is undoubtedly the collection of letters and diaries of Edward Charles Cocks, one of the most forward-thinking of Wellington's officers and a young cavalry officer who, fortunately for us, left extensive and very pertinent observations on the role of the cavalry.[2] His 'Observations on Piquets' and 'Of attacking small parties of the enemy' provide a valuable insight into military thought in the early 19th century regarding the operation of cavalry in the field. The 1796 cavalry regulations naturally provided the basis for cavalry movements but there was much that they simply did not cater for on campaign, and it was only through the experiences of intelligent cavalry officers in the field that the regulations were to evolve into something rather more practical. Cocks's observations were never published as official or unofficial regulations. He was killed at Burgos in October 1812, a great pity as there was much good advice in them, based upon over three years of campaigning in Spain and Portugal.

Cocks divided the duties of outposts into three categories; the first, those covering an army in position, the second, those covering an army extended in cantonments, and the third, those which cover a line or frontier. He did the same when dealing with patrols. The first category was patrols of reconnaissance or discovery, the second, patrols of security, and the third, patrols of communication. He also dealt with piquets and their duties. In all cases Cocks left advice on troop numbers, the most practical and safest way to conduct the various operations, details relating to procedures, timings, ruses, the use of terrain and, in fact, all manner of sound and very practical advice for cavalry officers on campaign.[3]

Cocks obviously knew that much was lacking in the capability of British cavalry officers in the Peninsula, most of whom had never seen active service, and it quickly became apparent at the outset of the campaign that it was going to be what might be termed a 'hands-on' approach for them, as they got to grips with the science of war, a very different science to that which they had been use to dealing with in England. Inevitably, mistakes were made but the more conscientious officers, like Cocks, learned from them and as a result things improved throughout the war, until by 1814 Wellington's cavalry were thoroughly adept in the art of mounting piquets and patrols. This is not to say that mishaps did not occur. Far from it. Indeed, one of the more notorious cases occurred in Macaye, southern France, in January 1814 and resulted in a Court Martial for the officer involved.[4] However, these were fairly infrequent episodes and it was only through the efforts of men like Cocks that they remained so.

In many ways, Cocks's notes can be compared with the famous Standing Orders written by Robert Craufurd of Light Division fame.[5] Craufurd, another 'scientific' officer as he would have been known, witnessed the breakdown of discipline in Sir John Moore's army during the ill-fated Corurina campaign of 1808–9. During the retreat Craufurd made copious notes relating to affairs during the episode, and upon his return to England these became the basis for an extensive set of orders which concerned all matters relating to the army on the march and in camp. As a result, the Light Division evolved into one of the finest and most highly disciplined divisions in Wellington's army and, indeed, the Standing Orders were later adopted by foreign armies. Cocks, too, was bent on seeing widespread improvements throughout the army, and particularly the cavalry. His observations are not as extensive as Craufurd's but they do, nevertheless, provide the basis for a far more efficient system of outposts and piquets. The tragedy is that they were never issued, of course. Even had he survived, they would have been published too late to have had any real effect, other than late in the war, but they were an acknowledgement that all was not well with the cavalry and some harsh lessons had to be learned before matters improved.

Although Grant, Cocks and Waters are the most famous intelligence officers, there were scores of others, mainly cavalrymen, who would spend long periods behind enemy lines, living with danger and obtaining information, often the hard way. These officers rarely attract the limelight and it is an important aspect of the role of the cavalry that is usually overlooked. The actual business of patrol, piquet and reconnaissance work was normally down to the light cavalry, although it was not uncommon for heavy cavalry too to be employed in such roles. Indeed, the carrying of despatches was often assigned to dragoons. In his small but fine book on the British light cavalry, the late John Pimlott points out the importance which 18th-century tacticians attached to these tasks. They regarded such work as the most important role of light cavalry.[6] Lighter equipment, uniforms and even horses reflected this, whilst the bitter experiences of the British Army in America only served to emphasise it. However, in the Peninsula, the practical uniforms worn by light dragoons were altered in favour of hussar-style uniforms, complete with outrageous fur caps which afforded little protection against either enemy or the elements. It would also appear that, like changes in equipment and uniforms, the tactical and operational functions of light cavalry, learned in America, were quickly forgotten and instead the 18th-century emphasis on the charge returned. The charge, however, was the role of the heavy cavalry who were employed as shock troops against enemy infantry and cavalry. We shall see later on just how effective the heavy cavalry were against both of these arms.

The light cavalry role, redefined to an extent at the end of the 18th century, lingered for just a few years, for although their role at the outposts and at reconnaissance work remained their main task, they still saw themselves in similar roles to the heavy cavalry and the charge as their 'ultimate' objective. In fact, the light dragoons and hussars would perform this function with great distinction, as we shall discover, at Sahagun, Campo Mayor, Orthes and at scores of other actions. However, during the six years of war in the Peninsula the main function of the light cavalry returned to that to which they were best suited, i.e. patrol, piquet and outpost work. This was not through any great intention on the part of the army's commanders, it was simply that experience on campaign led the light cavalry back to those vital tasks which must always accompany an army and it was those tasks which had to be performed by the light cavalry, for there was no other body which could perform the role as effectively. This may be stating the obvious but it is an important and often overlooked point. At the end of the Peninsular War the British light cavalry emerged as being very effective at skirmishing, piquet and patrol work, in addition to having got the better of the French on numerous occasions on the field of battle.

One of the other primary functions of the light cavalry and, for that matter, the heavy cavalry, was the pursuit of beaten enemies. Unlike the tasks dealt with above, pursuit was one aspect at which the British cavalry certainly did not prove adept. Indeed, it was rare for them to follow up any of Wellington's victories even when the opportunity presented itself. There were, of course, circumstances which invariably prevented this, namely the terrain or simply a lack of daylight, when battles had ended late in the evening and darkness brought the curtain down on the fighting. Salamanca and Waterloo stand out as examples. At Orthes it was the broken nature of the ground which prevented the hussars from getting in amongst Soult's fleeing army, but at Vittoria, where the greatest opportunity of all arose, it was the undisciplined conduct of regiments such as the 18th Hussars which thwarted any effective pursuit. True, the ground was not good, but there was enough daylight left and enough fresh British cavalry to have got in amongst Joseph's routed army to have engaged in a very profitable round-up of prisoners. But it was not to be and, as we shall see, Vittoria stands out as the one great example of the failure of Wellington's cavalry to pursue after victory.

Having outlined the perceived functions of the British cavalry in the Peninsula, and at Waterloo, other than its fighting role, it would be well to examine the important task of outpost and piquet work. In his edition of General Orders, John Gurwood, a Peninsular veteran, outlined this very vital role.

One of the most important services of an army in the field is that of the outlying piquet, particularly when in the presence of the enemy. It is then interesting from its peculiar importance, as not only the repose and tranquillity, but the honour and even the safety of a whole army are dependent upon the manner in which it is performed. When the outlying piquet is first posted it is done with a view that with small detached outposts from it, and double sentries, the whole of the front of the position of the division from which it is detached should be covered, and every possible approach so watched that nothing can attempt to pass the line of demarcation between two armies without its being seen and reported.[7]

Gurwood's definition of outpost duties is accurate and sensible enough and is as straightforward as one could wish. The implementation of the system, however, appears to have been very diverse and, as a consequence, was not always a success, as we shall see. Fortunately, these incidents were few and far between and, on the whole, the outpost system worked. For example, the vital manning of the line of the Agueda river in the spring and summer of 1810 was accomplished with complete success. The Light Division, which included the 1st Hussars KGL, and the 14th and 16th Light Dragoons, held an area of over 400 square miles with a front of over forty miles and not once did the prying French manage to penetrate the Allied line, so effective was the system of outposts. True, the British cavalry played only a supporting role in the operation but it does prove that the objective of outposts, as defined by Gurwood, was accomplished, not only on the Agueda but at other locations throughout the war.

Reference has already been made to the 'hands on' approach which, through necessity, the British cavalry appears to have been forced to adopt during the early years of the war. Proof of just how far they had come along this learning curve can perhaps be gauged by the comments of a British hussar, writing in March 1814. It is generally accepted that the KGL cavalry often remained in the saddle during moments of alarm and almost certainly kept their horses saddled. Their British comrades, however, often unsaddled their horses, at least at the beginning of the war, until they too realised the benefits of keeping their horses saddled. 'The uncertainty of our position,' wrote the hussar, 'and the constant change of scene and place, to which we are ever liable (even to the heart's content of a gypsy) almost always keeps *ennui* at a distance. We may be in our present quarters a week, or the bugle may call us to horse within ten minutes, and expectation thus keeps us ever on the *qui vive*. Should our spirits flag for a moment, in a few hours they are sure to be restored by some such unlooked-for event, as a pass-order being suddenly circulated "For the regiment to hold itself in readiness to move at the shortest notice," or for the horses to be saddled, and for every man to lie by his horse's head.'[8]

Although the hussar brigade had only arrived in the Peninsula at the beginning of 1813, they had obviously gained enough experience to learn that it was a prudent measure to keep the horses saddled when close to the enemy. Those British cavalry regiments, particularly the light dragoons, who had been in the Peninsula since 1809 also began to appreciate the wisdom of keeping their horses saddled. William Tomkinson, of the 16th Light Dragoons, wrote in July 1810, 'The duty at Gallegos was very severe. Every morning before 3 a.m. on the alarm ground, and the subalterns were nearly every other night on piquet. When off duty in the daytime, we had so many alerts that little rest could be had. The evenings, from the heat of the weather, were the pleasantest part of the day, and at first we did not lie down so soon as we ought, considering the early hour we turned out. We soon learnt to sleep in the day or at any time – never undressed – and at night all the horses were bridled up, the men sleeping at their heads, and the officers of each troop close to their horses altogether.'[9]

The anonymous British hussar, quoted earlier, also wrote extensively on the experience of piquet duty in the Peninsula, a passage which is worth quoting at length, for it contains many observations regarding the abilities of our cavalry at piquet work, the excitement of such duty and its importance.

When at the advanced posts (as we are at present) our time is delightfully passed in watching the movements of the hostile armies, and the enemy's posts 'en face,' not to say anything of the alert occasioned by his vicinity. I defy any one to name a more exhilarating sound (which can alone be compared to a tally ho! on unkenneling a fox) than that of a shot falling on the ear from the direction of the outlying picket. All attention is instantly concentrated in that direction, and all breathing is suspended until the doubts, as to the cause of the alarm, are either quieted by a failure of its repetition, or confirmed by two or more reports following each other in quick succession. In the latter case, anxiety is shown in the faces of all; some hasten the completion of what previously occupied them; others leave their pursuits for calls now most pressing; the pace of all strollers is accelerated, and the whole camp or quarters is in motion; while cries of 'Get my horse!' 'Where is the trumpeter?' 'Mount the in-lying picket,' or, 'Pack the baggage,' are reverberated to its utmost limits, proving all active in preparation for defence or retreat.

Since crossing the French frontier, we have been enlivened with foraging parties beyond our lines. These have occasionally produced affairs, though of little consequence, our object being solely to procure hay and grain from the vicinity of the enemy, and retreat having been previously ordered, the moment that any likelihood appeared of committing the troops in a serious skirmish.

The disposition of the vedettes, on these occasions, posted towards the enemy with a view to prevent surprise, while the men are off their horses collecting the hay and corn in the farm-houses and granaries, and, if interrupted, the subsequent retreat on our quarters, after an exchange of a few shots, have not only been mightily entertaining, but given opportunities of instruction to our young officers.

Being on picket is not agreeable, although even those in support are obliged to be almost equally alert. If during a march, this duty commences, of course, as soon as we arrive in our quarters or camp, and instead of laying in a stock of repose, we are pushed on a mile or two in front heartily jaded and tired. This is undoubtedly inconvenient, if we have before us the prospect of another march the next day, which insures for ourselves and horses thirty-six hours' duty without any rest whatever. If a line of posts is stationary, we are at the advance half an hour before daylight, in order to strengthen it, should the enemy attack, the dawn of the day being the hour at which they judiciously choose to come on, if they intend to act in earnest; in order, kind considerate souls, to have the whole day, and as much daylight as possible before them, to do us all the harm in their power between sunrise and sunset. It is not a post of any danger, if your men know their duty, and have their wits about them. Not that our nation are by any means suited for this kind of service, our soldiery being mere children of habit, and so seldom thrown on their own resources, particularly intellectual, that they are little capable of reflection, or of being trusted beyond their almost mechanical duties.

Picket is tedious during the day, and at night anxious. You cannot hide from yourself that on you not only the safety of all depends, as the army's watchman, but feel that your own credit rests upon your vigilance. I am always most anxious; and if a patrol (that is, two men who have gone a certain distance on the road towards the enemy) does not return at the usual time, I always mount my horse and go along the road to meet them.[10]

Despite these positive comments by the hussar, William Tomkinson, writing in the spring of 1812, still harboured great doubts as to the abilities of the British cavalry both on piquet duty and, indeed, in the field. Much of his own criticism was directed at the authorities at home in England whose methods of drill were found wanting when put into practice on campaign. I have already stated that it was one thing to practise manoeuvres on the parade ground but an entirely different prospect when putting it to the test in the field. Tomkinson, too, held similar beliefs.

We do everything so quickly that it is impossible men can understand what they are about. They have enough to do to sit their horse and keep in the ranks, without giving their attention to any sudden order. Before the enemy, excepting in charging, I never saw troops go beyond a trot, though in some cases it might be required, and therefore in some movements they should be taught to gallop. These are few, such as moving to a flank in open column of divisions or half squadrons, wheeling into line and charging without a halt. In England, I never saw nor heard of cavalry taught to charge, disperse and form, which, if I only taught a regiment one thing, I think it should be that. To attempt giving men or officers any idea in England of outpost duty was considered absurd, and when they came abroad, they had all this to learn. The fact was, there was no one to teach them. Sir Stapleton Cotton tried, at Woodbridge in Suffolk, with the 14th and 16th Light Dragoons, and got the enemy's vedettes and his own looking the same way. There is much to be learnt in service which cannot be done at home, though I do not mean to say nothing can be taught in England.[11]

Tomkinson's views are very important and give great insight into the military thought amongst British cavalry officers at home during the early 19th century. He emphasises the point that much of what was necessary by way of cavalry drill and procedure had to be learnt whilst on campaign. It was, therefore, the 'hands-on' approach which I have mentioned above. Like the anonymous British hussar, Tomkinson left notes on the procedure adopted by cavalry piquets for warning the inlying piquets of the approach of enemy troops.

'When the enemy appeared,' he wrote, 'the vedette put his cap on his carbine. When he only saw cavalry, he turned his horse round in a circle to the left; when infantry, to the right. If the enemy advanced quick, he cantered his horse in a circle, and if not noticed, fired his carbine. He held his post until the enemy came close to him, and in retiring kept firing.'[12]

This system would appear, on the face of it, to have been very haphazard and clumsy. For example, what happened in darkness, in foggy conditions or when visibility was poor? The procedure certainly appears to have been a non-regulation one, and yet, through the benefit of experience it worked. After all, the 16th Light Dragoons formed one of the regiments attached to the Light Division during the latter's holding of the line of the Agueda in 1810, during which the French failed to penetrate the forty-mile front. True, the bulk of the work on the Agueda was performed by the infantry but the cavalry attached to the division formed an integral part of the operation and I would suggest that the system described by Tomkinson worked here and in other areas, and who better to judge the merits and defects of the system than he himself?

Tomkinson's diary is full of incidents involving affairs at the outposts and is an essential read for anybody researching Wellington's cavalry. There are certainly far too many incidents to examine here. However, in order to see how the system failed we must turn to the south and two infamous incidents involving the 11th and 13th Light Dragoons, both of which occurred in the space of eleven weeks between 7 April and 22 June 1811. The two incidents demonstrated the failings of poor outpost work and coming so close together – and hot on the heels of the Campo Mayor action – they evoked severe criticism from Wellington who, with his faith in the ability of his cavalry already shaken, was driven to greater despair.

The first incident occurred before dawn on 7 April 1811, as Beresford advanced towards Badajoz to lay siege to the town. A squadron of the 13th Light Dragoons, consisting of the troops of Captains White and Serle, under the command of Major Morris was sent across the Guadiana in advance of the main army, and on the evening of 5 April had piquets placed in good positions from which they were able to observe any enemy movements from Olivenza. The following evening Morris's men were relieved by a squadron of Portuguese cavalry under Count Penefield, accompanied by a British officer, Major Foljambe, of the 20th Regiment, who was acting as Assistant Quartermaster General. Morris duly pulled back from his posts after receiving orders from Foljambe to bivouac in a small wood some distance in the rear in the direction of the Guadiana. Apparently, the men had not had any food since 4 April, and when provisions arrived on the evening of the 6th the men duly lit fires and began cooking their meal after first seeing to it that patrols were sent out to cover their right flank, Morris assuming that the Portuguese were covering their left. Sadly, he was mistaken, for at about 3 o'clock in the morning of the 7th, French cavalry, having spotted the fires of the 13th Light Dragoons, swept into their camp whilst the men were asleep, cutting at the British as they awoke. The men tried to defend themselves as best they could but there were around 400 French hussars in their midst and there was little they could do. Some British officers who were billeted in a small house managed to mount their horses, sped out into the night and managed to escape but the majority were not so lucky. Major Morris and Lieutenant Moss were taken prisoner along with one sergeant major, five corporals, two trumpeters, two farriers and forty privates, a total of fifty-two all ranks. Sixty-three troop horses and much baggage was taken also. Only twenty men managed to get away whilst eight were left behind wounded.[14]

Robert Ballard Long, Beresford's cavalry commander, was critical of Morris's arrangements. 'Major Morris seems to have been thrown off his guard so far,' wrote Long, 'as not to have paid attention to the nature of the ground he occupied which it deserved, and besides to have suffered his men to dismount and even unbridle at the very time they should have been prepared for such a rencontre as shortly afterwards took place. The French, on the look out, discovered these errors, and moved out of Olivenza... Their plan was well laid and ably executed... This was a sad blow upon us, a glorious triumph to the enemy. They got a beautiful lot of horses (officers and privates) worth in this country £2,500. But what I regret most is the temporary advantage they obtained over a corps which had a short time before given them a specimen of superiority they will not soon forget.'[15]

This last reference was, of course, to the fight at Campo Mayor, which we shall deal with later, where the 13th Light Dragoons defeated a superior French cavalry force, an action which set the tone for the rest of the year and instilled in the French a great deal of wariness of their British counterparts. The capture of Major Morris was, therefore, quite a setback for the British. Oman placed the blame on faulty staff work, for there was certainly some confusion between the outgoing piquet under Morris and the incoming unit of Portuguese under Penefield, whilst the order to bivouac in rear, given by Major Foljambe, probably only served to confuse things further. Whilst Long was critical of Morris, the historian of the 13th thought him to be the victim of much unjust criticism and claimed, with some justification, that Morris did not consider himself on piquet duty and therefore was entitled to light fires, something which certainly gave his position away to the French. But Morris was not new to the Peninsula, for the 13th Light Dragoons had been out since February 1810, and it is difficult to believe he would make camp without ensuring proper arrangements for its security. On this occasion, however, it would appear that he did not, although I believe his greatest mistake was placing too much faith in the ability of the Portuguese cavalry in front of him. It would and should have been prudent for him to have sent out proper piquets to cover his own position although even these precautions may have been upset by the fact that he lit fires which gave his position away. Given the fact that he and his men had not eaten for two days this is, however, understandable. Wellington himself, present with the main Allied field army farther north, was merely moved to write that he was much concerned to hear of the loss of the 13th Light Dragoons and particularly the cause of it.[16]

The incident at Olivenza should have put Beresford's cavalry on their guard but it was not to be. On 22 June yet another British cavalry piquet was taken wholesale by the French in what was to be a far more disastrous incident. This time it involved the 11th Light Dragoons, a regiment which had only arrived in the Peninsula in May 1811. Ironically, Lord Liverpool had written to Wellington on 11 April informing him of the impending departure from Britain of the regiment. 'I have directed the 11th Light Dragoons to be sent to you,' he wrote, 'for whether it shall be determined to reduce the British infantry or not, it must be a considerable advantage to you to have an efficient body of cavalry, especially as you are now again upon the frontier; and though infantry may be reinforced in a short time, it is impossible to transport suddenly any large body of cavalry, and to look to their arrival in an effective state.'[17]

Once again, the incident occurred close to the Guadiana river, very near the place where the 13th Light Dragoons had come to grief in April. Wellington had been forced to abandon his attempts on the fortress of Badajoz in June 1811 and pulled back to a position on the Caya river. The French force opposed to him, some 60,000 men, with marshals Soult and Marmont at their head, was far superior to the Allied force and on 22 June a strong reconnaissance force was despatched across the Guadiana to test the strength of Wellington's position. Three heavy columns were duly sent out from Badajoz, two of which, on the left and right flanks, encountered Allied outposts, drove them in and returned to make their report. The third column, however, under Latour-Mauborg, with fourteen squadrons of dragoons and lancers, forded the Guadiana south of Elvas at the ford at Jerumenha and soon came into contact with the Allied piquets opposed to them, consisting of the 2nd Hussars KGL on the right, and the 11th Light Dragoons on the left.[18]

The piquet of the KGL hussars, under Lieutenant von Stoltenberg, who had only just taken up their posts, began skirmishing with the French close to the river until they were joined by the main body of the regiment, under Captain Schulze and the relieved piquet under Lieutenant von Issendorf, some two squadrons altogether.[19] The hussars then retired a short distance before turning to charge the leading French regiment. Although the charge broke the French cavalry, it took the hussars into the midst of the main French body and, surrounded on three sides, the KGL hussars were forced to turn and fight their way out with some loss. Having regrouped, the hussars fell back towards a large house, the Quinta de Gremezia, where they were joined by the main body of the 11th Light Dragoons, which had come forward upon hearing the fighting. The French cavalry, having been brought to a halt by the combined force of the 2nd Hussars and the 11th Light Dragoons, turned to their right and made their way north back towards the Guadiana and Badajoz. By moving in this direction they immediately found themselves in the rear of the outlying piquet of the 11th Light Dragoons which was formed by Captain Lutyens' troop. Why Lutyens had paid little attention to the skirmish on his right between the French and the 2nd Hussars KGL is a mystery. Oman certainly blames Long, their brigadier, for not issuing any orders to Lutyens to watch his flank, whilst the historian of the 11th simply claims that Lutyens had been ordered to take up a most unsatisfactory and dangerous position. The situation was made worse by the fact that Lutyens appears to have mistaken the French for either Portuguese or Spanish cavalry which he assumed were coming up to relieve him. It was not until the French were right upon him that Lutyens suddenly realised, much to his horror, just who the approaching cavalry were. Lutyens immediately formed his troop and charged and, like the 2nd Hussars KGL, was successful in breaking the first French line. However, like the KGL, he found himself in the midst of a large enemy force and, after a brief struggle, virtually his entire troop of sixty-five officers and men, was taken, save for a single officer, Lieutenant Binney, who managed to escape. George Farmer was one of those captured.

A smart skirmish began; which lasted without intermission three hours, and the excitement of which hindered us from paying any particular attention to what was going on all the while in our rear. At last, however, some of us chancing to look back, beheld a formidable line drawn out, in such order as to bar our way completely, were we to think of retreating upon the regiment; for the left of the line rested upon a river, and the right leaned upon the wood from which the whole had, during the progress of our affair, emerged. It is marvellous how slow men are to perceive that they have got into a scrape. We never supposed for a moment that these were Frenchmen; we took it for granted that they were Portuguese brought up, we did not care to inquire from what quarter, but placed where they were manifestly for our support. On, therefore, we went with our amusement, till the enemy in our front suddenly called in their skirmishers, and with four squadrons advanced to charge. We were quite incapable of making head against such disparity of numbers; so we gave ground section after section, turning to check the advance, and still keeping up a warm skirmishing fire as opportunity offered. 'Retire upon the Portuguese, men,' exclaimed the captain, 'when they perceive that we are overpowered they will advance; and then, ho! for another push at these rascals.' We did retire upon what we believed to be Portuguese; neither did we discover our mistake till something less than a hundred yards of ground divided us; and then what was to be done. The odds were out of all calculation; yet we were nowise disposed to be taken; so at the captain's orders we closed our files, and rode right at them. Never were men so entirely confounded. It was clear that they expected nothing of the sort; for they sat still, looking us in the face, and never made a movement to meet us. The consequence was, that coming upon them at speed, with all the weight and activity of our more powerful horses, we literally knocked them down like nine pins. Over they went, the horse and rider rolling on the ground; while we, cutting and slashing as we rode, broke through. But, alas! for us, there was a second line behind the first, which behaved differently. We in our turn were charged, and the battle became in a few seconds a mere affair of swords, where there was no room to move either to the front or rear. The result could not be doubted for five minutes. Outnumbered and hemmed in, we were almost to a man cut off. Eight were killed on the spot, twenty were wounded, and sixty-three good soldiers on the whole, lost to the service. The only man, indeed, who escaped to tell the tale, was one of our officers, who, being particularly well mounted, made a dash at the enemy's line; and laying about him, opened a way for himself, though not till he had received a severe wound in the shoulder.[21]

Coming so soon after the mishap to the 13th Light Dragoons, the news of this latest disaster was received at headquarters with much indignation. Writing to Lord Liverpool, six days after the event, Wellington wrote, 'The loss of the piquet of the 11th Light Dragoons, and that sustained by the 2nd Hussars, were disagreeable circumstances; but they tend to show the difference between old and new troops. The old regiments of cavalry, throughout all their services, and all their losses put together, have not lost so many men as the 2nd Hussars and 11th Light Dragoons and 13th Light Dragoons, the former in a few days, and the latter in a few months. However, we must make the new as good as the old. Our cavalry are just now in very good condition.'[22] Here, Wellington did have a point. The 11th Light Dragoons had been in the Peninsula only a month and can certainly be excused for mistaking French for Portuguese troops. However, the fact was that the 11th appear to have been let down by both their own lack of training at home and, to an extent, by their brigadier, Long, who could possibly have done a little more to ensure that these fresh, inexperienced troops were given more by way of protection until they had got a little more used to conditions in the Peninsula. The KGL cavalry were very expert at outpost duties and perhaps Long thought the 2nd Hussars would prove up to the task. However, he appears to have overlooked the fact that the two squadrons of the regiment had arrived only in April and were hardly any more experienced than the 11th. Indeed, the 2nd Hussars would appear to have forgotten one of the basic principles of outpost duties, i.e. that they were to warn the main force of any approaching enemy. It was certainly not their business to go charging pell-mell at any enemy force, let alone a far superior one. The simple and most effective course would have been to draw off slowly, skirmishing as they went, whilst not forgetting to maintain contact with the piquets on the left, being the 11th Light Dragoons. This was simply not done, and the consequence for the 11th was the capture of Lutyens' piquet. Having said this, Lutyens himself was at fault for not looking to his own security. If we are to believe George Farmer's account, the skirmishing referred to by him lasted for around three hours, and this would have been entirely the exchange of carbine fire. For a skirmish of this duration to have been ignored by the commander of a piquet was a gross neglect of duty.

As for Long's part in the affair, Wellington was in no doubt that he was, in part, to blame. Long had evidently been told, and at least should have known, that large piquets were not as effective as smaller ones owing to the difficulty cavalry officers evidently had in controlling them. Whether this was in response to the incident involving the 13th Light Dragoons is not clear, but, judging from Wellington's despatch, the practice of employing large piquets was not the done thing. 'I beg you will order General Long to take up his ground in any convenient situation near Elvas, and that he will attend to the directions he received before from Sir Stapleton Cotton, to throw out small piquets of observation on the Caya and Guadiana. If he had had his whole brigade instead of a large piquet on the Caya, he could not have prevented the enemy from advancing, and the difficulty of retiring is increased in proportion to the numbers of which the body which is to retire consists. The principle is well known and understood in this army; and if it had not been acted upon invariably, we should have lost all our cavalry long ago in the way in which Captain Lutyens lost the piquet of the 11th this morning. To crown all, I understand that these large piquets were not able to give sufficiently early intelligence of the enemy.'[23]

Long himself, writing to his brother on 26 June, obviously thought himself blameless.

> All having been reported quiet in the morning I had rode out to wait upon Sir Wm. Erskine, who commanded en chef, at the time the posts were attacked, and therefore I did not see what passed nor was it in my power to prevent it. Had my orders been obeyed, it probably would not have occurred, but when young officers first come out with young men, they have not always their wits about them, and think only of showing their spunk instead of their judgement. The post occupied by Capt. Lutyens was certainly an unpleasant and indeed an extremely dangerous one; so much so that I had warned all the officers of the piquet I first placed there, by Sir Stapleton Cotton's orders, of their situation, and pointed out vigilance as their only security. I indicated the point by which I considered a retreat alone practicable. Lutyens had, unfortunately, but just relieved the post, when he was attacked, without having had time to prepare and look about him, and I understand the cause of his disaster arose from his mistaking the enemy for his friends, and leading his men in consequence into their very clutches. The loss at this time is to be lamented, but it will do good in the end.[24]

In the light of the above letter it is difficult to see what Long could have done in the circumstances once the action had begun. It was certainly not the business of brigade commanders to go around joining the outlying piquets. He had considered his duty to have been done in informing Lutyens of the dangerous position he occupied, a position of which we find no criticism from any of the major historians, such as Oman, Napier and Fortescue, although some eye-witnesses thought that Lutyens should have occupied some rising ground a little farther back from the Caya, but instead took post too close to the river itself. Writing on 27 June, William Warre wrote, 'It is attributed to some mismanagement in posting our Pickets, which I thought very apparent, and by no means the fault of the Officers commanding them.'[25] Another critic of Long – although an obvious one, given his allegiance to Beresford, one of Long's greatest enemies – was Benjamin D'Urban, who merely said that the whole affair was due to the blunder of a brigadier-general, meaning Long.[26] Edward Cocks, of the 16th Light Dragoons, wrote of Lutyens and his position:

> It is said that he was posted and remained near the Casa Comineda in a sort of punch bowl, that the cavalry which moved from the Puerte de Chico amused him in front while the remainder gained his flank and rear. I am unable to conceive how this could have happened in such a plain. It is said that Lutyens fell back on a column of dust, supposing it to be English and

it was French. But how could an officer allow a column to pass his right without seeing them? How could he fall back on dust without sending to ascertain what it was? How could the whole piquet surrender, one officer only having escaped? Had they either dispersed or endeavoured to make their way through in a body, many must have escaped.[27]

I think there is no escaping the fact that, whilst Long could do little once the fight started, he certainly did Lutyens no favours by placing him in a position which would have been dangerous even for an experienced piquet, let alone one consisting of troops who had been in the country barely a month. But if Long was guilty of faulty dispositions, Lutyens was certainly culpable by having very little knowledge of outpost duties. Cocks, writing on 30 June, echoed Long's sentiments as to the inability of British officers, fresh from England, to be able to mount an effective piquet. 'The 11th [Light] Dragoons have made a bad business of it,' he wrote.

This is to teach soldiers at home nothing but the fiddlestick duties of parade. John Bull, in his growling humour, sometimes talks of the great risk of keeping thirty or forty thousand troops abroad in case the enemy should attack him at home, but either we are to have an army or we are not. If we are, that army – officers, soldiers, generals and all – must learn their business among swords and bayonets or they will be no better than so many citizens. I believe the enemy will never be able to invade England or Britain but if he should, with a respectable army, a pretty business we should make of it if we had nothing to oppose but armies made of men like so many volunteers. To be sure, it is very provoking to lose 125 men of the 11th and 2nd Hussars but still I comfort myself that it will have its use by proving the necessity of training our troops in war itself, and altering our system at home to make it as like war as circumstances will admit. Barracks are the ruin of cavalry and the making of infantry.[28]

Cocks – quite uncannily – wrote in his journal of the business of piquets in such instances. Pre-dating Wellington's own later despatch regarding the strength and size of piquets he wrote:

Piquets may be established for two purposes and it should be always clearly understood which is the object in view, whether to watch the enemy or check him. In the first, a few men can be employed and these should be considerably advanced. In an open country eight or ten men cannot think of fighting and can always gallop away, whereas stronger piquets do not think it honourable to retreat without at least skirmishing with the enemy's advanced guard. Then they get men and horses wounded and, on trying to bring them off, the whole get into a scrape. If piquets are intended to check an enemy's line the most advanced should be very small, but immediately handy to these should be several squadrons forming a reserve, constantly saddled and accoutred. The small advance piquets should be posted with a view to looking out only, the reserve squadrons with a view to the strength and defensibility of the ground.[29]

The remarkable thing about Cocks's entry is that it was written precisely one day before Lutyens' piquet was taken. The irony was that had the latter officer employed just a modicum of Cocks's most sound advice, it is probable that his piquet would not have been taken.

The bottom line to the business was simple – a plague on both houses; Long for his faulty dispositions and Lutyens for his neglect in not knowing his business properly and in failing to secure sufficient intelligence as to just what was occurring away to his right once the 2nd Hussars KGL became engaged with the enemy. This latter regiment was also at fault for not falling back and sounding the alarm but instead getting itself involved in a needless fight. Ultimately, it was a combination of poor management and inexperience that led to the capture of Captain Lutyens and his piquet. It was a blow to Wellington and was, in the words of Cocks, 'the worst affront British cavalry has received in this country.'[30]

Having dealt with the piquet side of things it will be as well to take a look at patrols. The notes left to us by Edward Cocks are very precise as to the conduct and best procedures to be adopted for patrols which, as we have seen, he divided into three categories: the first category being patrols of reconnaissance or discovery; the second, patrols of security, and the third, patrols of communication. The business of piquet and outpost work appears to have been largely a hands-on business, as I have stated above. Patrol work, however, would appear to have been slightly more advanced, judging from a very fine account by George Landsheit, of the 20th Light Dragoons. Landsheit's regiment was the first cavalry regiment to serve in the Peninsula, fighting at Vimeiro where, as we shall see, the regiment was roughly handled when pursuing beaten French infantry. The patrol described by Landsheit took place prior to Vimeiro and so was extremely early in the war. One would be forgiven for assuming that, like piquet work, the British cavalry was not particularly adept at such work. However, Landsheit's account shows that this was not the case for it describes a very capable and effective patrol.

'I was ordered for piquet on the evening of the 20th [August 1808], and repairing to my post, found the General [Fane] mounted, and ready to lead us forth on a reconnoitring expedition. His object was to make us thoroughly acquainted with the localities in our front; so that, in pushing our patrols at night, from point to point, we should incur no risk of falling into error.'[31] Landsheit then describes how general Fane halted the piquet after a few miles before briefing the men and sending out the first patrol in order to gather intelligence. 'It was my business,' continues Landsheit, 'as senior sergeant, to take the command of this patrol – and I have never ceased to look back upon the circumstance as one of the most fortunate in my military life.

> The patrol, consisting of twelve men and a corporal, besides myself, mounted and took the road as soon as I had received my instructions. These were, to move very slowly to the front, keeping every eye and ear on the alert, till we should reach the Red Chapel – not to engage an enemy's patrol, should we fall in with one – to hasten back to the piquet on the first appearance of danger and on no account to trust ourselves beyond the limits which General Fane had marked out. Thus instructed, I ordered the men to march; and, as far as silence and an acute observation could go, we obeyed the officer's directions to the letter. Nor, indeed, would it have been easy, on such a night, and when so occupied, to indulge idle or ribald conversation. The moon shone full and bright, millions of stars were abroad, and the silence was so profound, that the very ripple of the stream could be heard as it wound its tortuous way along the base of the hill down the slope of which we were riding... The world seemed asleep; and we reached the Red Chapel, fully assured that no enemy was or could be within many miles of us. At the Red Chapel we halted, quitted our horses, and, holding the bridles over our arms, applied ourselves to the contents of our haversacks and canteens... My men again mounted, and taking every possible precaution, by sending forward a corporal and a file of troopers to feel the way, we pushed on. At the meeting of the roads the advanced file had pulled up, and once more we were all together; when I directed two men to pass to the right, two to the left, and, with the main body under my own command, I kept the centre. We were to meet in the square or open space round which the village was built, and to communicate each to the other the results of our investigations.
>
> Everything was done with the most perfect regularity. My party, having the shortest distance to travel, was the first to reach the village square, though the detachments were not long after us; and we found, on comparing notes, that the same tranquillity had prevailed here which had prevailed elsewhere.[32]

Landsheit then went to visit the local innkeeper who informed him that a friend from Lisbon had visited him an hour before and had passed the French army along the way, adding that he thought the French were expected in about an hour. Landsheit wrote:

> It was not our policy, however, to return to the camp with a vague rumour. We were inclined to believe the innkeeper, certainly, yet we wished to have his tale confirmed; so I halted the patrol as soon as we regained the Red Chapel and determined to wait the event. I knew that the advance of the enemy, if it did occur, would be made known to us clearly enough by the

clatter of their horses' hoofs when crossing the wooden bridge, by which alone they would enter the village; and being now within my prescribed limits, and having a good half-mile start of all pursuers, the thought of danger never crossed my mind. Accordingly, after placing a couple of vedettes somewhat lower on the slope, in such a situation that they could not be surprised, I directed the remainder to alight, and to keep their ears open. For a while all was still. Not a breeze moved the branches; not a beast or bird uttered a cry; indeed, the only sound distinguishable was the running water, which came upon us most musically. But by and by 'a change came over the spirit of our dream'. Wheels began to rumble; there was a dead heavy noise, like the tread of many feet over a soft soil; and then, the wooden bridge rang again with the iron hoofs of horses. Immediately the vedettes fell back, according to my orders, to report what they had heard, and to learn from us that we had heard it also; and then, after waiting a sufficient time, to leave no doubt upon our minds as to the formidable extent of the column that was moving, we vaulted into our saddles, and returned at a brisk trot towards the piquet. There was much challenging, of course, as we drew towards the vedettes, and demanding and giving the countersign; for we rode briskly; and whether we came as friends or foes, our people knew that there must be something in the wind.[33]

We could wish for no finer account of a routine but effective patrol. Landsheit and his men were in full grasp of their objectives prior to setting out and, having made arrangements during the patrol for securing the intelligence, it set about doing so, waited, obtained the information, and then returned to camp with the minimum of fuss and with no loss in either men or horses. It was, in effect, a typical patrol, although in this case vital intelligence was transmitted to Wellington – then Sir Arthur Wellesley – about the movements of Junot's army prior to Vimeiro. This illustrates just how important such patrols were and the conduct of the patrol would be repeated in the Peninsula for the next six years. Therefore, I would suggest that, given the fact that this patrol was conducted in August 1808, the knowledge of patrol work was more advanced than was that of piquet work which, as we have seen, was to an extent a hands-on learning process for much of the time.

Reading various accounts of military operations during this period would lead us to believe that British cavalry were not very adept at mounting patrols such as those described by Landsheit, particularly when compared to the French who are generally regarded as being masters of the art. But this is not quite the case. In fact, the supposed French superiority over the British is a bit of a myth. Whilst I have stated that this book is not intended to be a comparison between the British and French cavalry, it will be useful to cite a few incidents to demonstrate that the two sides were, in fact, on a par with each other and that French cavalry piquets were prone to the sort of mishap that befell the 11th and 13th Light Dragoons, as described in this chapter. They also go to show that British cavalry were more than capable of ambuscade and surprise. I am conscious of the fact that encounters between the opposing piquets took place almost daily and so are far too numerous to recall altogether. But, at the risk of appearing to be selective, the following incidents – typical, I might add, of those between 1808 and 1814 – demonstrate how good Wellington's cavalry were on patrol. They also show how lax French piquets could be on certain occasions.

The first example takes us back to 17 November 1810 and concerns two patrols of the 16th Light Dragoons. The first patrol, consisting of four men led by Sergeant Liddle of Captain Belli's troop, rode out from Alquentre heading for Rio Mayor whereupon it encountered a French patrol of an officer and fifteen infantry. Liddle shadowed them for a while before attacking them and forcing them to surrender. The incident is pretty insignificant, although typical, of the sort of encounters that took place in the Peninsula. However, it was a much grander surprise that same evening which is more worthy of note. Another patrol of the 16th Light Dragoons, again just four men, led by Sergeant Baxter, came across an enemy infantry piquet close to a house, with all their arms piled in front of it. William Tomkinson takes up the story. '[Baxter] got so near unobserved that he thought he might get to the arms before they could take them up. He galloped forward; they had time to turn out, gave him a volley, wounding one of his men. It was too late to turn back; he persisted in his charge, rode up to the enemy, who laid down their arms, he killing one man. In all, forty-one men and an officer, which he marched in. It was a most gallant thing; but though he succeeded, he was not justified in attacking them.'[34] The same day Sergeant Nichols' patrol took a further sixteen men. It was, therefore, a good day for the regiment. It is interesting that Tomkinson thought Baxter unjustified in his attack. Perhaps he was right, with Baxter having just four men opposed to nearly fifty Frenchmen. If the five British cavalrymen had been killed, wounded or taken, it would have been a disaster. But Baxter obviously thought his chances good and, in the event, that is generally what war is all about. The important aspect, however, is that Baxter was able to get close to the French without being discovered. The French piquet was, therefore, negligent.

A far more important case of French negligence occurred on 31 May 1813 at the passage of the Esla river. The crossing of the river and subsequent concentration on the right bank by Wellington's army was vital to the operations preceding the Battle of Vittoria. The river itself was crossed at various points, but with great difficulty as it was in full flood and many men were drowned. Given the state of the river, the French could have made things far worse for Wellington by disputing the passage but, for some inexplicable reason, they failed to do so. In fact, at Almendra they had a perfect opportunity to do so but were themselves surprised and taken by Grant's cavalry. The French cavalry piquet, of one officer and thirty-two men, lay at the next village, Val de Perdrices and was perfectly placed to dispute the crossing or at least raise the alarm. That it failed to do so is a mystery, but it demonstrates the lack of professionalism that British cavalry have often been accused of showing. Even Sir Charles Oman, no great disciple of Wellington's cavalry, was moved to write with incredulity of the French performance.

> This was certainly about the most extraordinary instance of carelessness on the part of outposts during the war, and reflects as much discredit on Digeon, whose dragoons were supposed to be watching the lower Esla, as on the wretched officer in charge of the piquet. How was it possible that such a large body as a brigade could approach in daylight the best known ford of the neighbourhood, at a spot where the course of the high road showed the convenience of the passage, without finding a single vedette on the bank? And why was such an important point watched (or not watched) by a half-troop, instead of by a force which could have offered at least a momentary opposition, and have passed the alarm to its regiment, which, as Digeon's report shows, was at Iniesta, only four miles to the rear?[35]

It was indeed a gross neglect of duty on the part of the French commander who could have made things far more difficult for Wellington's men. Given his feeble showing at Morales two days later, an episode which is dealt with in a later chapter in this book, it would appear that either Digeon did not have the stomach for a fight at this stage of the war or he was simply deficient in the ways of commanding cavalry.

A far better known incident concerning a British patrol occurred in the summer of 1812, in the days following the Battle of Salamanca. It has none of the consequences attending the failure of Digeon's piquet at Almendra but it does, nevertheless, demonstrate both the negligence of French piquets and the sheer audacity of a British patrol. The episode happened on 26 July when a four-man patrol from the 14th Light Dragoons, with four men of the 1st Hussars KGL, led by Corporal William Hanley, was sent out to observe the movements of the French. The patrol reached the small village of Blasco Sancho in which a party of enemy troops were busy foraging. As Hanley entered the village three French dragoons rode in from the adjacent field where they had also been foraging. The three dragoons were quickly taken, after which Hanley rode to a large house in which the main body of the enemy were busy feeding their horses and preparing for the night. The lock on the door was quickly forced with the aid of a carbine ball and then Hanley got his men to fire down the passage inside the house, apparently with the intention of giving the impression that his patrol was much larger than it actually was. The French officer in command fired at Hanley from a window in a room off the passage, but quickly came out and surrendered. There was no escape for the other Frenchmen and so Hanley called forward one of the German hussars, who could speak French, to tell them that unless they surrendered immediately his men would set fire to the thatched roof. The threat had the desired effect and, one by one, the French cavalrymen filed out of the house after first leaving their sabres behind them. As each man came down the passage and out through the door his carbine was taken from him and the stock broken and thrown away. Much to Hanley's surprise, there were no fewer than twenty-seven enemy troops who, upon seeing that they had given themselves up to just nine Allied troops, were understandably disgusted by it all. Hanley and his party quickly mounted and, with their prisoners in tow, rode back towards the Allied camp. His haul of prisoners was not yet done, however, for on his way back he met a French lieutenant-colonel who, upon seeing Hanley with so many French dragoons, naturally assumed that it was Hanley and his patrol who were the prisoners. 'Good-day, Englishman,' said the French officer, as he slapped Hanley on the back, at which Hanley quickly drew his sabre and, holding it to the shocked Frenchman's throat, made him a prisoner too. The colonel's orderly, with two mules and his baggage, were likewise taken. We may well imagine the sight and reaction back in the Allied camp when Hanley and his strange looking party rode in. Hanley was awarded a medal by the officers of the regiment for his gallantry at a full dress parade.[36]

The incident at Blasco Sancho again illustrates the fact that French piquets and patrols were prone to the same failings as British ones and that there was really no marked superiority on their part. The tardiness of the French patrol at Blasco Sancho is matched only by the audacity of Hanley in capturing it. Furthermore, like the two incidents on 17 November 1810, it is worth noting that on each occasion the British patrol was commanded by either a sergeant or a corporal. This says much for the skill of the NCOs in being able to accomplish so much without the assistance of an officer. One wonders also, given Tomkinson's view that Sergeant Baxter, of the 16th Light Dragoons, was ill-advised when attacking the French on this latter date, whether officers would have adopted the same course of action or whether they would have sent for reinforcements. Or was Tomkinson merely envious that such an attack should have succeeded so well? It is difficult to say, but these three incidents do serve to demonstrate the effectiveness of NCOs in the field.

The success of the sort of small-scale skirmishes mentioned above should not, however, obscure the failings of the system when reporting enemy movements, numbers and positions. This was, after all, one of the most important functions of the cavalry. Wellington prided himself on being able to know what was going on 'on the other side of the hill', and much of the intelligence came from cavalry officers and small patrols like

Hanley's. But if the information was not accurate it could often cause more problems for Wellington that it solved. The fact is that information was wrongly reported, leading to a General Order, issued on 7 May 1811 from Wellington's headquarters at Villar Formoso. In the order, Wellington wrote: 'The Commander of the Forces requests that when an officer makes a report of the movements of the enemy, he will specify whether consisting of cavalry, infantry or artillery; the number, as far as he could judge; the time when seen, and the road on which moving; from what place, and towards what place, if the officer can state it; and if reference should be made to the right or the left in the report, care should be taken to state whether to the right of our own army of that of the enemy.'[37]

This was sound advice, the result, almost certainly, of many erroneous reports which would have caused no end of problems. Cavalry officers and, indeed, NCOs, were therefore required to have a good appreciation of the facts requested by Wellington, and this often had to be done under dangerous circumstances. Captain William Light, for example, in a very famous incident in March 1814, feigned death by hanging down across his horse's neck before riding the length of a French column. The enemy skirmishers, taken in by the ruse, held their fire, assuming he was mortally wounded. Once Light had got to the far end of the column, having counted its numbers, he rode back before suddenly springing upright again and returned to Wellington with the required information. This was certainly not the usual manner of gaining information but it was an effective one.

We have seen that in the 1796 *Regulations and Instructions for Cavalry*, a copy of which every cavalry officer was to have, there is not a single reference to the gathering of intelligence, out-post duties or patrol and reconnaissance work, with the emphasis being firmly on manoeuvring, on charges and on drill and parades. How, therefore, was a cavalry officer to learn about these other duties? It was, of course, by virtue of the hands-on approach, what we might call today 'the school of hard knocks'. As I have already stated, it is difficult to quantify the success of Wellington's piquet and patrol work as it was happening each and every day in the Peninsula and on the outskirts of each and every camp, of which there were many. The notable successes are described above, as are the disasters. Ultimately, I would consider the British cavalry to have made a good job of their routine work in the Peninsula, from the early days of 1808 right up until the close of the war in 1814. This is not to say there were not setbacks at this latter stage of the war. Far from it. When Wellington entered France he was fighting on the enemy's home soil. Furthermore, many of the French cavalry bases, such as Tarbes and Bayonne, were situated in the south where the terrain would have been well-known to them. Fortunately, there were very few mishaps to the British cavalry, the most notable being Macaye in January 1814, but this did not result in any great loss although it did result in the Court-Martial of Colonel Quentin of the 10th Hussars.

Macaye simply brought to a head a series of disputes and mismanaged internal affairs between Quentin and his officers, hence the Court-Martial. That, however, is another story.

Let us finish this chapter with a passage from Sir Charles Oman, the great historian of the Peninsular War. As will be gauged from the subsequent chapters in this book, I consider Oman to be very critical of the British cavalry and a source of much myth and flawed research. However, when it came to his appreciation of the cavalry's outpost and piquet work, even he recognised their achievements. 'In short,' he wrote, 'the proper work of cavalry, apart from mere charging, had to be learnt on Spanish soil when any regiment landed. But it was in the end picked up by the better corps, and on the whole the outpost and reconnaissance work of the Peninsular Army seem to have been well done, though some regiments had a better reputation than others.'[38]

Notes

1 Grant's biography, *The First Respectable Spy: the life and times of Colquhoun Grant, Wellington's head of intelligence* was written by Jock Haswell and published in London in 1969.

2 Julia Page (Ed), *An Intelligence Officer in the Peninsula: the letters and Diaries of Major the Hon. Edward Charles Cocks, 1786–1812* (Tunbridge Wells, 1984).

3 Ibid. 212–23.

4 *The Trial of Colonel Quentin of the 10th, or Prince of Wales's Own Regiment of Hussars* (London, 1814).

5 See *Standing Orders as given out and enforced by the late Major General Robert Craufurd for the use of the Light Division during the years 1809, 1810 and 1811.* (Corfu, 1837, and various subsequent editions).

6 John Pimlott, *British Light Cavalry* (London, 1977), 33.

7 J. Gurwood, *The General Orders of Field Marshal the Duke of Wellington in the Campaigns of 1809 to 1818* (London, 1837), xli–xlii.

8 'A Hussar's Life on Service', *The United Service Journal*, 1829, part 1, 428.

9 James Tomkinson (Ed), *Diary of a Cavalry Officer in the Peninsular War and Waterloo Campaign, 1809–1815* (London, 1894), 30.

10 Ibid. 428–9.

11 Ibid. 135.

12 Ibid. 136.

13 The regimental history of the 13th Light Dragoons gives the officer's name as Morres.

14 By far the best account can be found in Barratt, *History of the 13th Hussars* (London, 1913), I: 141-3.

15 T.H. McGuffie (Ed), *Peninsular Cavalry General (1811–13): The Correspondence of Lieutenant Gener Robert Ballard Long* (London, 1951), 85–6.

16 Wellington to Beresford, 13 April 1811, *The Despatches of Field Marshal the Duke of Wellington during his various campaigns* (London, 1832), VII: 461

17 Lord Liverpool to Wellington, 11 April 1811, *Supplementary Despatches, Correspondence and Memoranda of Field Marshal the Duke of Wellington* (London, 1860), VII: 102

18 Oman claims that Latour-Mauborg crossed in front of Elvas but also states that his column formed the centre column. Given that he also states that Montbrun, forming the right-hand column, crossed by the bridge at Badajoz itself, it is almost certain that Latour-Mauborg and Broil, forming both the centre and left columns respectively, crossed the Guadiana at the same point, Jerumenha, as there are no other crossing points between here and Badajoz. It is an important point as it accounts for how Latour-Mauborg was able to get in the rear of the 11th Light Dragoons' piquet.

19 See N. Ludlow Beamish, *The King's German Legion* (London, 1832), II: 6. The remainder of the 2nd Hussars KGL were farther south at Cadiz having taken part in the Battle of Barrosa in March 1811.

20 Captain G. T. Williams, *The Historical Records of the Eleventh Hussars Prince Albert's Own* (London, 1908), 115.

21 George Gleig, *The Light Dragoon* (London, 1843), 93–6.

22 Wellington to Lord Liverpool, 28 June 1811, *Despatches,* VIII: 58.

23 Wellington to William Erskine, 22 June 1811, *Despatches,* VIII: 40–1.

24 McGuffie, *Peninsular Cavalry General,* 119.

25 The Rev. Edmund Warre (Ed), *Letters from the Peninsula, 1808–1812* (Staplehurst, 1999), 122.

26 I.J. Rousseau (Ed), *The Peninsular Journal of Major-General Sir Benjamin D'Urban, 1808–1817* (London, 1930), 226.

27 Page, *An Intelligence Officer in the Peninsula,* 121. Cocks goes on to claim that the 2nd Hussars KGL charged three squadrons of enemy lancers and suffered heavy casualties in bringing off General Long and his baggage, although I have no record of this being true. Long himself states that he was with Erskine at the time, so I would suggest that, as Cocks was not present, he was probably acting on hearsay.

28 Ibid. 125.

29 Ibid. 121.

30 Ibid. 121.

31 G. Gleig, *The Hussar* (London, 1837), 255.

32 Ibid. 257–60.

33 Ibid. 261–3.

34 Tomkinson, *Diary of a Cavalry Officer,* 59–60. The memoirs of both Tomkinson and Cocks are full of such attacks on French piquets.

35 Oman, *History of the Peninsular War,* VI (Oxford, 1902), 330–1.

36 Col.H.B.H. Hamilton, *Historical Record of the 14th (King's) Hussars* (London, 1901), 104–5, 109–11.

37 General Order, Villar Formoso, 7 May 1811.

38 Sir Charles Oman, *Wellington's Army, 1809–14* (London, 1913), 110–11.

CHAPTER VI

The Iberian Peninsula: 'The Grave of Horses'

SPAIN AND PORTUGAL

The Iberian Peninsula is no place for cavalry. From the rocky, rugged hills of Portugal to the mountain barrier of the Pyrenees, there are few places where cavalry can operate with any degree of effectiveness. And, unfortunately for the British cavalry, those areas where cavalry could be used, such as the plains of Leon around Salamanca, and in the south in Estremadura and Andalucia, were regions where Wellington spent very little time campaigning. Indeed, it is no coincidence that many of the actions which we shall be studying took place in the south, where the rolling plains afforded cavalry ample space both for manoeuvring and for ease of operation. Sadly, it was not an area of any great strategic importance, a fact borne out by Wellington's almost continual absence. The Commander-in-Chief paid only fleeting visits to the region, contenting himself with leaving his lieutenants, Rowland Hill in particular, to oversee operations while he remained farther north with his main field army.

It is important to grasp the diverse nature of the topography of Spain and Portugal if we are to understand some of the problems faced by the British cavalry and the limitations imposed upon it. For no matter how well equipped, strong, disciplined and experienced are your cavalry, none of these qualities can be best exploited if you do not have the country in which to operate.

When the British Army landed in Portugal in the summer of 1808 it did so with just 240 cavalry, a seemingly paltry figure with which to begin a campaign. On the face of it this does not seem to be too serious given the rugged nature of the country to the north of Lisbon. However, even though there would be little scope for cavalry in combat there is always a need for patrols and piquets. Moreover, given the fact that in the summer of 1808 the Peninsula was new to the army, one would have felt it only natural that this most vital arm of the army would have been much stronger. In the event, the shortcomings did not have too adverse an effect on the campaign which was won largely by the British infantry.

The terrain over which the 1808 campaign was fought is barely forty miles from east to west, bounded by the Tagus and the Atlantic. It is a similar distance from north to south, although, when we consider that the actual campaigning took place between the village of Roliça and the town of Torres Vedras, this distance is drastically reduced. This country is characterised by woods and rocky valleys, by winding roads and by small rivers and rivulets. It is no coincidence that it was here that Wellington later chose to build his Lines of Torres Vedras, the land affording good, rugged defensive qualities, the sort which rendered the Lines impregnable to Masséna's invading French army in 1810. In short, this was no place for cavalry. We need not concern ourselves with the area to the south of Torres Vedras as there was no fighting here during the war. North of Roliça, however, and as far as the Mondego, there was plenty of fighting, albeit of a fluid nature, during Masséna's retreat from the Lines in the spring of 1811. The terrain here is again of a rugged nature and stretches for about 100 miles until the Mondego is reached. There were several sharp fights during Masséna's retreat, notably at Pombal, Condeixa, Casal Nova, Redinha and Foz d'Arouce, but these were short, swift infantry actions fought between the French rearguard, commanded by Ney, and, more often than not, the Light Division, supported at various times by the 3rd and 6th Divisions. The final action, at Sabugal, falls within a different area altogether, so we will leave that for the moment. Wellington's cavalry was always at the forefront of the pursuit of Masséna's army but visibility was difficult at best, it being almost impossible to see over wide distances owing to the broken nature of the terrain. And, even when these wooded valleys gave way to more accessible country it was usually impossible for cavalry to deploy into fighting formation. The absence of any real French cavalry activity only serves to confirm how difficult it was for cavalry to operate to great effect.

North of the Mondego we find the long, dominating ridge of Busaco, which is certainly unsuitable for cavalry. Again, the only work engaged in by Wellington's cavalry during the days before and after Busaco, in September 1810, was of a purely reconnaissance and patrolling nature and, although present during the battle itself, the cavalry saw little if any action. There was no real campaigning between the Mondego and Douro rivers during the war which leaves us with very little of Portugal, save for a corridor running north-south, parallel with the Portuguese-Spanish border, and stretching fifty miles inside the latter. This corridor varies from very rugged country around Almeida and Sabugal, a wide area covered with woods and barren rocky plains, interspersed with rivers and small streams, to the greener areas to the south around. Elvas and Campo Mayor, where we find wide, rolling plains. Therefore, we find much activity in the south, with many small actions and skirmishes involving the British cavalry, whereas in the north, around Almeida, the cavalry

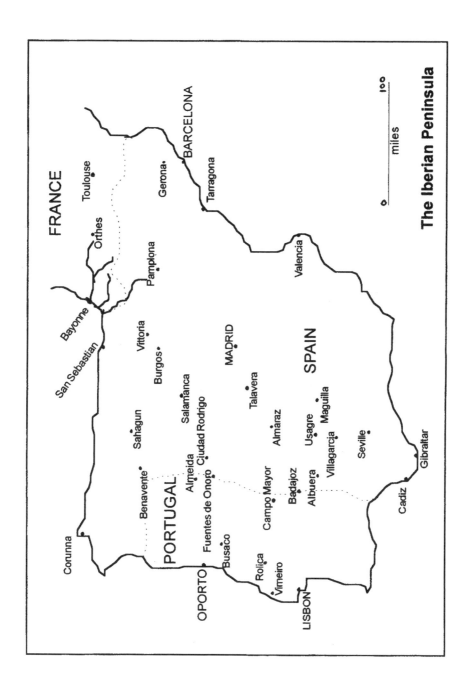

The Iberian Peninsula

operations were of a purely outpost and patrolling nature. This corridor was also the main route north-south for Wellington's army during the war, the Spanish equivalent being far bleaker and less hospitable or practical for large-scale army movements, as Junot had discovered to his cost in October and November 1807.

Spain itself presents a far more varied country as far as terrain is concerned. In the north west, we find the mountains of Galicia which prohibit cavalry activity in much the same way as the Pyrenees. The British Army spent just a few months in this region, during the Corunna campaign in the winter of 1808–9, during which there were just a few skirmishes and the Battle of Corunna itself. However, it was during this campaign that the cavalry achieved some of its finest successes, at Mayorga, Sahagun and Benavente. These latter two actions were fought on battlefields which were small but relatively flat, allowing the cavalry room both to deploy and fight, two conditions which were unfortunately absent on so many other battlefields. Once into the mountains there was little scope for satisfactory cavalry action and so, like the majority of the rest of the army, the cavalry regiments concentrated on reaching Corunna and the ships waiting to transport them back to England.

The main areas of Spain in which Wellington's army did most of its campaigning between 1810 and 1813 were in Estremadura and Andalucia, in Leon between Ciudad Rodrigo and Portugal, and between Ciudad Rodrigo and Burgos. Yes, the Vittoria campaign falls within this period, but it took just two months – May and June 1813 – before the army moved into the Pyrenees. The other three named areas saw much activity, particularly the border region between Ciudad Rodrigo and Almeida. This area is not ideal cavalry country but there are large tracts of wide open land which did allow Wellington's cavalry to operate efficiently. However, the nature of much of this took the form of outpost work, particularly during the spring and summer of 1810, and patrol and reconnaissance work, a vital task which the cavalry performed with great credit. The area to the east of Ciudad Rodrigo, between there and Salamanca and continuing on to Burgos is ideal for cavalry–large open expanses of rolling countryside with only a few rivers and streams to hinder operations. The problem was that the army spent very little time here, during the run up to the Battle of Salamanca in July 1812 and during the retreat from there in October and November of the same year, following the debacle at Burgos. Therefore, very few satisfactory actions took place here, although, once again, there was scope for the 'bread and butter' work, such as patrols, reconnaissance, piquet work and the gathering of intelligence.

The real cavalry country is to be found in the south, in Estremadura and Andalucia, where flat, rolling fields extend for mile after mile and where, in places, it is possible to gaze out over vast distances with nothing to obscure one's line of vision. It is here, in the south, that so many of the actions studied in this book took place – Usagre, Maguilla, Los Santos and Villagarcia. It is where Beresford almost lost the Battle of Albuera in May 1811, a battle which saw his British cavalry put their French adversaries to flight with successive charges. Unfortunately, it was also an area of lesser strategic importance to the Allied cause, hence Wellington's absence for almost the whole of the war.

The south provides us with the area of greatest interest for it is here that much of what went right – and wrong – for the British cavalry occurred. We can evaluate British piquets, see the cavalry in action against the much-vaunted French cavalry and put individual cavalry commanders in the spotlight, for the British cavalry was engaged in this particular theatre of war far more than their infantry comrades. Indeed, southern Spain emerges as the most concentrated area of cavalry activity in the Peninsula, which is perhaps no surprise given the nature of the terrain. And that brings us back to the original point; unless you have suitable campaigning country you will not see your cavalry at its best.

This leaves just three more regions to be discussed. The first includes the area of the Vittoria campaign, from the Douro to the Ebro, an area dissected by rivers and valleys and one where again Wellington's cavalry could not be used to its full capabilities. Despite this, the Vittoria campaign yielded one very successful cavalry action, at Morales de Toro, fought on a plain outside the town on the northern bank of the Douro. Unfortunately, the nature of Wellington's strategy – an outflanking move through the apparently impassable country to the north of the great road back to France – meant that his cavalry was never able to deploy on a wide scale, not that it was ever called upon to do so, the French remaining completely unaware of the whereabouts of the Allied army until it was almost upon them at Vittoria itself. Instead, the cavalry was used in the conventional role as part of the vanguard and on patrol work. As we shall see at Vittoria, Wellington held his cavalry firmly in check until late in the day when his hussars were launched against the breaking French army. Sadly, there was no effective pursuit as many cavalrymen stopped to help themselves to the enormous amount of treasure which had been abandoned by the French in their panic and Joseph's army was allowed to slip away towards Pamplona and France.

After the great victory at Vittoria Wellington pushed on to the Pyrenees where, given the mountainous nature of the region, the cavalry was sent into cantonments at Logroño, save for a few light dragoons and hussars who accompanied the army and who did sterling work at the piquets. Serious cavalry operations were definitely out in this region, however, and it was not until the spring of 1814 that Wellington's cavalry were brought forward once again to join the pursuit of Soult's army east towards Toulouse.

SOUTHERN FRANCE

The winter of 1813–14 saw some light cavalry units in action during the invasion of France and during the Battles of the Nivelle and Nive, but on the whole, the region bordering northern Spain and southern France, with its mountains, hills, rivers and hedges, holds few joys for cavalry. The Bidassoa crossing on 7 October 1813 was purely an affair for infantry with some small units of cavalry involved merely as supports. The steep cliff-like hills overhanging the river make it virtually impossible for cavalry, save at the western end where the main route into France ran. The following month saw the Battle of the Nivelle, considered by Wellington to be his finest achievement. But, once again, the very hilly nature of the ground over which the battle was fought precluded any cavalry activity. Indeed, it is interesting to note that some thirty-nine infantry regiments took part in the great battle, .suffering just over 1,200 casualties between them, whereas Wellington's cavalry suffered just one man – of the 12th Light Dragoons – wounded. And it was a similar story in December 1813 during the Battle of the Nive where virtually all of the fighting was done by the infantry, the area being of a very broken, wooded nature, with sunken lanes, tall hedges and small hills, all of which made it almost impossible for cavalry to act in any effective manner.

The last opportunity for Wellington's cavalry in the Peninsula came towards the end of the war, between Orthes and Toulouse, where several British cavalry regiments were involved in frequent skirmishes with the French. The countryside here resembles England, with valleys and rivers and with fields bordered by tall hedges, something noted by more than a few British soldiers in their diaries. It is not an area where cavalry can be used to great effect in battle but it did provide much more scope for the day-to-day operational tasks than had been afforded by the inhospitable region of the Pyrenees and by the hilly country along the Bidassoa and Nivelle rivers.

THE BATTLEFIELDS

Having dealt with the topography of the Peninsula on a much wider scale, we must make a survey of the individual battlefields in order to get an appreciation of some of the limitations imposed upon the British cavalry in battle. This may appear on the face of it to be a rather crude exercise in terms of re-appraising British cavalry, particularly when we consider that only a tiny fraction of the time spent in the Peninsula was spent fighting battles. But, given that so much myth has grown up around the cavalry's performance and that much of that myth stems from its performance on the battlefield, it would be as well to examine these battlefields themselves. I shall make only a brief allusion to the actual fighting as more detailed accounts follow in later chapters. Here, I want only to discuss the battlefields themselves.

Roliça and Vimeiro are perhaps not the best places to begin. True, they were the first battles fought by the British Army in the Peninsula, but as there were barely 240 cavalry present they are hardly worth our consideration–were it not for the fact that Vimeiro saw the first misadventure, when the 20th Light Dragoons charged too far in pursuit of beaten French infantry, only to be badly mauled in turn. This has little to do with the topography of the battlefield, however, and we shall examine this particular episode later on in another chapter. I would say that, even if there had been more British cavalry present at Roliça and Vimeiro, their contribution could not have been any more significant, as both battles were brought to a swift end after successful infantry actions. At the former the French fought a gallant rearguard action to make good their escape, whereas at the second Wellesley was superseded by Burrard and Dalrymple who decided that further action or indeed any pursuit was unnecessary.

With Wellesley, Burrard and Dalrymple back in England to face the inquiry into the Convention of Cintra, command of the British Army in Portugal devolved upon Sir John Moore whose brave campaign ended in tragedy both for him and his army. The retreat to Corunna remains one of the most harrowing of episodes in the history of the British Army with Moore and his men marching mile after mile through the snow-covered Galician mountains with Soult's French troops conducting a vigorous pursuit. The Battle of Corunna, fought on 16 January 1809, afforded little scope for the British cavalry, most of whom were in no condition for a fight after the retreat. However, during the retreat itself Lord Paget's hussar brigade – the 7th, 10th, 15th and 18th – fought some very creditable actions, at Mayorga, Benavente and Sahagun. These latter two actions were fought on relatively level fields with little to hinder either deployment or use. At Benavente, on 29 December 1808, the battle was fought over a plain stretching between the town and the Esla river which allowed Paget's hussars, supported by cavalry of the King's German Legion, to manoeuvre in successive charges against their opponents who were driven back with heavy loss upon the river; all this under the watching eyes of the Emperor Napoleon himself. Eight days earlier at Sahagun, Paget had achieved what Oman later called the most brilliant cavalry exploit of the war, when his hussars surprised, attacked and routed a force of French cavalry, again over ground suitable for cavalry in spite of the freezing temperatures which made conditions treacherous underfoot. The battlefield was small in comparison with other battlefields but, like Benavente, this was an all-cavalry affair and the chosen field was required to be nowhere near as large as 'regular' battlefields involving all arms. Both Benavente and Sahagun allowed the cavalry to deploy, charge and then fight without the need to worry about either broken ground, which might hinder a charge, or dead ground, in which enemy reserves might or might not be concealed. Sahagun was crossed by some drainage ditches, but apart from a deep ditch which skirted the western end of the field – which was quickly negotiated – there was really nothing to restrict movement. Hence, Paget's hussars were able to form up, charge and scatter their French enemies in a fair stand-up fight. It was the only time during the Corunna campaign when conditions allowed for such a fight.

The first battle upon Wellesley's return to the Peninsula was not so much a battle as a daring river crossing, the passage of the Douro on 12 May 1809. Here, there was no scope whatsoever for any cavalry action, although three light cavalry regiments formed part of Murray's force which was intended to cut off Soult's retreat from the town and, indeed, the 14th Light Dragoons were awarded 'Douro' as a battle honour.

The next major action we must concern ourselves with came on 27–28 July at the Battle of Talavera. It was the battle which earned for Wellesley the title 'Wellington'. It was also a battle which gave him further cause for concern over the conduct of his cavalry. The escapade of the 23rd Light Dragoons is dealt with later on, but as far as the battlefield is concerned we find a very broken, rocky field, dominated by two hills, the Medellin and the Cascajal, and strewn with vineyards and cork trees. There was certainly scope for the deployment of cavalry, but only to an extent, as the broken nature of the ground forming Wellesley's centre restricted forward movement, as did a ravine through which flows the Portina brook. To the north, however, there runs a valley along which the 23rd Light Dragoons charged, probably the only area over which Wellesley could have used his cavalry. But it is very rough ground, particularly around the middle of the valley which marked the demarcation between the two armies. Here, the ground falls away and rises very deceptively and, as we shall see, a deep, dry watercourse ran across the valley in 1809 into which the light dragoons tumbled. It can be said, therefore, that whilst it was possible to use cavalry along the valley, the regimental commanders had to ensure that control was asserted at all times and care taken during any charge, something which was sadly lacking.

The battlefield of Busaco, fought over on 27 September 1810, is certainly no place for cavalry, and despite the loss of four men amongst the 14th and 16th Light Dragoons, Wellington's cavalry played no part in the battle whatsoever. Anybody who has visited the battlefield will quickly understand why–the steep, rocky slopes proved difficult for infantry to climb, let alone cavalry. The ridge extends for some eight miles north from the Mondego and nowhere can you imagine cavalry being used there. No, Busaco was an infantryman's battle and thus, another battle is fought with little cavalry involvement.

Between Talavera and Busaco there was a great deal of cavalry activity, mainly on the Portuguese border, but this took the form of small combats and skirmishes between opposing piquets. The most notable fight which interests us was at Villar de Puerco, on 11 July 1810. Again, we shall deal with this episode later. And we have already discussed the ground on the border, an area strewn with rocks and rocky chasms with fords which rose and fell almost by the hour, a most difficult and unpredictable area for cavalry to operate in but one in which good light cavalry could and did excel at piquet work.

The spring of 1811 saw Masséna ejected from Portugal, his sorry army dragging itself back into Spain with the loss of thousands of men. The final French invasion was thwarted, but there still remained the fortress town of Almeida, garrisoned by a French force under General Brennier. It was an attempt by Masséna to relieve the garrison that led to the next great battle in the Peninsula, at Fuentes de Oñoro on 3–5 May 1811. This battlefield can be divided into three sectors; the northern sector, from the village of Fuentes de Oñoro itself to Fort Conception, being impassable for infantry, let alone cavalry; the middle sector, from the village to Poço Velho, much more accessible and certainly suitable for cavalry, and the southern sector, from Poço Velho to Nave de Haver, ideal for cavalry which is why there was such widespread cavalry activity during the battle. The sector forms a large, rolling plain, ideal for cavalry combat, with few obstacles to restrict or prevent movement.

In terms of activity and suitable battlefields, 1811 was a good year for cavalry. As well as the Battle of Fuentes de Oñoro there was a mass of activity in the south with several good skirmishes and other small incidents, not to mention the great controversies of Campo Mayor and Maguilla. As far as major battles go, however, there was also Albuera, fought eleven days after Fuentes. This savage battle too provided much scope for British cavalry to show what it could do, with low rolling hills and a vast plain to the west providing plenty of room for manoeuvre, the sort which had been lacking in so many of the earlier Peninsular battles.

We need not dwell on either of the great sieges which took place at the beginning of 1812, Ciudad Rodrigo and Badajoz, but move on instead to the battlefield which allowed Wellington's cavalry to achieve the most devastating results of any Peninsular battlefield, Salamanca. Virtually all of the conditions required by cavalry to operate effectively came together on 22 July 1812 with devastating effect; a good commanding officer, superb 'softening up' by the infantry and, finally, a great rolling plain on which to deploy. The battlefield of Salamanca actually varies a great deal, with dips and folds, small quarry-like depressions, long, ranging ridges and, of course, the two peculiar box-shaped hills, the Arapiles. But the chosen ground over which Le Marchant and his heavy dragoons charged was almost perfect, with a low ridge masking their initial advance and a wide, flat valley on which to fight once contact had been made with the French infantry. The pursuit afterwards was made easy by an extensive flat plain to the south and it was only a dense wood which saved the fugitives from further punishment. Sadly, the battlefield of Salamanca is a rarity, and the conditions on 22 July – which had never been met before – were not to be repeated.

The Battle of Vittoria, on 21 June 1813, was Wellington's next major action, although there had been several skirmishes after Salamanca – including the charge of the King's German Legion at Garcia Hernandez – and following the retreat from Burgos in October and November 1812. There had also been a notable triumph for Wellington's hussars at Morales de Toro, on 2 June 1813, during the preliminaries to the Vittoria campaign. Here, a sprawling plain provided a most suitable battlefield for the British cavalry and, as we shall see, a most handsome victory was gained. Unfortunately, the powers that be decreed that it would not stand either as a battle honour or as a clasp to the General Service Medal, as both Sahagun and Benavente were. Vittoria itself saw Wellington's cavalry finally take the field in great numbers but, sadly, the battlefield was far too broken for them to be used effectively. The valley of the Zadorra, through which the river flows, has a boundary formed of several small villages, each of which required infantry to flush out the defenders. And it was the infantry which did the majority of the fighting, suffering 4,000 casualties against a mere 150 suffered by the cavalry. In fact, the cavalry was only deployed and used towards the end of the day when Joseph's army had begun to crumble. The ground was not particularly suited to large-scale cavalry movements, but there are areas where they could have been used to greater effect. Another major factor in the ineffective pursuit afterwards – where Wellington's cavalry should have done some really good work – was the tremendous amount of treasure abandoned by the French which stopped virtually all of the advancing Allied units in their tracks, so eager were they to fill their pockets. In any case, the country to the east of Vittoria, across which Joseph's army retreated, is criss-crossed by numerous streams and cuttings which would have hampered any Allied pursuit.

I have already alluded to the battlefields of the Pyrenees, the Bidassoa, the Nivelle and the Nive in the section on the Iberian Peninsula above. We need not dwell on any of these battlefields as they are all totally unsuitable for cavalry. Indeed, it is no coincidence that, save for a few units of light cavalry, all of the British cavalry were sent back to the area around Logroño during the late autumn and winter of 1813, Wellington recognising the fact that there would be little use for them during this particular period of the war, taking place as it was in such inhospitable country.

The next major battlefield on which Wellington's cavalry fought was that of Orthes, fought on 27 February 1814. This, like the regions of the Nivelle and the Nive, is not altogether suitable for cavalry, with broad ravines and re-entrants leading up to a long, low ridge. Tall hedges and lanes also made it difficult for the cavalry to deploy. However, the cavalry did manage to take part in the battle, making several charges along the ridge in support of their infantry comrades. And of course, they were in their element during the pursuit of Soult's army afterwards. The last battle of the war took place on 10 April 1814 at Toulouse, an assault on a city bordered by a canal and by a low ridge. Again, this was no place for cavalry, save in a supporting role, but four cavalry regiments still did enough to be awarded 'Toulouse' as a battle honour.

So, what do we have at the end of all this? Well, as I said at the outset this is a fairly crude exercise, dealing with only the major Peninsular battlefields. But, as many historians have judged the British cavalry on its performance in battle, it is worth looking at them. The end result is that of all of the major battles only Fuentes de Oñoro, Albuera and Salamanca provided the cavalry with what might be termed a suitable battlefield with space to deploy, manoeuvre and fight effectively. Little wonder, then, that the achievements of the British cavalry on the field of battle are relatively small in comparison with the infantry. There is no denying the fact that the topography of the Iberian Peninsula is not good for cavalry on a general scale and that given the absence of large, flat battlefields, its performance must be judged largely by its routine day-to-day work, by its reconnaissance, forage and patrol work, and its success in numerous cavalry skirmishes. This is not to overlook the major actions but, as we have seen, the contribution made by the cavalry in battle was limited owing to the nature of the ground.

PART TWO
The Cavalry in Action

CHAPTER I

Wellesley, Vimeiro and a Bad Start

The Peninsular War was one of the most successful campaigns ever fought by the British Army and saw the forging of one of the finest armies this country has ever produced. It also saw the emergence of one of the greatest Britons ever to have lived, Arthur Wellesley, 1st Duke of Wellington. The names of the men who served under him, men like Picton, Craufurd, Hill, Graham, Cole and Leith, may not be household names today, nor were they particularly well known even in 1808, but to military historians these men represent some of the finest soldiers ever to have worn the uniform of the British Army. There are scores of such general officers, whilst the regimental officers are even more numerous, men whose memories live on today in the pages of the many memoirs and journals which were written by them. In 1808, however, these men, along with the British Army in general, had yet to prove themselves on a major battlefield. True, several of them had seen action in Egypt or in India, where Wellington himself, then Sir Arthur Wellesley, had stamped his mark on British military history. But, on the whole, the army that disembarked in Portugal in the hot summer of 1808 was a far cry from that which was to march triumphantly into France at the back end of 1813, having spent the previous five years driving Napoleon's armies back and forth across the Peninsula until, finally, they threw them back across the Pyrenees themselves.

The British Army entered the Peninsular War with what can best be described as a patchy record behind it. The campaign in Flanders at the end of the previous century was a distant memory, if it was worth remembering anyway, whilst Egypt and Sir Ralph Abercrombie were likewise nothing more than glorious names with which to light up many a bleak English night when Napoleon's armies were poised ready to invade from across the English Channel. Even Nelson's triumph at Trafalgar had been, to an extent, overshadowed by Napoleon's subsequent crushing victory at Austerlitz, but so long as the Royal Navy ruled the waves, Britain could be assured, at least, that any invading army would have a very difficult task to even get across the seas, let alone fight on our shores. It also meant that, wherever Britain's armies were needed, safe passage could be afforded. And so it was in 1806 and 1807, when the Royal Navy transported the army to such far-off places as South Africa, South America and, for a second time, Egypt, but at only one of these places, South Africa, was success to be found. At Buenos Ayres, in 1806, initial success had by the following year turned to disaster, matched only by the similar disaster of El Hamet in Egypt in the same year. Only in 1806, at Maida in southern Italy, did the British Army achieve anything of note with a fine but small and strategically insignificant victory over the French, whilst Copenhagen the following year similarly provided only a hint of what was yet to come.[1] It was, therefore, with this very patchy record that the British Army embarked for Portugal in the summer of 1808. Furthermore, preparations for the campaign were not particularly good, for as late as June the same year Wellesley was still making plans for an attack on South America.[2] Fortunately it was not to be and the inflammation of the volatile situation in the Peninsula was such that the British government decided to abandon its plans for what would have been a waste of valuable resources and instead send a British force to Portugal.

We need not trouble ourselves too much with the often complex causes that brought about the Peninsular War, or War of Independence as the Spaniards call it. Briefly, however, the French had marched through Spain and into Portugal under the pretext of enforcing Napoleon's so-called 'Continental System', whereby European countries were forbidden to trade with Britain. Portugal, which refused to comply with this, immediately became the object of Napoleon's attention, and in November 1807 the remnants of a French Army under General Andoche Junot, Duke of Abrantes, which had started out from France the previous month, finally reached Lisbon after a gruelling march across the Sierra de Gata. Unfortunately, Junot failed in his attempts to arrest the Portuguese royal family, who sailed for the safety of Brazil and thus eluded him. Portugal was then occupied and its army disbanded. In April 1808 internal affairs in Spain had reached crisis point, with a very heated dispute between King Carlos IV and his son, Ferdinand, whilst Manuel Godoy, the so-called 'Prince of the Peace' and lover of the hideously ugly Queen Maria Luisa, intrigued to the point at which Napoleon's help was sought by both parties. Napoleon, never slow to see an opportunity, promptly arrested both Carlos and Ferdinand and marched his army into Spain, whilst those French troops already in Spain promptly took control of the key fortress towns such as Pamplona and Barcelona, which allowed easy access through the Pyrenees for Napoleon's men. In May the people of Madrid rose up against Murat's men, but the insurrection, consequently known as the 'Dos de Mayo', ended in bloodshed, as Murat's men ruthlessly went about restoring order. Representatives from the Asturias had already travelled to England to ask for Britain's help, and when risings broke out all over Spain the British government decided to act, and instead of sending Wellesley to South America despatched him to the Peninsula.

When Sir Arthur Wellesley landed in Portugal on 1 August 1808 he did so with a small British Army of around 8,000 men of which just 394 were cavalry, of the 20th Light Dragoons, and of these only 180 had horses. Fortunately, the redoubtable Bishop of Oporto sent Wellesley a further sixty horses which increased the number of cavalry to 240.[3] Four days later Wellesley was joined by a further 4,500 men under General Brent Spencer, although these were infantry, save for 245 artillerymen. The omens were not good, therefore, with the British cavalry – at least those who were mounted – numbering just 240 out of an army of 12,500 men. Furthermore, the 20th had to provide the army with orderlies, whilst others were used to escort supply wagons and perform other duties which, although part of a cavalryman's job, were nevertheless detrimental to the regiment by reducing its actual strength even further. Portugal is not the most suitable country for cavalry, and it was as well that the opening campaign of the Peninsular War was a short one. However, it is a poor reflection on the arrangements for the campaign that this vital arm of the army was paid such scant attention.

The disembarkation of the army was not a smooth one, with the rolling Atlantic breakers upsetting more than a few of the boats which transported the troops from ship to shore. Norbert Landsheit was with the 20th Light Dragoons and we are indebted to him for the only account by a serving cavalryman at this stage of the war in which he provides an interesting insight into the problems faced by cavalry coming ashore.

> The shores of Mondego Bay are open and shelving, so as to produce, when the winds blow fresh, a heavy surf; and it so happened that we brought with us to our anchorage just enough of a breeze to render the task of disembarkation a difficult one. Several boats were upset, and out of the infantry corps which landed first, some men were lost, though I believe that the casualties were not numerous. But for us, we suffered nothing. We were directed to stand upright in the boats, with bridle in hand, and prepared, in case of any accident, to spring into the saddle; a judicious precaution, which proved in two or three instances eminently useful. One punt capsized upon the surf, but no lives were lost, because the horses sometimes swimming, sometimes wading, carried their riders ashore. We then formed upon the beach, and carrying each man his three days' provisions, ready cooked, pushed forward to a village, the name of which I have forgotten.[4]

The opening battle of the war, a skirmish by later standards, was fought on 17 August 1808 at Roliça, where Wellesley drove General Delaborde from successive positions south of the town of Obidos. It was a small but satisfying affair which earned for the army its first battle honour. It was also an all-infantry affair, with the light dragoons playing no part in the action although, as Landsheit describes, they were not completely idle.

We had watched the progress of the battle for some time, without sustaining any injury, except from a single shell, which, bursting over our column, sent a fragment through the backbone of a troop-horse, and killed him on the spot – when a cry arose, 'The cavalry to the front!' and we pushed up a sort of hollowed road towards the top of the ridge before us. Though driven from their first position, the enemy, it appeared, had rallied, and showing a line both of horse and foot, were preparing to renew the fight. Now, our cavalry were altogether incapable of coping with that of the French; and the fact became abundantly manifest, so soon as our leading files gained the brow of the hill – for the slope of a rising ground opposite was covered with them in such numbers, as to render any attempt to charge, on our part, utterly ridiculous. Accordingly, we were directed to form up, file by file, as each emerged from the road – not in two ranks, as is usually done both on parade and in action – but in rank entire. Moreover, we were so placed, that the French officers could not possibly tell what was behind us; and thus made a show which appeared to startle them; for they soon began to change their dispositions, the infantry moving off first, the cavalry following, upon which we likewise broke again into column of threes, and rode slowly after them. But we had no desire to overtake them. They therefore pursued their march unmolested, except by a few discharges of cannon; and we, after seeing them fairly under weigh, halted on the field of battle.[5]

Thus, the day ended with the first victory for the British Army in the Peninsula, albeit a modest one. The cavalry played a very small part in the battle and suffered no casualties, which is not surprising given the nature of the ground. However, their turn was to come four days later at the Battle of Vimeiro, a battle in every sense of the word fought between Wellesley's 16,000-strong British Army – he had received a further 4,000 reinforcements since Roliça – and a French Army of around 14,000 under the command of General Junot, whose own cavalry numbered 2,251.[6] Therefore, we are only four days into the war and already we see the disproportionate numbers of cavalry on both sides. The French cavalry represented 17% of Junot's army whereas the 20th Light Dragoons represented barely 1.5% of the British Army. The situation was not good, although a further 260 Portuguese dragoons, part of Trant's force, joined Wellesley prior to the battle.

The battle itself was extremely hard fought, with French columns meeting for the first time the strength of a British skirmish line and the power of a two-deep firing line. Successive French attacks had been driven off by the time Wellesley decided to launch his handful of cavalry. Colonel Taylor, commanding the 20th, had been sitting impatiently with his men whilst the infantry dealt with the French attacks.[7] Now, with the French advancing once again, General Fane rode up and called out to Taylor and his men, 'Now, Twentieth! now we want you. At them, my lads, and let them see what you are made of.'[8] Landsheit takes up the story again.

Then came the word, 'threes about and forward,' and with the rapidity of thought we swept round the elbow of the hill, and the battle lay before us. As we emerged up this slope, we were directed to form in half-squadrons, the 20th in the centre, the Portuguese cavalry on the flanks, and the brief space of time that was necessary to complete the formation enabled me to see over a wide extent of the field. The French were coming on in great force, and with the utmost show of confidence. A brigade of cavalry was in front, followed by a line of infantry, in rear of which again were some heavy columns and guns. On our side there were some infantry who had long and gallantly maintained the hill, but who were so overmatched, that our advance was ordered up for the purpose more effectually served.[9]

Wellesley now raised himself in his saddle and, turning to the 20th Light Dragoons, waved his cocked hat in the air as he would do more famously at Waterloo some seven years later, crying, 'Now Twentieth, now is the time!'. Taylor's moment had finally come and, drawing his sabre, he turned to his men and ordered them to charge. The Portuguese dragoons remained with them for a short while until a few round shots sent them panicking to the rear, leaving the 20th Light Dragoons to charge on alone. Landsheit later described the charge and, for its detail, it is worth quoting at length;

'Now, Twentieth! Now!' shouted Sir Arthur, while his staff clapped their hands and gave us a cheer; the sound of which was still in our ears, when we put our horses to their speed. The Portuguese likewise pushed forward, but through the dust which entirely enveloped us, the enemy threw in a fire, which seemed to have the effect of paralysing altogether our handsome allies. Right and left they pulled up, as if by word of command, and we never saw more of them till the battle was over. But we went very differently to work. In an instant we were in the heart of the French cavalry, cutting and hacking, and upsetting men and horses in the most extraordinary manner possible, till they broke and fled in every direction, and then we fell upon the infantry. It was here that our gallant Colonel met his fate. He rode that day a horse, which was so hot that not all his exertions would suffice to control it, and he was carried headlong upon the bayonets of the French infantry, a corporal of whom shot him through the heart... We were entirely ignorant of the fall of our commanding officer, and had the case been otherwise, we were too eager in following up the advantages which we had gained, to regard it at the moment. Though scattered, as always happens, by the shock of a charge, we still kept laying about us, till our white leather breeches, our hands, arms, and swords, were all besmeared with blood.[10]

Watching Taylor and the 20th Light Dragoons was one of the most famous Peninsular diarists, Benjamin Harris, of the 95th Rifles, who later wrote:

During this day I myself narrowly escaped being killed by our dragoons, for somehow or other, in the confusion, I fell whilst they were charging, and the whole squadron thundering past just missed me, as I lay amongst the dead and wounded. Tired and overweighted by my knapsack and all my shoe-making implements, I lay where I had fallen for a short time, and watched the cavalry as they gained the enemy. I observed a fine, gallant-looking officer leading them on in that charge. He was a brave fellow, and bore himself like a hero; with his sword waving in the air, he cheered the men on, as he went dashing upon the enemy, and hewing and slashing at them in tremendous style. I watched him as the dragoons came off after that charge, but saw him no more; he had fallen. Fine fellow! his conduct indeed made an impression upon me that I shall never forget.[11]

The charge by Taylor and his men had taken them straight through the French dragoons opposed to them and into the fleeing ranks of infantry. Here, the 20th Light Dragoons were in their element, hacking and hewing in all directions as they cut their way through. Up to this point everything had gone well but now, with both men and horses tiring, it was time to bring the charge to a halt and return to British lines. Unfortunately, things did not work out that way, for their blood was up, and their ensuing forward movement was to be the first example of what would later drive Wellington to distraction as the 20th continued pressing forward deep into French positions until they were brought up by the wall which blocked their path. With all momentum lost, with French infantry firing at them and, worst of all, with two regiments of fresh French cavalry coming at them, Taylor's men suddenly found themselves in an extremely perilous situation and he was left with little option but to turn and fight his way back to the British lines.

As the enemy gave way we continued to advance, amid a cloud of dust so thick, that to see beyond the distance of those immediately about yourself, was impossible. Thus it was till we reached a low fence, through which several gaps had been made by the French to facilitate the movements of their cavalry; and we instantly leapt it. The operation cost some valuable lives, for about twenty or thirty of the French grenadiers had laid themselves on their bellies beneath it, and now received us as well as they could upon their bayonets. Several of our men and horses were stabbed, but of the enemy not a soul survived to speak of his exploit – we literally slew them all and then, while in pursuit of the horse, rushed into an enclosure, where to a man we had well nigh perished. For the fold in which we were caught was fenced round to a great height, and had but a single aperture – the door of which, the enemy, who hastened to take advantage of our blunder, immediately closed. Then was our situation trying enough, for we could neither escape nor resist; while looking over the wall we beheld that the French had halted, and were returning in something like order to the front.[12]

The 20th eventually managed to regain their original position, largely through the intervention of their comrades of the 50th Regiment who advanced with fixed bayonets, forcing the enemy back and releasing the 20th from the perilous situation, but not before they had lost twenty men dead, twenty-four wounded and a further eleven taken prisoner. Among the dead was Colonel Taylor himself. The fifty-five casualties sustained by the 20th Light Dragoons represented just under a quarter of their strength and it is as well that the opening campaign came to a swift and controversial end with the Convention of Cintra, otherwise the British Army would have been severely lacking in cavalry with which to provide vital advance guard duties, patrols and piquet work.

Taylor paid for his enthusiasm and lack of experience with his life. He had seen action previously in the West Indies in 1805 and during the ill-fated Buenos Ayres fiasco of 1807. However, on both of these occasions there was little or no scope for the use of cavalry. Indeed, in South America the 20th numbered just 191 all ranks, most of whom were dismounted, and were hardly used at all. It is easy to imagine what was going through Taylor's mind as he sat with his regiment watching the Battle of Vimeiro unfolding around him. The urge to get his men into the action and charge must have been almost unbearable, the battle being the first time they had seen what might be termed 'conventional' action for many a year. In front of Taylor was a body of French infantry. What finer opportunity was there for the sort of charge of which he had probably dreamt for most of his career? This misplaced enthusiasm amongst the British cavalry typifies the cavalry spirit of the day and is something which would continue throughout the war. It would occur again at Waterloo with the charge of the Union Brigade, two out of three regiments of which had seen no action overseas during the previous twenty-odd years. The 20th Light Dragoons could claim that there were mitigating circumstances, not least the loss of their commanding officer, as well as the fact that, in the confusion of battle their view was obscured by the dust kicked up by the various combatants on both sides. Nevertheless, as Landsheit himself pointed out, the 20th did admit to having committed a blunder, which is undoubtedly what it was.

Vimeiro had seen the British cavalry get off to a bad start, making the sort of fundamental error that was to be repeated on several more infamous occasions before the end of the war. It should not be forgotten however, that in a stand-up fight with French cavalry the 20th Light Dragoons had broken their enemies before they embarked upon the reckless forward course which was to prove their downfall. We will continue to discover that, in spite of all of their misadventures, British cavalry rarely found themselves outfought during the initial fight, and it was only during the pursuit when both horses and men were exhausted that the French cavalry – and usually their fresh reserves – managed to match them and defeat them. The Battle of Vimeiro also highlighted two of the great problems which bedevilled the cavalry in the Peninsula, the first being a lack of numbers and the second being unsuitable campaigning country, although, as we have seen, the opening campaign was of such a short duration that this hardly mattered. Fortunately, things were to improve during the second phase of the war with the arrival in the Peninsula of Henry, Lord Paget and a strong contingent of hussars. Two of the problems were, therefore, rectified, albeit temporarily as it was to prove, and whilst the terrain of the Corunna campaign generally was certainly unsuitable for satisfactory cavalry, they did manage to find a handful of battlefields on which they were to demonstrate that they were more than equal to the challenge thrown down by their much-vaunted French adversaries.

Notes

1 British successes in Egypt in 1801, Cape Town and Maida, 1806 and Copenhagen, 1807, were comparatively minor ones compared with the forthcoming success of Wellington's army in the Peninsula. However, the first-class groundwork done during these campaigns should not be overlooked, particularly in Egypt and at Maida where significant lessons were learned by many British officers who would later serve in the Peninsula.

2 Memorandum for the Expedition against Spanish America, *Supplementary Despatches, Correspondence and Memoranda of Field Marshal Arthur Duke of Wellington* (London, 1857), VI: 80–2.

3 Sir Charles Oman, *A History of the Peninsular War* (Oxford, 1902), I: 231. However, at the Court of Inquiry into the Convention of Cintra, Wellesley stated that he had '210 mounted men of the 20th [Light] Dragoons', which makes the situation even worse for the British cavalry. 'Court of Inquiry,' *The Despatches of Field Marshal the Duke of Wellington during his various campaigns* (London, 1834), IV: 168.

4 Gleig, *The Hussar* (London, 1837), 248–9.

5 Ibid. 252–3.

6 Oman, Peninsular War, 1: 247.

7 Landsheit wrote that Taylor 'repeatedly asked leave to charge, but was on each occasion held back by the assurance that the proper movement was not yet come.' Gleig, *The Hussar*, 267.

8 Ibid. 267–8.

9 Ibid. 268.

10 Ibid. 269–70.

11 Henry Curling (Ed), *Recollections of Rifleman Harris* (London, 1929), 53–4. Another rifleman who witnessed the charge was Jonathan Leach, author of *Rough Sketches of the Life of an Old Soldier* (London, 1831), 52.

12 Gleig, *The Hussar*, 270–2.

CHAPTER II

Paget, Moore and the Corunna Campaign

The British cavalry had got off to an unfortunate start with the disappointing performance of the 20th Light Dragoons at Vimeiro. However, there was no further fighting in what may be termed the opening phase of the Peninsular War as the two sides sat down to conclude the notorious Convention of Cintra, under the terms of which French troops gave up all their possessions in Portugal but were allowed to sail home to France in British ships along with all of their accumulated plunder. Junot's army had, therefore, been kicked out of Portugal by the stroke of a pen, but it was an episode which left a sour taste in the mouths of both people and politicians back home. Enemy armies were there to be beaten and destroyed, they cried, not to be shipped back home in our own ships.[1] Indeed, such was the outcry that two of the three British commanders who were party to the treaty, Burrard and Dalrymple, were recalled to face a court of inquiry, the third, Wellesley, already having returned to England. In the meantime, the army reverted to the command of Sir John Moore and it was under his command that the British cavalry enjoyed two of its finest successes.

It will not be necessary to go into the detailed background of the ill-fated Corunna campaign of the winter of 1808–9, suffice to say that in an attempt to assist his Spanish allies, Moore decided upon a bold course of action which involved marching north-east towards Burgos, a march which would threaten French communications between Madrid and France. The move was intended to draw Napoleon, who for once was present in the Peninsula, away from Madrid and by doing so try to give the defenders of the Spanish capital time to regroup. Unfortunately, when Moore began his advance on 11 December he did so not knowing that Madrid had fallen seven days earlier. He was joined at Mayorga on 20 December by reinforcements under Sir David Baird and the following day Henry, Lord Paget, fought the first of two fine cavalry actions.

One of the characteristics of the early stages of the Corunna campaign was the lack of reliable intelligence and the almost complete ignorance on both sides of the whereabouts of each other. Consequently, on 20

December 1808, when Paget – commanding the cavalry – discovered that two French regiments were idling away at Sahagun, unaware of his presence, he resolved to attack them. The ensuing fight was to become what Oman later called, 'perhaps the most brilliant cavalry exploit during the whole six years of the war'.[2]

Paget's force consisted of the 10th and 15th Hussars, along with thirteen men of his own regiment, the 7th Hussars, presumably his own escort, and six guns of the Royal Horse Artillery. There is no accurate record of the number of sabres Paget had under his command although the 15th Hussars, who were destined to play the leading part in the fight, returned some 527 men two days earlier. The 10th Hussars numbered roughly the same, although they were to play little part in the fight.[3] The French cavalry consisted of two regiments, the 8th Dragoons and the 1st Provisional Chasseurs à Cheval, who between them numbered around 450 men, and were commanded by General Debelle.

Paget had established his headquarters at Melgar de Abajo, twelve miles to the south-west of Sahagun where Debelle resided completely unaware of the close proximity of the enemy. The plan was quite simple. John Slade, whom we shall come across many times, with the 10th Hussars and two of the horse artillery guns, was to attack the French from the west and drive them through the town into the waiting arms of Paget and the 15th. The plan involved a hazardous night march in freezing conditions along hard, frozen roads which caused many a horse and rider to slip and fall. Indeed, many took to dismounting and leading their horses through the snow which was falling and which was several feet deep in places. Slade himself wrote, 'A more dreadful night the troops could not be exposed to, as it was particularly dark, a severe frost, with sleet falling, and the snow drifted in many places to the depth of four feet. Many horses fell, and one man had his leg broken.'[4] The 10th Hussars were late starting, primarily because of Slade first insisting upon making a very stirring speech to his men which ended with the now famous words, 'blood and slaughter, march!'[5]

James Tale was with the 15th Hussars and he left a vivid description of the night's march:

> It was bitterly and intensely cold, and as far as I can judge was conducted and corkscrewed throughout as it were by paths and narrow lanes, now à cheval, now à pied. Sometimes we had to lead our horses in single file even over a narrow bridge that daylight might have made one shudder to look upon. All was silent; the stillness of night was only interrupted by the continuous pattering of the horses' hoofs upon the snow, the muffled clink (we were cloaked) of spur and scabbard, scabbard and spur, or an inner growl accompanied by a naughty word at the stumbling of man or animal on our uneven track.[6]

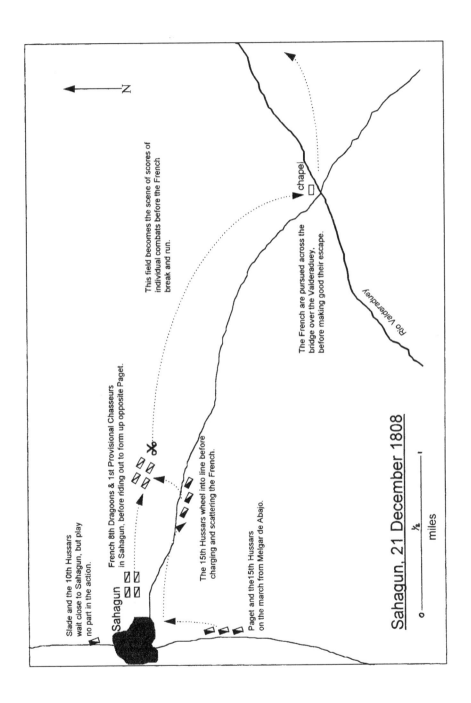

Slade and the 10th Hussars wait close to Sahagun, but play no part in the action.

Sahagun

French 8th Dragoons & 1st Provisional Chasseurs in Sahagun, before riding out to form up opposite Paget.

This field becomes the scene of scores of individual combats before the French break and run.

chapel

Rio Valderaduey

The French are pursued across the bridge over the Valderaduey, before making good their escape.

The 15th Hussars wheel into line before charging and scattering the French.

Paget and the 15th Hussars on the march from Melgar de Abajo.

Sahagun, 21 December 1808

0 ½ 1
miles

N

107

The two columns, Slade's and Paget's, parted from each other somewhere around Galleguillo de Campo, Slade marching off to the left in order to approach Sahagun from the west, whilst Paget continued north. Any hopes Paget may have harboured of a surprise were dashed between five and six o'clock in the morning when his column fell in with a dozen or so French cavalry, which was either Debelle's outlying piquet or simply a patrol. The French were quickly overcome, but one man managed to escape into the freezing night to raise the alarm. Undeterred, Paget hurried on until the houses at Sahagun appeared, silhouetted against the dawn sky. Suddenly, Debelle's cavalry, which had turned out with great speed after the alarm had been raised, loomed out of the gloomy, grey dawn, drawing up in close column of squadrons behind a deep ditch.[7]

> As the grey morn dawned upon us, we seemed to emerge from our narrow path into more open ground. The silence hitherto maintained was now inter-rupted by hummings, buzzing, whispering, and indistinct sounds of human voices. Then followed the words of command – 'Form divisions! Wheel into line!' A dark living mass was in front, not to be plainly distinguished by the eye; onward we rushed. The followed a plunge – a crash – a clatter – hacking and hewing, and the devil to pay.[8]

Apparently, Debelle was still not certain whether the enemy cavalry were Spanish or British. His men moved to their left, that is, to the south, with the intention of deploying into two lines in order to charge Paget's advancing column. Paget made a corresponding movement to his right until he drew up opposite the French who had deployed into their lines, the eight squadrons forming with the 1st Provisional Chasseurs in front and the 8th Dragoons in rear, but even as they moved into line Paget was giving the order for his own hussars to swing to their left into line and, shouting 'Emsdorff and Victory!', the 15th Hussars charged directly at the French.[9] Captain Alexander Gordon wrote:

> The shock was terrible, horses and men were overthrown, and a shriek of terror, intermixed with oaths, groans, and prayers for mercy, issued from the whole extent of their front. Our men, although surprised at the depth of the ranks, pressed forward until they had cut their way quite through the column. In many places the bodies of the fallen formed a complete mound of men and horses, but very few of our people were hurt. Colonel Grant, who led the right centre squadron, and the Adjutant who attended him, were amongst the foremost who penetrated the enemy's mass; they were both wounded – the former slightly on the forehead, the latter severely in the face. It is probable neither of them would have been hurt if our fur caps had been hooped with iron like those of the French Chasseurs, instead of being stiffened with pasteboard.[10]

James Tale wrote:

> Hard knocks indeed were given and received, and when the curtains of dark-
> ness were fairly withdrawn, frightful gashes and streams of gore were made
> visible, as also other features consequent upon such a sharp rencontre. Horses
> galloping about sans riders, riders à pied running after their horses; the moans
> and tortures of the wounded writhing in anguish from a cold and freezing
> atmosphere – the dying and the dead! The onslaught and carving of the first
> course scarcely exceeded twenty minutes, and before we had re-formed, the
> head of a column was observed shooting from the end of a street into the main
> road. A view halloo was pealed forth from hundreds of throats, and troops
> were knotting together for a second course. The troop to which I belonged
> – Captain D's – happened to be nearest the *débouchement* of the enemy. When
> a score or two had mustered, up galloped our Adjutant with his head tied up,
> and ordered chase to be given. Away we went. The inequalities of the ground
> were masked by snow; and dashing at what appeared a ridge of that fragile
> material, we were precipitated into a broad ditch, not deep certainly, but suffi-
> ciently so to put us *hors de combat* for a few minutes. Saddles were ingloriously
> emptied, and men and horses rolled in the snow. My animal, anything but a
> plucky one, fell on his side, and pinned me to the earth for some seconds.[11]

The British charge saw Paget's men crash through the first French line,
throwing the enemy back upon the dragoons who turned tail and fled
with the British hussars close behind them. In fact, the relatively small battlefield was covered with isolated groups and individuals who engaged in
combat with each other as the French made for the small bridge over the
Valderaduey river which lay a few hundred yards to the south.[12] Scores of
British hussars and French dragoons tumbled and fell in the confusion as
they galloped across the field which was criss-crossed by several drainage
ditches. The French were finally driven over the bridge and a rather disorderly pursuit took place before Paget ordered the recall to be sounded.[13]

> The mêlée lasted about ten minutes, the enemy always endeavouring to gain
> the Carrion road. The appearance of their heavy dragoons was extremely
> martial and imposing; they wore brass helmets of the ancient Roman form,
> and the long black horsehair streaming from their crests as they galloped
> had a very fine effect. Having rode together nearly a mile, pell-mell, cutting
> and slashing each other, it appeared to me indispensable that order should
> be re-established, as the men were quite wild and the horses almost blown;
> therefore, seeing no superior officer near, I pressed through the throng until
> I overtook and halted those who were farthest advanced in pursuit. As soon
> as I had accomplished this object, the bugles sounded the 'rally'. Whilst we
> were re-forming our squadrons, the enemy also rallied and continued their
> flight by different routes.[14]

The end result of the fight at Sahagun was the virtual destruction of the Provisional Chasseurs who lost two lieutenant-colonels, eleven other officers and 157 men taken prisoner, whilst twenty men were killed and nineteen others wounded. The 15th Hussars lost two killed and twenty-three others wounded, including the colonel, adjutant and quartermaster.

The small but brilliant action by Paget was the first triumph of the war for the British cavalry although one of the hallmarks of later misadventures was in evidence, being the pursuit afterwards which, while not being the wild, overblown gallop of later years, was still sufficient for Paget to give his regiment 'a good scolding'.[15] The fight also highlighted the inferiority of the British hussars' head-dress which, being mere fur caps, offered little protection compared with the French dragoons' brass helmets.[16] By all accounts, the fur caps, if not protected by oilskin covers, would quickly turn very soggy when wet. As a consequence, enemy sabre cuts were likely to cause more numerous and more dangerous wounds, a fact confirmed by Dr Adam Neale, who considered the wearing of the brass helmet to be a great advantage. 'I have examined all the wounded,' he wrote, 'and find that while our men are desperately wounded about the face and head, there is not a single Frenchman cut deeper than the hairy scalp.'[17] The brass helmets worn by the French did indeed provide more protection for the wearer although, as Colonel Chamourin of the 26th Dragoons was to discover to his cost at Campo Mayor, even that was not sufficient at times to protect the head from the power of the 1796-pattern   light cavalry sword. And yet, commenting on the fight at Sahagun, Fortescue considered the British sabre to have been inferior to the French sword, being shorter, too broad and blunted by their metal scabbards.[18] This is a subject dealt with in another chapter of this book.

There were further skirmishes between the French and British cavalry during the next few days, notably at Villada, where the 18th Hussars killed fourteen and took a further six Frenchmen prisoner. Five days after Sahagun the two sides' cavalry clashed again, this time at Mayorga, where Paget came up with part of Marshal Ney's advanced guard, consisting of two squadrons of the 15th Chasseurs à Cheval which were positioned on a plain close to the town. Advancing with the 10th Hussars, and with the 15th and 18th Hussars in support, Paget found the Mayorga occupied by enemy cavalry piquets who were quickly flushed out by two squadrons of the 10th after which Paget ordered them to make their way through the town and drive away the main French force on the plain beyond it. The order was obeyed with relish and the 10th advanced uphill through the slush before coming into sight of the French who were drawn up about a mile away across the plain.

When we had got clear of the town, two squadrons of chasseurs à cheval were discovered, formed on a rising ground about a mile distant. Lord Paget directed General Slade to attack them with a squadron of the Tenth, supported by the remainder of the regiment. The General moved off at a trot, but had not advanced far when he halted to have some alteration made in the length of his stirrups. An aide-de-camp was sent to enquire the cause of the delay, and the squadron was again put in motion; but the General's stirrups were not yet adjusted to his mind, and he halted again before they had advanced a hundred yards. Lord Paget, whose patience was by this time quite exhausted, then ordered Colonel Leigh to take the lead. The Tenth charged gallantly, routed the enemy, and took between forty and fifty prisoners, with little loss on their part.[19]

The French opened fire on the 10th Hussars as soon as they came within range, but the British hussars charged and threw their opponents into complete disarray, killing several and taking over 100 prisoners at a cost of just a few men wounded. British cavalry had, therefore, beaten the French twice within the space of just a few days and, more noteworthy, had defeated an enemy upon ground of his own choosing. The fight also showed Slade in a less than favourable light which, coming after his poor showing at Sahagun, did not agur well for one of the British cavalry's more senior officers, one who would play a prominent part in the forthcoming Peninsular campaign under Wellington.

The events at Sahagun and Mayorga put some fire back into the bellies of an otherwise very fagged and fatigued British cavalry force as the weather grew colder by the day. On 29 December Paget led his men to yet another fine victory, this time at Benavente. By now Moore's army was in retreat with the French advanced guard closing in on the hard-pressed British rearguard until the two sides clashed at the bridge over the Esla river close to the village of Castrogonzalo. The bridge had been partially destroyed by Robert Craufurd's Light Brigade, forcing the French, under General Lefebvre-Desnouettes, one of Napoleon's own personal favourites, to look for another way across. A suitable ford was duly found close to the village and soon French cavalry were splashing and swimming through the icy waters to reach the opposite bank where Paget's piquets were hovering. Lefebvre-Desnouettes had with him four squadrons of chasseurs of the Imperial Guard, about 600 in all, who were faced initially by around 100 men of the 7th, 10th and 18th Hussars under Colonel Otway who rode forward to meet them. The British hussars were driven back and, letting off their carbines and keeping a respectful distance, retired to be joined by three troops of the 3rd Hussars KGL under Captain von Kerssenbruch and Lieutenant Jansen. At this point, General Charles Stewart arrived on the scene and took command from Otway. Stewart charged the French a second time and his men cut their way through the first French line before being brought up by their second, whereupon, being outnumbered, they hacked their way out and fell slowly back. Stewart rallied the men and drew them off carefully towards the town of Benavente, about three miles back, where he knew Paget was lying in wait with his reserves.

Paget, who sat on his horse 'twirling his moustachios', had been watching intently from behind some houses and was waiting patiently for Stewart to buy him some time in order for him to get the 10th Hussars organised and ready for the charge. Meanwhile, Lefebvre's chasseurs came on confidently, continuing their forward movement under the watchful eyes of Napoleon himself, who had come forward to view the action from some heights overlooking the Esla. The Emperor was not to enjoy the spectacle that unfolded before him, however, for as his chasseurs neared Benavente the 10th Hussars, with Paget at their head, came charging out from their concealed position amidst the cheers of the locals who turned out to watch. With the 18th Hussars in support, Paget and the 10th swept forward, driving the French back pell-mell towards the Esla where they were forced to turn and fight. Many of the French chasseurs plunged into the river and tried to swim back but others, whose horses were blown after the chase back from Benavente, could not do so and were forced to fight. In the mêlée that followed over fifty chasseurs were cut down and either killed or wounded with the British hussars suffering a similar number of casualties. In addition, seventy-two French cavalry were taken prisoner including two captains and the most famous prisoner of them all, Lefebvre himself. It was a small but well-executed attack by Lord Paget which, coming as it did just a few days after Sahagun, confirmed his status as the finest cavalry commander the British Army possessed.

With the onset of January 1809, the real miseries of the retreat to Corunna began in earnest. The Galician mountains must have seemed like an impenetrable barrier to the poor wretches who now had the task of dragging themselves through the snow and ice and the cold, biting winds if they were to escape from the clutches of the pursuing French cavalry who showed little mercy to any stragglers unfortunate enough to fall into their hands. Sadly, hundreds of them did, mostly drunken stragglers who had stopped to plunder the few Spanish hovels dotted along the route through the mountains. Villafranca and Bembibre witnessed the worst of the disorders as hordes of drunken British soldiers broke from the ranks in search of plunder and drink, and when Franceschi's cavalry rode in afterwards they found it all too easy to sabre the straggling British troops who, too inebriated to fight back, were put out of their misery with a slash or thrust of an enemy sabre. Not everybody gave up the ghost, however, and there were several hard fought skirmishes along the way, particularly at Cacabellos and Constantino.

There was little in the way of real fighting for Paget's cavalry, however, and the fights at Sahagun, Mayorga and Benavente were momentarily forgotten as the hussars' priority became the struggle for survival in the terrible conditions. But they still had a task to perform, of course, forming part of the rearguard keeping the French at bay, and skirmishing almost daily, usually with their carbines whilst ammunition lasted. The retreat was particularly hard on the cavalry for not only did the men have to look to themselves but they had to see to their horses also and forage was virtually non-existent. Scores of horses were shot or simply dropped dead in the cold from exhaustion. Even Paget and Stewart became victims, both being put out of action by ophthalmia which as good as blinded the unfortunate victims. Both men were led through the mountains to Corunna with handkerchiefs bound over their eyes whilst command of the cavalry passed into the hands of Slade.

The British cavalry began to come in sight of Corunna on 11 January and four days later they began to embark aboard the ships of the Royal Navy which had arrived from Vigo. The majority of the men were embarked the following day but very few horses were with them.[20] In fact, Gordon records that whilst the officers were allowed to take their horses with them, few troop horses went aboard. The 7th and 10th Hussars embarked just ninety horses, the 15th Hussars embarked thirty and the 18th Hussars and 3rd Hussars KGL not a single horse between them. Hundreds of other horses were shot to prevent them falling into the hands of the French. And then, whilst the infantry turned to fight for their survival just outside Corunna on 16 January, the remains of the once proud hussar brigade sat aboard the ships, waiting and watching anxiously as the battle raged on the heights to the south of the town. Fortunately, the battle petered out with Moore's men in possession of their positions and with Soult's army beaten back. It was a victory which gave the British Army the opportunity to re-embark and sail away for England. Sadly, Moore was not with it, having died of the wounds sustained during the fighting around the village of Elviña.

The exhausted and shattered British Army sailed away from Corunna on 17 January but for many the ordeal was not over yet, for several ships were wrecked by storms on the homeward journey, including the *Despatch* which went down with the best part of two troops of the 7th Hussars. The last few days of January saw the arrival at Falmouth, Plymouth and other south-coast ports of the ships bringing home the British Army, and during the first week of February the various units of the hussar brigade began to arrive at their respective headquarters.

It had been a short but gruelling campaign during which Paget and his hussars had cut a splendid reputation for themselves and had demonstrated that, even in tremendously difficult and extreme conditions, they were more than a match for their more numerous French adversaries. In all three of the main fights, at Sahagun, Mayorga and Benavente, the British hussars had broken their enemies and had resisted the urge to indulge in the sort of reckless and disaster-prone pursuit that would dog so many of the later fights in the Peninsula and which would lay the foundations for the bad reputation the British cavalry acquired in Spain. The hussars had also shown themselves to be skilled at their job of acting as part of the rearguard of Moore's retreating army, skirmishing, patrolling and gathering in stragglers along the way. Granted, many of the cavalry stopped to join in the plundering and were lost but, on the whole, discipline remained good among the four regiments of hussars during the retreat to Corunna. In fact, of a total strength at the beginning of October 1808 of 2,645 officers and men of the 7th, 10th, 15th and 18th Hussars, no fewer then 2,423 returned to England in January 1809, a deficiency of just 222 and these included some fifty-six men who were drowned when their transport ship was wrecked during the voyage to England.[21] Such a low loss, just 166, is quite remarkable given the three actions and the almost continual skirmishing which took place during the retreat, let alone the rigours of the retreat itself.

Upon their return to England the hussars could reflect with some satisfaction on a job done well, particularly after the disastrous start which the British cavalry had got off to at Vimeiro. Unfortunately, these experienced troops would be sorely missed in the Peninsula and it would be four more years before the hussars returned, during which time they would kick their heels in frustration as Wellington's army fought the war without them.

Notes

1 See Lord Moira's very strong views on this, printed in Sir Charles Oman, *History of the Peninsular War* (Oxford, 1902), I: 628–30.
2 Ibid. I: 536.
3 Fortescue claims 700 French cavalry based upon Spanish reports. Sir John Fortescue, *A History of the British Army* (London, 1899), VI: 336.
4 Slade, quoted in *The Military Memoirs of Lieut.-General Sir Joseph Thackwell* (London, 1908), 15.
5 Captain A. Gordon, *A Cavalry Officer in the Corunna Campaign* (London, 1913), 99. Gordon's account of the Corunna canpaign is by far the best from the cavalryman's perspective.
6 William Tale, *Jottings from my Sabretasch* (London, 1847), 77.
7 This ditch appears in most accounts of the fight although it does not appear to have provided Paget and his men with any great obstacle.
8 Tale, *Jottings*, 77–8.
9 Fought on 16 July 1760, the Battle of Emsdorff was an action fought during the Minden campaign and involved the 15th Light Dragoons (in their pre-hussar guise) who played a major part in the defeat of a French division. The battle honour 'Emsdorff' is unique to the regiment.
10 Gordon, *A Cavalry Officer*, 102–3.
11 Tale, *Jottings*, 78–9.
12 This river is invariably refered to as the river Cea, mainly due to an error in the map featured in Gordon's *A Cavalry Officer*, 103.

13 'The pursuit was sadly disorderly,' wrote Paget afterwards. 'I gave the Regiment a good scolding for it after the affair was over.' The Marquess of Anglesey, *One Leg* (London, 1961), 80.

14 Gordon, *A Cavalry Officer*, 107.

15 Anglesey, *One Leg*, 80.

16 Dr Adam Neale, *Letters from Portugal and Spain* (London, 1809), letter XLV, 266.

17 Ibid. 266.

18 Fortescue, *British Army*, VI: 336–7.

19 Gordon, *A Cavalry Officer*, 134.

20 Ibid. 199.

21 Oman, *Peninsular War*, I, 646.

CHAPTER III

Wellington and his Cavalry: The Early Years

Although a British force had remained at Lisbon throughout the Corunna campaign, the Peninsular War had, as far as Britain was concerned, come to a temporary halt. However, having escaped censure following the enquiry into the Convention of Cintra, Wellesley was re-appointed as commander of the British Army in Portugal, and in April 1809 he returned to resume the campaign he had begun eight months earlier.

The morning state of the British Army on 6 May 1809 shows a great improvement in the ratio of cavalry to infantry. Altogether, Wellesley commanded 18,881 infantry, which included 1,268 men stationed at Lisbon. The cavalry consisted of two brigades, the 1st Brigade, numbering 1,668 and commanded by Stapleton Cotton, being the 14th and 16th Light Dragoons, two squadrons of the 20th Light Dragoons, and one squadron of the 3rd Light Dragoons KGL. The 2nd Brigade, 1,466 strong and commanded by Henry Fane, consisted of the 3rd Dragoon Guards and the 4th Dragoons. The return shows how the situation as regards the number of cavalry with the army had improved, the two brigades, 3,134-strong, representing almost fifteen percent of Wellesley's army. These two brigades were to be the nucleus of the British cavalry force in the Peninsula, for although the two squadrons of the 20th Light Dragoons and the single squadron of the KGL cavalry would be gone from the Peninsula by July 1809, the remaining four regiments would go on to make a major contribution to the British campaign in the Peninsula, fighting their way across Portugal, Spain and southern France until the war ended in April 1814.

Wellesley's first action upon his return to the Peninsula came on 12 May 1809 when, in one of the most daring operations of the war, he crossed the Douro river at Oporto, right under the nose of a very careless Marshal Soult who failed to realise what was going on until it was too late. The ensuing fight resulted not only in the driving of Soult from Oporto but also in the expulsion of the French from Portugal. Wellesley had, therefore, brought the second French invasion to the same conclusion as the first. Naturally, there was no scope whatsoever for the British cavalry at Oporto, but the 14th Light Dragoons did, in fact, manage to involve itself in the pursuit of the retreating French army, and did enough for 'Douro' to be added to the regiment's battle honours.

Two squadrons of the 14th, along with two battalions of KGL infantry and two guns, had crossed the Douro by ferry at Barca d'Avintas, a few miles to the east of Oporto. The small force was commanded by Major General John Murray[1] whose task it was to cut the French retreat eastwards. Unfortunately, he was not up to the job, for when he saw the French army strung out along the road to Vallongo, he hesitated instead of putting himself across their path and the French were allowed to pass unscathed. At that moment, Charles Stewart rode up, determined not to let the French get away without a fight, and, taking command of the two squadrons of the 14th Light Dragoons, galloped along the road after the enemy.[2] The two squadrons, Felton Hervey's leading with Charles Butler's in reserve, crashed into the rear of the French column causing havoc among them. In the confusion the French general, Delaborde, was knocked from his horse, whilst General Foy, who was to become one of Wellesley's most enduring adversaries in the Peninsula, was wounded. The French infantry suffered at the hands of the light dragoons' sabres and were badly mauled, over 300 of them being taken prisoner. The 14th did not get off lightly, however, and suffered thirty-five killed and wounded, including Hervey who lost an arm. It was a creditable action for the light dragoons, and although no enemy cavalry were involved it demonstrated what cavalry could do against retreating infantry. Fortunately for the French, they were protected to a large extent by the nature of the ground, the road being lined with stone walls which restricted the 14th's movements.

By the end of the following month, a further brigade of cavalry had joined Wellesley's army, consisting of the 23rd Light Dragoons and the 1st Hussars KGL, commanded by George Anson and numbering 910 sabres. As we shall see, the two regiments were to enjoy vastly contrasting fortunes. When Wellesley's army lined up alongside the Spanish army under the ageing General Cuesta at Talavera, on 27 July 1809, it did so with three brigades of cavalry. The 1st was Fane's 1,070-strong brigade of the 3rd Dragoon Guards and 4th Dragoons. The 2nd Brigade consisted of the 14th and 16th Light Dragoons, some 989 men under Cotton, whilst the 3rd Brigade, 910-strong, consisted of the 23rd Light Dragoons and the 1st Hussars KGL, both of whom had recently arrived in the Peninsula. The cavalry as a whole was commanded by Lieutenant General William Payne, an officer who does not figure largely in the subsequent annals of the Peninsular War.

Like Vimeiro, the Battle of Talavera was largely an affair of infantry and artillery, although the light cavalry, particularly the 14th Light Dragoons, did assist in seeing off some of the French infantry attacks. Nevertheless, the battle was to provide us with the second, and one of the most infamous, examples of the recklessness of British cavalry in the Peninsula,

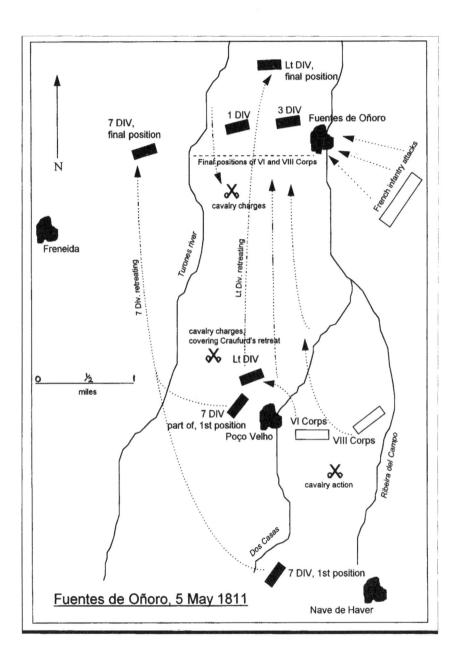

Fuentes de Oñoro, 5 May 1811

which came towards the end of the battle, during the hot, sweltering afternoon of 28 July, the second day of the battle. Both French and British infantry had been heavily engaged throughout the day, with the artillery of both sides pounding away at each other. Fortunately for Wellesley, his relatively untried army was up to the challenge thrown down to it by the more experienced French army which attacked it on several occasions, the long dark-blue columns being driven off by the controlled musketry of the steady British line. Only once, when the two battalions of Foot Guards pursued their beaten enemies too far, to be badly mauled themselves, did Wellesley face anything like a crisis, and even that was averted when the resulting gap was suitably plugged by the 48th Regiment.

After seeing his infantry thrown back time after time, Marshal Victor, the French field commander, decided to test the mettle of Wellesley's men one last time and sent the remnants of Ruffin's division and three battalions under Villatte to attack the British line at its northern end, along the valley to the north of the Medellin, the long hill from where Wellesley had directed the battle throughout the day. Ruffin's men had been in action the previous evening and had already been sorely tried earlier in the day, and it was with some reluctance that they advanced along the valley, something which was not lost on Wellesley who decided to meet this threat with Anson's brigade of cavalry.

The 23rd Light Dragoons duly trotted out in two lines with the 1st Hussars KGL on their left and a little to their rear.[3] Fane's brigade of heavy cavalry was to support the two regiments. The cavalry advanced at first at an easy pace whilst ahead of them, some way to the front and mounted on a white horse, rode Colonel Sir John Elley, his job as Adjutant-General being to pick out a suitable line of advance for the cavalry. The French infantry saw the advancing cavalry at quite a distance and duly formed themselves into squares whilst on the hills to the east, French gunners trained their pieces on the approaching British cavalry. In fact, the French artillery fire was hot enough to cause the 23rd to veer to their left and increase their pace whilst the KGL cavalry did likewise.

To anybody who has visited the battlefield of Talavera, the charge of Anson's brigade bears some resemblance to the later charge made by the Light Brigade at Balaclava, at least from the observer's perspective, with a long, fairly narrow valley and heights to both north and south which provided a wonderful grandstand view of the events unfolding in the valley. The valley itself is very broken and undulating and it is difficult to imagine the cavalry travelling at anything more than just a swift canter. It is almost inconceivable to imagine them travelling at a furious gallop but they were obviously travelling at a fast enough pace for them not to see the source of the disaster which was about to befall them, a dry watercourse, some twelve feet wide and about six feet deep at its deepest, which lay directly in their path. Elley certainly saw it as it loomed out of the long, parched grass but even he only just managed to get his horse to clear the obstacle. Once on the other side, Elley halted his horse and tried, in vain as it happened, to signal to the 23rd Light Dragoons who were by now almost on top of the ditch. Many of the cavalrymen saw it and, approaching at speed, managed to jump the obstacle, but the majority of the 23rd simply had no chance of avoiding it and tumbled headlong into it. Horses and men rolled on top of each other and many suffered broken limbs whilst others tried desperately to scramble out before the second line crashed into them. In fact, whilst many of this second line did manage to halt in time, they could not avoid charging into the disorderly ranks which were struggling out of the ditch and the chaos increased. Also, the French 27th regiment, the closest enemy infantry to the stricken light dragoons, opened fire, adding to the confusion.

The KGL cavalry, meanwhile, being farther to the left and a little to the rear, were able to negotiate the ditch with far greater ease although even they suffered some disorder from the obstacle. To their immense credit, the 23rd managed to extricate themselves and reformed along with the KGL to attack Ruffin's infantry who were drawn up to meet them.[4] No cavalry ever stood much chance of breaking squares formed of steady infantry, however, and after making a few attempts the KGL fell back having suffered thirty-seven casualties. Remarkably, the 23rd continued forward, passing between the enemy squares and charging the leading brigade of Merlin's cavalry division, the 10th and 26th Chasseurs. The French allowed them to pass and turned against them once they had done so, forcing the 23rd to fight their way out, which they did but at some cost to themselves. Indeed, Elley, at the head of around 170 men, found himself cut off and surrounded and while the remnants of Drake's and Allen's squadrons were virtually wiped out Elley managed to cut his way out along with just seven others.[5] In all, the disaster in the valley at Talavera cost the 23rd Light Dragoons two officers and forty-seven men killed, four officers and forty-six men wounded and three officers and 105 men taken prisoner. This, out of a strength of 459 present at the start of the battle, represents an alarming casualty rate of almost fifty percent.

The mishap that befell the 23rd Light Dragoons at Talavera is one of the better known episodes of the Peninsular War and is one which has contributed enormously to the bad reputation of the British cavalry in the war. On the surface it would appear that the lessons of Vimeiro were evidently not heeded; for the 20th Light Dragoons read the 23rd Light Dragoons. However, whilst the episode has clearly been detrimental to the reputation of the British cavalry, closer examination shows that the facts are slightly more at odds with the accepted version than we would imagine. At Vimeiro the 20th simply refused to be held in check and charged on into strong enemy positions when they should have reformed and returned to their own lines instead. The same happened to the 23rd at

Talavera. However, the criticisms which the regiment has since attracted are based not on the charge but on a large slice of bad luck in not being able to see the dry watercourse until the last moment. This was not the reason for the regiment's heavy losses during the battle. At the end of the day it matters little what the real cause of the mishap was. The main thing is that the regiment did charge too far and suffered accordingly. However, it is worth nailing the 'myth of the watercourse'. Closer inspection of the battlefield confirms that it would have been almost impossible for any body of cavalry to come on at anything faster than a brisk trot.[6] The ground is very broken and the 23rd had not covered any great distance to reach the watercourse, their starting positions being just a few hundred yards to the west. My contention is, therefore, that they were not coming on in a disorderly manner, nor could they have been coming on at break-neck speed, as many latter-day historians would have us believe. 'In the most perfect order' was how one eye-witness, Schaumann, described the charge,[7] adding that clouds of dust were thrown up by the horses. Perhaps this was an additional factor that contributed to the regiment's inability to see what lay in front of it. Schaumann never mentions anything like a reckless charge and describes the 23rd as being 'in full swing' only when they came across the watercourse. Certainly, Elley, riding ahead to see the lie of the land, was not charging at full pelt, and even he failed to see the obstacle until the very last moment, looming as it did out of the long grass. The major reason for the accident was just bad luck in that they failed to see what was undoubtedly a hidden obstacle.

To enter into a deep discussion of the events at the watercourse is, in my opinion, simply adding to a myth, for I believe the episode to be a 'red herring' which should be discarded as having obscured the real reason behind the losses incurred by the 23rd Light Dragoons at Talavera. This may come as a surprise, but consider the facts. The 23rd suffered 207 casualties during the battle and the vast majority of these were sustained not during the fall at the watercourse but in the action against both the French infantry and cavalry shortly afterwards. Supporting this is the evidence of Sir John Elley himself who said that of the 170 men he led against the French cavalry just seven or eight, plus himself, managed to cut their way out and rejoin Wellesley's line. Therefore, if we assume that the 23rd took casualties whilst attacking and passing the French infantry squares, and add to these the casualties sustained by them when they were cut off by French cavalry, it becomes clear and undeniable that the 23rd Light Dragoons suffered mainly during their attack after they had pulled themselves out of the watercourse, and that the said watercourse has had far too great an influence on the analysis of their performance, being little more than an insignificant – if well-documented – accident. It was not, however, anything like the sort of disaster which successive historians have led us to believe. The attack itself was, ironically, successful, in that it halted the reluctant advance of Ruffin's infantry. Even French reports claim that such was the power of the British charge that Generals Villatte and Cassagne were almost captured when they were caught outside the infantry squares.[8]

Fortescue calls it a 'mad exploit'[9] although I think it unfair to call the whole episode mad. There is little doubt that the 23rd were at fault in charging on beyond the French infantry to engage the French cavalry without any infantry support of their own and with all momentum and order gone. It was simply a reckless repeat of the 20th Light Dragoons' charge at Vimeiro the previous year. The lesson had patently not been learned. But even had the regiment not come to grief, is there really any reason to suspect that they would have been able to accomplish what was to prove a virtually impossible feat, of breaking an infantry square? I doubt it. The final verdict may lie with the commander-in-chief himself for, in his despatch to Castlereagh, Wellesley writes, 'although the 23rd [light] dragoons suffered considerable loss, the charge had the effect of preventing the execution of that part of the enemy's plan.'[10] (i.e. Ruffin's attack on the northern end of Wellesley's line). He went on to thank successive generals, citing 'Lieut. General Payne, commanding the cavalry, and particularly Brigadier General Anson's brigade.'[11] This is hardly the sort of praise one would expect if the charge had been so disastrous, particularly when we consider the sort of damning censures handed out to the cavalry later in the war.

The Battle of Talavera ended in a rather costly victory for Wellesley who, in September the same year, first signed his name 'Wellington' after being awarded the title Viscount Wellington of Talavera in recognition of his victory. This no doubt gave him great satisfaction, although the consequent retreat of his army to the Portuguese border and the complete lack of co-operation from the Spaniards did not. And while he could reflect with great satisfaction upon the performance of his infantry he may have began to wonder, after two major battles during which they had come to grief on two occasions, whether he would be able to utilise his cavalry to the same effect.

The victory at Talavera yielded few positive results for Wellington and by the end of 1809 his army had retreated to the relative safety of Portugal. The rugged nature of the country meant that there would be little work for the cavalry over the next few months and the majority of the regiments withdrew to the Tagus valley where forage was easily obtainable. In November the 23rd Light Dragoons returned to England, largely as a result of their losses sustained at Talavera. They were replaced in Anson's brigade by the 16th Light Dragoons who were transferred from Cotton's brigade. The 16th themselves were replaced by the 1st (Royal) Dragoons who had arrived in Lisbon in October. Cotton himself assumed his duties as second-in-command to Payne, commanding the cavalry division, whilst Cotton's place was taken by Slade.

There was little work for the cavalry during the next few months, or, for that matter, for the army itself, and there would be an interval of fourteen months between the Battle of Talavera and Wellington's next major battle, at Busaco in September 1810. However, these months proved to be the most anxious time of the war for Wellington. He was beset by internal problems, caused largely by a group of officers who considered the campaign in the Peninsula a waste of both their time and Britain's resources. These 'croakers', as they were called, advocated a swift return home and an abandonment of the campaign. The whinging of a few junior officers was nothing new, but as the 'croakers' included such senior officers as Robert Craufurd and Charles Stewart, the problem was a very real one for Wellington. MPs in Parliament also questioned the wisdom of remaining in the Peninsula, having seen few benefits from the victory at Talavera. Was it a fluke, they wondered, and should they leave their Spanish and Portuguese allies to their fates? It was all something which Wellington could do without, particularly as the French commander, Marshal Masséna, along with the fiery Marshal Ney, was massing his force for a third invasion of Portugal.

Just as the spring and summer of 1810 proved to be a very trying period for Wellington, so it also proved a great opportunity for the Light Division to demonstrate its prowess as Wellington's finest division, holding the line of the Coa and Agueda rivers against a vastly superior French force. The chosen route for Masséna's invasion lay through the northern corridor between Spain and Portugal, which was guarded by the twin fortresses of Ciudad Rodrigo and Almeida. The Light Division contained some of the finest regiments in Wellington's army and was commanded by arguably its finest – and most controversial – commander, Robert 'Black Bob' Craufurd, so called because of his black, violent temper, but a man uniquely suited for the task which his chief had entrusted to him. With the French looking to force the northern corridor it was Craufurd's task to prevent the prying and probing French forces from piercing his chain of outposts and obtaining information on troop numbers, dispositions, etc. in Wellington's army. It was also his job to encourage, by the presence of the Light Division, the garrisons of the two fortresses, the resistance of which Wellington hoped would buy him time for the completion of the defences across the Lisbon peninsula. These fortifications would become known as the Lines of Torres Vedras, the construction of which had begun in secret in October 1809. Wellington had resigned himself to a retreat to the Lines but the timing of it depended largely upon just how long Ciudad Rodrigo and Almeida could hold out. Allied to this was Craufurd's maintenance of the line of the Coa and Agueda rivers, some forty miles of front with a depth of ten miles. The task of holding this area of 400 square miles fell squarely upon the shoulders of the infantry, the 43rd and 52nd light infantry regiments and the 95th Rifles, supported by the 1st and 3rd Caçadores.

Attached to the division were the 14th and 16th Light Dragoons and the 1st Hussars KGL. This latter regiment was wonderfully adept at piquet duties and it was upon them that the bulk of the cavalry work in the area devolved. Indeed, they proved themselves to be the finest cavalry Wellington possessed for this kind of work. The two British light cavalry regiments arrived in the area in June, by which time the rest of the Light Division had gained an intimate knowledge of this most rugged of campaigning areas. It is a very rocky country, the roads were – and still are – bad, and, in general, the area was totally unsuitable for cavalry to be employed in any manner other than on piquet and patrol work. There were few places where cavalry could be deployed in any great strength, and huge boulders and rocks strewn about characterised the area. Nevertheless, the cavalry still found themselves busy on most days and were engaged in a number of skirmishes.

This brings us to yet another controversial cavalry action which has tended to overshadow the good work the 14th and 16th Light Dragoons did during the summer of 1810. It happened on 11 July at Villar de Puerco, or Bexmeiro, or Barquilla, depending upon which account you read, as the action took place in a sort of triangle formed by these three small villages.

Although the rough nature of the land on the Agueda and Coa rivers prohibits agriculture of any great extent, there are areas where crops can flourish. The wide, rolling expanse of land, albeit relatively small, where crops do flourish begins to the east of Ciudad Rodrigo and opens out at Salamanca and beyond. But there was still enough forage in the area to attract the attention of the French who regularly made incursions across the Agueda and into the territory held by Craufurd's Light Division. Irritated by this practice, Craufurd made plans for an attack on the French who regularly made it their business to plunder the villages of Villar de Puerco and Barquilla. At midnight on 10 July Craufurd led twelve companies of infantry, six squadrons of cavalry and two of RHA guns east across the Dos Casas river to cut them off, and by dawn on the 11th had got his infantry into position on some low hills to the west of the villages with his cavalry in support. The French detachment before them consisted of between 200 and 300 men of the 22nd Line,[12] commanded by a Captain Gouache, accompanied by thirty dragoons. The French spotted Craufurd's men shortly after dawn and hastily prepared to move off. Craufurd, on the other hand, had not yet located the infantry but sent some of the KGL hussars in pursuit of the enemy dragoons. Leading the hussars was Captain Krauchenberg who, as he was leading his men through the high-standing corn, spotted the glint of bayonets ahead of him, a fact which was duly reported to Craufurd who ordered the KGL to charge them. The advance of the German hussars was hampered by a stone wall which prevented them from forming correctly and certainly took away the momentum of the charge. Moreover, by the time Krauchenberg had got his men past the wall the French infantry had disappeared, having been ordered to lie down in the corn. Suddenly, when the KGL hussars were just fifty yards from them, the French got to their feet, and presented a square formation to the surprised hussars, eleven of whom were sent tumbling from their saddles as the French opened fire. Krauchenberg did not stop but led his squadron past the square in pursuit of the enemy cavalry, all of whom were taken. Meanwhile, a squadron of the 16th Light Dragoons, under Captain Bellis, was ordered to charge, but he too met with the same result after having experienced difficulties in passing the defile. Craufurd, seeing the prize escaping his grasp, ordered Lieutenant Colonel Talbot to charge with his squadron of the 14th Light Dragoons. Talbot led his men forward at the charge and had got within pistol-shot when the French fired a volley again which sent several men and horses crashing to the ground. Among them was Talbot himself who was killed, having been shot eight times. Others, whose horses had been shot, got to their feet but were spared by Gouache who ordered his men not to fire. Edward Charles Cocks was with the 16th Light Dragoons:

As the sun rose we discovered the infantry beyond Villar de Puerco, and the cavalry to their right. The whole of the country was open in front, and to our left covered with corn. To the right were some woods. We had a defile to pass, by the village, in order to get to the plain. We advanced in column of divisions from the right; the hussars first, followed by the 16th, and then the 14th. The infantry were just opposite the defile, behind the brow of a hill, and nearly concealed by the corn. The hussars endeavoured to form to the front and charge, as did the 1st squadron (Ashworth's) of the 16th. They got a heavy volley, which knocked down thirteen or fourteen men and nearly as many horses. They then wheeled to the left, and made at the cavalry. The 3rd squadron (Bellis') followed their example. The sun was directly in our eyes, and from that circumstance and the dust we could see nothing, and, except the two squadrons who had charged, no one knew whence the volley had proceeded. Then three squadrons rode at the cavalry, and took nearly forty with their horses. Very few got away. The 4th squadron (Brotherton of the 14th) was stopped by General Crawford [sic] and ordered to charge the infantry. It is impossible to do justice to the intrepidity of this body of men. They stood the second charge as well as the first, knocked down some by a running fire, and bayoneted others. Colonel Talbot led the squadron. When he saw the enemy had formed an oblong, he endeavoured to bring his right flank forward and charge the upper face of the square. He moved like a lion, had his horse killed close to the enemy, and fell himself fighting sabre in hand in the middle of the square. This was not broken, and the 14th was repulsed. In the dust and confusion which ensued the enemy got off through the corn into the woods.[13]

Having repulsed successive attacks, Gouache was able to draw his men off towards the village of Sexmeiro and eventually rejoined French lines where he was greeted as a hero. In fact, when Masséna heard his account of the fight, he awarded him the Legion of Honour. Craufurd, on the other hand, was left to count his dead and wounded, which totalled thirty-two, including Talbot, the most senior casualty.

The affair at Villar de Puerco quickly became the talk of the army, with Craufurd the target of a great deal of criticism. It did not help matters that so many future diarists, such as Simmons, Leach, Costello, Cocks and Tomkinson, and even Napier, were present, all of whom recorded their version of events in their journals. For once, it was not the cavalry who were criticised but Craufurd and his handling of the fight, with the majority of opinion being that he should have simply brought forward his infantry and artillery, which would certainly have decided the business in his favour. Nevertheless, the mishap to the 14th and 16th Light Dragoons has still tended to appear in the debit column of the British cavalry in the Peninsula although, as we have seen, it comes with massively mitigating circumstances. The cavalry was not properly formed owing to the route of advance chosen by Craufurd, the stone wall breaking their formation, whilst the French themselves, hidden away in the corn, proved to be very steady and, in square formation, were relatively safe from cavalry as long as they remained so. We cannot, therefore, hold Talbot or his men responsible for the incident. It was quite simply a mishandled affair by the commander of the Light Division.

With the fall of Ciudad Rodrigo to the French in July 1810 and Almeida the following month, Wellington began to withdraw his army deeper into Portugal to what he hoped would be the safety of the Lines of Torres Vedras, the finishing touches to which were being put even as he fell back. There was little for his cavalry to do during the next few months, other than provide the army with a rearguard and with the usual tasks of escort, piquet and patrol work. On 27 September Wellington brought Masséna to a standstill at Busaco, although the battle was never intended to be more than a delaying action, and the retreat continued afterwards. The Battle of Busaco was yet another action which was fought almost exclusively by the infantry and artillery with the 14th and 16th Light Dragoons sustaining just four wounded between them. From then on it was a steady withdrawal to the Lines, although on 8 October there was a little scrap between Cocks's squadron of the 16th Light Dragoons and two regiments of French cavalry who had entered the village of Alcoentre, where two troops of Horse Artillery were resting.

About 2 we heard some shots fired near the village, and Captain Cocks' squadron, being the first for duty moved down as quickly as possible with the first mounted dragoons we could collect, in all not fifty men. On our way down we met five of the guns coming up in the greatest confusion, some with four, some with six horses to them, having got away how they could. On the other side of the village ran a considerable brook, which was not passable excepting at the bridge on the entrance to the town. The enemy had two regiments of cavalry close up, and Captain Murray's people were all withdrawn over the bridge. Our party formed up ready to charge down the street. There was a howitzer and two ammunition waggons without a horse to them, commissariat mules and men in the street in the greatest confusion. The enemy did not long remain idle, and detached two squadrons from the 14th [French] Dragoons into the village; they passed the bridge, driving in Captain Murray's people, and came half-way up the street to where we were formed. The enemy's two squadrons were close to each other, in sixes, completely filling up the street. From the bridge to where we were formed, the street makes a right angle; the head of the column passed the turning, the other squadron in the rear, not seeing how we were formed. In this situation they halted, when we charged them; they instantly went about and wished to retire. There was the greatest noise and confusion with the enemy, their front wishing to get away, and their rear, not seeing what was going on, stood still. They got so close together that it was impossible to get well at them. We took twelve and killed six, driving them over the bridge again, and by this means allowing time for what remained in the town to get clear away.[14]

In spite of their numerical superiority the French were driven off with the loss of eighteen casualties in what was another creditable affair for the British cavalry. In fact, Anson's brigade did much good work during the latter days of the retreat, protecting the infantry from attack and generally keeping the French at arm's length. There were almost daily skirmishes and, as Fortescue says, 'as usual, in every conflict of the small bodies engaged the Allies had the better'.[15]

Wellington's army reached the safety of the Lines of Torres Vedras during the second week of October 1810, and for the next few weeks watched and waited while Masséna sat before them, no doubt brooding upon the problem Wellington had set him, namely, how to get through the impenetrable range of fortified hills before him. The situation remained this way until 15 November when Masséna pulled his starving troops back to Santarem, where he hoped to find food and forage, his men having stripped the land elsewhere of its resources. The following day Wellington emerged from the Lines, shadowing Masséna as they moved back. There was daily contact between the British vanguard and the French rearguard, during which Wellington's cavalry engaged in numerous skirmishes. Typical of these was a small affair, again at Alcoentre, on 17 November when Anson's cavalry brigade overtook the French rearguard and enjoyed itself during the day, mauling isolated groups of French.[16] The 16th Light Dragoons took two officers and seventy-eight men prisoners, most of whom were taken during a particularly daring exploit by Sergeant Baxter who, with just five men, surprised a French outpost consisting of no fewer than fifty men, most of whom had stacked their arms and were busy cooking. One officer and forty-one men were taken prisoner at a cost of just one trooper of the 16th wounded.[17]

The situation on the Tagus remained in a state of deadlock until 5 March 1811 when Masséna finally admitted defeat and began the long haul north, his half-starved, ragged army dragging itself along wreaking havoc on the way. Indeed, the route taken by Masséna as he retreated north to the Mondego was marked by a series of burning villages and outrages against the local population. It was one of the most harrowing episodes of the war.

There was the usual cut and thrust of cavalry skirmishing during the French retreat whenever the British vanguard made contact with the French rearguard. The larger actions came at Pombal, Casal Nova, Redinha and Foz d'Arouce, although the nature of the ground precluded any real effective cavalry operations, other than those of a supporting nature to the infantry. By the first week of April, Masséna had been pursued to the very borders of Spain and with the Battle of Sabugal, on 3 April, Wellington brought about an end to the third French invasion of Portugal.

The year 1811 was an important one for Wellington. He had come through the most trying period of the war, the spring and summer of 1810, and had witnessed the success of the Lines of Torres Vedras. The 'croakers' had largely been silenced, whilst at home the politicians appeared to be more disposed towards the cause in the Peninsula. However, Wellington was still far from secure in the Peninsula. The French still held the two great fortresses of Ciudad Rodrigo and Badajoz, the possession of which was vital before he could even consider moving deeper into Spain, whilst the fortified town of Almeida, in Portugal, remained in French hands also. 1811 was all about consolidation, therefore, after the retreats of the previous two years. Furthermore, his Spanish allies needed a demonstration of his commitment to the cause against France – after all, they had seen little from him during the past two years other than retreats. The next six months were, therefore, to prove an important time for Wellington.

As for the cavalry, it had been organised into three brigades. The 1st, consisting of the 3rd Dragoon Guards and the 4th Dragoons, was commanded by Colonel the Hon. George de Grey. The 2nd Brigade consisted of the 1st Royal Dragoons and the 14th Light Dragoons under Slade. The 3rd Brigade, commanded by George Anson, consisted of the 16th Light Dragoons and the 1st Hussars KGL, with the 13th Light Dragoons being unbrigaded. The whole was commanded by Stapleton Cotton. The 1st Brigade of cavalry would spend most of its time with Hill and Beresford in the south, the other two remaining with Wellington. There would be changes during the year and additions, including the 2nd Hussars KGL and the 11th Light Dragoons.[18]

The problem of retaking Almeida from the French was resolved on 11 May 1811, when the garrison, under General Brennier, absconded during the night and made off towards their own lines, leaving the badly damaged town in Wellington's hands.[19] However, this was not before Masséna had made one final attempt at relieving the place with a three-day battle which was to prove his final act before he was recalled to France by Napoleon. The battle, fought on 3-5 May, took place on the Spanish-Portuguese border, at Fuentes de Oñoro, to the south of which a large rolling plain allowed the cavalry of both sides to deploy and fight in strength. Indeed, it was one of the great cavalry fights of the war.

Masséna's army numbered around 47,000 men, with Wellington's Anglo-Portuguese army weighing in at around 37,500.[20] The battlefield of Fuentes de Oñoro stretches for some twelve miles, from Fort Conception in the north, to the village of Nave de Haver in the south, although the eight miles from Fuentes de Oñoro to Fort Conception is covered by a ravine for its greater part and was not, therefore, fought over. Indeed, this section was held by just the 5th and 6th Divisions. The main infantry battle took place in the village of Fuentes de Oñoro itself, a maze of alleyways and small streets which became the scene of much bitter hand-to-hand fighting as successive French attacks swept forward. The fighting at the village subsided towards the end of the first day with the village remaining in Allied hands. On 4 May there was very little fighting. The following day, however, was one of the most desperate of the war for Wellington who faced a stern test of his resolve when Masséna launched a large-scale attack against his right flank, an attack which was designed to provoke Wellington into moving his men south to meet the threat. This, naturally, would uncover Almeida, which would allow the waiting convoys of supplies to get forward and revictual the place. The choice for Wellington was simple; he gave up either his communications across the Coa or the blockade of Almeida. In the event, Wellington was not to be moved and he simply adopted the expedient of refusing his right flank. He realised that by doing so he risked losing both his baggage and artillery as the only bridge over the Coa, which lay at his back, was at Castello Bom, and this was situated at the bottom of a very narrow, winding descent. It did, however, ensure that Almeida remained covered and this was the object of the game.

The attack on Wellington's right flank at Nave de Haver was delivered at dawn by 3,500 French cavalry and three divisions of infantry. The village was held by Julian Sanchez and his Spanish irregulars who were driven from the village by the sheer weight of enemy numbers thrown against them. The plain to the north of Nave de Haver, stretching as far as the next village, Poço Velho, is ideally suited to cavalry, being open, rolling country. It extends beyond the latter village also, and it was across this plain that the British cavalry, under Cotton, fought against an enemy twice their number, some 1,500 British and KGL against 3,500 French. The ensuing cavalry action bore testament to the contrasting conditions of the horses of the two sides. Cotton's cavalry were relatively well mounted, upon horses which had benefited from a winter and early spring behind the Lines of Torres Vedras, whereas Masséna's cavalry had endured quite the reverse, having spent the winter and spring starving before the Lines. Hence, when the two sides met at Fuentes de Oñoro the British cavalry, whilst being totally outnumbered were, nevertheless, far better mounted, which gave them a distinct advantage in individual combat. Atkinson, the historian of the Royal Dragoons, also points out that, 'all accounts emphasise the want of determination about the French attacks, and clearly neither commanders nor men faced the British with any confidence.'[21] We can well imagine this French reluctance owing to the poor condition of their horses, but the Campo Mayor factor should not be forgotten either, the fight there having set the tone for the war as far as British-French cavalry combats were concerned.

With Sanchez having been driven out of Nave de Haver, the brunt of the French attack fell upon two squadrons of the 14th Light Dragoons who found themselves hopelessly outnumbered and were duly forced to fall back. They were joined before Poço Velho by a squadron of the 16th Light Dragoons and one squadron of 1st Hussars KGL but, again, they were forced to turn about by sheer weight of numbers. It was at this point that Robert Craufurd arrived with his Light Division in order to relieve the hard-pressed 7th Division, a new division under Houston, which found itself in a particularly tight spot. While the 7th Division fell back, Craufurd covered its retreat, his division being drawn up in squares, supported by Royal Horse Artillery and by Cotton's cavalry which kept the ever menacing French cavalry at bay. Cotton's cavalry consisted of two brigades; Slade's, the 1st Royal Dragoons and the 14th Light Dragoons, and Arentschildt's, the 16th Light Dragoons and the 1st Hussars KGL. Between them, they made several effective charges, retiring and charging by alternate squad against a superior French cavalry force to prevent them from interfering in Craufurd's withdrawal across the plain. The magnificent achievement of the Light Division – an orderly retreat across an open plain for almost three miles, all the way surrounded by French cavalry – has justly been praised as one of the finest achievements in the history of the British Army.[22] However, the supporting role played by Cotton's cavalry has long been overlooked, which is a great oversight, for if they had not prevented the French cavalry from closing upon Craufurd's infantry, the story might have been very different. The 14th and 16th Light Dragoons and the Royal Dragoons, along with the 1st Hussars KGL, deserve far greater credit for their part in the retreat of the Light Division. Indeed, Fortescue was of the opinion that Craufurd succeeded in drawing off his division only 'by sheer skill and resolution on the part of himself and Cotton'. He went on to add that, 'If the French brought their guns forward, it was the cavalry and Bull's battery that suffered; and the British dragoons, remembering how the infantry had saved themselves earlier in the day, willingly sacrificed themselves. The French squadrons, some three thousand strong, swarmed round the squares at a respectful distance, shouting and gesticulating, but never dared to deliver their threatened attack. Hardly a cannon-shot can have touched them [the Light Division], for their casualties when the day ended amounted to sixty-seven among the seven battalions of British and Portuguese, so nobly did the cavalry fulfil their duty.'[23] Tomkinson, of the 16th Light Dragoons, wrote:

On the enemy's first advance the army was very differently posted, the 7th Division being in a wood to the right rear of Possa Velha [sic] Our two brigades of cavalry scarcely amounted to 900, and these in bad condition. The enemy had 4,000 fresh cavalry, and were driving ours back on the infantry. The 7th Division in the wood waited too long, and Lord Wellington thought it was all over with them, the enemy's cavalry being on each of their flanks, and they had ground to pass on which cavalry could act. They, however, got away into the rocks, and the enemy's advance charged up the rising ground on which our horse artillery was posted, and passed two guns of Captain Bull's troop. Their advance was not well supported. Our cavalry came on and took a lieutenant-colonel and some prisoners... On the right, before the 7th Division evacuated the Possa Velha wood, Major Myers of the Hussars was in advance with two squadrons – one from the 16th, and one of his own regiment. Captain Belli had joined from England the day before, and taken command of Captain Cocks' squadron. Cocks commanded the left. Captain Belli's squadron (late Cocks'), with one of the Hussars, was in advance; and the enemy having sent forward two or three squadrons, Major Myers attempted to oppose them in front of a defile. He waited so long and was so indecisive, and the enemy came up so close, that he ordered the squadron of the 16th to charge. The enemy's squadron was about twice their strength, and waited their charge. This is the only instance I ever met with of two bodies of cavalry coming in opposition, and both standing, as invariably, as I have observed it, one or the other runs away. Our men rode up and began sabring, but were so outnumbered that they could do nothing, and were obliged to retire across the defile in confusion, the enemy having brought up more troops to that point.[24]

Cotton's cavalry retired behind the new line which Wellington had adopted, running west from the village of Fuentes de Oñoro along the top of a ridge. In effect, the Allied line now formed a sort of inverted 'U' shape. But if the British cavalry thought its work done for the day they were mistaken, for two squadrons of the 1st Royals and the 14th Light Dragoons were called upon to charge some French hussars who had cut off a large group of British skirmishers, including scores of Foot Guards. Fortunately, the majority were freed by this gallant charge and, in fact, some twenty-five French prisoners were taken including Lieutenant Colonel Lamotte, of the 13th Chasseurs.[25] It was during the French shelling of the Allied line that followed this last episode that the 14th Light Dragoons, who had lost their commander, Talbot, at Villar de Puerco the previous year, suffered the loss of another much-loved officer, Captain Knipe, who had a theory that artillery could take an enemy battery provided they charged it head-on. The theory proved sadly flawed, however, as Knipe discovered to his cost when the French gunners brought him crashing to the ground, dead, along with several other men.

Cotton's cavalry suffered 149 casualties on 5 May, ten percent of their strength, mainly in providing invaluable protection from French cavalry and artillery for Craufurd's Light Division.[26] Once again, their actions demonstrate that not all British cavalry actions in the Peninsula were wild, reckless charges. Here we find them outnumbered two-to-one, and yet they charged time and time again, dispersing their enemies and proving themselves equal – if not superior – in sword play and horsemanship. They were commanded steadily by Cotton and by good regimental officers and, apart from the mishap to Knipe of the 14th, the day passed with nothing but praise for them in performing a task without fuss, or accident and without too great loss to themselves. The Battle of Fuentes de Oñoro was, there-fore, one to be put firmly in the credit column of the British cavalry in the Peninsula and represents one of their greatest days of the war. Wellington himself, whilst not entirely happy with the way the battle had been fought –'if Bonaparte had been here we should have been beaten,' he later said – had nevertheless thwarted Masséna's plans to relieve Almeida, ostensi-bly the reason for the battle being fought. Shortly afterwards, Masséna was recalled to Paris and was replaced by Marshal Marmont.

Attention now switched to the south, with Wellington's attempts to take the fortress of Badajoz, an attempt which failed in May and June 1811. The accounts of cavalry actions in this theatre of war are to be found in the next three chapters, which deal with the operations of both Hill and Beresford. Having been thwarted in his attempts to take Badajoz Wellington turned his thoughts to the northern fortress of Ciudad Rodrigo, duly marched north once again, and established his headquarters at Fuenteguinaldo in August. During the next few months Wellington would engage in much manoeuvring and counter manoeuvring with Marmont to the south and south-west of Ciudad Rodrigo in order to be ready for the attempt on the place. Wellington's cavalry would find themselves embroiled in several small skirmishes during September 1811 and two are worthy of particular mention.

The first combat came on 25 September, close to the village of Carpio. There is nothing particularly dramatic about the fight but it is significant in that it was the first time that British cavalry had ever fought enemy lancers in the Peninsula.[27] The fight came about when Marmont sent forward a strong force of cavalry to discover the exact positions of Wellington's troops which lay to the south and west of Ciudad Rodrigo and to see whether Wellington was actually preparing for the siege. The French cavalry consisted of around 1,300 men in all, mainly from the Lancers de Berg and the 26th Chasseurs, who left Ciudad Rodrigo on the morning of the 25th and quickly came up against the outlying piquets of the 14th Light Dragoons which were driven from Carpio and over the Azava river, which runs north-south a few miles west of Ciudad Rodrigo. The 14th retired to the safety of some heights above Carpio, in the direction of Espeja, where they joined two squadrons of the 16th Light Dragoons. The French commander, Wathier, left six squadrons of his cavalry in Carpio itself while the remaining eight squadrons crossed the Azava in pursuit of the British cavalry. The latter were now supported by the light companies of the 11th, 61st and 53rd, from Hulse's brigade of the 6th Division, which Sir Thomas Graham had ordered forward to a wood situated upon the heights. Wathier advanced very cautiously, not seeing any British troops in the woods, but evidently concerned lest there be any hidden from sight. He sent forward four of the eight squadrons which had crossed the Azava and these were suddenly charged by the squadron of the 14th Light Dragoons and one of the squadrons of the 16th. The French rallied, however, and advanced again, this time with all eight squadrons. Wathier's caution was not without good cause, for, as the French passed close to the wood, the light companies of Hulse's brigade opened fire into them, taking them by surprise and bringing them to a halt, upon which the 14th and 16th Light Dragoons charged once more, this time driving the French cavalry back for a distance of about two miles until they had driven them across the Azava with the loss of around fifty casualties. The British light dragoons sustained just a dozen casualties in what was, in Fortescue's words, 'a brilliant little affair'.[28]

The fight at Carpio is quite remarkable for its obscurity. Indeed, when one considers the numbers involved – three British squadrons against eight French, with a further four enemy squadrons in reserve – the achievement of the 14th and 16th Light Dragoons deserves to be up there alongside such affairs as Sahagun, where Paget's cavalry were nowhere near as outnumbered. Notwithstanding the part played by Hulse's light companies in bringing the French cavalry to a virtual standstill, the charge of this very small British cavalry force ranks as one of the finest of the war, with no reckless pursuit or great loss of life, but with measured and steady control, with discipline determination and, more important, with a satisfying end result, being the repulse of a strong French reconnaissance. Once again, it was a demonstration of what British light dragoons could do in a stand-up fight. Sadly, it has all but been forgotten and has certainly been overshadowed by the more famous fights at Sahagun and Benavente. This is not to denigrate the fine achievements of Paget's cavalry in 1808 but one is certainly moved to wonder why the fight at Carpio quickly disappeared into the mists of time, unlike the other two named actions which are continually being held up – quite correctly – as examples of what British cavalry could achieve on the field of battle, although this almost certainly has much to do with the dramatic circumstances surrounding Paget's two actions. As well as demonstrating the bravery and skill in action of the British cavalry, the fight at Carpio is also an example of their effectiveness at piquet work, a task at which they did not always excel and, indeed, is an aspect of their work which is often regarded as being woefully inadequate. The fight therefore demonstrates a combination of fighting ability, timing and manoeuvrability in the field and effective piquet work, all of which was achieved in the face of a numerically superior enemy cavalry force.

25 September 1811 was quite a busy day for Wellington's cavalry, for whilst the 14th and 16th Light Dragoons were busy at Carpio, another British force was being attacked by a much larger French force at El Bodon, a few miles to the south. As the 3rd Division of Wellington's army was drawing back towards Fuenteguinaldo it was attacked by four brigades of French cavalry, 2,500 men altogether, under Montbrun. The Allied situation was made worse by the fact that the 3rd Division was split into three with the main thrust of Montbrun's attack being made against two battalions of Colville's brigade, the 1/5th and 77th, whilst the other two battalions of his brigade, the 2/83rd and the 94th, were positioned some two miles away to the west. The other brigade of the 3rd Division, Wallace's, consisting of the 1/45th and 1/88th, was three miles to the south-west at Pastores. A successful attack by Montbrun against Colville would cut off both him and Wallace from the main body of the army which lay around Fuenteguinaldo, about five miles to the south-west. It was vital, therefore, that Colville and this very weak infantry force held the high road along which the French were advancing. Fortunately, they were assisted by two Portuguese batteries – Picton's divisional artillery – and five weak squadrons of cavalry, three of the 1st Hussars KGL and two of the 11th Light Dragoons.

The fight at El Bodon is famous for the charge made by Major Ridge and the 5th Regiment, a charge made in line against French cavalry in order to recover four guns which the Portuguese had lost. This went against all conventions of warfare as it was normal practice for infantry to fight in square formation against cavalry. Ridge was successful, however, and the guns were recovered. But apart from the infantry fight, we should not lose sight of the part played by both the KGL cavalry and the 11th Light Dragoons who made single-squadron charges against a numerically superior French force to drive them off on no fewer than forty separate occasions. The Allied cavalry may have fought under a numerical disadvantage but they did enjoy a topographical advantage as they were able to make their charges downhill and it was the momentum of their attacks which helped enormously in putting the French cavalry to flight. It is important to note that on no occasion did they pursue the beaten French cavalry farther than was necessary, and there was no repeat of the Vimeiro incident. The charges were controlled and very business-like, the men appreciating they had a job to do, and an important one at that, and they did it well. They protected the infantry and artillery as they fell back along the high road to Fuenteguinaldo for five miles, all the time under intense pressure but never failing to keep at bay the French cavalry until the whole reached the safety of the Fuenteguinaldo position, by which time several other Allied units had arrived in support. The whole episode was a repeat of the withdrawal of the Light Division at Fuentes de Oñoro the previous May, with the squadrons of Allied cavalry preventing the French from interfering with the retreat. Once again, they had demonstrated their ability to carry out a task under great duress and accomplish it with great credit, under the watching eyes of Wellington himself.[29] The fight cost the 11th Light Dragoons and the 1st Hussars KGL sixty-eight casualties out of a total of 149 suffered at El Bodon.[30] Montbrun's losses, on the other hand, were around the 200 mark.

Wellington found himself in a very dangerous position on 26 September, with superior enemy numbers before him. Fortunately for him, Marmont was reluctant to attack, fearing the same treatment that Masséna had been given at Busaco the previous year. It was a classic example of the psychological hold Wellington was developing over his enemies, developed largely through his battlefield tactics and, in particular, by the reverse slope position, by which he shielded his troops from enemy view and thus denied them the chance to forge any accurate understanding of either his strength or his true dispositions. Masséna had come to grief at Busaco; Marmont, suspecting that Wellington had again hidden large numbers out of sight – which was far from the real situation – was not willing to become a similar victim of this very simple but effective strategy and passed up the opportunity to attack which, if he had done so, may have been to his advantage. Wellington was reinforced during the next few days when his army concentrated around Fuenteguinaldo and so a great French opportunity was spurned. There was yet another small affair on 27 September, at Aldea de Ponte, which involved Slade's and De Grey's cavalry, but it was a very minor one. The fighting on 25 September all but brought down the curtain on the year's campaigning, and in October Wellington put his army into winter quarters, as did Marmont. Hill would continue to be active during the same month, but on the whole Wellington's campaigning in 1811 had come to a close. 1812, on the other hand, would begin in a blaze of glory, as we will see in another chapter.

Notes

1 Sir Charles Oman, or at least the person who compiled the index for volume 2 of his great history, makes the mistake of confusing the inept John Murray with George Murray, a much underrated soldier who became Quartermaster General of the army. *History of the Peninsular War* (Oxford, 1902), II: 661,

2 There is some confusion over the number of squadrons of the 14th involved. Hawker, who was present, claims only a single squadron was involved, *Journal of a Regimental Officer* (London, 1811), 58. and has been followed by Oman, *Peninsular War*, II: 340–1. The regimental history, however, has both squadrons involved. Col. H.B. Hamilton, *Historical Record of the 14th (King's) Hussars, 1715–1900* (London, 1901), 58, Wellesley's despatch states only one squadron was involved. Wellesley to Castlereagh, Oporto, 12 May 1809. *The Despatches of Field Marshal the Duke of Wellington during his various campaigns* (London, 1832), IV: 299 & 300.

3 The map in Hawker's *Journal* places the KGL directly behind the 23rd Light Dragoons.

4 The officer who appears to have rallied the 23rd was Major Frederick Ponsonby, who later served throughout the war with the 12th Light Dragoons. He was severely wounded whilst commanding the regiment at Waterloo and left a gripping and frightening account of his experiences during the night as he lay wounded on the battlefield.

5 Elley later wrote of the charge to his sister. 'The charge of the cavalry, so much talked of in your newspapers, was led by your humble servant, at the head of two squadrons of the 23rd Light Dragoons, and so desperate was the undertaking, out of the two squadrons, consisting of about 160 men, all were either killed or wounded, with the exception of myself and six or seven dragoons. This affair was witnessed by the whole British Army with a mixture of exultation, anxiety, and astonishment.' Elley, quoted in Combermere, *Memoirs and Correspondence of Field Marshal Viscount Combermere* (London, 1866), 1:124. There are good accounts of the charge in Schauman, *On the Road with Wellington* (London, 1924), 186–7, and Gray, *The Trumpet of Glory* (London, 1985), 77–80. Hawker's account is disappointing.

6 It is impossible to place the exact position of the watercourse today because of the lake that now covers this section of the battlefield. However, I believe the water of the lake ends almost at the point where the watercourse ran originally, evidence of which can be seen on the southern side of the valley where reeds and small watercourses now run down into the lake.

7 Schaumann, *On the Road*, 186.

8 Oman, *Peninsular War*, II: 549.

9 Sir John Fortescue, *History of the British Army* (London, 1899), VII: 253.

10 Wellesley to Castlereagh, Talavera, 29 July 1809, *Despatches*, IV: 507.

11 Ibid, IV: 508.

12 Hamilton says the regiment was the 61st Line Regiment. *History of the 14th Hussars*, 67.

13 Cocks, quoted in Combermere, *Memoirs and Correspondence of Field Marshal Viscount Combermere* (London, 1866), 1:143–4. A very similar account is to be found in Cocks's own diary, edited by Julia Page, *Intelligence Officer in the*

Peninsula (Tunbridge Wells, 1986), 64. The book is very important in studying Wellington's cavalry in the Peninsula.

14 Tomkinson, *Diary of a Cavalry Officer*, 50–1.

15 Fortescue, *British Army*, VII: 539.

16 Oman makes the point that these were not stragglers but piquets and convoy escorts. *Peninsular War*, III: 469.

17 Tomkinson, *Diary of a Cavalry Officer*, 59–60. Curiously, Tomkinson says that although Baxter succeeded he was not justified in attacking them, as if it was a sort of underhand business.

18 On 7 May 1811 Lord Liverpool wrote to Wellington informing him of much-needed reinforcements for the cavalry. 'I am desirous of informing you as soon as possible of the arrangements we have made for keeping your cavalry effective. The 11th Light Dragoons are embarked for Lisbon, and only waiting for a fair wind; they are one of the most complete, best appointed, and best disciplined regiments in the service. The severe shock which the cavalry received in Sir John Moore's retreat in 1808 has placed us in this predicament, that the 12th Light Dragoons is now the only regiment of that description in this country which has seasoned horses. If the other regiments are suffered to remain in their present state till next year, they will be fit for any service; but it would be a serious detriment to them, and no adequate advantage to you, to move them at present. It has therefore been determined to dismount the 12th Light Dragoons, and to send the greater part of their horses to complete the light dragoons regiments at present in Portugal. A remount to a certain extent can likewise be supplied without much difficulty for the heavy regiments in Portugal from those which are at home; and the Enniskillen regiment will be ordered to hold itself in readiness for foreign service, and will be stationed at Cork, so that it will be ready to proceed to Portugal if you should be desirous of receiving an augmentation of your cavalry, and will send horse transports to Cork for them. I trust that this arrangement will effectually keep up your proportion of cavalry for the present campaign. I have been particularly anxious on this subject, because I know from experience that though infantry may be sent out at a very short notice, it is very difficult to keep a body of cavalry effective without a great deal of foresight and previous preparation.' Liverpool to Wellington, 7 May 1811, *Supplementary Despatches, Correspondence and Memoranda of Field Marshal Arthur Duke of Wellington* (London, 1857), VII: 119–20.

19 The escape of the garrison of Almeida was one of the more infuriating episodes of the war for Wellington. In fact, it was one which he later claimed turned the victory at Fuentes de Oñoro into a defeat. 'I was quite sure of having Almeida,' he wrote, 'but I begin to be of opinion, with you, that there is nothing on earth so stupid as a gallant officer. They [the British blockading force] had about 13,000 men to watch 1400; and in the night of the 10th, to the infinite surprise of the enemy, they allowed the garrison to slip through their fingers and to escape, after blowing up some of the works of the place! There they were all sleeping in their spurs even; but the French got off. Pray read my despatch and letter to Lord Liverpool on this subject. We have taken, killed, and wounded, however, about three-fourths of the vagabonds.' Wellington to Pole, 15 May 1811, *Supp. Despatches*, VII: 123. It has been claimed that one of

the main reasons for Wellington's annoyance was that Brennier, the garrison commander, owed Wellington £500, a debt which went back to the days of Vimeiro where Brennier was taken prisoner. Wellington loaned Brennier the large amount but never saw it again. With the Frenchman bottled up inside Almeida, Wellington can be forgiven for believing his money was on the point of being repaid but, sadly, it was not to be as Brennier escaped. Little wonder, therefore, that the Frenchman made such a daring break-out!

20 Fortescue, *British Army*, VII: 153–5.

21 C.T. Atkinson, *History of the Royal Dragoons*, 1661–1934 (Glasgow, 1935), 263.

22 Fortescue wrote of the episode, 'No more masterly manoeuvre is recorded of any general; no grander example of triumphant discipline is recorded of any regiments in the history of the British Army.' *British Army*, VII: 166.

23 Ibid. VII: 165–6.

24 Tomkinson, *Cavalry Officer*, 100–1. Tomkinson's diary has the cavalry action on 3 May whereas it took place on 5 May.

25 Atkinson, *Royal Dragoons*, 264.

26 Oman, in his appendix XI of Allied casualties on 5 May 1811, curiously states that not a single British cavalry officer was killed, and all of this after a discussion of the Knipe incident on page 327. Oman, *Peninsular War*, IV: 624.

27 British cavalry had come up against Polish lancers at Albuera on 16 May 1811 but appear never to have actually engaged them. The lancers advanced in support of infantry attacks on the bridge in front of Albuera but retired when the attacks floundered. Carpio was the first time British cavalry had actually fought enemy lancers.

28 Fortescue, *British Army*, VIII: 260.

29 Fortescue makes the comment, 'in both actions the same features are conspicuous, namely the powerlessness of the French cavalry against the British squares, and the ease with which it could be thrust back by a handful of British or German horse.' Ibid. VIII: 263.

30 Oman, *Peninsular War*, IV: 648.

CHAPTER IV

Campo Mayor: The Great Controversy

Much of the research carried out into the Peninsular War tends, naturally, to focus upon the operations of Wellington himself. After all, he was the most dominant personality of the war, with the main Allied field army being under his personal command. There were, however, senior British officers who were given independent commands, such as Robert Craufurd, Sir Thomas Graham, Rowland Hill and William Carr Beresford. We need not dwell upon the operations on the east coast as these did not really come within the sphere of Wellington himself. These four officers carried out their tasks with varying degrees of success. Craufurd, in spite of one or two lapses, held the line of the Agueda and Coa rivers with his Light Division throughout the anxious spring and summer of 1810. It was a task to which his men were well suited and although Craufurd came to grief at Villar de Puerco on 11 July and, more dramatically, at the Coa river on 24 July, his prevention of any French penetration during this period was one of the great achievements of the war. Indeed, Wellington duly acknowledged Craufurd as being the finest leader of light troops he possessed and, when the latter was killed at Ciudad Rodrigo, Wellington called his death 'a great blow'. Graham proved a capable commander and, indeed, won the Battle of Barrosa on 5 March 1811 and supervised the siege of San Sebastian in July and August 1813. However, he was dogged by ill-health as the campaigning took its toll on this elderly but brave soldier.

Beresford's main contribution to the Peninsular War is almost certainly his re-organisation of the Portuguese army. His handling of troops on the battlefield, however, was severely called into question after the slaughter at Albuera on 16 May 1811, a victory won purely by the staying power of the British infantry who, in Soult's own words, 'did not know they were beaten and would not run'. Beresford was, nevertheless, Wellington's own choice as his successor in the event of anything happening to himself, which is probably the greatest testament to Beresford's abilities. By far the most successful independent commander was Rowland Hill, who not only won fine victories at Arroyo dos Molinos, Almaraz and St Pierre, but proved himself a most effective operator, about whom Wellington had no need to worry throughout the long periods when he was detached from the main Allied field army.

With the focus of so much study being Wellington himself, it is rather ironic that many of the fine actions in which the British cavalry were involved, as well as the two most controversial incidents of the war, took place not under his command, but under those of Hill and Beresford. All of the actions studied in the next three chapters occurred in the south, in Estremadura and Andalucia, an area to which Wellington paid only fleeting visits during the Peninsular War, as the overwhelming majority of his time was spent farther north or in Portugal. The period of study extends from March 1811 to June 1812, during which time the British cavalry fought such notable actions as Campo Mayor, Usagre, Los Santos, Villagarcia and, of course, Maguilla, the fight that prompted Wellington to accuse his cavalry of 'galloping at everything'. The cavalry also performed most creditably at Albuera, albeit in a supporting role. What we have in these chapters is, therefore, of crucial importance to the case for the British cavalry, for we have probably the two greatest controversial cavalry actions of the entire war, Campo Mayor and Maguilla. Indeed, so controversial was Campo Mayor that it provoked a furious row between the two central characters, Robert Ballard Long and William Carr Beresford, as well as a most vitriolic correspondence which continued between the supporters of both men long after the war had ended. Campo Mayor, in fact, is probably the most important cavalry battle studied in this book, for it represents everything that is wrong with the way in which the British cavalry have been misrepresented in the Peninsula, owing to the failure on the part of successive historians to come up with anything other than flawed research. So damaging have the judgements been on the performance of the British cavalry – and Long in particular – at Campo Mayor, that the action, like that at Maguilla, needs to be examined in a separate chapter in this book.

With Soult besieging Badajoz in March 1811, Wellington despatched Beresford, in Hill's absence,[1] to march south to its relief, although the place fell before he got anywhere near it.[2] Nevertheless, on 18 March he was ordered south again, this time to attack Soult. On 25 March Beresford, approaching from the north, closed in first of all upon the small and badly fortified town of Campo Mayor, a few miles to the north of Badajoz. His approach forced the French to abandon the place rather hurriedly, and in his efforts to scoop up the withdrawing French garrison Beresford set in motion a chain of events which were to end in the most controversial cavalry action of the war.

Beresford's force, which numbered around 18,000 men, consisted of the 2nd and 4th Divisions, Hamilton's Portuguese, De Grey's brigade of heavy dragoons, being the 3rd Dragoon Guards and the 4th Dragoons, and two and a half squadrons of the 13th Light Dragoons who were unbrigaded.

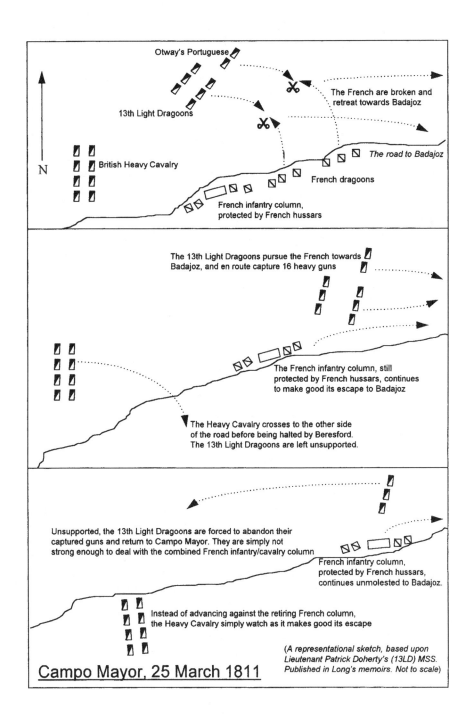

Otway's Portuguese

13th Light Dragoons

The French are broken and retreat towards Badajoz

N

British Heavy Cavalry

The road to Badajoz

French dragoons

French infantry column, protected by French hussars

The 13th Light Dragoons pursue the French towards Badajoz, and en route capture 16 heavy guns

The French infantry column, still protected by French hussars, continues to make good its escape to Badajoz

The Heavy Cavalry crosses to the other side of the road before being halted by Beresford. The 13th Light Dragoons are left unsupported.

Unsupported, the 13th Light Dragoons are forced to abandon their captured guns and return to Campo Mayor. They are simply not strong enough to deal with the combined French infantry/cavalry column

French infantry column, protected by French hussars, continues unmolested to Badajoz.

Instead of advancing against the retiring French column, the Heavy Cavalry simply watch as it makes good its escape

Campo Mayor, 25 March 1811

(A representational sketch, based upon Lieutenant Patrick Doherty's (13LD) MSS. Published in Long's memoirs. Not to scale)

Commanding Beresford's cavalry was Robert Ballard Long, who was to become one of the central figures of the cavalry action at Campo Mayor and, indeed, several others that followed. Campo Mayor itself had fallen to the French under Marshal Mortier on 20 March after a siege lasting seven days, a most praiseworthy achievement given the crumbling nature of the town's defences. Mortier had no intention of repairing the defences but instead withdrew most of his troops to Badajoz whilst others began dismantling the defences and destroying the antiquated Portuguese guns. Mortier was still engaged in this operation when, on 25 March, one of his patrols brought him the news that an Allied force was bearing down on him. Mortier appears to have been taken completely by surprise by the news, unaware as he was of Beresford's approach, which says little for the effectiveness of the French cavalry screen provided by Latour-Maubourg. Mortier's force consisted of around 2,400 men, 900 of whom were cavalry of the 26th Dragoons and the 2nd and 10th Hussars. In addition, there was half a battery of horse artillery and the entire siege train of sixteen heavy guns which had lately been used against Campo Mayor. These had set off from the town much earlier and were well on their way along the road to Badajoz. It was, therefore, quite a tantalising prize that was dangling in front of Beresford, and with such a force as he possessed the chances of his capturing it were extremely favourable.

It should be noted that Beresford approached Campo Mayor with a stem warning from Wellington on the need for maintaining a tight hold on the cavalry. In fact, it is essential that this advice is quoted at length as it would have a major influence on Beresford's handling of the fight which was about to happen. 'I recommend to you to keep your troops very much en masse', he wrote. 'I have always considered the cavalry to be the most delicate arm that we possess. We have few officers who have practical knowledge of the mode of using it, or who have ever seen more than two regiments together; and all our troops, cavalry as well as infantry, are a little inclined to get out of order in battle. To these circumstances add, that the defeat of, or any great loss sustained by, our cavalry, in these open grounds, would be a misfortune amounting almost to a defeat of the whole; and you will see the necessity of keeping the cavalry as much as possible en masse, and in reserve, to be thrown in at the moment when an opportunity may offer of striking a decisive blow.'[3] One can imagine, therefore, just how Beresford felt when, at around 10.30 on the wet and rainy morning of 25 March, Campo Mayor hove into view with the French garrison making off in the direction of Badajoz, having been warned of the Allied approach by Latour-Maubourg's cavalry.

On the face of it the cavalry combat at Campo Mayor is straightforward; Beresford approaches the town at the moment when the French garrison are in the process of abandoning the place. Long is sent with the light cavalry to make a detour around the town to cut off the French retreat, drive off their cavalry and detain the French infantry long enough for the British infantry and artillery to come up. Long, with the 13th Light Dragoons, scatters the French dragoons escorting the infantry whereupon the British light dragoons pursue the French in a mad gallop over ten miles as far as the gates of Badajoz where they are brought up by the cannon fire of the garrison there. The 13th then turn around and, with the rest of the French cavalry and infantry approaching, are forced to relinquish the sixteen heavy guns that they captured en route. They then return to Campo Mayor to face the wrath of both Beresford and Wellington, the latter having been apprised of the affair by a very annoyed Beresford. The 13th are then censured by the commander-in-chief and are threatened with an early return to England should they repeat their hair-brained escapade. Simple? No, far from it. This is exactly the sort of misrepresentation which the British cavalry have suffered over the years as generations of historians have painted the sort of picture that depicts them as inept, brainless gallopers.[4]

The following version of the cavalry combat at Campo Mayor is based upon various accounts, both eye-witness and secondary. Existing accounts of the combat are frequently at odds with each other. Indeed, such was the fall-out afterwards that the ensuing arguments provoked a flood of correspondence between various participants and a great deal of animosity grew between Beresford and Long. More fuel was poured on to this fire during the years after the war following the publication of Napier's *History of the War in the Peninsula*, in which the author criticised Beresford's handling of the affair. The result of this was the publication of the infamous *Strictures and Further Strictures*, amongst other pamphlets, which were written by the various disputants, each refuting the charges made by their opponents. Long himself was defended by his nephew as he had died some years earlier. All of this has served to throw up a great number of red-herrings and confusion but it has also enabled us to examine the events of 25 March 1811 in more detail as a result of all of this correspondence, for no other cavalry action in the Peninsula has attracted more attention, much of it resulting in erroneous conclusions. Napier's account of the action at Campo Mayor is very short and sweet and would probably have remained so had it not been for the publications by Beresford and his defenders.[5] These prompted Napier to lay before the public much more detail than he had originally published and which certainly confirm some of the events which we shall now examine.

With Beresford's force approaching Campo Mayor the French retreated, the infantry marching in column with one of the hussar regiments in front and the other bringing up the rear. The 26th Dragoons rode in front of the whole. According to Long's account, he asked Beresford whether he should attack to which the latter replied that the French were very strong and that he should not commit himself, although he added that if a favourable opportunity of striking a blow should occur, he was to avail himself of it.[6] Wellington's warning to Beresford to keep his cavalry together must have been echoing in his mind and yet, in spite of this, he immediately detached Long with the five troops of the 13th Light Dragoons and the five weak squadrons of Otway's Portuguese cavalry to 'turn and gain the rear of the town', that is to say, to march away to the east of the town and turn south, with the intention of cutting across the road ahead of the retreating French force. This was duly done by Long who, however, passed too far to the east of the town, prompting Beresford to send one of his aides, Henry Hardinge, after him with an order, telling him to circle nearer the town. Long continued his wide circuit, however, and once again Hardinge was sent after him, 'to express the Marshal's displeasure.'[7] Apparently, Long took the wider circuit to avoid some sort of ravine which blocked his original route. The detour is seized upon by the author of the *Further Strictures* in an attempt to blot Long's copybook but it is another red herring. The issue has no real relevance and certainly has no bearing on the course of the fight. Upon reaching the top of a ridge to the east of the town, Long looked down into the valley along which the road to Badajoz ran, and saw before him the French column retreating along the road. At the foot of the valley was a bog with what Long described as an impassable ditch, although this does not appear to have affected his line of march. At the bottom of the valley floor, meanwhile, on Long's right and a little to his rear, came the heavy brigade. Altogether, the cavalry force under Long was, at his own estimate, about 1,200 strong and of sufficient strength for him to consider an attack upon the French. It was, he thought, the 'favourable opportunity' that Beresford had mentioned earlier.

Long's cavalry marched in column with the Portuguese in front and the 13th Light Dragoons bringing up the rear. His plan was quickly formed and involved detaching the 13th from the rear of the column to take up a position on the right, whilst the five squadrons of Otway's Portuguese were to cover his left flank and get themselves between the French cavalry and Badajoz. The heavy cavalry, meanwhile, were in support on Long's right rear a little to the east of the main road. Commanding the 13th Light Dragoons was Colonel Head who, as he sat watching the French move slowly along the road, was joined by Long who said, 'Colonel Head, there's your enemy. Attack him', adding, 'and now, Colonel, the heavy brigade are coming up on your rear, and, if you have an opportunity give a good account of these fellows.' Head replied simply, 'By gad, sir, I will.'[8]

Latour-Maubourg, seeing the 13th Light Dragoons forming to charge, immediately turned the 26th Dragoons, formed them in line and upon his order charged whilst the 13th did likewise, both sides giving a great cheer as they did so. The advance of the 13th took them past the French infantry who opened fire and caused a little mischief before the two cavalry units crashed into each other. Accounts differ as to exactly what happened at this point. Both Napier and Barratt, the historian of the 13th, state that the 13th charged through the enemy before wheeling about and making a second charge. On the other hand, the author of *Further Strictures*, wrote, 'the whole of this tale is supposititious', adding that the 13th 'never rallied to bar the enemy's advance. They never drew up, nor indeed ever stopped.'[9] Oman follows this version with a mêlée, ruling out a second charge. However, when one considers the facts, it is clear that there must have been a second charge otherwise the French dragoons would have been trapped on the wrong side of both their supports and the road to Badajoz.

Lieutenant Dudley Madden, of the 4th Dragoons, wrote in his diary that the 13th 'charged their flank several times', whilst John Burgoyne, of the Royal Engineers, claimed the 13th 'went through them [the French]; the enemy closed and faced to the right about, the 13th rode through them again, and again a third time, when the enemy's cavalry went off in confusion.[10] It is almost certainly the case that the French wheeled about after passing through the 13th Light Dragoons to make a second charge. The 13th did likewise and it was after this second charge that the mêlée took place. Indeed, one eye-witness, quoted by Napier in his Justification, stated that, 'every horse was let out, and the men cheered; the enemy did the same. The crash was tremendous; both parties passed each other, and at some short distance in the rear of the enemy, the 13th came about; the enemy did the same, and a second charge took place with equal violence, when the conflict became personal with the sabre.'[11]

The fight at this point was between the two and a half squadrons of the 13th Light Dragoons and the three squadrons of the 26th Dragoons. Long himself took personal command of three squadrons of the Portuguese cavalry whilst the two other squadrons covered the 13th's left flank. One of the 13th's officers later wrote:

> The road from Campo Mayor to Badajoz runs across the great plain of Badajoz, and has not even a thistle or briar to intercept the prospect. The French manoeuvred most beautifully all the way, and sustained three charges of our cavalry without breaking. The 13th behaved most nobly. I saw so many instances of individual bravery, as raised my opinion of mankind in general many degrees. The French certainly are fine and brave soldiers, but the superiority of our English horses, and more particularly the superiority of swordsmanship our fellows showed, decided every contest in our favour; it was absolutely like a game at *prison bars*, which you must have seen at school... The whole way across the plain was a succession of individual contests, here and there, as the cavalry dispersed... it was certainly most beautiful.[12]

With the two opposing units having clashed there ensued a furious mêlée with sabres clashing in individual combats. It was real man-to-man stuff.

During the fight Corporal Logan, of the 13th, cut down one of the French dragoons whereupon the 26th's commanding officer, Colonel Chamorin, engaged him in single combat to exact revenge for his slain countryman. Logan was obviously a good swordsman for, not content with slaying the first Frenchman, he quickly got the better of Chamorin, cutting him about the face twice and sending his helmet spinning from his head. Logan then brought down his sabre with a mighty blow upon Chamorin's head, splitting the skull open completely, and exposing the brain.[13]

The French dragoons were scattered in all directions before making off along the road to Badajoz, pursued by the 13th whose blood was well and truly up. Long himself was following up behind and described what happened next. 'I followed as rapidly as I could to support this attack, still supposing the heavy brigade in my rear, occupying the attention of the remaining part of the enemy's force, but, to my utter astonishment, when, at the point where I first met the Badajoz road, I halted, and looked round to see what was next to be done, I found they had quitted altogether the line of direction I had pointed out, and at the suggestion of one of Marshal Beresford's aides-de-camp, had marched by their right to the other side of the valley and road, and were halted a mile and a half off, on the opposite and elevated ground, quite abandoning me to myself, and completely oversetting all my plans.'[14] It was true. Instead of coming forward in support of Long, de Grey's heavy dragoons were halted by the side of the road. It was at this point that the trouble really began.

Having placed himself at the head of the three reserve Portuguese squadrons, Long did not see what happened to the 13th Light Dragoons after they disappeared from view over the hill in front of him as they set off in pursuit of the French. Although his position prevented him from getting a decent view, he did nevertheless manage to despatch Otway and his two squadrons which were covering the 13th's left flank, to support them and rally them. However, Otway too disappeared over the hill and out of sight, following hard on the heels of the 13th. With the heavy cavalry halted by the roadside the French infantry and hussars were allowed to move off unmolested towards Badajoz. There was little Long could do but send for the heavy brigade, although at this point he was unaware that Beresford had actually forbidden them to advance. In the meantime he determined to advance with his three Portuguese squadrons in order to detain the French long enough for the heavy brigade, along with the infantry and artillery, to get forward. However, a few shouts and some carbine shots from the French were enough to put the Portuguese to flight and they turned tail and fled in panic with Long himself trying to rally them with the assistance of Captain Doyle of the quartermaster general's department. It was apparently Doyle, in fact, who was sent by Long to get the heavy brigade forward but he was met by an alarmed Beresford who came forward and enquired somewhat angrily of the whereabouts of the 13th. Doyle told him that the 13th had scattered the French and that it was imperative that the heavy brigade were brought forward to bring about the surrender of the French infantry. Beresford, on the other hand, already knew, or thought he knew, what had become of the 13th, having already been given the news that the 13th had all been taken prisoner. This false information was given to Beresford by one of Long's aides, a Dutch émigré officer named Baron Tripp who, upon seeing the 13th disappear, thought they had been captured wholesale by the French, and so returned to inform Beresford who in turn ordered the heavy brigade to halt. Doyle meanwhile returned to Long and told him who was responsible for halting the heavy brigade. 'For the first time,' wrote Long, 'I learned from Captain Doyle that Marshal Beresford himself was with the brigade of heavy cavalry, and had himself halted them in the situation I have described. I had nothing further to say.'[15]

Beresford, believing that the 13th Light Dragoons had been lost, ordered the heavy brigade to move to their right, whereupon they crossed the road and formed up to the west of it, with their left flank upon it. By now, Colborne's infantry were fast approaching, as were Cleeve's KGL artillery.[16] In fact, Cleeve managed to get two of his guns forward, under Major Hartmann, who threw a few shells into the midst of the retreating French. Hartmann wanted to get the guns even closer to the French but he was ordered to halt and remain where he was, again by Beresford. The French infantry, meanwhile, was allowed to continue along the road to Badajoz. The whole thing seemed unbelievable to Colborne, coming up fast with his infantry.

> From my position, [he wrote] I could plainly see the French evacuate the town, and I saw an admirable operation of the 13th Light Dragoons, who passed through the French cavalry and dispersed them, and if they had been supported by the heavy cavalry, a most excellent coup de main would have been achieved, and the whole French force might have been made prisoners. But just at the moment General Lumley, who commanded the heavy cavalry, to my great mortification, sent me a message by his aide-de-camp that the infantry must halt, as it was useless in the face of the superior strength of the enemy to continue the engagement. 'The whole of the 13th,' it was added, 'are taken.' I told the aide-de-camp that I had seen the contrary with my own eyes, and that I should do no such thing. The aide-de-camp said, 'Shall I take the general this message?' to which I replied, 'Yes, he thinks the 13th are taken, but there they are.' However, through this error, the heavy cavalry were halted, and the whole operation failed.[17]

Whether or not the heavy cavalry would have been able to break the French infantry square is open to debate, and as such an event was extremely rare it is unlikely that De Grey's heavies would have been able to do so. But, the important factor now was the arrival of Colborne's infantry and Cleeve's artillery who, if the heavy cavalry had been allowed to get forward, if only for the purpose of detaining the French infantry, must surely have forced the latter to surrender. But it was not to be. Alexander Dickson, of the artillery, also considered the surrender of the French infantry as a certainty had the artillery and infantry been allowed forward. 'General Long who commanded the cavalry had made such a disposition, that it was inevitable the French must have laid down their arms, at least the infantry. But somehow or other the business was marred and the enemy got off although not without heavy loss.'[18]

It seems astonishing that Beresford had not been able to see what had happened to the 13th whereas Colborne, coming upon the field after him, managed to see the whole episode, and was most indignant at seeing an opportunity spurned. However, Beresford appears to have acted in good faith, believing the loss of the 13th to be true. I would suggest that, like Long, he had taken up an unsatisfactory position, one which did not afford him a suitable overview of the events happening in front of him. The issue of who actually spread the false rumour has been the source of much debate and controversy but it is, I believe, a red herring and has no bearing on the business whatsoever. However, what is important is that such a report was spread in the first place for it was to have dire and lasting consequences for the 13th Light Dragoons. When Tripp – assuming that he was the bearer of the information – informed Beresford of the loss of the 13th Light Dragoons the latter ordered the heavy brigade to halt, in the same way that Lord Lucan would do later with the heavy brigade at Balaclava, both men being unwilling to see their precious brigades swallowed up like the light cavalry had been. The problem was that unlike the light brigade at Balaclava, the light cavalry at Campo Mayor was far from in difficulty. In fact, Colonel Head and the 13th had accomplished one of the finest cavalry achievements of the war, or at least it would have been but for Beresford's lack of support and for generations of historians whose own research has gone no further than Wellington's subsequent censure which, by his own admission, was erroneously given, following Beresford's report to him.

So, what had actually happened to the 13th Light Dragoons? Well, as we have already seen, they had charged through the ranks of the French dragoons before wheeling round to charge once more. The two sides clashed a second time and, following a great deal of swordplay the French broke and fled in the direction of Badajoz, pursued by the 13th. It was now that the great pursuit began, the British light dragoons being joined by Otway's two Portuguese squadrons. The 13th galloped after the beaten French, taking a few casualties from the French infantry who were still making their way along the road to Badajoz. The French dragoons did manage to put up some resistance initially, but this appears to have been just token resistance and the pursuit continued for nearly ten miles to the tête du pont over the Guadiana at Badajoz. It was, as the historian of the 13th put it, an 'extraordinary pursuit', but was not, as Oman described it, 'incredibly long and disorderly, quite in the style of Prince Rupert at Edgehill.'[19]

Somewhere along the road to Badajoz, almost certainly in the vicinity of Fort San Christobal, situated on the northern bank of the Guadiana, Head and the 13th Light Dragoons caught up with the section of the French convoy drawing the sixteen heavy guns towards Badajoz. As well as the guns themselves there were eight mules, a number of wagons and 'immense quantities of stores, baggage of all descriptions, provisions, stores, horses, mules – in fact, the whole camp equipage which had been early that morning despatched from Campo Mayor towards Badajoz.'[20] When the light dragoons caught up with the convoy the gunners and drivers, with no other mounted supports, surrendered without a fight, but as they neared Badajoz they tried to escape and most of them were sabred. Troopers were then mounted on the mules in order to bring the guns back to Campo Mayor. In the meantime, Head had rallied the 13th, some of whom had been wounded by artillery fire from Fort San Christobal.[21] These were joined by Otway's two squadrons of Portuguese cavalry which had arrived on the scene and together they organised the removal to Campo Mayor of the guns, stores and equipment and the French prisoners they had taken. Colonel Head can be forgiven for having mixed feelings at this moment. After all, he had just seen his regiment charge and defeat the 26th Dragoons and had pursued them virtually to Badajoz itself. Furthermore, he must have felt elated at having captured no less than sixteen heavy guns, let alone the vast quantity of stores. However, he must have wondered what had happened to the heavy brigade, for his men were exhausted and their horses blown and they now had the task of getting the haul back to Campo Mayor. What if a French force suddenly appeared from the gates of Badajoz itself? After all, there was still a sizeable garrison inside the town and Head's two and a half squadrons would hardly be likely to be able to get away with the guns if the French tried to rescue them in force. In the event, the threat to Head and the 13th came not from Badajoz but from his rear, from the direction of Campo Mayor.

Colonel Head and the 13th Light Dragoons began to make their way back along the road to Campo Mayor, their trophies being drawn along by mules with troopers of the 13th mounted upon them. But if they thought they were to return as heroes to the Allied camp their hopes were to be quickly dashed, for after having got about halfway along the road they were met by a trooper of the 13th with a message from Lieutenant Holmes, also of the 13th, who had been wounded during the initial charge and had not taken part in the pursuit. The message to Colonel Head told him that the French hussars and infantry were approaching him and that there were no Allied infantry or cavalry to give him support. One can imagine Head's astonishment at this message and, apparently, it was concluded that it must be a mistake and that the French infantry were, in fact, Portuguese from the similar colour of their uniforms. However, as Head and his men continued along the road another messenger galloped up with a second message, again from Lieutenant Holmes, confirming the first. This second message also informed Head that the French cavalry which had earlier surrendered had regained their arms and horses and were even now approaching him. This second message placed Head in a difficult situation. He had altogether fewer than four and a half squadrons of British and Portuguese cavalry, most of whom were blown after their exertions and would be no match for some 1,200 French infantry supported by a superior body of French cavalry. And yet, he had with him sixteen heavy guns as well as the large quantity of wagons and supplies captured from the French. Was he now, after having made such a great effort to secure them, about to simply give them up just because he had received no support from either the heavy brigade of cavalry or from the Allied infantry? Sadly, he had little choice and, indeed, barely had his men remounted their own horses and the captured convoy been abandoned than the French columns hove into view, marching hurriedly and unmolested along the road. And then, as the French approached, Head and his men made off to their right, making their way across the rolling plain, leaving their trophies standing by the roadside. The French could not believe their luck, and when the column came up the guns and wagons were secured whilst Mortier sent out from Badajoz a force of 2,000 infantry and one cavalry regiment to assist in bringing the guns back inside the town.

The 13th Light Dragoons lost twelve men killed, and three officers and twenty-six men wounded. Fifteen others were recorded as missing, presumably taken prisoner by the French close to Badajoz.[22] Total Portuguese casualties were one officer and thirteen men killed, and thirty-five men wounded. A further fifty-five were recorded as missing. Between 222 and 232 officers and men of the 13th Light Dragoons took part in the fight at Campo Mayor. Therefore, their casualties represented about twenty-four percent of their total strength. This may appear to be high, but when one considers their achievements it is a mere trifling number. The 13th captured sixteen guns and a large quantity of wagons and supplies as well as inflicting the majority of the 200-odd French casualties. Sadly, the guns were not to remain in their hands although, as we have seen, this was not through any error on their part. The pursuit after the initial mêlée was carried out over a long distance but there is no record of it being of the sort that Oman described. Furthermore, as there were no eye-witnesses to the actual pursuit it is difficult to see where such reports could have come from. Having said that, there is no record of the pursuit not having been conducted in a disorderly manner. If Colonel Head was guilty of one error it was in not ensuring that the heavy brigade was coming forward in support at the moment the pursuit began. On the other hand, it has to be said that any delay at the moment he had scattered the French dragoons would have almost certainly meant that they would get away unmolested. As commanding officer of the 13th, Head had to make a decision and he had to make it fast. He had seen his men break the 26th Dragoons and was aware that the heavy brigade had joined him. There was no reason to suspect that they would be ordered to halt and so he pressed on with the pursuit, disappearing out of sight as he lead his men off in the direction of Badajoz. From that moment on, the 13th accomplished everything that could have been expected of them. After all, it was not their fault that Beresford took the astonishing step of ordering the heavy brigade to halt.

There is no record of what happened when Colonel Head met Beresford after returning to the British camp. The historian of the 13th, however, records that Head was received with 'coldness and somewhat bitter sarcasm.'[23] Given the stern warning that Wellington had issued to Beresford prior to the operation, one can easily imagine Wellington's feelings when the report of the fight was received by him. In fact, the commander-in-chief was so enraged that he was moved to issue a strong reprimand to Head and the 13th. Wellington's despatch to Beresford shows quite clearly how little he knew of the real facts behind the fight. 'I wish you would call together the Officers of the dragoons', he wrote, 'and point out to them the mischiefs which must result from the disorder of the troops in action. The undisciplined ardour of the 13th [Light] dragoons, and 1st regiment of Portuguese cavalry, is not of the description of the determined bravery and steadfastness of soldiers confident in their discipline and in their Officers. Their conduct was that of a rabble, galloping as fast as their horses could carry them over a plain, after an enemy to whom they could do no mischief when they were broken; and the pursuit had continued for a limited distance, and sacrificing substantial advantages, and all the objects of your operation, by their want of discipline. To this description of their conduct I add my entire conviction, that if the enemy could have thrown out of Badajoz only one hundred men regularly formed, they would have driven back these two regiments in equal haste and disorder, and would probably have taken many whose horses would have been knocked up. If the 13th [Light] dragoons are again guilty of this conduct I shall take their horses from them, and send the Officers and men to do duty at Lisbon. I beg that you will tell De Grey how well satisfied I was with the conduct of his brigade.'[24] He also issued a General Order which again censured the 13th 'for their impetuosity' and want of discipline, although he did give the regiment credit for its 'bravery and resolution.'[25]

Wellington's despatch to Beresford and his verdict upon the fight at Campo Mayor are so damning that they have prejudiced the case against the British cavalry ever since. Indeed, it is one of the most influential despatches Wellington ever wrote and, like that written after Slade's affair at Maguilla, is a despatch which is remarkably similar in both tone and content, and is seized upon time after time as an example of the alleged misbehaviour of his cavalry. And yet, given the true facts concerning the fight, Wellington's despatch to Beresford is clearly incorrect and totally unfair to the 13th Light Dragoons. The charge that they galloped like a rabble cannot be substantiated, nor can the charge of their want of discipline. And as to the 'sacrificing substantial advantages, and all the objects of your [Beresford's] operation', well, this was clearly Beresford's own fault for not supporting the 13th with the heavy brigade. The final sentence, in which he praises De Grey's conduct simply emphasises how little Wellington really knew of the true facts. After all, the heavy brigade, through no fault of their own, did nothing at all but watch at Campo Mayor. Was inactivity really what he wanted from his cavalry? This was something which irritated Long, who said of Wellington's praise for De Grey, 'the Heavy Dragoons and Col. Grey have received his particular thanks for having, under the Marshal's personal directions, done nothing but look on, and suffer that enemy to escape unmolested from their swords who in ten minutes might have been annihilated!' The officers of the 13th were understandably stung by the rebuke, not only for its tone and content, but by the obvious misrepresentations contained within it. The upshot was that they wrote a letter containing the full and true facts of their exploit which was signed by all of the regiment's officers and given first to Long and then passed on to Wellington himself. The commander-in-chief read it and apparently said that had he known the full facts of the fight at Campo Mayor he would never have issued the reprimand. However, as he had already issued it he characteristically refused to withdraw it. The l3th's historian also wrote that Beresford himself later 'changed his opinion as regards the conduct of the regiment at Campo Mayor.'[27] Long, meanwhile, read out Wellington's General Order, censuring the conduct of the 13th, to all of the assembled officers of the regiment, although he went on to say that he would never allow it to be entered in the regiment's Orderly Book. In the meantime, the army sided with the 13th and felt they had been treated unfairly by the various reprimands. However, as Napier wrote, 'the unsparing admiration of the whole army consoled them.'[28]

In his treatment of the fight in his great *History of the Peninsular War*, Oman wrote of the casualties, '... the moral effect of a combat is not judged by a mere comparison of losses, and the British officers were much disappointed.'[29] However, what he failed to understand was that by their defeat of the 26th Dragoons during the mêlée before the pursuit, and indeed by the very pursuit itself, the 13th had set the tone for the entire cavalry war in southern Spain. The French cavalry, who had for so long regarded the British cavalry as their inferiors, would be forever wary of them and would never again underestimate them, save for Lallemand at Villagarcia, and that, as we shall see, was to his cost. The fight planted the seeds of doubt firmly in the minds of the French cavalry and during the campaigns in the south and, indeed, elsewhere in the Peninsula, the British cavalry would rarely be defeated in a fair stand-up fight. It was a point which Fortescue realised when writing of the French losses at Campo Mayor: 'But more important than all was the admission of the French that they could not stand before the British cavalry.'[30]

As for the performances of both Long and Beresford, well, both men were guilty of faults at Campo Mayor. Long, in taking up a defective position during the fight, was unable to see the full extent of the events unfolding before him and as a consequence was never in a position to control his cavalry. However, he can certainly be excused for thinking the heavy brigade was coming forward behind him in support. That having been said, he should have ensured that they really were coming forward before sending the 13th Light Dragoons forward. Like Craufurd at the fight on the Coa river in July 1810, his control of the battle, once it had started, was quickly lost and the subsequent tide of the battle was dictated by both Colonel Head and the 13th and by a series of bad decisions made by Beresford. These decisions were, however, based on false information and it is the source of this information, being the inaccurate report of the loss of the 13th, that has been the source of great controversy and mystery ever since. Ultimately it is of no particular importance who made the report. What is important is that Beresford acted upon it, halted the heavy brigade and in so doing deprived the 13th Light Dragoons of much needed support. Much of the correspondence between the various disputants after the war concerned the source of the report but it really is a red herring. In effect, it provided an escape clause for Beresford who stands guilty of not supporting the 13th and, like Long, for adopting a position on the battlefield which prevented him from getting a clear and accurate view of what was happening to his front. Other officers, like Colborne, saw what was happening. Why couldn't Beresford? Any analysis of Beresford's performance in the Peninsula usually runs along the lines of how effective he was at re-organising the Portuguese army. On the field of battle, however, it was a different story, as Albuera was to prove. Like Soult, he was, as Wellington once said of the French marshal, good at getting his men to the battlefield, but once there he didn't know what to do with them. The analogy may appear to be harsh on Beresford, perhaps, but the similarities are there. Indeed, in his analysis of Campo Mayor Fortescue, touching upon Beresford's abilities, wrote, 'The truth is that, with many merits, he was unfit for independent command, as Wellington soon discovered, and that he first betrayed his unfitness on the day of the combat of Campo Mayor.'[31]

We may also ask what influence Wellington himself had upon the action at Campo Mayor, for it was his warning to Beresford that weighed very heavily on the Marshal's mind. We have already seen how Wellington had experienced for himself two flawed performances by the cavalry under his command, at Vimeiro and Talavera, whilst Craufurd's notoriously bungled affair at Villar de Puerco had, of course, come to his attention. As a result, we may well imagine with what trepidation Wellington despatched Beresford on his first real independent command. Indeed, it was, in effect, the first time any of Wellington's commanders had exercised independent command in the Peninsula away from their master. Graham at Barrosa cannot be included in this category as his force was, essentially, part of the garrison of Cadiz, whilst Craufurd, covering the frontier during the spring and summer of 1810, was still part of Wellington's main field army. Therefore, Wellington, still busy driving Masséna from Portugal, was understandably very anxious that part of his precious army did not suffer any setback. Thus, Beresford was given strict orders relating to his operations against Badajoz and, in particular, to the cavalry. As we have seen, Wellington's 'advice' regarding the cavalry virtually paralysed Beresford once the action developed at Campo Mayor and thus his influence, borne out of his own experiences with cavalry, can be said to have had a major bearing on the events of 25 March 1811.

Robert Ballard Long was an argumentative man at the best of times and the cavalry action at Campo Mayor did little for relations between himself and Beresford, something which was to sour many a coming action during the next two years as both men served together in southern Spain. I have already stated that it is not my intention to discuss the unholy row which ensued between Beresford's and Long's supporters after Napier's publication in his *History of the War in the Peninsula* of the events at Campo Mayor. There remain, however, one or two final points concerning the action. The first is that, for the first time in the Peninsula, the British cavalry had room to manoeuvre, the ground between Campo Mayor and Badajoz being a vast rolling plain. Dickson described the countryside as 'perfectly open with gentle rises and falls, and excellent for the operation of cavalry'.[32] This undoubtedly contributed to the enthusiastic gallop by the 13th Light Dragoons by way of providing a wonderful battlefield, free of the sort of obstacles and constraints that had dogged the cavalry so far. As we shall see in the next chapter, the campaign country in the south was well disposed towards cavalry, and it is largely as a result of this that so many actions took place there. The second point provides us with a follow up to Campo Mayor, for on 16 April Long and the 13th Light Dragoons again defeated a French cavalry force at Los Santos. We shall deal with it in more detail in the next chapter but, briefly, on this second occasion Beresford, perhaps mindful of errors on his part at Campo Mayor, allowed Long to get two heavy cavalry regiments forward in support. Together, the British cavalry regiments pursued their broken enemies for some ten miles until Long brought them to a halt. If only Beresford had acted in the same manner at Campo Mayor things may well have turned out quite differently there. In the event, we are left, as we must always be in these instances, wondering what might have been. Given the amount of detrimental publicity which the British cavalry has attracted over the years following the action at Campo Mayor and, indeed, as a result of flawed research into the episode, it is worth ending this particular chapter with the verdict of Sir John Fortescue, the historian of the British Army, and no mean judge of characters and events both in the Peninsula and elsewhere. 'Of the performance of the Thirteenth,' he wrote, 'who did not exceed two hundred men, in defeating twice or thrice their numbers single-handed, it is difficult to speak too highly. Indeed, I know of nothing finer in the history of the British cavalry... if he [Colonel Head] had been supported and his trophies had been secured, the action would no doubt have become a classic in the annals of cavalry.'[33]

Notes

1 Hill had been forced to return to England sick.
2 Badajoz fell to the French on 11 March after a protracted defence by its tenacious governor, General Menacho, who was killed during a sortie on 3 March. His successor, José Imaz, failed to emulate him and, indeed, surrendered the town most treacherously to the French without offering anything other than a token defence.
3 Wellington to Beresford, 20 March 1811, *The Despatches of Field Marshal the Duke of Wellington during his various campaigns* (London, 1834), VII: 374–5.
4 Wellington himself can be largely credited with beginning this myth following his damning verdict of the 13th at Campo Mayor which, as we shall see, he later regretted, and with his condemnation of Slade at Maguilla. Other historians who have come to the wrong conclusion at Campo Mayor include Oman himself, who went no further than Wellington's censure. Modern historians who have come to the wrong conclusion about the affair include Michael Glover, *Wellington as Military Commander*, 225, Julian Rathbone, *Wellington's War*, 134, Brent Nosworthy, *Battle Tactics of Napoleon*, 274 (he contradicts this view five pages later), Jac Weller, *Wellington in the Peninsula*, 157, and, most recently, Rory Muir, in his *Tactics and the Experience in the Age of Napoleon*, 119. Muir, in fact, typifying the attitude towards the British cavalry, goes so far as to say that Campo Mayor was a famous defeat for the British cavalry. Few historians have ever bothered to take anything other than a superficial look at the action, believing it to be a clear-cut case of cavalry behaving badly. Among them is Sir John Fortescue himself, the historian of the British Army, whose examination of the causes and the culprits in his *History of the British Army* (London, 1899), VIII: 132–5, runs to four pages, far longer than the above named historians put together in their incorrect, generalisation. His own verdict, 'I know of nothing finer in the history of the British cavalry', is probably too grand but reflects his own opinion on the matter.

5 Napier's account of Campo Mayor can be found in his *History of the War in the Peninsula*, III: 500–2. It is barely two pages in length. However, some of the points relating to Campo Mayor answered by him in his *Justification* of his third volume, which are printed at the front of the 2nd Edition, run to almost five pages, being found on pages xxi–xxv. One wonders why he did not include this detail when he wrote his account of Campo Mayor in the 1st edition of the third volume.

6 Long to his brother. T.H. McGuffie (Ed), Peninsular Cavalry General; *The Correspondence of Lieutenant General Robert Ballard Long* (London, 1951), 74.

7 See *Further Strictures which relate to Colonel Na pier's History of the Peninsular War* (London, 1832), 38.

8 C.R.B. Barratt, *History of the 13th Hussars* (London, 1913), 1:130.

9 *See Further Strictures*, 44.

10 'The Diary of Lieutenant Charles Dudley Madden, 4th Dragoons, 1809–11', in the *Journal of the Royal United Service Institution*, LVIII: 1914, 511 and G. Wrottesley, *Life and Correspondence of Field Marshal Sir John Burgoyne* (London, 1873), I: 127. Madden's account of the fight at Campo Mayor is a very descriptive piece although it contains nothing of great significance relating to any of the controversies thrown up by the fight.

11 Napier, 'Justification', in his *History of the War in the Peninsula* (London, 1833, 2nd edition), Ill: xxii–xxiii.

12 'The Courier', 20 April 1811, kindly supplied by Philip Haythornthwaite.

13 On the day after the fight a French burial party came out from Badajoz under a flag of truce. An officer of the 13th wrote of the incident in 'The Courier' for 20 April 1811; 'Yesterday, a French Captain of Dragoons brought over a trumpeter, demanding permission to search among the dead for his Colonel; his regiment was a fine one, with bright brass helmets, and black horse hair, exactly like the old Romans are depicted with; the Captain was a fine young man and had his arm in a sling. Many of us went with him – it was truly a bloody scene, being almost all sabre wounds, the slain were all naked, the peasants having stripped them in the night; it was long before we could find the French Colonel – he was lying on his face, his naked body weltering in blood, and as soon as he was turned up, the Officer knew him, he gave a sort of scream, and sprung off his horse, dashed his helmet on the ground, knelt by the body, took the bloody hand and kissed it many times in an agony of grief; it was an affecting and awful scene... The French Colonel I have already mentioned, was killed by a corporal of the 13th; this corporal had killed one of his men, and he was so enraged, that he sallied out himself and attacked the corporal – the corporal was well mounted and a good swordsman, as was also the Colonel – both defended for some time, the corporal cut him twice in the face, his helmet came off at the second, when the corporal slew him by a cut which nearly cleft his skull asunder, it cut in as deep as the nose through the brain. The corporal is not wounded.' The 13th's paymaster, Gardiner, later purchased Chamorin's brass helmet from Logan and presented it to Colonel Head. Barratt, *History of the 13th Hussars*, I: 139. See also Madden's *Diary*. He was one of the officers of the 4th Dragoons who escorted the French burial party that came out from Badajoz to see to their dead. 'The Diary of Lieutenant Charles Dudley Madden', 511.

14 Long, *Peninsular Cavalry General*, 76.

15 Ibid. 78. In the row that followed the fight Beresford alleged that it was Long himself who told Tripp that the 13th Light Dragoons had been taken. Although Long had taken up a poor position during the fight he was hardly likely to be the source of the report. The issue of who actually spread the false rumour is another red herring, however, and has no bearing on the business. According to Lieutenant Madden, of the 4th Dragoons, the heavy brigade was halted just 200 yards from the French column. 'The Diary of Lieutenant Charles Dudley Madden', 511.

16 Colborne's infantry are put at various distances from the scene of the action. Oman, for example, claims that Colborne was still two miles away (see *History of the Peninsular War*, IV: 259) although Colborne himself saw the whole action, and must, therefore, have been very close. It certainly appears that the 66th Regiment, in addition to some light troops, were with Colborne.

17 Moore-Smith, *The Life of John Colborne, Field Marshal Lord Seaton* (London, 1903), 152–3. Colborne later told Long that, 'he was detached round the town, and observing the enemy with the baggage, etc., was quitting it, he sent back word to beg he might be supported and that he was in a situation to cut them all off. The answer he received was a positive order to halt, in consequence of which the opportunity was lost, and could not be again recovered.' Long, Peninsular Cavalry General, 151–2.

18 Alexander Dickson, in *The Dickson Manuscripts* (Woolwich, 1905), 25 March 1811, 367.

19 Barratt, *History of the 13th Hussars*, 1: 132. Oman, *History of the Peninsular War*, IV: 261. It is rather surprising that, unlike Fortescue, Oman appears never to have gone beyond Wellington's censure of the 13th Light Dragoons when he wrote about the Campo Mayor combat. This is symptomatic of many historians when dealing with the fight and of the British cavalry in general.

20 Barratt, *History of the 13th Hussars*, I: 132.

21 Some suggestions have been made that the 13th sustained casualties from the guns in Badajoz itself. This seems very unlikely, however. Badajoz was never threatened from the north owing to the Guadiana river which prevented any attacking force from approaching from this direction. Therefore, few guns, if any, were ever placed facing north. Furthermore, there are no ramparts on the northern side of Badajoz. It is simply a wall. The fire which caused casualties in the ranks of the 13th Light Dragoons almost certainly came from Fort San Christobal, as they would have had to pass it in order to approach the bridge to the town.

22 These figures are from Barratt, *History of the 13th Hussars*, I: 138.

23 Ibid. I: 135.

24 *Despatches*, Wellington to Beresford, 30 March 1811, VII: 412.

25 Barratt, *History of the 13th Hussars*, I: 136.

26 McGuffie, *Peninsular Cavalry General*, 89.

27 Barratt, *History of the 13th Hussars*, I: 136, and Fortescue, *History of the British Army*, VIII: 133.

28 Napier, *History of the War in the Peninsula*, III: 502. Napier's comment is quoted twice by Philip Haythornthwaite, first in his *Armies of Wellington*, 245, and again in his *British Cavalryman*, 51. On both occasions the latter adds, 'it is a

measure of the lack of tactical awareness among most of the cavalry that this fiasco was regarded as a triumph.' I feel this is missing the point once again and that the author is giving way to generalisations about the cavalry rather than looking deeper into the true facts. The army did feel that the 13th *had* achieved something very fine, that they had been let down by Beresford and, finally, that Wellington's General Order and Despatch were unfair to them. If the fight at Campo Mayor was a fiasco, it was not the fault of the 13th Light Dragoons. Burgoyne wrote in his Journal, 'The army under Marshal Beresford, from all accounts, appear much discontented with this affair.' Wrottesley, *Life and Correspondence*, I: 128.

29 Oman, *History of the Peninsular War*, N: 264.
30 Fortescue, *History of the British Army*, VIII: 136.
31 Ibid. VIII: 135.
32 Dickson, *The Dickson Manuscripts*, 25 March 1811, 367.
33 Fortescue, *History of the British Army*, VIII: 132.

Above left: **1** Arthur Wellesley, 1st Duke of Wellington.

Above right: **2** William Carr Beresford. Noted for his reorganisation of the Portuguese army in the Peninsula, he was, nevertheless, less than able on occasion in the Peninsula, notably at Albuera. He was also one of the central figures of the fight at Campo Mayor.

Right: **3** John Gaspard le Marchant. One of the most influential soldiers of his day, he was killed at Salamanca, 22 July 1812.

Above left: **4** Henry, Lord Paget, one of the great cavalry commanders. His affair with Wellington's sister-in-law barred him from serving with Wellington's army in the Peninsula, although as Lord Uxbridge, he commanded the Allied cavalry at Waterloo with great skill.

Above right: **5** Stapleton Cotton, later Lord Combermere. He possessed none of Paget's flair and dash but proved Wellington's most reliable cavalry commander.

Above left: **6** John 'Black Jack' Slade. Generally considered to be one of the more inept cavalry commanders in the Peninsula, he was responsible for the debacle at Maguilla.

Above right: **7** Robert Ballard Long an underrated cavalry commander and one of the central figures of the fight at Campo Mayor.

Above left: **8** Trumpet Major William Wheldon, 13th Light Dragoons, one of the great Peninsular War cavalry regiments. Wheldon was Lord Hill's orderly trumpeter during the latter stages of the Peninsular War. He is seen here wearing his Waterloo medal.

Above right: **9** Colonel Taylor, 20th Light Dragoons, killed in action at Vimeiro, 21 August 1808.

Above left: **10** Sir Hussey Vivian. He served with distinction in the Peninsula and at Waterloo.

Above right: **11** Loftus Otway, who commanded the Portuguese squadrons during the fight at Campo Mayor.

Above left: **12** Colonel Peter Hawker, 14th Light Dragoons. He fought at Oporto and was wounded at Talavera.

Above right: **13** Lt Col Henry Webster, 9th Light Dragoons. A good depiction of a Peninsular War cavalry commander, complete with Marmaluke sabre.

Above left: **14** Private, 1st (Royal) Dragoons, one of the most distinguished of Peninsular and Waterloo cavalry regiments. This picture shows the uniform worn at Waterloo.

Above right: **15** An unknown officer of the King's Dragoon Guards, 1812.

Above left: **16** Officer, 6th Inniskilling Dragoons, *c*. 1811. The regiment saw no service in the Peninsular but this is a good depiction of the sort of uniform worn by heavy dragoons in Portugal and Spain with their unusual watering cap.

Above right: **17** A private of the 7th Hussars on patrol in the Peninsula.

Right: **18** A fine study of a 15th Hussar, *c*. 1810.

19 Paget's hussars charge at Sahagun, 21 December 1808.

20 They repeat the exercise at Benavente eight days later. Both actions were fought during the ill-fated Corunna campaign of Sir John Moore.

Above left: **21** 10th Hussars on patrol during the Corruna campaign.

Above right: **22** The same regiment skirmishing, also during the Corunna campaign.

23 The 23rd Light Dragoons come to grief in the dry watercourse at Talavera, 29 July 1809.

24 Corporal Logan kills Colonel Chamourin of the 26th Dragoons at Campo Mayor, 25 March 1811. Logan is depicted wearing the later 1812 pattern uniform.

25 The battlefield of Campo Mayor, as seen from just outside the town. The 13th Light Dragoons charged over the hills to the left of the picture, whilst Beresford halted the heavy dragoons by the side of the road in the foreground.

26 The bridge at Usagre, where Lumley's heavy dragoons 'chastised' their French opponents.

27 The scene of the fight at Villa de Puerco, 11 July 1810. Gouache and his infantry formed square in this field successfully to repulse attacks by British light dragoons.

28 Light dragoons gathering intelligence in the Peninsula. A fine illustration of the sort of work which occupied them for a great deal of their time on campaign.

29 A superb study of a light dragoon on patrol in the Peninsula. This very accurate painting is a wonderful depiction of a cavalryman on active service.

30 The scene of the fight at Villagarcia. Le Marchant and the 5th Dragoon Guards charged out of the olive groves away to the right of this photo before engaging the French across the plain.

31 Maguilla, showing the broken ground and river in front of the village where Slade was brought up by Lallemand's reserves.

32 Salamanca. British light dragoons charge French cavalry, 22 July 1812.

33 The scene of Le Marchant's charge at Salmanca, as it looks today. The heavy brigade came charging over the crest from right to left before smashing first Maucune and then Brennier in the valley to the left.

34 Vittoria. British hussars crash into the routed French rearguard, 21 June 1813.

35 The crossing of the Bidassoa, 7 October 1813. British hussars, infantry and horse artillery cross the river to set foot on Napoleon's 'sacred soil'.

36 The 7th Hussars coming into action at the battle of Orthes, 27 February 1814.

37 The battlefield of Morales, as seen from the heights occupied by Digeon's infantry and artillery. Grant's hussars chased Digeon's dragoons across this plain after breaking them at Morales, which can be seen on the horizon.

38 Captain Clarke-Kennedy, of the 1st (Royal) Dragoons, captures the eagle of the French 105th regiment at Waterloo, 18 June 1815.

39 An unusual painting showing the beginning of Uxbridge's heavy cavalry charge at Waterloo. Wellington watches as the Household Brigade begins its charge.

40 A wonderful depiction of Sergeant Charles Ewart, of the Scots Greys, taking the eagle of the 45th Regiment at Waterloo, 18 June 1815.

CHAPTER V

Operations under Hill and Beresford

Much of the fighting in the Peninsula revolved around the control of the two great fortress towns of Ciudad Rodrigo and Badajoz, for whoever commanded these controlled the two main corridors between Portugal and Spain. After Wellington had driven Masséna from Portugal in April 1811 he set about blockading Ciudad Rodrigo, which controlled the northern corridor. The British siege train had yet to be landed, however, and a regular siege was not yet possible. In the south, the fortress of Badajoz was held by a Spanish garrison under its redoubtable leader, Menacho, but when he was killed during a sortie from the place on 3 March 1811, the garrison came under the command of Brigadier-General José Imaz who very treacherously gave up the place to the French eight days later. It would be a whole year before the town fell to the Allies, during which time two further attempts were made on the place, both of which failed, but fall it did and in spectacular and bloody style. The significance of the Allies' presence in the south, as far as we are concerned, was not the siege of Badajoz but the various cavalry actions that it led to.

We have already studied the cavalry action at Campo Mayor on 25 March 1811 in the previous chapter. Now we must move on to the series of other cavalry fights in the south. By the beginning of April Beresford's force consisted of the 2nd and 4th Divisions and Hamilton's Portuguese. The cavalry division under Long which was attached to the force consisted of the 3rd Dragoon Guards, 4th Dragoons and the 13th Light Dragoons, under De Grey, and two regiments of Portuguese cavalry, the 1st and 7th, under Otway. Essentially, Beresford's task was to lay siege to Badajoz, although this would not be possible until the first week in May owing to a lack of supplies and equipment. In the meantime, he planned to advance south across the Guadiana in order to drive the enemy back to the Sierra Morena.

Beresford got his force across the Guadiana by the end of the first week in April and on the 9th set about besieging the small fortified town of Olivenza, which was carried out by the 4th Division. On 15 April the town surrendered, at which the 4th Division crossed the Guadiana and marched to join the rest of Beresford's force at Santa Marta. The following day Beresford marched south towards Zafra but had got no farther than Los Santos, some three miles to the north of the place, when, at around noon, he received reports that between 500 and 600 French cavalry had been sighted to the south, some of whom had actually entered the village. Long wasted little time in getting his cavalry forward, the 13th Light Dragoons leading with the Portuguese cavalry and De Grey's Heavy Brigade in support. Unfortunately, the 13th were somewhat disordered at first when Beresford and his staff came riding into them, having fled in the face of the advancing French cavalry. The 13th soon righted themselves, however, and, passing to the left of the village, charged with the Portuguese in line behind them. The French cavalry carried little weight with them when they met the 13th and after a brief skirmish were driven back, stopping now and then to fire their carbines in order to keep the 13th Light Dragoons at a respectful distance.[1] At the same time Long ordered the Heavy Brigade to get around the flank of the enemy force in order to cut off their retreat. The 13th pressed in on the French centre, and when the heavy brigade charged their right flank the French suddenly lost heart, panicked and bolted with Long and his cavalry in pursuit. There followed another very long pursuit, this time for around ten miles, with the British cavalry cutting down any French stragglers too blown to keep up with the main body, until the chase ended close to Usagre, by which time all those concerned were simply too exhausted to go on. Long returned to Los Santos with his men and with over 150 prisoners, all of which had been secured at a cost to the 13th Light Dragoons of barely six casualties.

Lieutenant Charles Madden was present with the 4th Dragoons and wrote:

> The cavalry instantly advanced at a quick trot, and on our passing the town a small distance we saw them [the French] drawn up in column ready to receive us; the 13th was in the centre, and the heavy brigade on the right flank. The French charged the right squadron of the 13th on our advancing near them, which was returned. We then went up to charge them on the flanks, on which they went about and galloped off as fast they could. We pursued them for about two leagues, most part of which time the French were completely dispersed, and as their horses brushed up we picked them up... We should have destroyed most part of them had we not come off a march of five leagues, without corn, and the French having in the head of their column a considerable start of us.[2]

The action at Los Santos was a very creditable one by the British cavalry and the 13th Light Dragoons who showed that they were not to be discouraged by the controversies surrounding the fight at Campo Mayor. Indeed, such was the treatment handed out to the French by the 13th at

Campo Mayor that the 2nd Hussars, one of the French regiments present at the latter fight, displayed a marked reluctance at Los Santos to engage a regiment that had beaten their comrades soundly only three weeks before. Once again, a British cavalry force had routed a French one in a fair, stand-up fight. There are some parallels between Campo Mayor and Los Santos. The pursuit at the latter was not dissimilar to that at Campo Mayor, and, if anything, was conducted over an even greater distance. Long, who was present during the pursuit, wrote afterwards that it was nevertheless conducted at a pace which allowed the 13th to preserve order, not that a lack of order had been the cause of the controversy at Campo Mayor. Furthermore, Long was in a position to order a recall if any French reserves ever appeared which, in the event, they did not.

With typical bitterness, following the affair at Campo Mayor, Long wrote:

> We pursued them at such a rate as enabled us to preserve something like order, and at the same time pressed them so hard by pursuers that as their horses were passed, blown, or left behind we came up and secured them. Never was there such a fox chase, but I did not enjoy it, because I knew the ignorans [sic] expected us to take every man of them, which I knew was impossible, without disbanding every soldier I had in pursuit; and this, after the thanks I experienced at Campo Mayor, I did not feel inclined to do. Had I had my will, I should have detached a Corps to the left by a road which intercepted the line of the enemy's retreat, and would infallibly have been fatal to them. But here again I was over-ruled. Thus success is not left at my disposal, but I shall be made amply responsible for all failures.[3]

The main difference at Los Santos was that Beresford was in a position to see everything happening in front of him and, observing no danger to his cavalry, allowed De Grey's heavy brigade to get forward and sup-port Long. The end result was a victory, albeit a small one, for Long who thought he could have achieved more had a corps marched to the left of the road from Los Santos to cut off the French retreat. In this, however, he was over-ruled. In spite of his irritation, Long could at least console himself with Beresford's commendation afterwards and his thanks, which were duly mentioned in his report to Wellington on the affair.

On 5 May Beresford finally began the first siege of Badajoz, but just seven days later came the news that Soult had arrived at Llerena with the relieving force, causing Beresford to abandon the siege and make prepa-rations to march south in order to meet him. The two sides met astride the road to Badajoz at the small village of Albuera where, on 16 May, the bloodiest battle of the Peninsular War was fought. The numbers on each side were not particularly great – 34,000 Allies, of which around 10,000 were British, against 24,000 French, but the casualties were horrendous.

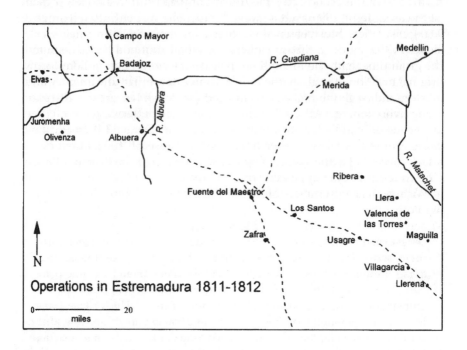

Operations in Estremadura 1811-1812

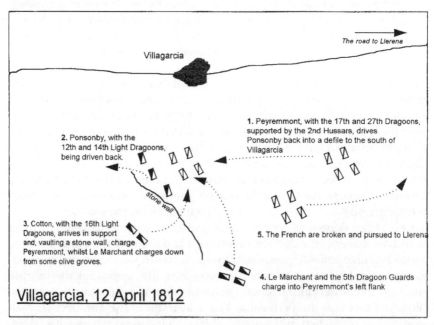

The road to Llerena

Villagarcia

1. Peyremmont, with the 17th and 27th Dragoons, supported by the 2nd Hussars, drives Ponsonby back into a defile to the south of Villagarcia

2. Ponsonby, with the 12th and 14th Light Dragoons, being driven back.

3. Cotton, with the 16th Light Dragoons, arrives in support and, vaulting a stone wall, charge Peyremmont, whilst Le Marchant charges down from some olive groves.

5. The French are broken and pursued to Llerena

4. Le Marchant and the 5th Dragoon Guards charge into Peyremmont's left flank

Villagarcia, 12 April 1812

By the end of this bloody day, the Allied army had suffered no fewer than 5,956 casualties, 4,199 of which were British. The French suffered around 7,000 casualties. Most of these occurred on the undulating fields and slopes to the south of Albuera where the infantry of both sides disputed the ground beneath the low hill on the extreme right flank of Beresford's original position. It was a battle fought almost entirely by the infantry and artillery, although the French cavalry, and the Polish lancers in particular, made a very telling and deadly contribution to the proceedings when they all but destroyed Colborne's brigade of the 2nd Division. Indeed, they caused some 1,300 casualties out of a total strength of 1,600 in a ferocious attack following a hail and rain storm which blinded the British infantry who were caught in line, unable to fire their weapons. The British cavalry also made an important if less dramatic contribution to the battle protecting both a ford and bridge against threats from French troops in addition to checking enemy cavalry. As Madden later wrote, 'our advances had the effect of checking their cavalry', although he was of the opinion that the British cavalry would have been able to make a more telling contribution had they not been so few in number. He also claimed that the British cavalry engaged Polish lancers, which would make it the first occasion that such an encounter occurred in the Peninsula. 'The charge of our right wing was made against a brigade of Polish cavalry, very large men, well-mounted; the front rank armed with long spears, with flags on them, which they flourish about, so as to frighten our horses, and thence either pulled our men off their horses or ran them through. They were perfect barbarians, and gave no quarter when they could possibly avoid.'[4] The day ended in victory for Beresford, although he himself had little hand in it, the crucial decision for the decisive advance of the 4th Division being made by Cole and Hardinge. In fact, Beresford appears to have lost control of the battle fairly early on and the day was saved only by the extreme bravery of the British infantry who refused to give an inch in the face of a terrible French onslaught until their assailants themselves gave up the struggle, unable to endure further punishment.

If Albuera was the bloodiest battle of the war it was also the most controversial. The vitriolic pamphlet war waged afterwards between Beresford, Long's nephew and Napier, the great historian of the war, and their respective supporters, which we have come across in the previous chapter, concerned not only Campo Mayor but Albuera also. Much of the controversy centred on Beresford's handling of the battle and, in particular, his choice of position, something which was severely criticised by Napier who, unfortunately, never visited the actual battlefield and was not, therefore, qualified to pass judgement. There was no love lost between the two men, and the now famous *Strictures* and *Further Strictures* which were published in the wake of the publication of Napier's account of the battle in his classic *History of the War in the Peninsula*, was the end result. Long, too, was a party to the pamphlet war, although it was his nephew who championed his cause, Long having died in 1825. There are all sorts of arguments and controversies surrounding Long and Beresford at Albuera, not least of which was the way in which Beresford replaced Long as commander of the Allied cavalry with William Lumley, an able officer but essentially an infantryman. It was not so much his removal that hurt Long, but the way in which it was done, and the timing of it, coming as it did soon after the battle had begun, an outrageous moment for such a decision to be made.

Successive historians, including Weller and Oman, have criticised Long and his cavalry for giving up too much ground to the south of Albuera in the face of the French advance, and giving it up all too hastily.[5] This criticism is ill-founded, for Long was simply obeying orders he believed had come from Beresford but which, in effect, had come first from Beresford's Quartermaster General, Benjamin D'Urban, and second, from his Adjutant General, Colonel Rooke. The first ordered Long to remain on the right bank of the Albuera river, in front of the Allied position, and not to cross until hard-pressed. Rooke, on the other hand, ordered Long to cross the river and form on the left bank, which he duly did. The explanation of the above is very clearly set out by Fortescue, who quite accurately states that the blunder, 'thus unhandsomely attributed by Beresford and D'Urban to Long, was really due to one of Beresford's own staff officers.'[6] As in the previous chapter, it is not my intention to join the great Albuera debate which was waged in the volumes of the Strictures and Further Strictures, as the whole affair did not really have any bearing on the performance of the British cavalry during the battle. However, the issue has certainly tended to place a slur on Long's service in the Peninsula and has long since been a factor which historians have seized upon when analysing the performance of Long and his command of the cavalry. As to Long's removal from command on the day of the battle, we have his own explanation, which, unlike Oman and Weller, Fortescue again picks up on. The real reason for Long's replacement in favour of William Lumley was to ensure that the Allied cavalry remained under the command of a British officer, for Long, in command before the battle, was junior in rank to some Spanish officers who may well have asked for command of the whole Allied cavalry, something which Beresford certainly would not have wanted but would have found difficult to refuse. The dilemma was actually pointed out to Beresford by Long himself, who wrote after the battle, 'In consequence of the union of the Spanish cavalry, and to prevent disputes about rank, General Beresford directed Major-General Lumley to take command of the whole cavalry, and, in my opinion, rather indelicately permitted this command to be assumed after the action commenced, and whilst I was manoeuvring the troops'.[7] Thus, we have Long being replaced, not as a result of any ineptitude, but to avoid disputes with the Spaniards about rank. There is little doubt that the decision was also made on a personal basis, the two men having been at loggerheads ever since the Campo Mayor business, but to claim that Long was removed for his lack of resolve is incorrect.

The role of the British cavalry at Albuera was similar to that played by the light cavalry at Waterloo, with successive charges being made over short distances in order to usher away the enemy cavalry who had in turn made attacks on Allied infantry. Losses amongst the 1,164–strong British cavalry contingent at Albuera were slight, just forty-eight in fact, but what short work they did was done well. When the battle opened at 8am, the French sent down a brigade of infantry, supported by a brigade of light cavalry and a further infantry brigade, to attack the bridge over the Albuera river in front of the village. Long, still to be replaced by Lumley, sent down the 3rd Dragoon Guards against the Polish lancers accompanying the attack, and drove them back. It was the first time British cavalry had seen enemy lancers in the Peninsula, a fight which resulted in the lancers being thrown back. The 13th Light Dragoons were also sent down to assist in the defence of the bridge before they were all recalled when Soult changed the direction of his attack. The battle then devolved upon the infantry, although the British cavalry were active on the extreme right of the Allied position and, as already stated, saw off several threatening advances by the enemy cavalry.

All in all, the British cavalry played little more than a supporting role in the great act of the Battle of Albuera, but it is important that we understand something of the controversies mentioned above, surrounding Beresford, his handling of the battle and his decision to replace Long as Allied cavalry commander, for they have had a significant bearing on the way in which Robert Ballard Long, a major figure in the history of the British cavalry in the Peninsula, has been portrayed.

Soult's army had given its all at Albuera but had failed to achieve its objective, namely to relieve Badajoz, and on 17 May Soult limped away south in the direction of Seville. This allowed Wellington, who had arrived at Elvas on 20 May, to resume the siege of Badajoz, although it took him a little time to get forward the remnants of the British force shattered at Albuera. In the meantime, Beresford's cavalry set off in pursuit of Soult to ensure that he was driven back a good distance from Badajoz and to ensure that he could not pose any threat during the siege operations. Irritated by this pursuit, Soult determined to send back his cavalry in order to discover the size and composition of the force coming on behind him, and on 25 May ordered Latour-Maubourg to turn about and attack the pursuing cavalry.

Beresford's cavalry was still being commanded by William Lumley and consisted of the 13th Light Dragoons, 3rd Dragoon Guards and 4th Dragoons, four weak regiments of Madden's[8] and Otway's Portuguese cavalry and two squadrons of Spanish cavalry under Penne Villemur. Altogether, this cavalry force numbered around 2,200 sabres. Pitted against this force were some 3,000 French cavalry of the brigades of Bron, Bouvier des Eclats, Vinot and Briche, who easily drove back the Spanish piquets in and around Villagarcia, a small village which was to be the scene of another British cavalry triumph the following year. The Spaniards were pursued for around five miles until they reached the town of Usagre where Lumley had drawn up his British and Portuguese cavalry, having been alerted to the news of Latour-Maubourg's approach.

The French commander, upon seeing Allied cavalry, halted his own in order to determine the strength and dispositions of the force in front of him, and opened up with his artillery on the Allied cavalry as they retired from the town. Latour-Maubourg, in fact, could see very little as Lumley had hidden his heavy dragoons on the reverse slope of a hill which lay a few hundred yards to the north of the town. He would have to tread warily before he moved owing to the fact that he would have to pass through the town and then cross a very narrow bridge over a small river before gaining the northern bank, held by Lumley. In effect, Lumley was aping Wellington's infantry tactic of keeping his men hidden from view to prevent the enemy from discovering their true strength and positions. All that Latour-Maubourg had seen were the retreating Spaniards and a few units of Portuguese cavalry, those of Otway and Madden. Otway had been sent originally by Lumley, who had already very diligently sounded the various crossing points, over the steep-sided river, crossing by way of a ford to the east of the town, the 13th Light Dragoons going with him. To the west of the town Madden had likewise crossed the river, again using a ford. However, upon the approach of the French cavalry, all of these retired the way they had come and quickly disappeared from sight behind the crest of the heights on the northern bank of the river. The retiring British and Portuguese cavalry did not go undetected by the French, although they were afforded such a fleeting glimpse that it was impossible for Latour-Maubourg to determine either their true strength or positions. He did, however, decide to proceed with caution and, accordingly, decided not to pass over the bridge but sent Briche's brigade of light cavalry to the east of the town in order to discover the ford used by Otway. Once this had been accomplished, Briche was to cross with his brigade and turn Lumley's left flank, whereupon Latour-Maubourg would send across his remaining three brigades.

Briche had with him the 10th Hussars and 21st Chasseurs, and after going about a mile, came across the ford by which Otway had crossed and recrossed the river. He was prevented from crossing, however, by Otway who had evidently appeared on the northern bank ready to dispute it. Briche, reluctant to try crossing the steep-banked river in the presence of an enemy force, continued farther east along the bank in an effort to try and find another suitable place to cross, and in doing so became more and more detached from the main body of French cavalry under Latour-Maubourg who was completely unaware of his whereabouts. In fact, Latour-Maubourg, having received no reports at all from Briche, came to the erroneous conclusion that Briche must have crossed the river according to plan and decided to pass the river by the narrow bridge at the town itself.

Taking the lead was Bron's brigade of dragoons, the 4th, 20th and 26th, all of whom passed through the narrow streets before approaching the bridge which lay at the end of a sharp bend in the street. It was, and still is, a very narrow bridge which allows barely two riders abreast to cross. At length the 4th and 20th Dragoons passed the bridge and began to deploy, the former on the right and the latter on the left, on the slopes on the northern bank of the river, It is not clear where Bron himself was positioned, but he was evidently unaware of the close proximity of Lumley's heavy dragoons, who sat waiting out of sight on the back of the slopes a few hundred yards away. Lumley's timing could not have been more perfect, for just as the last files of the 20th were passing the bridge, he launched the 3rd Dragoon Guards and 4th Dragoons, who suddenly appeared on the skyline above the shocked and surprised French dragoons, who quickly tried to deploy to meet them. Everything was in Lumley's favour – surprise and ground, not to mention the fact that Lumley's plan was without fault and the order of his men good.[9] Charles Madden was with the 4th Dragoons, and wrote, 'We charged them with great rapidity, having a good descent in our favour; we broke them with the shock and they retired in the greatest confusion. Those in front of the 3rd endeavoured to get over the wall, and were nearly to a man cut down or taken prisoners; the 4th cut them down in the lane leading to the bridge, till it was blocked up with men and horses. Numbers made their escape by leaping off their horses and getting over a high wall into an olive grove'.[10]

The 4th Dragoons hit the French head on, whilst the 3rd Dragoon Guards struck them in their flank, throwing them back towards the bridge at the very moment that Bron's third regiment, the 26th Dragoons, were crossing it. The confusion is easy to imagine with Lumley's dragoons pushing the French back to the bridge where they were jammed in and, unable to form or move, were simply cut down by the British dragoons who hacked and hewed at an enemy paralysed by their predicament. In an attempt to escape the carnage, many of the French cavalrymen simply jumped from their horses over the low walls that led from the bridge, whilst those able to wield their swords struck back at their assailants. It was a short but bloody fight which spread along the banks of the river as the French tried to escape the confusion at the bridge. The Portuguese and Spanish cavalry came forward also and pursued isolated enemy riders to their deaths. Eventually, the helpless French cavalry were relieved from their predicament by Bouvier's brigade, the 14th, 17th and 27th Dragoons, who threw themselves down along the southern bank of the river and opened fire with their carbines on the Allied cavalry, forcing them back and allowing the French to recross the bridge. Four enemy guns were likewise brought forward, but these were silenced by a battery of British guns under Lefebure, which Lumley had brought forward on to the slopes above the town.

The action ended with Latour-Maubourg watching helplessly as his cavalry – at least those who were not being hunted down by the Spanish and Portuguese – were driven back across the bridge having lost over 250 men killed or wounded, whilst a further six officers and seventy-two men were taken prisoner, including the colonel of the 4th Dragoons. There is no record of it happening, but one cannot help wondering whether the British 4th Dragoons played host to their captive that night, as was often the case when similarly-numbered opposing units met in battle. Lumley himself suffered not more than twenty casualties in this superb little action, dubbed by Oman as, 'the most satisfactory of its kind that the British horse in the Peninsula had been engaged in since the combats of Sahagun and Benavente.'[11]

The action at Usagre is a wonderful example of the planning and execution of a trap, the likes of which the British cavalry have generally been accused of being incapable of mounting.[12] Everything went according to plan; the initial moves, the choice of ground, the planned withdrawal and the timing and execution of the final attack. Surprise and a downhill charge were certainly to the British cavalry's advantage but numbers were equal. In fact, it may be overlooked that by having the French jammed against the bridge, the majority of Lumley's dragoons probably never got within striking distance of them, the fighting in such situations being done by the front ranks whilst those in the rear struggled to get forward. The mere impetus of the British charge, the confusion and the lack of room to wield their swords all conspired to leave the French hopelessly overpowered as the casualty figures demonstrate. There was never any danger of a reckless pursuit either, with the town occupied by more French cavalry. Therefore, control of the victorious British dragoons was never an issue. Lumley simply had to let them loose and have them lay into the French at the bridge. Once the damage had been inflicted they simply pulled back, allowing the French to disengage and count their losses. Lumley then withdrew and joined the Allied cavalry screen formed from Hinosa to Fuente Cantos, with the ravine at Usagre forming the boundary between the two sides for the next month or so. Sadly, Lumley fell sick and returned home to England in August 1811, and so we shall never know how he would have fared in subsequent campaigns.

The siege of Badajoz was renewed towards the end of May but was prosecuted with little success. Indeed, such was the want of success that on 10

June Wellington gave up the siege and drew up his army on the Caya river, with his right resting upon Elvas, his centre about Campo Mayor and his left at Ouguela. It was a period of no great activity for the army as a whole, but the cavalry were as busy as usual, providing the piquets for the army and engaging in the usual crop of minor skirmishes. On 23 June there occurred the notorious capture of almost an entire piquet of the 11th Light Dragoons, under Captain Lutyens, an affair which annoyed Wellington greatly. This episode is covered in Part One, Chapter Five.

During the autumn and early winter of 1811 Wellington's main field army moved north to get itself into position for the projected siege of Ciudad Rodrigo which Wellington hoped would begin early in 1812. The cavalry engagements in this area are dealt with in a previous chapter. In the south, meanwhile, Hill had replaced Beresford as commander of the Allied army watching the southern corridor between Portugal and Spain. The year seemed to be coming to an end with very little in the way of action, prior to the army going into cantonments for the winter, when Hill decided to launch a raid against a French force under General Girard which was operating in the vicinity of Merida and the northern districts of Estremadura, mainly for the purpose of gathering forage. This irritating unit was the object of Hill's famous raid at Arroyo dos Molinos on 28 October, during which Long was once again party to events as commander of Hill's cavalry.

Girard's force consisted of around 6,000 men, including infantry, cavalry and artillery, and on 27 October were reported to be at Arroyo dos Molinos, a small village which sits at the foot of the south-western end of the Sierra de Montanchez. It was, in fact, the situation of the village itself which dictated Hill's plan. Quite simply, anybody occupying the village did so at the risk of being cut off and surrounded if any enemy force decided to cut the three roads from the village which branched off to Truxillo, Medellin and Merida. By simply cutting these roads any force in the village would be trapped with only the steep mountains behind, and it was such a plan that Hill adopted. Hill's own force consisted of around 10,000 men, with Howard's Brigade; the 1/50th, 1/71st and 1/92nd, Wilson's Brigade; the 1/28th, 1/34th and 1/39th, five regiments of Portuguese; the 4th, 6th, 10th and 18th Line, and the 6th Caçadores, and Long's cavalry brigade; the 9th Light Dragoons, 13th Light Dragoons and the 2nd Hussars KGL. In addition, there was Morillo's Spanish infantry and Penne Villemur's Spanish cavalry. It was a force more than strong enough to deal with Girard and, with good planning, Hill hoped to take the whole French force.

By the evening of 27 October Hill had got his force into position in front of the village of Alcesquar, with Allied units astride all of the main roads leading from Arroyo dos Molinos. On the morning of the 28th he himself would lead a frontal attack on the village, his force acting as the 'beaters' to drive the French into the waiting arms of the other Allied units. Hill gathered his attacking troops around him at Alcesquar during the stormy and tempestuous night of 27–28 October before advancing. He got his men to within about half-a-mile of the French before they were discovered by an enemy piquet which, although overcome, managed to raise the alarm. Two French regiments had got off an hour before dawn, accompanied by a cavalry regiment, but the majority of the remaining 4,000 French troops were just making preparations to depart when the 71st and 92nd Highlanders burst into the village, driving the surprised French through the streets and out the other side of the village. General Bron, who commanded a brigade at Usagre, was taken prisoner, as were scores of other men whilst Girard himself, seeing the road to Merida blocked, ordered his cavalry to hold back the British infantry in order to allow his own infantry to escape. It was during this phase of the fighting that the 9th Light Dragoons and the 2nd Hussars KGL became embroiled in the fighting, scattering their opposing numbers and taking scores of them prisoner.

Whilst this fighting was going on Girard's infantry hurried off along the Truxillo road but, to their horror, saw it blocked by Wilson's brigade which was hurrying to cut them off. Seeing the trap into which his men were falling, Girard ordered his men to abandon the idea of retreating to Truxillo and led them instead up the mountains behind the village, scrambling up the precipitous rock face with Morillo's Spanish infantry in hot pursuit. In the event, Girard managed to escape, but with just 500 of his men. Over 1,300 French troops were taken prisoner, including Bron and the Prince of Aremberg, the colonel of the 27th Chasseurs. Girard's command had, in effect, ceased to exist. Hill's force, on the other hand, had lost just seven men killed and seven officers and fifty-seven men wounded, the Spaniards suffering a further thirty casualties.

The work of Long's brigade of cavalry involved the 9th Light Dragoons and the 2nd Hussars KGL, who engaged Girard's cavalry, who were in turn being assailed by Spanish cavalry. Apparently, just one squadron each of Long's two regiments were involved in the fight, but they still managed to scatter their enemies and take over 200 of them prisoner. Long, meanwhile, was ordered personally by Hill to gallop after the three guns which were getting away from the village and take them, which was duly accomplished by the 13th Light Dragoons. Long himself was of the opinion that he could have prevented Girard's escape had he been allowed to do so by Hill. However, he was ordered to take the guns instead, and by the time he had returned to the fray Girard had made good his escape. It was something about which Long complained in one of his letters although he did not labour the point. Indeed, it appears that Long was unable to fight a single action without managing to find some cause for complaint afterwards. His bravery, enthusiasm and dedication to duty were matched only by his complaining, bitterness and his constant rowing with Beresford. Fortunately, after Arroyo dos Molinos he managed to avoid such a fallout with Hill. The British cavalry again did good work at Arroyo dos Molinos, although their task was fairly straightforward and there was nothing too difficult about it. They dispersed the French cavalry when called upon to do so – again in a stand-up fight – and duly captured the three enemy guns when ordered to do so by Hill. Their job was well done, therefore, with a minimum of fuss and with little cost to themselves, although it has to be said that this was very basic work for them.

The same could not be said, however, of an action which brought the year of 1811 to a close. Indeed, the affair, at Membrillo, bore too many uncomfortable resemblances to Craufurd's action at Villar de Puerco on 11 July 1810. The action, on 29 December, came about when Hill embarked on another of his famous raids, the object on this occasion being the French 5th Division, commanded by General Dombrouski, which lay in and around Merida, on the Guadiana river. In order to surprise the French Hill had to approach from the north, and by 28 December had reached the village of La Rocca, just twenty miles from Merida. As luck would have it, Dombrouski had sent out a foraging party in this very direction, and it was this group of French troops that Hill's advance guard, consisting of one squadron of the 2nd Hussars KGL,[13] ran into on the 29th near the village of Navas de Membrillo. Escorting the foraging party was a group of hussars who managed to ride off in order to raise the alarm, thus denying Hill the element of surprise. The French infantry consisted of three companies of the 88th Regiment under Captain Neveux, some 400 men in all, who, upon being apprised of the approaching Allied cavalry, formed up and began to make off in some haste for Merida. Hill then ordered the 2nd Hussars KGL, along with two squadrons of the 13th Light Dragoons, to pursue them and take them if possible, but by the time they came up with the enemy infantry, Neveux had got his men off the road and had formed them into square in a cork wood. Naturally, the Allied cavalry found it almost impossible to get themselves into any real order in which to charge the French square, protected as it was by the low cork trees. The resulting charges carried no weight and the French square held firm against them, giving as good as they got with fairly accurate musketry at close range. In all, five charges are said to have been made, all without success, and the only casualties sustained by the French, two killed and nine wounded, were caused by Hawker's battery which only arrived on the scene when the French were well on their way along the road to Merida. The 2nd Hussars KGL suffered two men killed and one officer and seventeen men wounded. The 13th Light Dragoons lost one man killed and nineteen officers and men wounded.[14]

According to the account of Captain Gubbins, of the 13th Light Dragoons, Hill, his staff and the 13th were, apparently, 'extremely vexed and annoyed', at the way in which the affair fell out.[15] Indeed, it was by far the most unsuccessful of Hill's affairs and pales into insignificance when compared with his exploits at Arroyo dos Molinos, Almaraz and St Pierre.[16] Comparisons between the affair at Membrillo and Villar de Puerco are obvious and there are plenty of them. On both occasions British and German cavalry failed to break the French infantry squares and were driven off with loss. The French also had the advantage of ground which they used to good effect, particularly at Membrillo, in restricting the operational frontage of the cavalry attacks. As a consequence the cavalry were unable to bring their horses to the charge and the attacks that were delivered went in at little more than a trot. At Villar de Puerco the ground was not as bad, but even so there were a series of stone walls that had to be negotiated before the squares could be approached. The main difference between the two actions was that at Membrillo Hill had the excuse of not having either infantry or artillery, which almost certainly would have decided the issue had they been present. The only Allied guns to be involved came upon the scene very late in the day when the French were almost within sight of Merida and safety. At Villar de Puerco, on the other hand, as we have seen in a previous chapter, Craufurd had the use of all arms but failed to take advantage of them, preferring instead to use only his cavalry but to no avail.

The French commander at Membrillo, Neveux, deserves much credit for his conduct during the fight in getting his men under the protection of the wood, on high ground, and getting them away in good order to the safety of Mérida with the loss of just a few men. Ultimately, we must return to Wellington's own verdict on the Villar de Puerco business, which is equally applicable at Membrillo, in that such attacks were rarely liable to succeed if the enemy infantry remained formed and steady, which was the case on both occasions. As we will see when we come to look briefly at the heavy dragoons of the King's German Legion at Garcia Hernandez, it would take something very extraordinary for cavalry to break into a formed infantry square. Wellington's British cavalry never succeeded in the Peninsula and neither did the French.[17] Nor did they succeed at Waterloo in 1815 despite hours of relentless attacks on the Allied squares. Membrillo, therefore, ranks as one of the more disappointing cavalry episodes in the Peninsula and a rare failure for the otherwise very successful Lord Hill. His 'vexation and annoyance' were, however, probably due to the fact that the alarm had been raised and the whole raid therefore failed, rather than the conduct of the cavalry who could not really have been expected to perform any better than they did.

The year 1811 ended in slight disappointment for Hill, but it had been an otherwise very successful campaigning season for him. Prior to his assuming command, Beresford had performed very patchily and certainly blotted his copybook with his command of the Allied army at Albuera. Overall there was little for him to write home about and his tenure was to provoke much controversy between himself, Long and Napier, the historian of the war who introduced Beresford into his six-volume masterpiece as 'a devil', after the latter had accused him of portraying Napoleon as a sort of 'god'. The arguments between the various disputants have only a small bearing on our study of the British cavalry in the Peninsula and, as I have already stated, it is not my intention to enter into the controversy, other than when it affects the performance or reputation of the British cavalry. As for them, the year had witnessed some fine performances – Lumley's brilliant action at Usagre, Long's workmanlike performance at Albuera and Arroyo dos Molinos, and his very creditable action at Los Santos. Even the most controversial cavalry action of the all, Campo Mayor, whilst ultimately a lost opportunity, was attended initially with success. Membrillo was the one real disappointment, as was the capture of Captain Lutyens' piquet of the 11th Light Dragoons, which we have studied in a previous chapter.

It was traditional during the winter months for both armies to go into cantonments when the unsuitable weather brought a curtain down on the year's campaigning. Not so during the winter of 1811–12, however, when Wellington demonstrated that, far from being the defensive-minded commander that some historians would have us believe, he leapt on to the offensive, taking advantage of the withdrawal of several thousands of French troops under Dorsenne, who marched east to assist Suchet in dealing with the Spanish guerrillas, to lay siege to Ciudad Rodrigo, which town controlled the northern corridor between Portugal and Spain. The town was taken by storm on the night of 19 January 1812, after which Wellington turned his attention once again to the mighty fortress of Badajoz, which controlled the southern corridor and which had eluded him in June 1811.

Whilst his main field army laid siege to Badajoz in March and April 1812, Hill remained, as usual, watching the eastern approaches to Badajoz from the direction of Merida. His 14,000-strong force was to prevent any interference from this direction which might come from Marmont, whilst Sir Thomas Graham, with a further 19,000 men, kept an eye on Soult, still in Andalucia. Badajoz was stormed on the momentous night of 6 April and was sacked mercilessly for the next seventy-two hours by Wellington's victorious, battle-maddened troops who had gone above and beyond the call of duty to deliver the town to their commander. A threat to Ciudad Rodrigo by Marmont caused Wellington to return to the north to deal with it, and the end result was the Salamanca campaign, which we shall deal with in a later chapter. Immediately after the capture of Badajoz, Hill, who was to remain in the south, was pushed forward to drive back the French – who were returning south after their failure to intervene at Badajoz – to give Soult the impression that Wellington's next step was an invasion of Andalucia. It was a business that was to involve Hill's cavalry in two very notable actions, one being a very successfully planned and executed trap, and the other one of the most controversial cavalry actions of the war, second only to Campo Mayor.

The first action, at Villagarcia on 11 April, was not only a very successful one but it saw the debut in the Peninsula of John Gaspard Le Marchant, a most forward-thinking cavalry officer with the potential to be one of the finest soldiers the British Army ever produced. His career is dealt with in an earlier chapter but, to recap briefly, Le Marchant, an experienced soldier, had not only designed the 1796-pattern sabre, which all of Wellington's light cavalry regiments employed in the Peninsula, as well as his famous sword-drill which accompanied it, but had been instrumental in forming the Staff College at Marlow, the forerunner of today's Sandhurst.

The fight at Villagarcia came about when D'Erlon, whose two divisions were set by Soult to form a communication between his Army of the South and the Army of Portugal, clashed with the British cavalry who were pushing him back in the direction of Seville, which was where Soult himself had gone. If he was unable to form this communication, D'Erlon was ordered not to stand and fight any serious action but was to fall back towards his chief at Seville, but only if Hill pressed him too hard. As it turned out, D'Erlon was indeed pushed hard by Cotton's cavalry, consisting of Ponsonby's brigade being the 12th, 14th and 16th Light Dragoons, Le Marchant's heavy brigade,[18] being the 3rd and 4th Dragoons and the 5th Dragoon Guards, and Slade's heavy brigade, the 1st (Royal) Dragoons, the 3rd Dragoon Guards and the 4th Dragoon Guards. On 10 April Cotton's cavalry lay between Los Santos, Villafranca and Ribera, with D'Erlon occupying Llerena about twenty-five miles to the south east. About fifteen miles from Llerena is the small town of Bienvenida, and it was to here, on 10 April, that both Cotton and Le Marchant rode and, climbing the tall steeple of the church, managed to get a glimpse through their telescopes of some French cavalry resting close to the village of Villagarcia, ten miles away.[19] Cotton may not have been the dashing cavalryman in the style of Paget, but on this occasion he was quick to form his plan of attack.

Cotton ordered Ponsonby, Le Marchant and Slade to concentrate at Bienvenida before dawn the next day in order to begin his move against the French cavalry, which consisted of the 2nd Hussars and the 17th and 27th Dragoons, the whole being commanded by General Lallemand. By nightfall, however, it was learned that the French had pulled out of Villagarcia, prompting Cotton to order Ponsonby to send two of his squadrons into the village the next morning and to throw out patrols to find the whereabouts of the French. The three British cavalry brigades duly moved between midnight and one o'clock on the morning of 11 April, making their way along difficult roads in the darkness. During the march it suddenly occurred to Cotton that the advance of Ponsonby might drive the French back and thus elude him, and so he sent an aide-de-camp after him, telling him to delay his advance, in order to allow Le Marchant to get his heavy cavalry brigade round the French left flank and so sever their escape route to Llerena. Unfortunately, the aide arrived too late to prevent Ponsonby from throwing his men, two squadrons of the 12th and 14th Light Dragoons under Charles Cocks, into the village at dawn. These drove Lallemand's piquets out on to the plain beyond where they came across the main French cavalry force. Naturally, the two squadrons were brought to a halt and were driven back towards the village, being joined en route by Ponsonby with two squadrons each of the 12th Light Dragoons and the 14th Light Dragoons, whilst the 16th Light Dragoons were still with Cotton and had yet to appear on the field. These six squadrons, around 600 men in all, began skirmishing with the much larger French cavalry force, two regiments of which, it will be remembered, were heavy cavalry regiments. Despite putting up a good fight, Ponsonby's light cavalry were driven steadily back upon Villagarcia by a delighted Lallemand who had suddenly noticed the presence in some olive groves away to his left of a large number of men in dusty, red jackets, black cocked hats and tall, knee-length boots. It was Le Marchant with four squadrons of the 5th Dragoon Guards. Lallemand rode back to inform General Peyremmont, commanding the 2nd Hussars, of the presence of enemy cavalry, but the latter arrogantly stated that, 'the officer commanding the British detachment must be a blockhead, and was throwing himself upon certain destruction'.[20] Apparently, Lallemand, a more experienced soldier, considered this far from the case, but Peyremmont continued advancing, unaware of the trap into which he was being lured.

The heavy dragoons had made their way unseen along the back of some heights to the south west of Villagarcia, picking their way over very rough and broken ground to appear on Lallemand's left flank. In fact, the ground was so difficult that the other two regiments of Le Marchant's brigade, the 3rd and 4th Dragoons, were unable to get up in time and took no part in the action. As Le Marchant looked out on to the rolling plain before him he saw, at a distance of about a quarter of a mile, the six squadrons of light cavalry being driven steadily back into a defile or enclosure formed of low stone walls, whereupon he quickly got his men through the olive groves and formed them in line for the charge. It was just as well that Le Marchant had arrived when he did, for things were beginning to get somewhat difficult for Ponsonby's light dragoons who were faced with around 2,300 French cavalry. Then, just as Ponsonby approached the wall, Cotton and the 16th Light Dragoons appeared behind him, on his right, trotting forward over a low hill. The 16th apparently took the wall in line, after which they charged the French head on.

William Tomkinson, of the 16th Light Dragoons, described the action in his diary:

When we came to the top of the hill, there were the 12th and 14th on our left, close in front of Villagarcia. The enemy formed a quarter of a mile from them, and a small stone wall betwixt the 16th (our regiment) and the French. We came down the hill in a trot, took the wall in line, and were in the act of charging when the 5th Dragoon Guards came down on our right, charged, and completely upset the left flank of the enemy, and the 12th and 14th, and 16th advancing at the same moment, the success was complete. The view of the enemy from the top of the hill, the quickness of the advance on the enemy, with the spirit of the men in leaping the wall, and the charge immediately afterwards, was one of the finest things I ever saw.[21]

It was indeed a formidable attack by the British cavalry. At the same time as the 16th leaped the wall Le Marchant and the 5th Dragoon Guards came charging down the hill from out of the olive groves to hit the French left flank with a mighty crash, the front ranks of the French dragoons being ridden down. Caught between these two attacks, Lallemand's cavalry were thrown back and completely broken by the power of this well-timed charge.[22] There followed a short but stiff fight as the French defended themselves against the blows of the powerful if unwieldy heavy cavalry swords and against the cuts of the far more superior light cavalry sabre, designed by Le Marchant himself. Indeed, Le Marchant must have viewed the combat with a great deal of satisfaction as it was almost certainly the first time he had seen his sabre used in action.

Lallemand's cavalry, being assailed on two sides and having now realised they had ridden into a trap, broke and fled in the direction of Llerena, where D'Erlon's infantry and artillery lay. They were pursued with much gusto by the British cavalry who cut and hacked at any French stragglers they came up with on the wide, rolling plain over which the pursuit took place. Indeed, the whole region makes for superb cavalry country and Cotton's men took full advantage of it, taking four officers and 132 men prisoner. Tomkinson again:

We pursued, and made some prisoners; and in the place of pushing them on, the enemy were allowed to form in rear of a ditch halfway between Villagarcia and Llerena. Here we delayed a little, when Sir Stapleton ordered the right and left squadrons, 16th (which had got together), down the road, turning the enemy's left flank. They did not halt one instant. The 12th and 14th advanced at the same time, and charged with three squadrons (12th). We drove them quite close to Llerena, and Cookson, of Captain Cocks' troop, was killed in the town. To check us, the enemy fired (from the ground they held with 10,000 infantry close to the left of Llerena) a few cannon shots over our heads, not daring to hit us, being so intermixed with their own people. . . The prisoners were dreadfully cut, and some will not recover. A French dragoon had his head nearer cut off than I ever saw before; it was by a sabre cut at the back of the neck.[23]

The pursuit went on for a full two miles before Lallemand drew his men up behind a large ditch, which caused Cotton to bring his men to a halt in order to have them reform. He then ordered two squadrons of the 16th Light Dragoons to get round the left flank of the French, whilst the 12th and 14th charged for a second time, supported by Le Marchant's heavy dragoons. Once again the French were sent flying and the pursuit ended only when French artillery opened fire on the British cavalry when they were almost at the gates of Llerena itself. Cotton then had the recall sounded, whereupon the whole retired with their prisoners to Villagarcia, having inflicted fifty-three casualties upon the French in addition to the prisoners taken, at a cost of just fourteen killed and thirty-seven wounded. Slade's brigade did not get forward in time and took no part in the action, described by Fortescue, as 'a brilliant little affair'.[24]

The action at Villagarcia throws up several issues as regards the performance of the British cavalry. First of all the planning was good. Cotton was quick to form his plan and seize upon the opportunity of attacking the French cavalry at Villagarcia. He was also quick to amend the plan once he discovered that Lallemand had withdrawn his main force from the village. However, where he did err was in the timing of Ponsonby's orders to wait until Le Marchant had got into position to threaten the French escape route to Llerena. The idea of taking the French force whole appears not to have entered his mind until his original orders had gone off to Ponsonby, and by the time the fresh orders reached him he had already become engaged with the enemy and thus the element of surprise was lost, as was the opportunity of cutting off Lallemand's retreat. He later blamed Ponsonby for engaging the enemy too soon, but one can hardly blame Ponsonby for this as he did not receive the new orders until it was too late. As it turned out, it could be argued that Le Marchant still had the opportunity to get behind Lallemand when the latter was engaged in driving Ponsonby back, but he revealed himself on the left flank of the French instead. Overall, the planning was good, therefore, as was Cotton's later idea. It was only the late despatch of his revised orders to Ponsonby which let him down, but this did not have any adverse effect on the outcome of the fight.

Once Cocks's squadrons had become engaged at Villagarcia the execution of the plan was without fault. The 12th and 14th Light Dragoons did their job, drawing the French into the trap whilst Cotton and the 16th remained out of sight. Le Marchant, too, did wonders in getting the 5th Dragoon Guards into position after a very tiring night march over very difficult ground. The hill to the south-west of Villagarcia is very broken and is far from ideal ground, and it is to his great credit that the men got forward into position in time to make the telling contribution to the victory. Cotton himself, having realised that his orders had not reached Ponsonby in time, proved flexible enough to be able to revert to his original plan, and brought the 16th Light Dragoons on to the field at the precise moment they were needed, and in good order, and with Le Marchant falling upon the left flank of the French at the same time, the attack was delivered with precision and was attended with great success.

The curse of the British cavalry in the Peninsula was, of course, its habit of engaging in a reckless pursuit of a beaten enemy. At Villagarcia there was again a lengthy pursuit of about five miles between that village and Llerena, including the halt at the ditch halfway between the two, and, indeed, Le Marchant actually ordered the recall to be sounded, wary no doubt of the failings of the 20th and 23rd Light Dragoons earlier in the war and of the fallout over the Campo Mayor affair the previous year. However, at Villagarcia there was no French reserve, other than the artillery and cavalry at Llerena, and the British cavalry was perfectly within its rights to pursue the beaten enemy as far as it did. Indeed, when Le Marchant ordered the recall to be sounded Tomkinson, of the 16th, pointed out to him the confusion the enemy were in and, no doubt aware of the absence of any French reserve, continued the pursuit. 'The desire of General Le Marchant to halt after the charge, my urging the men on, the enemy being in confusion; and his after acknowledgement that I was right. He said, "Halt, and form your men." I said, "The enemy are in greater confusion." "You must halt." "Must I call out, 'Halt'? I asked. Seeing the general hesitated (he would not give the order), I called to the men to come on, and we drove the enemy a mile, in the greatest confusion, into Llerena.'[25] This seems to me to be a flagrant breach of orders by Tomkinson, although in the event there was never any danger from French reserve cavalry. Furthermore, if there had been any French reserves, the British cavalry could have fallen back upon their own, as Slade's brigade was in support and had yet to be engaged.

It seems rather surprising that Villagarcia was not awarded either as a clasp on the General Service Medal, or the status of a battle honour. We have already discussed Paget's fine actions at Sahagun, which was indeed credited as a battle honour, and Benavente, which was awarded as a clasp, and yet the numbers involved at these actions were much smaller. Apparently, Wellington refused to allow medals or honours to be awarded for any actions which did not involve musketry,[26] which is curious given the awards accredited to both Benavente and Sahagun. But of course, Wellington was not there. Is this a further indication of his suspicious nature towards his cavalry? Villagarcia was just one of several fine cavalry combats which have undoubtedly been largely forgotten as a result of not being awarded their deserved honour, and whilst the men themselves would not have fought for medals or reward, it would be nice to think that the memory of their actions was perpetuated along with the better-known actions such as Sahagun and Benavente.

The last action which we shall examine in Estremadura came two months after Villagarcia and is at the heart of much of the myth surrounding the performance of the British cavalry in the Peninsula. In fact, it was, like Campo Mayor, so controversial that it demands examination in a separate chapter. The action was, of course, Maguilla.

Notes

1 Hon. J.W. Fortescue, *History of the British Army* (London, 1899), VIII: 141, says that the French regiments involved were those which had suffered at Campo Mayor, although Oman claims that only the 2nd Hussars were involved in the fight. Charles Oman, *History of the Peninsular War* (Oxford, 1902), IV: 277.

2 'The Diary of Lieutenant Charles Dudley Madden, 4th Dragoons, 1809-1811', *Journal of the Royal United Services Institution, 1914,* LVIII: 515.

3 T.H. McGuffie (Ed), *Peninsular Cavalry General: The Correspondence of Lieutenant General Robert Ballard Long* (London, 1951), 91.

4 Madden, *Diary,* 518.

5 See Jack Weller, *Wellington in the Peninsula* (London, 1962), 171, and Oman, IV: 372.

6 Fortescue, *British Army,* VIII: 186. Fortescue goes on to say, 'Beresford's accounts of his own proceedings at this period are so contradictory that it is safer to believe that he knew nothing and was doing nothing'. Ibid. 187. See also McGuffie, *Peninsular Cavalry General,* 104–5, for another accurate explanation of the events.

7 McGuffie, Peninsular Cavalry General, 106.

8 Not to be confused with Lieutenant Charles Madden, extracts from whose *Diary* are included in this chapter.

9 Long afterwards claimed that the 3rd Dragoon Guards were broken and in some confusion as they advanced, which prompted him to launch the 4th Dragoons, supported by the 13th Light Dragoons, adding that he gave the order personally as Lumley was away to the left and was probably unsighted. He also claimed that these were formed in line for the attack before the 3rd Dragoons. See McGuffie, *Peninsular Cavalry General,* 109 & 123. The point is not particularly relevant and is debatable, although if true certainly enhances Long's own part in the action. Madden makes no mention of it in his diary.

10 Madden, *Diary,* 521.

11 Oman, *Peninsular War,* IV: 411.

12 There are striking similarities between the fight at Usagre and the action at Venta del Pozo, during the retreat from Burgos on 23 October 1812, where Cotton's cavalry, after having pulled back to a position on one side of the Hormaza river, waited for the pursuing French cavalry to cross, only to find his guns masked by some British cavalry who were falling back. On this occasion the trap failed to work and the French cavalry, having gained the Allied-held bank of the Hormaza, were able to form and drive the Allies back. Perhaps this says even more about the planning and timing of Lumley's attack at Usagre.

13 N.L. Beamish, *King's German Legion* (London, 1837), II: 25. Oman, *Peninsular War,* V: 131, has two squadrons.

14 These figures are those quoted in Oman. His differ from Beamish and from those quoted in Barrett's *History of the 13th Hussars* (London, 1913), I: 165. They

are roughly equal, however, and do not make for any particularly contentious issue.

15 Gubbins. Quoted in Barrett's *History of the 13th Hussars*, I: 165.

16 The raid on Almaraz took place on 19 May 1812 and the Battle of St Pierre on 13 December 1813, the final day's fighting during the Battle of the Nive.

17 When Colborne's brigade was destroyed at Albuera it was still formed in line and had not seen the approaching French and Polish cavalry owing to a torrential rainstorm that suddenly occurred. The 31st Regiment, on Colborne's left flank – farthest away from the point of initial contact at Albuera – did have time to form square and consequently got off relatively unscathed.

18 Frederick Ponsonby, whom we have already met at Talavera, where he charged with the 23rd Light Dragoons, commanded the brigade in the absence of George Anson, who had gone home on sick leave.

19 It seems hard to believe that it was possible to see this distance, but the country is very flat and with no heat haze, and with a good telescope, ten miles was no great distance to distinguish enemy troops. For an interesting discussion of period telescopes see Appendix IV in the Reverend Edmund Warre's edited version of Lt. Gen. William Warre's *Letters from the Peninsula, 1808–1812* (Staplehurst, 1999), 209–11.

20 Denis Le Marchant (Ed), *Memoirs of the late Major-General Le Marchant* (London, 1841), 213.

21 Lt Col W. Tomkinson, *Diary of a Cavalry Officer, in the Peninsular and Waterloo Campaigns, 1809–1815* (London, 1894), 150.

22 According to Fortescue, *British Army*, VIII: 414, the first charge of the 5th Dragoon Guards, who were blown after their long march, was beaten back by French carbine fire, forcing them to reform and charge a second time, which charge succeeded. It is not mentioned by Tomkinson, however, who charged with the 16th Light Dragoons, nor does Le Marchant make any mention of two charges.

23 Tomkinson, *Diary*, 150–1.

24 Fortescue, *British Army*, VIII: 415.

25 Tomkinson, *Diary*, 153.

26 P.F. Stewart, *History of the 12th Lancers* (London, 1950), 71.

CHAPTER VI

Maguilla: The 'Unluckiest' Cavalry Combat of the Peninsular War

There is often a very narrow margin between success and failure, and at Villagarcia the fortunes of war were firmly with Cotton who managed to get all the elements of his plan to combine on time and give him a fine victory. Had Le Marchant been late or lost his way things may have fallen out rather differently. But such is war. Just to prove how narrow the margin is we must move on exactly two months to June 1812 and the notorious combat of Maguilla, called by Oman, 'the unluckiest combat that was ever fought by the British cavalry during the Peninsular War.'[1] It is also a combat which is shrouded in controversy, with the various accounts of the action being at odds with each other. It is also of great importance when we consider Wellington's damning verdict on the business, a verdict which has cast a cloud over the whole of the British cavalry and which has since had a great influence on the study and reputation of the British cavalry in the Peninsula. The action at Maguilla, therefore, like that at Campo Mayor, demands much deeper analysis than it is generally afforded.

The central figure was General John Slade, whom we have met on several occasions already in this book. Indeed, he had played a minor role at Villagarcia. His brigade consisted of the 1st (Royal) Dragoons, the 3rd Dragoon Guards and the 4th Dragoon Guards; although this latter regiment played no part at Maguilla. The fight came about shortly after Hill, who was still maintaining the Allied presence in the south, had, on 3 June 1812, established his headquarters at Zafra, just over forty miles south-east of Badajoz. Just over fifty miles farther to the east lay the small town of Fuenteovejuna, where D'Erlon had likewise established his headquarters after having fallen back from Medellin on the Guadiana. Hill decided to keep the pressure on D'Erlon and resolved to follow him, whereupon he sent Penne Villemur's Spanish cavalry off in reconnaissance from Llerena in the direction of Azuaga and Fuenteovejuna in order to collect the harvest of Estremadura. Supporting the Spaniards on their left flank was Slade, who started out farther north from Llera in the direction of Maguilla and Granja, apparently with orders not to 'commit himself to any serious engagement.'[2] By a strange quirk of fate, D'Erlon had sent out a strong cavalry force from Granja, heading in the direction of Llera by way of Maguilla, the French cavalry being commanded again by Lallemand. The two opposing sides were, therefore, placed unwittingly upon a collision course by their respective commanders. Lallemand started from Granja on 10 June with around 800 men of the 17th and 27th Dragoons and the following morning had reached Valencia de las Torres, about five miles south of Llera from where Slade, having received news of the French approach, got his own brigade, some 700 men of the 1st (Royals) and 3rd Dragoon Guards, under orders and began to march to meet them.

The exact details of the action at Maguilla are sketchy at best, and it is not clear where the two fights actually took place, although we do know the routes taken by each side prior to the action and the ground over which Slade's pursuit and Lallemand's counter-attack took place. There are certainly no maps or sketches. The account published here follows the accepted version of events fairly closely, in which Slade, after having broken Lallemand, pursues him for a few miles before being brought up at the defile at Maguilla where the French reserve comes into action, prompting a speedy flight by Slade. Oman and Fortescue differ in their accounts[3] and, indeed, the accounts by these great historians would appear to contradict those of the actual participants who place the fight at Maguilla. Nevertheless, we can be fairly certain of the sequence of events which led to the fiasco. First of all Lallemand, no doubt wary of British cavalry tactics since Villagarcia two months before, advanced with just one of his regiments, the 17th Dragoons, and soon came across Slade's picquets close to a wood, somewhere between Valencia de las Torres and Llera, in which the latter's main force was drawn up. Whether or not Lallemand suspected another trap is not clear but he turned around and began to draw off at a fairly quick pace in the direction of Valencia de las Torres and Maguilla, with his own picquets skirmishing with Slade's. It may well have been during this phase of the action that Slade attacked, which he claims to have done in his report to Lord Hill.[4] Both Fortescue and Tomkinson, of the 16th Light Dragoons, neither of them an eye-witness, have the bulk of the French casualties occurring at this point. However, Slade then states that he pursued Lallemand for about three leagues, 'to within a short distance of Maguilla', where he charged again, this time breaking the French line and killing and wounding several enemy cavalry, as well as securing many prisoners. Radclyffe, who was present with the 1st (Royals), also claims the main fight took place at Maguilla, where he says 'nothing could have been more successful than this charge at first, the enemy losing ground and losing many men'. Oman las Lallemand turning to fight close to Maguilla, which is probably correct, but then has Slade pursuing him for 'several miles' until they passed the defile at Maguilla, which is a contradiction in itself. Slade could hardly have fought 'close' to Maguilla if he then pursued Lallemand for several miles before finally reaching Maguilla.[5]

It is evident from the accounts of both Radclyffe and Slade that there had been a substantial clash of piquets before Lallemand drew off towards Maguilla, several miles away. This must have been the pursuit phase. Then, when Maguilla was reached, Lallemand was charged again by Slade, and another fight took place. Now, whether the bulk of the French casualties occurred during the initial fight, as claimed by Fortescue, Tomkinson and Oman, or at Maguilla, as claimed by Radclyffe and Slade, is not certain. If we believe Radclyffe, who, after all, was there with the 1st (Royals), the main fight undoubtedly occurred at Maguilla. Indeed, Radclyffe claims that he begged Slade not to allow Lallemand to reach the broken ground around Maguilla before charging him. Slade apparently rejected his pleas and did charge the French at the village, close to 'the uneven ground by the river'.[6] What is certain, however, is that from start to finish Slade pursued the French for about eight miles, from close to Valencia de las Torres to the defile of Maguilla, where the French reserves were waiting. This is backed up by Slade's statement that, during the fight at Maguilla itself, a captain of the 27th Dragoons was taken, and it was the 27th that provided Lallemand's reserve. Both Oman and Fortescue have the 'wild and reckless' pursuit taking place between the first fight, during which they claim the majority of French casualties occurred, and the defile at Maguilla. In the event, it really matters little where the main fight took place. The fact remains that, whether it occurred close to Valencia or at Maguilla, Slade pursued Lallemand for about eight miles between the two, before coming up against the French reserve which lay in wait beyond the defile of Maguilla.

It was at this point that Slade's problems really began, for his men were blown after their long ride during which they had evidently engaged the French at least twice. According to Radclyffe the main fight, which he says took place at Maguilla, was going well when suddenly, a shout went up, 'look to the right', which was passed from mouth to mouth upon the appearance of Lallemand's reserve. Interestingly enough, Radclyffe goes on to say that the French reserve was drawn up not for the purpose of attacking Slade, but to cover the flight of the beaten French cavalry who were 'flying in all directions'. Their sudden appearance then caused panic in the British ranks. 'All was now confused. Every man turned and made for the rear, and for a few seconds the extraordinary sight was to be seen of two forces running away from each other.'[7] The French appreciation of the situation was obviously quicker than Slade's, however, for with the arrival on the field of the 27th Dragoons, the 17th Dragoons turned and together the two regiments charged in pursuit of both the Royals and the 3rd Dragoon Guards, and it was during this pursuit that Slade lost all control and the damage was really done. Captain Hulton's squadron had been kept back as a reserve and in fact charged Lallemand, checking him, if only very briefly, before himself being forced to turn and retreat after looking round 'to see where his support was' but seeing none present was forced to 'yield to circumstances and put threes about'.[8] The French quickly released the prisoners who had been taken by Slade earlier in the fight, in addition to taking two officers and 116 men themselves from the fleeing British regiments. Slade's brigade also suffered twenty-two killed and twenty-six wounded.

During the pursuit, Slade was seen riding in all directions, begging his men to remain with him and fight. In fact, it is said that he went so far as to offer £50 to any man who would stand with him, not that any did. Instead, Slade and a few of his officers were left, desperately trying to rally their men, but to no avail. They were hell bent on survival and would not stop to fight for anybody. Lallemand's dragoons pursued the British for about eight miles, chasing them back the way they had come, although it is doubtful whether the pursuit was conducted at any great pace, given the distances that the majority of the combatants had already ridden that day. Only the 27th Dragoons were anything like fresh. It was during this phase of the action that the majority of the British losses were sustained, as is always the case when one exposes one's back to an enemy. Indeed, there is nothing a cavalryman likes better than the sight of a fleeing enemy. When Slade reached Valencia de las Torres the pursuit and the fighting came to a halt. It was then time for the repercussions to begin.

The combat of Maguilla quickly became the talk of Hill's army, as did Slade's report of the affair to Hill in which he praised the gallantry of both his officers and men. The report was considered a joke by the army, whilst his report to Cotton was mockingly referred to by Tomkinson as, 'the best I ever saw'.[9] Slade's report to Hill hardly does justice to the episode, mentioning the advance of the French, the initial fight, the main fight at Maguilla and the French counter-attack. He did, however, hit upon the root cause of the fiasco: 'the enemy brought up a support, and my troops being too eager in pursuit, we were obliged to relinquish a great number of prisoners which we had taken, and to fall back on this place [Llera].'[10] He then sent a second report to Hill accompanying the casualty return. Again, he left out the bulk of the story and added that, 'our misfortunes arose from too great eagerness and zeal in the pursuit, after having broke the enemy's first line, each regiment vying with each other who should most distinguish itself, which gave him an opportunity of bringing up fresh troops, and of charging us at a time when we were in confusion.'[11] It as not a good report and merely confirmed many officers' beliefs that Slade, 'a byword for ineptitude in the army', was not fit for command.

Maguilla was ultimately the most discreditable cavalry fight of the war, with Slade's men demonstrating everything that was wrong with the British cavalry in the Peninsula. And yet it was, as Oman himself said, an 'unlucky affair', which could have been quite the reverse had Slade demonstrated just a modicum of control over his men. It is interesting to note how Oman has treated Maguilla in comparison with Campo Mayor. This latter action he condemns unequivocally as a complete failure. However, with support from Beresford, it could have been a great success, as we have seen in the chapter which deals with the action. In my opinion Maguilla was by far the greater disappointment as no factors were involved other than a failure by those present. It was completely down to Slade, whereas the 13th Light Dragoons at Campo Mayor were badly let down by Beresford. And yet, Oman calls Maguilla 'unlucky'. One cannot help feeling that Oman reveals a certain lack of consistency in his treatment of the British cavalry, unlike Fortescue who shows a far greater appreciation of the situation and a more balanced view.

The whole affair was, in many ways, a reversal of the situation at Villagarcia, with Slade being lured into an ambush instead of Lallemand. At Maguilla, Lallemand showed a great deal of caution, probably due to his experience at Villagarcia two months earlier, and wisely drew off at the approach of Slade's two regiments. There was evidently some sort of fight at this point, although as I have already pointed out, the evidence does not indicate whether or not this was the main fight. If it was, Slade made a grave mistake in pursuing instead of securing his prisoners, reforming and returning to Llera having satisfied himself with a job well done. The matter almost certainly would have rested at this point but for the pursuit of Lallemand to Maguilla.[13] Slade's second mistake, once he embarked upon the pursuit, was in rejecting the advice of officers like Radclyffe, who advised him to attack Lallemand before he could reach Maguilla. The ground over which the pursuit took place forms a wide open plain, with few positions affording any advantage to either side, but Slade had the French on the run and outnumbered them at this point. Hence, the advantage lay firmly with him. Radclyffe obviously knew the area fairly well as his regiment had spent much time patrolling as far as Berlanga as well as in the vicinity of Maguilla. Here the ground is very broken, with its south and west covered by a defile, a small river, with a narrow bridge across it. The ground would certainly not allow any room for the deployment of large numbers of cavalry.[14] It is interesting to note that, in the various accounts of the action at Maguilla, there is only one mention of the river, although, of course, this may be what is referred to as the defile. The obvious route from Valencia de las Torres to Maguilla is, therefore, to the west of the town if one wishes to avoid this steep defile. Radclyffe knew this but was unsuccessful in trying to persuade Slade not to pursue Lallemand that far. But perhaps Slade's greatest error was in not deploying the 3rd Dragoon Guards a good way in rear of the 1st (Royals) as his reserve. Upon the appearance of the 27th Dragoons he could have fallen back upon them, in accordance with accepted practice. By allowing the 3rd Dragoon Guards to charge and get involved in the fight at Maguilla he deprived himself of this most vital element, and so had nothing to fall back upon, save for Hulton's squadron of the Royals which appears to have been kept back almost as an afterthought, rather than as a pre-determined reserve. The image of Slade riding about in an attempt to get his men to stand is a somewhat sad and pathetic one, although it is hard to imagine his brigade being able to withstand the enemy attack even if they had stood and fought as the ascendancy was firmly with the French, one regiment of which was fresh, having not endured the pursuit from Valencia de las Torres to Maguilla. It is perhaps a measure of the bad situation in which the troopers found themselves that, despite having already broken the French cavalry on two occasions, they were not willing to stand and fight once they realised the predicament they were in.

It is interesting to note what the officers of the 1st (Royals) thought of the Maguilla business, for no sooner had they dusted themselves down than they began a post-mortem into the cause of the fiasco. Slade, naturally, was the centre of their findings, and for a number of reasons. Some thought he should have charged sooner, which was what Radclyffe thought, whilst others blamed him for not organising a reserve. Both were correct of course, but no amount of good planning could compensate for the loss of morale and confidence that the Royals displayed during the fight, something which must have been quite disturbing amongst the army, given the fact that the British cavalry had beaten their French counterparts on numerous occasions in stand-up fights in the Peninsula. Why should they suddenly turn and bolt like frightened rabbits at the mere sight of just one French regiment of dragoons? The answer almost certainly lies in the steady erosion of morale amongst the men, something which was noted by the regimental historian, Atkinson, who wrote, 'Slade's responsibility lies less in his tactical errors on June 11th than on his undermining of the regiment's morale before the action, for which Erskine must share the blame.'[15] The regimental *Journal*, compiled from entries made by officers who served in the Peninsula, supports this view, blaming 'the bad education received from Slade, the poison of which had slowly and silently gained ground'.[16] Atkinson, drawing on the *Journal*, went on to write that the misfortune at Maguilla was,

> mainly to be attributed to the mishandling of Slade and Erskine. Nervous, excitable and irresolute, Erskine was in constant alarm of an attack on his cavalry screen. He 'would order picquets in every direction but that from which danger was to be expected', and then abuse Brigadiers, Staff officers and Colonels for not carrying out his express orders. The merest rumour of a French advance would make him decamp without waiting for it to be confirmed. Slade was equally liable to sudden alarms. 'No sooner was it announced that the French were in motion, no matter where or at what distance, than an order was given to turn out, Jack [Slade] running about crying out, "Bridle up, bridle up. The first dozen men for God's sake. God

damn you, trumpeters: blow, damn you. Haste, haste. Gallop. God damn you, Corporal, tell those fellows to turn out and never mind telling off. Turn out, turn out: the baggage to Azinshal." The consequence was that all was confusion: curbs were lost, surcingles were forgot, some of the men threw away their corn, others in the act of cooking threw aside their tins and meat and camp-kettles, while the batmen with the baggage half-tied on, by dint of beating, urged stubborn brutes into a jog.[17]

'By fidgeting and worrying the men,' wrote Atkinson, 'and by disturbing and depressing them with false alarms and unnecessary retreats, they [Slade and Erskine] had robbed them of their confidence and of their sense of superiority over their enemies.'[18] We can well understand this as Slade's odd behaviour had not gone unnoticed by either Sir John Moore or Lord Paget during the Corunna campaign during the winter of 1808–9.

A more sympathetic, if a little self-satisfied, view was expressed by Robert Ballard Long, himself a victim of misunderstanding and controversy following his fight at Campo Mayor the previous year. Writing to his brother, Charles Beckford Long, he wrote:

This circumstance compared with what we have lost has of course created some regret, and will give rise, I doubt not, to much malicious remark and insinuation. The failure is, in my opinion, decidedly to be attributed to the indiscreet manner in which the reserve or supporting body was conducted, for they cease to fulfil that character the moment they join in the attack or pursuit of an enemy's rear-guard, and in doing so advance so far and with such speed, as to destroy all order, blow their horses, and necessarily become the prey of fresh troops brought against them. General Slade it appears observed this error, and endeavoured to provide against the consequences by directing a squadron on the right of his line to halt and stand fast, but by some fatality the order was not complied with, and consequently the men, when obliged to turn about, found nothing to rally upon, and therefore continued their flight to what may be considered an unfortunate and perhaps disgraceful distance. Thus you see how much depends with us upon the Chapter of Accidents, and how much we are the creatures of chance. A day that promised to be a brilliant one, and if successful would have established Slade's fame for ever, has turned against him, and left only recollections of the most painful description.

And no doubt with Campo Mayor in mind, Long went on:

I know from experience how difficult it is to contain a British victorious cavalry in sight of a fugitive enemy, and I know equally well how much better the enemy has his men under his hands than we. Knowing this, although I must lament with others the result of this unfortunate day, I do not see what

Slade could do more to prevent it than he did, for in all such affairs, which are more or less extensive, one man cannot be everywhere to control every individual, and of course something must be left to, and depend upon, the discretion of others.[19]

Long's impressions were not too far off the mark and he certainly makes one or two very valid observations. However, what he does not take into account is the deeper effect that Slade's constant 'fidgeting and worrying' had had on the men's morale. It is one thing to lament the absence of formed reserves etc., but when the men have had their confidence stripped away it matters little. Such appears to have been the case with the 1st (Royals). Slade's reports to Hill and Cotton were quite inadequate and reflect his pale attempts, not to cover up the affair, but certainly to minimise the fiasco by mentioning the good conduct of some of his officers. However, the total lack of control demonstrated by them and by himself serves only to bring them discredit. Ultimately, any lengthy discussion of Slade's report is neither here nor there as the deed was already done and it is not my intention to enter into any deep discussion of it. The importance of Maguilla lies in the analysis of the fight itself.

Although it was the talk of the army, the unhappy affair at Maguilla might have been laid to rest had not a furious Hill been moved to hold an inquiry into the business, the findings of which were passed on to Wellington himself. Craufurd endured but survived much criticism of his handling of the bungled affair at Villar de Puerco in July 1810, and maybe Slade could have done likewise. However, Wellington could not disguise his extreme displeasure when he read the reports of the affair, and his damning comments afterwards have since become almost universally quoted by generations of historians when referring to the alleged ineffectiveness of the British cavalry in the Peninsula. The passage is worth quoting in full, as it has had such an influence on the reputation of the British cavalry.

To Lieut. General Sir R. Hill, KB
    Salamanca, 18th June 1812[20]
My Dear Hill,
I have received your letters of the 13th and 14th. I have never been more annoyed than by General Slade's affair, and I entirely concur with you in the necessity of enquiring into it. It is occasioned entirely by the trick our officers of cavalry have acquired of galloping at everything, and their galloping back as fast as they gallop on the enemy. They never consider their situation, never think of manoeuvring before an enemy; so little that one would think they cannot manoeuvre, excepting on Wimbledon Common; and when they use their arm as it ought to be used, viz., offensively, they never keep nor provide for a reserve.

All cavalry should charge in two lines, of which one should be in reserve; if obliged to charge in one line, part of the line, at least one-third, should be ordered beforehand to pull up, and form in the second line, as soon as the charge should be given, and the enemy has been broken and has retired. The Royals and the 3rd Dragoon Guards were the best regiments in the cavalry in this country, and it annoys me particularly that the misfortune has happened to them. I do not wonder at the French boasting of it; it is the greatest blow they have struck.[21]

Such was the caustic nature of Wellington's comments that they have since tended to prevent any rational analysis of the cavalry's performance. Successive historians have seized upon the passage, taking the easy option of utilising the phrase and blowing it up out of all proportion in relation to the actual damage done to the cavalry at Maguilla. It has become one of the most oft-quoted of Wellington's remarks and, indeed, forms the title of this very book, although it is hoped that these pages afford a far more sober analysis of the British cavalry than is usually to be found. Indeed, I cringe whenever historians arrive at the point where they have to deal with Wellington's cavalry, for we are almost universally treated to the words 'Campo Mayor', 'Maguilla' and 'galloping at everything'. This is not only short-sighted but betrays a marked lack of research into the subject. The inescapable fact remains that Maguila was a great calamity for the British cavalry, attended not only by a measure of bad luck but by an overwhelming display of ineptitude on the part of Slade who, despite his showing at Maguilla, remained in command of his brigade for a further year. But to use the affair as a typical example of the exploits of the British cavalry in the Peninsula is not only unfair to them but is totally inaccurate.

To be fair to Wellington he was only stating the obvious when pointing out to Hill the prerequisites for a correct cavalry charge. In an ideal world, these should occur on every occasion and, indeed, would occur in the Peninsula. Sadly, the misadventures of the British cavalry in the Peninsula were usually attended by a lack of such a reserve. We have seen, there was no such reserve at Vimeiro or Talavera, two other disasters which he himself had witnessed. Conversely, there was a reserve at Los Santos, Villagarcia, Usagre and Benavente, for example. There was even a reserve at Campo Mayor, although as we have seen, Beresford refused to allow it forward. To tar his entire cavalry with the same brush after Maguilla was unfair to the majority of his cavalry who had turned in much good work in the Peninsula although, significantly, Wellington was not present during the majority of the successful actions and had been relying heavily on his infantry up until this point. Another factor which contributed to Wellington's annoyance was, as he himself stated, that the two regiments involved were the best in the country. The question of just which was the best regiment is open to debate, of course, as is always the case when one ventures to make such a statement – some of the light cavalry regiments, for example, had been turning in consistently good performances – but one can understand the logic behind Wellington's statement. Ultimately, I think Maguilla was one mishap too many for Wellington and, coming as it did at the beginning of the important Salamanca campaign, it was the last thing he needed. He had a perfect right to be angry, and with some justification, but for historians to take his despatch and forever trot it out whenever an opinion of the British cavalry is required is to do them a great disservice and to make a generalisation of the true facts.

The postscript to the whole sorry saga came two days after the fight at Maguilla when Slade received information that twenty of his men, taken prisoner and too badly wounded to be moved, had been left at Maguilla when the French retired. Undaunted by his experiences two days before, Slade decided to send a small unit to the village to bring them away. The unit consisted of fifty men from the 1st (Royals) and the 3rd Dragoon Guards, the two units involved in the Maguilla fight, under the command of two officers, a Lieutenant Strenowitz, of the latter regiment, and Lieutenant Bridges, of the Royals. The party duly arrived and were preparing to move off with their wounded when some locals appeared, informing them that a large body of French cavalry were approaching the village on a foraging expedition. Bearing in mind the repercussions that followed the fight at the village two days earlier, Strenowitz would have been forgiven if he had saddled up and moved out of the place. However, he decided that here was an opportunity to strike back at the French and quickly got his men under cover of a wall and waited. The French duly arrived at the village, whereupon Strenowitz launched the fifty British heavy dragoons at the surprised French cavalry who, taken unawares, were very badly mauled and pursued for some distance before Strenowitz ordered the recall to be sounded. The French suffered several killed and wounded as well as about twenty prisoners, whilst the British wounded who had been left at Maguilla were brought back. Thus, the debacle at Maguilla on 11 June had been, in part, avenged and without the reckless pursuit of two days earlier. Indeed, Fortescue was moved to write, 'This brilliant little enterprise did something to redeem the fame of the British horse.'[22]

The action at Maguilla was the last of the real cavalry actions in the south under Beresford and Hill. There were still one or two good little fights, such as that at Albuera, close to the old battlefield, on 1 July, and at Ribera on 24 July where Long surprised Lallemand and 'made him pay dearly for his lunch'. This latter action featured Long's cavalry, the 2nd Hussars KGL, and the 9th and 13th Light Dragoons, with some horse artillery and four squadrons of Portuguese cavalry. Ribera lies at the foot of a low range of hills and is covered by a small river. Lallemand had occupied the place but gave up all of the high ground above the river without a fight, thus opening the way for Campbell's Portuguese cavalry to get across, upon which Long brought forward his horse artillery which played upon the French to good effect. The French soon began to give way and, once the river had been passed by Long's cavalry, they turned and fled with the British and KGL cavalry in hot pursuit. The pursuit, in fact, went on for over six miles over very broken ground, but it was never of the reckless sort, with Long handling his cavalry well and ordering the recall before his men became too blown. The fight cost the French thirty-nine killed and as many wounded, whilst eighteen men were taken prisoner. Long reckoned his own casualties to have been just seven Portuguese.[23]

Two days before Long's action at Ribera, Wellington gave Marmont a real drubbing at Salamanca, and when Skerrett took Seville the following month affairs in the south began to take a turn for the worse for the French. Wellington entered the Spanish capital, Madrid, on 12 August, and the following month sent orders to Hill to cross the Guadiana at Almaraz and join him farther north. Hill arrived at Aranjuez during the first week of October, by which time Wellington was engaged in the abortive siege of Burgos. The operations of the main Allied army under Wellington in 1812 are dealt with in the next chapter.

The Allied army would never return to the area south of the Guadiana, and there would be no repeat of the series of cavalry actions which took place in Estremadura. The area was one of the few regions in the Peninsula where cavalry could operate effectively, and it is no coincidence that so many of the actions, both successful and unsuccessful, were fought in the area. The wide open, undulating plains of Estremadura gave way to the plains of Leon and Castille, but the army would not fight at all across these vast plains as it would be engaged in the terrible retreat from Burgos, which ended in November 1812 on the Portuguese border. When the Vittoria campaign began in May 1813 there would be little scope for cavalry action, other than at Morales de Toro, and with the Pyrenees beyond, Wellington's cavalry were destined for a long period of relative inactivity. The period of greatest interest to us had come to an end and a new phase of the war had begun.

Notes

1 Sir Charles Oman, *History of the Peninsular War* (Oxford, 1902), V: 522.
2 Sir J W Fortescue, *History of the British Army* (London, 1899), VIII: 451.
3 Fortescue's account of Maguilla makes no mention of any reckless pursuit and has Slade pursuing only after the initial fight. He then has Lallemand being pursued to Maguilla, beyond which the French had drawn up their reserves. Both Slade and Ratcliffe, an officer with the 1st (Royals), place the main fight at Maguilla and, significantly, neither makes any mention of any reckless pur-

suit afterwards. Tomkinson, on the other hand, places the main fight a good distance before Maguilla with the pursuit and mauling of Slade coming at the village itself where he says that the French had placed a chasseur regiment in reserve. Tomkinson, however, was not an eyewitness and, certainly, no mention is made anywhere else of a regiment of French chasseurs. Oman's account also has the main fight at Maguilla but then introduces the reckless pursuit, which he claims went on for several miles, which is rather ludicrous. Based upon eyewitness accounts, I would suggest that the first clash came a good way before Maguilla, with the main fight between (*Wellington's Despatches*, IX: 242), in which he says the first charge was made near Valencia with the second clash coming at the defile of Maguilla. Oman, on the other hand, has Lallemand turning to fight at Maguilla with Slade's pursuit of the beaten French going far beyond the town, for several miles in fact, which is quite ludicrous. The point at which Lallemand's reserves came upon the Royals is undoubtedly very close to Maguilla, probably to the south of the town, where the broken ground gives way to an undulating plain. See Fortescue, *History of the British Army*, VIII, 451–3, and Oman, *History of the Peninsular War*, V: 523.

4 Slade to Hill, Llera, 11 June 1812, *Supplementary Despatches, Correspondence and Memoranda of Field Marshal Arthur Duke of Wellington* (London, 1857), VII: 348.

5 See Oman, *History of the Peninsular War*, V: 523.

6 CT. Atkinson, *History of the Royal Dragoons, 1661–1934* (Glasgow, 1935), 279–80.

7 Ibid. 279.

8 Ibid. 279.

9 James Tomkinson (Ed), *Diary of a Cavalry Officer, in the Peninsular and Waterloo Campaigns, 1809–1815* (London, 1894), 173.

10 Slade to Hill, 11 June 1812, Supp. *Despatches*, VII: 348.

11 Slade to Hill. 12 June 1812, Supp. *Despatches*, VII: 348. 243.

12 Bragge, of the 3rd Dragoons, actually calls the episode an 'ambuscade'. SAC. Cassels (Ed), *Peninsular Portrait, 1811–1814: The letters of Captain William Bragge, Third (King's Own) Dragoons* (London, 1963), 55.

13 Oman in his *History of the Peninsular War*, V: 523, comments that the pursuit was as reckless as that of the 13th Light Dragoons at Campo Mayor the preceding year. This is simply not the case, however, as was demonstrated in the chapter on the action at Campo Mayor. The circumstances which, at first glance, may appear to have been similar, were in fact far different.

14 Apparently, one officer of the Royals, Radclyffe, begged Slade not to allow Lallemand to reach the broken ground in front of Maguilla before he charged. Unfortunately, Slade attacked at that precise point. Atkinson, *Royal Dragoons*, 278–9.

15 Ibid. 280.

16 Ibid. 280.

17 Ibid. 276–7.

18 Ibid. 279.

19 Long, in McGuffie, *Peninsular Cavalry General*, 196.

20 It is quite ironic that exactly three years on from the date of this Despatch, Wellington would see his heavy cavalry repeat the same old failings on the

field of Waterloo, the 1st (Royal) Dragoons being one of the regiments present on that great day.

21 Wellington to Hill, 18 June 1812, *Despatches*, IX: 238. The reference to the 1st (Royal) Dragoons as being one of the best cavalry regiments in the Peninsula did little to ease the regiment's pain after Maguilla. Atkinson calls the fight, 'the most disastrous incident of their five years in the Peninsula'. Atkinson, *Royal Dragoons*, 276.

22 Fortescue, *History of the British Army*, VIII: 453.

23 For accounts of the neat little action see McGuffie, *Peninsular Cavalry General*, 206–7, and C.R.B. Barrett, *History of the 13th Hussars* (London, 1911), I: 181–2.

CHAPTER VII

Mixed Fortunes: From Salamanca to Burgos and Back

We last saw Wellington and his main field army settling down for the winter as 1811 came to a close, for it was traditionally a time when armies stopped campaigning and went into cantonments. But not this winter. Wellington, the man regarded by the French as the epitome of a defensive-minded and cautious general, was poised to strike at Ciudad Rodrigo, the fortress town which controlled the northern corridor between Portugal and Spain. Preparations were well under way for the siege as the last days of December dwindled away, and all that remained was for Wellington to fix the exact time for his advance. The window of opportunity was suddenly opened to him by the withdrawal of around 18,000 French troops under Dorsenne, who marched east to assist Suchet in his struggle against the Spaniards at Valencia. Wellington was quick to seize the opportunity and by 8 January 1812 his men were encircling Ciudad Rodrigo. The history of the sieges in the Peninsula was not unlike that of the cavalry, being an unsatisfactory business at times, punctuated with bloody but successful assaults. And so it proved at Ciudad Rodrigo which was by far the most successful siege. Indeed, the town was stormed after just eleven days of open trenches, and all this in freezing conditions.[1] Wellington's men laboured under the disadvantage of not having enough tools for the job, but when it was time for the place to be stormed on the night of 19 January the 3rd and Light Divisions made short work of it, gaining access to the town without too much difficulty. Control of the vital northern corridor was, therefore, safe in Wellington's hands, and he now turned his attention to the mighty fortress of Badajoz which controlled the southern corridor, a town that had denied him in 1811 and would come close to doing so again when he marched south to lay siege to it in March.

There was, naturally, little for the British cavalry to do throughout the siege of Ciudad Rodrigo, other than keeping a watchful, eye out for any French force which might interfere with the siege operations. As it turned out, Ciudad Rodrigo was left to its fate by Marmont, who did nothing to prevent its falling into Allied hands. For the next few weeks the cavalry was employed in maintaining not only a screen of outposts, but a sufficiently strong presence to give the impression that Wellington's army was still close to Ciudad Rodrigo, whereas it had begun to slip away to the south during the first few days of February. Marmont knew soon enough of the move, however, and after leaving Ciudad Rodrigo in the care of a Spanish garrison, Wellington moved his cavalry south, and by the middle of March they were engaged in the covering operations at Badajoz, once more watching for any offensive movements by the French who might try and relieve the place.

There was no snow or ice at Badajoz but the conditions throughout the siege were much worse, the rain falling in torrents for days on end, making for a thoroughly miserable existence for the infantry digging away in the parallels or 'trenches' as they were called. Indeed, the conditions endured by their descendants in Flanders a century later were not dissimilar to those before Badajoz. Of course, there was no heavy artillery or trench raids, but there was still plenty of shot and shell to kill and maim, whilst the French made one very effective sortie, filling in and destroying as much of the works as was possible during their short raid. The siege of Badajoz came to a terrible climax on the night of 6 April when the 3rd, 4th, 5th and Light Divisions stole forward in the darkness to begin one of the most awesome and horrendous episodes in the history of the British Army.[2] No fewer than forty assaults were made on the breaches, and not one of them met with any success. Instead, each attack was bloodily repulsed, leaving behind an ever-increasing pile of dead and wounded British and Portuguese soldiers. Incredibly, the 3rd Division, making a supposed diversionary attack by escalade at the castle, managed to get over the walls, whereupon resistance began to tail off, and when the 5th Division managed to do likewise on the other side of town, all French resistance ended and the town was won. But at such a cost. No fewer than 3,500 casualties were sustained during the assault, mainly by the 4th and Light Division at the breaches. It was such a bloody episode that even Wellington wept when he saw the shattered remains of the cream of his army in the breaches on the morning after the storming. By this time the victorious, maddened troops were venting their fury on the town and its inhabitants, an orgy of violence, destruction and debauchery that lasted a full seventy-two hours before they exhausted themselves and returned to their camps. It is difficult to defend their behaviour, but perhaps they deserved to sack the town after having gone above and beyond the call of duty in taking the place. Certainly, some of the men claimed that their officers had promised them the pleasure of sacking the town should they be successful in their attacks. Nevertheless, Badajoz was won, and with both corridors in his hands Wellington could set his mind to an advance deeper into Spain.

The obvious route was along the Guadiana and up the valley of the Tagus, but before Wellington could move he received information that

Marmont was threatening Ciudad Rodrigo once more. This news did not cause him any great alarm as he knew that Marmont possessed no siege train, it having been taken when Ciudad Rodrigo fell. Nevertheless, he decided to return north, and by doing so set in motion the chain of events that was to lead to the Battle of Salamanca, the one battle in the Peninsula where the British cavalry proved just how destructive and decisive they could be when the fates were with them.

Wellington arrived before Ciudad Rodrigo on 24 April, and on 13 June began his advance upon Salamanca with an army of around 43,000 men. On 17 June he reached Salamanca but discovered that, although Marmont had retreated to the north, the French had left 800 men in the town manning three strong forts, La Merced, San Vicente and San Gaetano, all of which proved a great nuisance before they fell on 27 June after being besieged by Clinton's 6th Division. Wellington, meanwhile, headed north with his main field army, and on 21 June took up a position along a low range of hills at San Christobal. Here, Wellington outnumbered Marmont by around 8,000 men and hoped the French commander would attack him, for not only did he have numerical superiority but he had chosen a wonderful position. There is nothing between San Christobal and the Douro but wide open plains and nothing for Marmont to fall back upon in the event of a failed attack. It is wonderful cavalry country and, indeed, Wellington is reputed to have said, 'It's damned tempting. I've a good mind to attack 'em.' It was not to be, however, and after some skirmishing Marmont withdrew to the northern bank of the Douro. The Salamanca campaign was one of great movement with Marmont continually trying to outflank Wellington. The manoeuvring began on 16 July when Marmont threw Foy's and Bonnet's divisions across the Douro at Toro, causing Wellington to shift his own troops to their left. Having deceived Wellington into moving his troops, Marmont then brought Foy and Bonnet back to the northern bank of the river and quickly started to get his army across the river farther to the east, Wellington having moved to the west. It was a wonderfully planned and executed move by the French which immediately threw Wellington back on the defensive.

The first clashes between the two sides came on 18 July at Castrejon and Castrillo. The fight at Castrejon came about when Cotton ordered forward some cavalry patrols to ascertain the strength of the French forces moving south upon Wellington's right flank. The first patrol, commanded by Tomkinson, of the 16th Light Dragoons, ran into enemy cavalry almost at once and was forced to fall back along with the Allied picquets towards Castrejon, falling in with a squadron of the 11th Light Dragoons along the way. The French pressed so hard that Tomkinson was forced to turn and charge, during which fight Captain Deakin, Cotton's ADC, was wounded. Eventually, the British cavalry arrived at Castrejon, a small village situated on the Trabancos river, where they found Anson's brigade, consisting of the 11th, 12th and 16th Light Dragoons, drawn up on the high ground above along with Ross's and Bull's troops of the Royal Horse Artillery. It was not long before the enemy's cavalry and artillery arrived, and the latter began shelling the British cavalry and artillery, who returned the fire. 'The enemy brought 16 guns against us, which obliged our guns to retire,' wrote Tomkinson. 'The guns being gone, they directed the whole of their fire against my troop, and before I could move off killed Corporal Hardiman and Dragoon Stone (the shot, round shot, hit him on the belly, and sent pieces of his inside all over the troop – a piece on Lieutenant Lloyd's shoulder, the first time he was ever in action – he lived an hour), wounding four others and five horses.'[3]

At around seven o'clock in the morning Wellington arrived on the scene accompanied by Beresford and their staffs, and together the two rode out to the skirmishing line where Ross's two guns were in action, supported by a squadron each of the 11th and 12th Light Dragoons. Suddenly, a squadron of French cavalry charged and broke the squadron of the 12th Light Dragoons, whereupon a member of Beresford's staff, perceiving Ross to be in danger, cried 'Threes about!' to the retiring squadron, in order to get them to turn around and charge. Unfortunately, the cry was heard by the squadron of the 11th instead who turned about and made for the rear instead of advancing to help the 12th. Both squadrons now fell back, with the French close behind, and in the confusion both Wellington and Beresford were carried away and had to draw their swords to protect themselves. Fortunately, the 11th, realising their mistake, turned around and put matters to right with a charge which sent the French reeling back towards their own lines.[5] The French guns continued pounding away at Anson's brigade for the next hour or so but little damage was done, the cavalry taking shelter in dead ground below the plain above Castrejon. Presently, Wellington perceived that Marmont was feeding his infantry through to Alaejos, which turned his left flank, causing him to fall back farther south.

Wellington fell back with the 4th and Light Divisions, picking up the 5th Division along the way, until he came to a halt on a good defensive position between Castrillo and Canizal, on the road to Salamanca, whilst the right flank was covered a few miles farther south by the 1st and 7th Divisions around El Olmo and Vallesa. Up until this point, the French had been held off by Le Marchant's heavy cavalry and by Anson's light cavalry, but at Castrillo the two sides adopted lines of battle. It was to be an affair involving the 4th Division and Victor Alten's cavalry, being the 14th Light Dragoons and the 1st Hussars KGL, and it is the fight involving the cavalry which interests us most of all.

Clausel, commanding the French at Castrillo, sent a brigade of dragoons across the Guarena river to the west of the village, whilst Brennier's division attacked the 4th Division at the village itself. The movement brought on a very sharp cavalry fight which ended in triumph for Alten's cavalry. The two regiments of French dragoons, the 15th and 25th, crossed the Guarena to the west of Castrillo, according to Clausel's plan, but they had been watched all the while by Anson's light cavalry. Alten then waited for the French to form and advance up the long slopes in front of him before he gave the order to charge. The ensuing charge completely overturned the French dragoons as Alten had the advantage of charging down the slope. The fight was a fierce one but, as in so many other instances in the Peninsula, the Allied cavalry came out on top, routing the French and causing losses to the French of eight officers and over 150 men, including ninety-four prisoners. Among the latter was General Carrie, commanding the French cavalry at Castrillo. The 14th Light Dragoons did not get off lightly, losing seventy-five killed and wounded, whilst the 1st Hussars KGL lost sixty men.[5] Whilst Alten was engaged away to the west of the town, Cole's infantry were seeing off Brennier at the village itself, breaking up the French infantry attack and sending them reeling back across the Guarena. As they retreated Alten sent his brigade of cavalry in pursuit, bringing back six officers and 240 men as prisoners, whilst scores of others were cut down as they fled back across the river. The fight ended with around 700 French casualties, with Cole losing 500. On the following day, Wellington continued his retirement until he reached his old position at San Christobal on 21 July.

The two actions at Castrejon and Castrillo were not large-scale affairs, although the latter fight was quite fierce. The British cavalry did a good job, as they had ever since the retirement from the Douro, in keeping the pursuing French army in check. When it came to the stand-up fight at Castrejon, the 11th and 12th Light Dragoons showed once again that they were more than a match for their French counterparts in throwing them back, and it was only when a member of Beresford's staff gave the order for the retiring squadron of the 12th to turn around that the confusion arose, thus this mistake cannot be put down to any cavalry officer. Fortunately the error was corrected, and quickly. At Castrillo, Alten's handling of the cavalry bears similarities to Lumley's at Usagre, waiting for the French to come on up the slopes until he gave the order to charge, which was done with great success. Again, Wellington's cavalry got the better of the French dragoons and when they pursued the beaten French infantry later on they showed good discipline in not pursuing them too far, but returned when they had done their job and with a good haul of prisoners. Neither was there was to be any repeat of Taylor's misadventure at Vimeiro. Good work was done, therefore, in two separate fights.

But of course, all of this was just the build up to the great battle on 22 July. Throughout the afternoon of 21 July Marmont began to get his army across the Tormes at the great bend in the river at Huerta, and Wellington duly followed suit by crossing the river at the fords of Cabrerizos and

Santa Marta, with only the 3rd Division under Edward Pakenham, Wellington's brother-in-law, and D'Urban's Portuguese cavalry remaining on the north bank.[6] By nightfall the two opposing armies were in battle array, Wellington's army facing east with its line running north to the Tormes and Marmont's facing west, with its left flank at Calvarassa de Ariba, and its right likewise resting near the Tormes. During the night a tremendous storm blew up, rain fell in torrents and bolts of lightning sent horses scattering in all directions. Indeed, the 5th Dragoon Guards lost thirty-one horses during the storm whilst eighteen men were badly hurt when their horses trampled on them.

The battle itself was one of Wellington's greatest strokes of the war. Marmont, seemingly blind to the fact that Wellington was capable of offensive manoeuvres, sent some of his skirmishers to occupy the Greater Arapile, one of two very distinctive hills around which the battle would revolve. Wellington already occupied the Lesser Arapile, and by taking the Greater, would have had possession of two bastions against which Marmont would have to move if he were to realise his objective of cutting off Wellington's escape route to Portugal. For this is what Marmont's plan was. He had manoeuvred around Wellington's right flank at the San Christobal position and, once across the Tormes, was in a position to head west and move across Wellington's front with the object being to sever the road back to Portugal and to catch Wellington with his back to the Tormes. It was a sound enough plan and all went well at first when his men duly occupied the Greater Arapile. This gave him a pivot around which he was able to swing his divisions, Maucune leading, followed by Thomières. The two divisions marched south before turning west once they had passed behind the Greater Arapile. To counter this, Wellington re-aligned his own army, swinging it around using the Lesser Arapile as a hinge and forming his army into a sort of inverted 'L' shape, with the village of Los Arapiles as his new front centre. Meanwhile, he sent orders to Pakenham, still on the north bank of the river, to march from Salamanca using the ford at Cabrerizos and the old Roman bridge in the town itself and march to Aldea Tejada, a small village away to the north of Los Arapiles and hidden from French view by a long hill.

The last few days of parallel marching by both armies appear to have placed the French troops firmly in the frame of mind that the day would be no different from the last few days, and they simply carried on marching to their front, seemingly in the misguided belief that they were still in some kind of race with the Allies. They were to be sadly mistaken. Maucune's division halted on some heights to the south of Los Arapiles and, while his artillery began to shell the ground behind it, his skirmishers went down to dispute the village, which was held by the light companies of the Coldstream Guards and the 3rd Foot Guards. Meanwhile, Thomières' division, which had been behind Maucune, continued marching west.

Suddenly, a considerable gap was opened up between the two divisions, something which was not lost on one of Wellington's aides, who rushed off to inform him of the fact. Wellington formed his plan in an instant and was soon galloping hard towards the village of Aldea Tejada to tell Pakenham what was to be done. Quite simply, the 3rd Division was to march straight ahead and drive the enemy before them. Then, returning to the village, he gave orders to Leith and Cole to attack Maucune directly in front of them.

Wellington also rode up to Cotton with instructions to charge at the first favourable opportunity, at which Cotton deployed his brigades with Le Marchant in front followed by Anson and then Victor Alten. Cotton then rode forward and, noticing the gap between Maucune and Thomières, ordered Le Marchant forward.[7] It is not necessary to go into too much detail of the battle as we are really only interested in the cavalry. But, briefly, Pakenham arrived close to Thomières, unseen until the last moment, and launched a devastating attack which destroyed the French division in a short time. The 3rd Division then began to drive the fugitives of Thomières' division back towards the main fighting area. Leith and Cole, meanwhile, advanced up the slopes to the south of Los Arapiles to launch their attacks. What followed was an example of the perfect attack, for advancing to the right rear of Leith's advancing infantry came 1,000 heavy dragoons under John Gaspard Le Marchant. Leith arrived at the crest of the low heights to find the French drawn up in squares, which was not the sort of formation you would wish to be in when faced with a powerful, two-deep British infantry line. It is almost certain, therefore, that the mounted officers had seen Le Marchant approaching with George Anson's brigade in support from the direction of Las Torres, a small village to the north of Los Arapiles. The two opposing infantry forces apparently fired almost at the same time with scores falling on both sides. Leith's leading brigade, Greville's, suffered some loss at this point, but their own well-disciplined volleys soon began to roll from end to end of their line, breaking the squares and sending the French reeling to the rear. It was at this precise moment that Le Marchant appeared on the crest with his heavy dragoons, the 5th Dragoon Guards and 4th Dragoons in front with the 3rd Dragoons in support. The infantry had done their job and now it was the turn of the cavalry. It was the perfect attack.

Le Marchant must have waited all his life for this moment. Sixteen years had passed since he designed the sabre being wielded elsewhere on the battlefield by the light cavalry, whilst the same period had elapsed since the publication of his famous sword drill. Destiny seemed to bring him to this point in his life; a hot, dusty battlefield, leading a brigade of heavy cavalry against a division of broken enemy infantry. He had seen action at Villagarcia but this was different, this was a major battle. His hour had come and he was about to put into practice all those years of training and thought. Tragically, the hour was to be all too short.

When the heavy dragoons came thundering over the crest, Maucune's division was still reeling from the devastating volleys of Leith's infantry. There was no escape for the French infantry as Le Marchant charged in diagonally against the left flank of Maucune's left brigade. Here, the 66th Line were able to get off a few loose shots, but the majority of them were simply ridden or cut down by the British dragoons who were wielding their fearsome heavy cavalry sabres. Hundreds gave up and, throwing down their muskets, ran to the relative safety of Leith's infantry for protection, whilst those who chose to fight on were brutally cut down, unable to defend themselves amidst the chaos and violence of the attack. With the 66th devastated, Le Marchant reformed his brigade and charged the next regiment, the 15th, which, despite managing to empty more than a few saddles, disappeared in much the same manner as the 66th. Two French infantry regiments had, therefore, been virtually wiped out, whilst scores of refugees streamed away to the south.

Next up was Brennier's division, the leading elements of which came rushing breathlessly to Maucune's aid. The men of the leading regiment, the 22nd Line, were exhausted by their march but to their credit managed to get themselves into some sort of order and sent more than a few men of the leading files of the 5th Dragoon Guards tumbling from their saddles. But even this well-controlled fire could not stop the cavalry and they burst into the French ranks, cutting and hewing as before. The 22nd likewise dissolved into a bunch of fugitives, fighting for survival, but the massive effort put in by Le Marchant's brigade was beginning to tell upon his men. They had lost all order and even Le Marchant could no longer control them for their blood was up and, with no French cavalry opposed to them at this point, they were determined to enjoy themselves. Le Marchant himself cut down several French infantrymen and was always in the midst of the fighting. He failed to keep control of his men but did manage to gather around him half a squadron of the 4th Dragoons for a charge against some enemy infantry drawn up on the edge of a wood. As Le Marchant charged in amongst them one of the Frenchmen fired and the British cavalry general was sent reeling from his horse, the ball having entered his groin and broken his spine. Thus the British cavalry, and indeed the army, was deprived of a man who had the potential to become one of the greatest soldiers in its history. Wellington, meanwhile, was so 'fired with unusual enthusiasm at the cavalry charge, rode up to Cotton and exclaimed, "By God, Cotton, I never saw anything more beautiful in my life! The day is yours."'[8]

The devastation of the centre of the French army did not, however, bring an end to the battle. Indeed, Clausel performed heroics in turning back Cole's 4th Division, after which he made a gallant attack on Wellington's centre, but the 6th Division came forward at the vital moment to drive back the French. The battle ended in semi-darkness, with the dying embers of the action illuminated only by the flashes of musketry as the French rear-guard fought to hold back the advancing red tide. And then, suddenly, all resistance collapsed and the French army turned into a fleeing rabble, retreating into the safety of an extensive wood, into which no Allied soldiers entered. The Battle of Salamanca was one of Wellington's greatest and most crushing victories, although the war would continue for the best part of two more years. The Allies suffered 5,200 casualties against some 14,000 French, although this figure included several thousand prisoners.

The death of Le Marchant at the height of the battle was one of the greatest losses the British Army suffered in the Peninsula. His brigade had destroyed no fewer than eight infantry battalions and had devastated the centre of the French army. The heavy brigade had achieved all of this at a cost to themselves of just 105 killed and wounded, just under ten percent of their total strength, an astonishingly low figure considering the carnage and havoc they had wreaked amongst Brennier's and Maucune's divisions. Elsewhere, the light cavalry had been in action, mainly in support of the infantry. Indeed, their losses – just thirty-one amongst Anson's and Victor Alten's brigades – perhaps reflect their part in the battle. Amongst the wounded was Cotton himself, who was shot by a Portuguese piquet who, in the darkness, mistook his party for the enemy. The ball shattered one of the small bones in Cotton's left arm, and for a while it was feared that it might have to be amputated. Fortunately, this did not prove to be the case and Cotton subsequently recovered although he endured many weeks of pain.

Salamanca was undoubtedly the first and last time that British cavalry played such a decisive part on the field of battle in the Peninsula. Unlike Fuentes de Oñoro or Albuera, where they had played just a supporting role, the British cavalry had taken the lead, and the destruction of Maucune's and Brennier's brigades was the proof that, on their day, they were more than a match for anybody, although it should be said that Le Marchant appears to have come up against no enemy cavalry, which was just as well given the exhausted state his brigade was in towards the end of their incredible charge. One may raise criticisms of Le Marchant for not controlling his cavalry and of his officers and men themselves for galloping out of control. Has the old failing of the British cavalry been overlooked owing to the overwhelming success of their charge? Perhaps, but there was never any danger of the heavy brigade galloping along the 20th or 23rd Light Dragoons' road that was taken so disastrously by these two regiments earlier in the war. No, here was a brigade of experienced heavy cavalry, led by an excellent commander, coming up against broken and semi-formed infantry and, without the threat from enemy cavalry, they were allowed to go about their job with gusto and to great effect. The ground was good also, with the wide undulating plain allowing plenty of room for the heavy brigade to deploy. All the required elements conspired to make Salamanca the greatest blow struck by the British cavalry in the Peninsula.

We shall never know how much the army missed the talents of John Gaspard Le Marchant, but it should be said that from the beginning of the Vittoria campaign in the spring of 1813 until the end of the war, the scope for good cavalry action was extremely limited, mainly due to the restraints placed upon them by the nature of the terrain over which the latter months of the war were fought. Le Marchant was essentially a heavy cavalry commander and there would be little use for them beyond the plains of Leon and Castille.

With Le Marchant dead, William Ponsonby, of the 5th Dragoon Guards, took over command of his brigade, whilst Bock assumed overall command of the cavalry in Cotton's absence, the commander having been wounded at Salamanca. Bock, in fact, was at the helm during what is possibly the most famous cavalry exploit of the Peninsular War and even the Napoleonic Wars themselves, the famous charge of the King's German Legion cavalry at Garcia Hernandez. The object of this book is essentially the study of the British cavalry in the Peninsula and not the KGL or Portuguese cavalry. However, it would be wrong to pass over the Garcia Hernandez incident without at least some words on it.

The great charge came on 23 July, the day after Salamanca, during the pursuit of the French rearguard under Foy, whose division had not been very heavily engaged during the actual battle. Foy had crossed the Tormes at Alba de Tormes and was making for Penaranda when Anson's light cavalry brigade, apparently with Wellington riding with them, caught up with him at the small village of Garcia Hernandez. Immediately the British light dragoons came into sight, Foy drew up Curto's light cavalry and a battery of artillery to meet them, whilst his infantry began to make for the heights of Serna, a short way to the north of the village. Unfortunately for the infantry, Curto's cavalry turned and fled, leaving them to fend for themselves. At the same time Bock, riding at the head of the 1st and 2nd Dragoons KGL, swung around the western end of the heights and began to set off in pursuit of Curto when they were hit by infantry fire from three French squares away to their left.[9] The squares, formed from two battalions of the 6th Léger and one of the 76th Line, numbered about 2,400 and should, under normal conditions, have been more than able to hold their own against the KGL cavalry, but what followed went against all normal practice, due partly to the gallantry of the KGL cavalry and partly to a stroke of good fortune.

Once they saw the French squares at the foot of the heights, the KGL dragoons turned to their left and charged them, Decken's squadron of the 1st Dragoons leading. As they closed on the square of the 76th Line, they were hit by a volley of musketry from the infantry which emptied a number of saddles. The dragoons pressed on, however, until they got to within about twenty yards of the square, whereupon the French fired another volley, one of their shots wounding Decken and mortally wounding his horse. It was at this point that the dragoons were handed their huge slice of good fortune, for the dying horse, rather than simply tumbling to the ground, kept going and crashed into the front of the square, creating an opening through which Decken's comrades charged. The square dissolved in an instant as the heavy dragoons set about the French, cutting and hacking with their long swords, until just fifty men out of a square of battalion strength were left to surrender. Watching the destruction of the 76th was the 1/6th Léger who had managed to get some way up the slopes. However, they were not quick enough to escape the 2nd Dragoons who swept past the 76th and charged after them. Two companies of the 6th actually turned to meet them and, indeed, brought several of the riders down, but when the 2nd Dragoons closed with them the two companies were quickly dealt with. This resistance gave the remaining companies of the 1/6th Léger time to gain the summit of the heights where they bundled their way into a square which had been formed by the 2/6th Leger. The survivors of the 1st battalion threw the square into some disorder, and two squadrons of the 2nd Dragoons were quick to charge home and once again the square was smashed. The survivors of this charge ran along the heights and threw themselves under the protection of some squares formed by the 39th and 69th Line, with Foy himself in the centre of one of them. By now the KGL dragoons were blown by their exertions and could not make any impression on these last squares, formed as they were of steady infantry, and the attack finally came to a halt.

The attack by the 1st and 2nd Dragoons KGL had lasted barely forty minutes, but during that time they had broken two squares and virtually destroyed three battalions of French infantry at a cost to themselves of 127 killed and wounded. The heavy dragoons of the King's German Legion achieved what no other cavalry force, British or French, managed to do during the war.[10] Indeed, instances of cavalry breaking infantry squares are rare enough during the Napoleonic Wars as a whole. However, there is little doubt that the attack by the dragoons was attended with a huge slice of good fortune when the dying horse pummelled its way into the square. We will never know what might have happened if the horse had come crashing down in front of the square, leaving the infantry formed and unscathed. On the other hand, the second square to be broken did not need any dead horseflesh being hurled into it to create the breach, although there is little doubt that the sight of the 76th's square being demolished before their eyes did much to unnerve the 6th Léger. As Wellington's infantry were to prove at Waterloo, steady infantry were always at their safest against cavalry when they formed square and, provided they held their nerve, the cavalry had little chance of breaking into it. A horse will simply not charge four ranks of bristling steel. The fight at Garcia Hernandez changed nothing tactically and both sides probably viewed it as a fluke and carried on adopting the same formation with success for the remainder of the war. Ultimately, the KGL dragoons succeeded where the 14th Light Dragoons had failed at Villar de Puerco and the 13th Light Dragoons and 2nd Hussars KGL had failed at Membrillo, owing to a combination of bravery and good luck. The British cavalry never lacked courage at either of these places, but what they did lack was the good fortune enjoyed by the KGL dragoons at Garcia Hernandez.

With Marmont thrashed at Salamanca, Wellington was able to march on Madrid, which he entered on 12 August. The day before Wellington entered the Spanish capital there was a fierce cavalry fight at Majalahonda, but as this involved only Portuguese and KGL cavalry we shall move on, not that there is a great deal to study at this point because it was in September that Wellington chose to march north to lay siege to Burgos. It was the one great failure of the war for him, undertaking the business as he did with just three heavy guns and with relatively inexperienced troops. The whole sorry saga at Burgos finally came to a close on 22 October, when the Allies crept silently away from the town having failed completely in their attempts to prise the place from the French.

The subsequent retreat from Burgos, and thence to Ciudad Rodrigo by way of Madrid and Salamanca, was the bitterest pill Wellington had to swallow in the Peninsula. Indeed, the retreat, conducted amidst chaotic conditions in rain and mud, and with a vigorous pursuit being conducted by Souham, was said by those who experienced both the retreat from Burgos and that of Sir John Moore to Corunna three years before, to have been by far the worse of the two. There is little for us to study of cavalry operations during this period, as the majority of the time Wellington's cavalry operated in much the same way as they had done in 1808, in a covering role, keeping back the French as best they could. There was little scope for open cavalry combat, although the 14th Light Dragoons and Alten's KGL hussars did fight a small but creditable action against some Polish lancers, 2nd Hussars and the 5th and 27th Chasseurs at Matilla on 16 November.

The most memorable fight during the long and miserable retreat came right at the outset, on 23 October, and took place on the main road from Burgos between Cellada del Camino, Venta del Pozo and Villodrigo when Cotton's cavalry, consisting of Bock's and Anson's brigades, clashed with Souham's advance guard, consisting of Curto's light cavalry brigade and Maucune's infantry division. Accounts of the fight at Venta del Pozo are as confusing as the fight itself, with some placing the combat at Venta del Pozo and others at Villodrigo. In fact, the fight began just in front of the village of Cellada del Camino, on the main road, in front of which runs a small stream, the Hormanza. Here, Cotton had left the 11th Light Dragoons and some Royal Horse Artillery guns under Ramsay and Downman, with

Halkett's two battalions of KGL infantry in support on the south side of another small stream farther west, at the small village of Villadelmiro. Parallel with the main road runs the Arlanzon river and on the south of the river, on the Allied right, lay Julian Sanchez's guerrillas, whilst another unit of guerrillas, under Marquinez, occupied some heights away to the Allied left. The pursuing French troops quickly drove in the light cavalry piquets of Anson's brigade, and pushed on towards Cellada del Camino, from where Major Money led out the 11th Light Dragoons, throwing back the leading troops of French cavalry, whilst the British guns opened fire on those behind. Away to Anson's left, on the heights, Marquinez was charged by two French brigades, Curto's hussars and Boyer's dragoons, and was quickly scattered, the Spaniards making for the bridge over a marshy rivulet at Venta del Pozo on the main road.[11]

Even as Marquinez was being driven from the heights, pursued by Curto's hussars, Anson's light cavalry was being pushed back to the stream at Villadelmiro, covered by Halkett's KGL infantry, whilst the guns went off in the direction of Venta del Pozo.[12] This was as a result of French cavalry outflanking the 11th Light Dragoons by passing through Cellada del Camino on the main road, whilst the 11th engaged other French cavalry to the left of the village. Once across this first stream at Villadelmiro, Anson fell back, with the 16th Light Dragoons covering the withdrawal. But as they neared the second bridge at Venta del Pozo, with French dragoons pushing hard after them, Marquinez's guerrillas came charging in on the left flank of the 16th with Curto's hussars right behind them. The charging horsemen threw the 16th into complete disorder, and about thirty men of the 16th were taken prisoner, whilst the remainder fell back fighting towards the bridge. Fortunately, the chaos forced the French to draw back and reform which gave Anson sufficient time to get his light cavalry across the bridge where Halkett's infantry and Bock's heavy KGL dragoons were drawn up, with the horse artillery in support. Cotton was on the spot also, and it was at this point that he attempted an operation similar to that employed so successfully by Lumley at Usagre in 1811.

With all of Cotton's force now on the left bank of the stream at Venta del Pozo, the French cavalry were able to approach, all the time under fire from the horse artillery guns. By now, Caffarelli's cavalry had come up also, consisting of the lancers du Berg, fifteen squadrons of dragoons and some squadrons of gendarmes. It was quite a formidable force and, making a sudden move to their right from the main road, they galloped over the bridge and began forming up on the Allied side of the stream. It will be remembered how Lumley, at Usagre in May 1811, allowed Latour Maubourg's cavalry to cross the bridge in the town before charging with his heavy dragoons, throwing back the French and inflicting heavy loss on them. At Venta del Pozo, Cotton appears to have attempted something similar, although on this occasion his cavalry were slow to cross and Caffarelli's cavalry crossed close behind them. Anson's brigade was apparently ordered by Cotton to form up on the left of Bull's guns, whilst Bock's KGL dragoons remained in position on Bull's right, between the Arlanzon river and the main road. However, somehow Anson's cavalry, in passing in front of Bull, managed to mask the guns and so prevented them from firing until they had passed, which allowed several French squadrons to get across the bridge. It was a costly mistake, for, unlike Lumley who charged at the very moment that the French were getting their troops across the bridge at Usagre, Cotton allowed too many French squadrons over the bridge at Venta del Pozo, and when Bock's dragoons made their charge, they could make little headway against a much larger enemy.[13] Anson's light cavalry joined the fight but they had been fighting all morning and their horses were fairly tired. Oman quotes eyewitness accounts, both English and French, who claim that 'this was one of the most furious cavalry mêlées ever seen'.[14]

The fight was indeed a most fearsome one, with British light dragoons and heavy German dragoons on one side, about 1,000 in all, against 1,200 French, consisting of lancers, gendarmes, hussars, chasseurs and dragoons. Oman's account of the fight has the business being settled by the intervention of two squadrons of French gendarmes that came up from the rear, crossed the bridge and hit the 2nd Dragoons KGL in the flank. Napier, on the other hand, puts it down fairly and squarely to the ferocity of the French onslaught, adding that Boyer's dragoons, who had crossed the stream farther north at Balbaces, came 'thundering in on the left', thus breaking the British ranks and sending the whole to the rear in confusion. Whatever the cause, it had been a hard-fought contest and is one of the few occasions where French cavalry, of relatively similar strength, fought and defeated British and KGL cavalry in a fair stand-up fight. In fact, it was only Wellington's personal intervention and the support the cavalry received from Halkett's infantry and Bull's guns that saved them from further punishment, and the whole force was finally allowed to retreat through Villodrigo and on to Quintana de la Puente, where they spent the night, whilst the French camped at Villodrigo. Allied losses were put at 230, including five officers and sixty men taken prisoner. French casualties were estimated to have been around 300.[15]

The fight at Venta del Pozo was not particularly satisfying for the British cavalry.[16] True, Anson's light cavalry, and the 11th Light Dragoons in particular, kept the French at bay on the Hormanza river for the best part of three hours before falling back to Villadelmiro and then Venta del Pozo, during which time they turned and made several successful charges.[17] However, they were outflanked on successive occasions and were disordered by Marquinez's guerrillas after the latter were routed by Curto and Boyer. When they finally managed to get across the bridge at Venta del Pozo, the comparison with Usagre becomes quite obvious and says much for Lumley's command at the latter fight that he managed to bring off his attack, unlike Cotton who through an error, committed either by one of his staff or by the leading light cavalry regiment, failed. This was the main difference between the two actions and once again illustrates the fine line between success and failure.[18] Curiously enough, the fight at Venta del Pozo affords another comparison, this time with Cotton's cavalry at Fuentes de Oñoro, when the 1st Royal Dragoons, 14th Light Dragoons, 16th Light Dragoons and the 1st Hussars KGL performed superbly in preventing Latour-Maubourg's cavalry from interfering with the retreating Light Division. At Venta del Pozo it was Cotton's cavalry again, this time the 11th and 16th Light Dragoons, that performed well, enabling Halkett's two battalions of KGL infantry to retreat over a similarly long distance towards Villodrigo without ever coming under serious threat. Credit, then, to the British light cavalry for performing good work, and all this after having skirmished for nearly three hours beforehand at Cellada del Camino.

The action between Cellada del Camino and Villodrigo on 23 October marked the opening stage of a long and terrible retreat that was to continue until 19 November, when Wellington's bedraggled and starving army reached Ciudad Rodrigo. It was ten months to the day since Wellington's men had stormed the town, on the night of 19 January, since when his army had stormed Badajoz, defeated Marmont at Salamanca and occupied Madrid. And yet, here they were once again, back where they had started, having overstretched themselves at Burgos, and it must have been hard to credit the fact that such a wonderful army at the outset of the campaign could have performed such tremendous feats and yet finished the year where they had started it, and in such a terrible condition.[19] The retreat from Burgos had been particularly hard for the cavalry, having not only themselves to fend for but also their horses, and with such a shortage of forage and supplies, they were in a poor condition when they reached Ciudad Rodrigo. The retreat had also brought on almost daily skirmishes with the French, the fight on 23 October being the sharpest of them all for the cavalry. There were other smaller fights, at Alba de Tormes, Matilla – where Wellington's cavalry again engaged Polish lancers – and San Muñoz, but these involved fairly routine work for the cavalry and are not really worthy of detailed study.

The retreat from Salamanca to Ciudad Rodrigo cost Wellington about 3,000 casualties, mainly stragglers taken by the French along the way, and this, combined with the fiasco at Burgos, which cost a further 1,500 men, conspired to make it the most unhappy episode of the war for Wellington. Among the prisoners was General Edward Paget, sent out ostensibly to act as Wellington's second-in-command, who was taken by a French cavalry patrol just east of San Muñoz. Wellington himself was furious with the conduct of his army during the retreat, and on 28 November issued his infamous 'Memorandum', in which he severely criticised his officers and NCOs for not controlling their men and maintaining discipline.[20] Given the circumstances, the army's recovery was a relatively speedy business, and by the end of the year Wellington's divisions were in winter quarters, with little on their minds but the following year's campaign, whilst Wellington himself reflected on the past year's events, determined that there would be no repeat during the next campaign. As we shall see, his wish was granted and the 1813 campaign in the Peninsula, culminating in the battle of Vittoria, proved to be the decisive campaign of the war.

Notes

1 See Sir J.T. Jones' *Journal of the Sieges carried on by the Army under the Duke of Wellington in Spain between the Years 1811 and 1814, etc.* of which the 3rd edition, published in London in 1846, is by far the best.
2 See Ian Fletcher, *In Hell Before Daylight: The Siege and Storming of the Castle of Badajoz* (Staplehurst, 1994, 2nd edition), for an account of the siege and storming.
3 James Tomkinson (Ed), *Diary of a Cavalry Officer, in the Peninsular and Waterloo Campaigns, 1809–1815* (London, 1894), 181.
4 Ibid. 181.
5 Sir Charles Oman, *History of the Peninsular War* (Oxford, 1902), V: 405.
6 Pakenham commanded the 3rd Division in Picton's absence, as the wound which the latter had received at Badajoz had opened up again.
7 Mary, Countess Combermere & Capt. W.W. Knollys, *Memoirs and Correspondence of Field Marshal Viscount Combermere* (London, 1866), I: 274. Apparently, Le Marchant, unsure of the direction of the advance, asked Cotton, whereupon the latter replied somewhat sharply, 'To the enemy, Sir'. The two men then exchanged 'high words' and Cotton's biographers claim that the matter would not have rested here had Le Marchant not been killed.
8 Ibid. 275.
9 It is said that Bock was so short-sighted that he asked somebody to point out the enemy to him. Sadly, Bock and his son were drowned when their ship was wrecked on the way back to England in 1814.
10 Colborne's brigade at Albuera were caught in line and had no time to form square.
11 The rivulet is also referred to as a ravine and a marshy stream.
12 The stream referred to in this account is based upon Napier's version of the fight at Venta del Pozo. It is curious that neither Oman nor Fortescue mentions the presence of this stream across which there was a bridge with a small village behind. Napier calls it 'a broad ditch with a second bridge in front of a small village.' (*History of the War in the Peninsula*, V: 295.) Napier actually means the 'first bridge' as the one at Venta del Pozo was the second bridge. Both Oman and Fortescue mistake this first bridge and ditch for the stream which runs to the east of Cellada del Camino, the Hormanza, which was Anson's first defensive position. Napier says that Anson skirmished with the

French on the Hormanza whilst Halkett's infantry 'was in the little village behind the bridge' (i.e. the broad ditch). He does not name this village but it is undoubtedly Villadelmiro, which lies, as Napier says, 'halfway between this stream [that at Venta del Pozo] and Celiada'. There is also much difference between Napier and Oman in their accounts of the fighting. For example, Napier has Marquinez's men being driven off by Curto and Boyer, whereas Oman says it was Merlin's brigade (Oman, *History of the Peninsular War*, VI: 71). Ultimately, this detail is not important and I do not think that we need get bogged down with a discussion as to who did what. What is important, however, is the correct movements of the respective troops and the conduct of the British cavalry.

13 Weller, typifying historians' approach to the British cavalry says of the incident, 'All was going well until Cotton and Anson collaborated in a blunder not unusual for British cavalry'. *Wellington in the Peninsula* (London, 1962), 238.

14 Oman, *Peninsular War*, VI: 74.

15 Ibid. VI: 75–6.

16 The fight was, however, awarded to the KGL dragoons as a battle honour and was worn on German picklehaubes during the First World War, alongside other Peninsular battle honours such as Garcia Hernandez.

17 See Wellington Despatch, Wellington to Earl Bathurst, 26 October 1812, *The Despatches of Field Marshal the Duke of Wellington during his various campaigns* (London, 1834), IX: 515–7.

18 Uxbridge, formerly Lord Paget, tried something similar to Lumey at Genappe, during the retreat from Quatre Bras during the Waterloo campaign. He charged with the Life Guards to send a unit of French lancers, who had crossed the bridge in the town, reeling back in all directions.

19 Typical of many officers' views as to the conduct of the business at Burgos were those of John Mills, an ensign with the Coldstream Guards. Writing from Salamanca on 3 November, Mills said, 'Our want of success at Burgos and the subsequent retreat will cause a great deal of dissatisfaction in England. I think it has turned the tide of affairs here and Spain I think is lost. If ever a man ruined himself the Marquis [Wellington] has done it; for the last two months he has acted like a madman. The reputation he has acquired will not bear him out, such is the opinion here.' Ian Fletcher (Ed), *For King and Country: The Letters and Diaries of John Mills, Coldstream Guards, 1811–1814* (Staplehurst, 1995), 253.

20 'Memorandum', 28 November 1812, *Despatches*, IX: 582–5.

CHAPTER VIII

The Vittoria Campaign:
The Return of the Hussars

Throughout the winter of 1812–13 and the following spring Wellington's army recovered its strength after the energy-sapping traumas of the retreat from Burgos, until by the beginning of May 1813 the whole sorry chapter was firmly behind it. The period of recuperation saw a number of improvements to the army, with the various departments, and in particular the Quartermaster General's and the Commissariat, undergoing reorganisation and improvement. There were changes in personnel, with Wellington finally ridding himself of several ineffective officers, some of whom returned to England immediately, whilst others did so later on in the year. He also managed to replace the inefficient Willoughby Gordon, the villain of the retreat from Burgos, with George Murray, as Quartermaster General. A much undervalued officer, Murray was the key to many of Wellington's most successful campaigns and was sorely missed during the 1812 retreat. Wellington also won his battle to retain the Provisional Battalions, formed of units whose strength had been so reduced both through sickness and action that, under normal circumstances, they would have returned to England. Wellington, however, appreciating the value of experienced troops, formed them into what he called Provisional Battalions and, in spite of the Duke of York's preference for them to return, they would serve Wellington faithfully for the remainder of the war.[1]

The cavalry also underwent some reorganisation with the recall to England in March 1813 of the 9th Light Dragoons and the unfortunate 11th Light Dragoons, a regiment that had suffered its fair share of accidents. The 4th Dragoon Guards and the 2nd Hussars KGL were likewise ordered home at the same time. All of these regiments were ordered to distribute their horses amongst the cavalry regiments remaining in the Peninsula.[2] These reductions in the cavalry were offset by the arrival of two new brigades. The first, the Household Brigade, consisted of two squadrons each of the 1st and 2nd Life Guards and the Royal Horse Guards, the brigade being placed under the command of General Rebow, although he returned to England shortly afterwards and command passed to Sir Robert Hill. The other new brigade saw the return to the Peninsula after a gap of four years of the Hussar Brigade, consisting of the 10th, 15th and 18th Hussars under Colquhoun Grant.[3] These three regiments had seen much good service under Henry, Lord Paget during the Corunna campaign but had not been out to the Peninsula since their return to England in January 1809. The three regiments would be joined in September 1813 by a fourth hussar regiment, the 7th Hussars.

The cavalry during the Vittoria campaign was commanded by General von Bock, whose cavalry had broken the French squares at Garcia Hernandez. This was in the absence of Stapleton Cotton who was in England and who did not return to Spain until a few days after the Battle of Vittoria. Two of the officers whom he would have to do without were Robert Ballard Long, the cavalry commander at the centre of many a controversial action in the south, including, of course, Campo Mayor, and John 'Black Jack' Slade. Long returned to England in August 1813 and, in fact, was present at Vittoria at the head of the 13th Light Dragoons. Slade, on the other hand, was ordered home in April and played no part in the campaign, his brigade of heavy dragoons being passed on to Fane. With the return to the Peninsula of five of his senior infantry commanders, all of whom had been in England at the end of 1812 on sick leave, the army could be said to have been in a very good condition on the eve of the Vittoria campaign.

Wellington's plan for the campaign involved an advance by his army in two wings, the left under Sir Thomas Graham with six divisions, and the right under Rowland Hill with three divisions. Graham was to cross the Douro well inside Portugal at Braganza and Miranda, the move being scheduled for 21–24 May. Hill, meanwhile, was to move north from his headquarters at Coria and advance on Salamanca. Upon arrival there he was to march to his left and head for the Douro at Toro. There, he would join Graham who should have crossed the Esla north of Zamora, and by doing so would complete the concentration of Wellington's army. More important, however, was the fact that once the two wings had established themselves on the north bank of the Douro, they would have turned the right flank of the French position on that river without having had to engage in a single serious combat. The advance would bring on either a general engagement in front of Valladolid, Joseph's new capital, or force him to retire upon Burgos. The sweep north of the great road to France would also allow Wellington to move his supply base from Lisbon to northern Spain.

The plan was set, and on 31 May Graham's troops began crossing the Esla which they found in full flood, and much equipment and more than a few men were lost in passing the river.[4] One criticism frequently levelled at the British cavalry is their apparent inability to perform adequate piquet duties. Well, when Grant's hussar brigade got across the Esla at Almendra it was the turn of the French cavalry to show that even they were guilty of the same crime when the hussars surprised a piquet of one officer and thirty-two men at the village of Val de Perdrices, about a mile beyond Almendra. It seems incredible that with the whole of Graham's wing of the army poised on the left bank of the Esla, the French did not have piquets on the right bank to dispute the crossing. Fortunately for Graham, there were no piquets at Almendra and Grant's hussars got ashore without meeting any enemy resistance. It reflects nothing but discredit upon Digeon's dragoons, who were supposed to be guarding the ford but who allowed instead first Grant to cross and then themselves to be taken prisoner. Digeon, in fact, retreated from Zamora in the direction of Toro with two regiments of dragoons and half a battery of horse artillery, leaving the town free of enemy forces.

The small town of Toro lies on the north bank of the Douro and is situated high above the river with a long, Roman bridge spanning the river itself. The French had broken the bridge in July 1812 during the Salamanca campaign, for it was here that Foy and Bonnet had feinted to Wellington's left before recrossing the river. Now, almost a year on, it was the concentration point for the two wings of Wellington's army and the commander-in-chief duly established his headquarters there on 2 June. With Digeon retiring to the east Grant's hussars followed in the same direction, scouting for any signs of French forces, whilst Bock and Anson patrolled to the north. The reconnaissance brought on a sharp action at Morales, on 2 June, the first action in which the British hussars had been engaged since the retreat to Corunna, four years earlier.

Digeon may not have been capable of mounting guard over the ford at Almendra, but he certainly knew when it was time to retreat, and with 40,000 Allied troops now converging upon him from the direction of Zamora, that time had come, for he had no more than 6,000 troops, infantry, cavalry and artillery, with which to dispute the Allies' advance. Digeon retired to some heights beyond the small town of Morales de Toro, which in turn lay some six miles east of Toro itself. He left behind one of his two brigades of cavalry in front of the town and placed the other behind the town, at about two miles to the east, on the far side of a wide open plain which culminates in a small bridge over the marshy Bayas river, beyond which lay the heights where his infantry and artillery were drawn up. Digeon's reconnaissance party, about 100 men of the 16th and 21st Dragoons, were actually disturbed in Toro whilst cooking their breakfast, whereupon they immediately saddled up and began to make off along the road to Morales, in front of which were two more squadrons of the 16th Dragoons, drawn up across the road. The dragoons were followed closely by Grant and the 10th Hussars, whilst the 18th Hussars came on behind them.

The two British units immediately began skirmishing with the French, pushing them back, until Gardiner's two horse-artillery guns were brought forward, and the skirmishers called in. The guns played upon the French

dragoons, forcing them back to Morales itself where the hussars discovered two further squadrons of dragoons who were formed to the north of
the town. The 10th Hussars now charged the retreating French squadrons,
with Grant and Major Robarts at their head, but as soon as the French
neared the two squadrons of their comrades placed in reserve at the town,
they turned around and charged the 10th, 'in high stile[sic] according to
Woodberry of the 18th Hussars.[5] 'All was now bustle and confusion,' he
continued, 'the French tried to make their best way off, while the 10th was
hacking and cutting them about in all directions.'[6]

The two squadrons to the north of the town now retreated, and at the
same time the right squadron of the 18th Hussars moved round the south
of the town, whilst the 10th drove the other French dragoons 'pell mell'
through the centre of it. It would appear that it was the intervention by the
18th that caused the French to panic and run. The French were overturned
and pursued for over two miles across the plain, which quickly became
the scene of scores of individual combats.

> The whole plain in 10 minutes presented a dreadful scene; dead, wounded
> and prisoners in all directions, for as fast as our men could get up with them,
> they were cut down and out of the four squadrons a very few made their
> escape to the hills in front of this plain, where the enemy had eight squad-
> rons more and a column of infantry with artillery. These never came from the
> hill, but upon our closing upon them, and being in the act of following them
> up the hill, they fired their artillery at us. It was here our centre squadron
> came up with the remains of their flying force and commenced the carnage.
> I had a cut at one man myself, who made point at me, but which I parried...
> I gave him a most severe cut across the eyes and cheek and must have cut
> them out. However, in the scene of confusion, when the enemy fired their
> first shot, he and many other prisoners made their escape. The bullet [shell]
> from their second fire fell within a foot of my horse, and nearly smothered
> me with dust. But as the saying is, every bullet has its billet. We in turn were
> obliged to retreat back out of range of their artillery, which after firing about
> a dozen times and throwing two bombs, they retreated.[7]

It had indeed been a very sharp action with the British hussars being
brought up only by the sight of Digeon's main force sitting upon the
height on the right bank of the Bayas. Nevertheless, some of the hussars
still managed to get across the marsh and over the small bridge to attack
the French on the heights. Here, however, they were very badly mauled by
the French and several were taken prisoner. The French were then able to
move off towards Pedroso del Rey, covered by their cavalry and artillery
which made no effort to prolong the fight on the plain, nor did Grant's
hussars make any attempt at pursuing them. Instead they returned to
Morales to see to their wounded and make their reports.

The fight cost Grant twenty-one officers and men killed, wounded and taken prisoner. Set against this were over 200 officers and men of the French 16th Dragoons taken prisoner, in addition to the killed and wounded, of which there are no exact figures, although Fortescue thought this to be around the 150 mark.[8] It was, in Fortescue's words, 'a brilliant little affair', although it is interesting to speculate on what might have happened had not the French guns and infantry brought the pursuit to an abrupt end. Indeed, Woodberry wrote, 'I never saw men so mad for action as the hussars before and after the skirmishing, and all appeared disappointed when ordered to march into this place [Morales] to take up their quarters.'[9] It was the hussars' first action for four years and, after having spent the intervening time no doubt reading reports of the Peninsular campaigns whilst at home in England, we can well imagine their sense of frustration being vented upon Digeon's hussars after the long spell of inactivity. However, the presence of Digeon's infantry and artillery probably saved them from making the same mistake as Slade at Maguilla, Taylor at Vimeiro and Elley and the 23rd Light Dragoons at Talavera, although at least the 15th Hussars appear to have been in reserve at Morales, not through design, but merely by virtue of not being able to get forward as fast as the 10th and 18th Hussars. The pursuit over the two miles of open plain was not unlike Long's affair at Campo Mayor, with the French being soundly beaten, broken and pursued on both occasions, although Grant's hussars at Morales retired in good order after having beaten their enemy, a fact which is borne out by the very low casualties suffered by them during the fight. Ultimately it was a fine victory for the British hussars and a good way for them to begin their second campaign in the Peninsula.

With Wellington's army having concentrated around Toro, the great march to the north began, with Wellington outflanking successive French positions by simply keeping to the north of the great road to France instead of along it. In this way, the Esla and Douro were passed, as was the Ebro, whilst Burgos, such a thorn in Wellington's side in 1812, was quickly blown up and abandoned by the French on 13 June when they realised that Wellington had slipped past to the north of it. There would be no stumbling block this time. Given the nature of the advance and the terrain over which it took place, it is not surprising that there were no further fights of any significance along the road to Vittoria. Indeed, the French barely knew where the entire Allied army was, let alone the cavalry. The French, commanded by King Joseph and his chief of staff, Jourdan, considered the area to the north of the great road to be virtually impassable to both cavalry and artillery and yet, there was Wellington's army, threading its way through the rugged countryside in three great columns, under Graham, Hill and Wellington himself, with Giron's Spaniards joining them further to the north. There were a few clashes between opposing piquets as the two armies neared each other, but on the whole, the British cavalry, at least the light cavalry, were employed in the traditional role of piquet and patrol work, acting as the eyes and ears of the great army which was converging upon Vittoria.

By 20 June Wellington had reached Subjiana de Morillos, a small village to the west of the great plain of the Zadorra river, where the battle would be fought the following day. It is not my intention to give a blow by blow account of the battle. Suffice it to say that it was the greatest of the Peninsular War, with Joseph's combined force of the Armies of the South., the Centre and of Portugal, putting up a brave show but ultimately being outfought by Wellington's Allied infantry, British, Portuguese and Spanish, for this was one battle where his army could truly be said to have been an Allied army. Wellington's plan involved splitting his force into four columns: the right, under Hill, which attacked the heights of Puebla on the French left; the centre, under Wellington himself; the left centre, under Lord Dalhousie, and the far left under Sir Thomas Graham. Timing was of the greatest importance and, in fact, it did not come off as well as it could have done, with Dalhousie becoming delayed and Graham hesitating somewhat, which, in the event, mattered little as far as the end result was concerned, although it did cause Wellington some anxiety during the battle. The French line was attacked at various points, with Picton's 3rd Division delivering the telling blow in the centre, which effectively created a gap between Gazan's Army of the South and D'Erlon's Army of the Centre, a gap quickly exploited by Wellington's divisions which presented an awesome array, strung out across the centre of the battlefield in a long, unstoppable line. Elsewhere, Hill's 2nd Division and Morillo's Spaniards threw back the French left, whilst on the extreme right of the French position, Longa's Spaniards took Durana, and by so doing made perhaps the most important contribution to the day's fighting by severing the great road to France and Joseph's logical escape route to the north of Vittoria. Graham, meanwhile, held the attention of Reille's Army of Portugal on the French right, his 5th Division becoming engaged in the fiercest fighting of the day at Gamarra Mayor. With successive attacks being successfully delivered, along Joseph's line, and with both French flanks coming under severe pressure from Hill and Graham, the French finally buckled and broke, their retreat to the east turning into a total rout once all resistance had collapsed.

To the east of Vittoria, Joseph's crushed army made off in the direction of Salvatierra and Pamplona, abandoning 151 guns in addition to hundreds of wagons containing over 5 million francs as well as the greatest treasure that had ever been captured on a battlefield. It was a crushing victory for Wellington but it could have been far greater had his men pursued Joseph's beaten army instead of setting to work plundering the enormous baggage train left by the French. This, ironically, proved to be Joseph's saviour, for had he not abandoned such a vast treasure to the clutches of Wellington's

men, they would surely have succeeded in taking thousands more prisoners than they eventually did.

The Battle of Vittoria decided the outcome of the Peninsular War, for
with the crushing defeat suffered by Joseph's army all chances of a French
victory in Spain disappeared. From then on the French turned from offence
to defence as Wellington's army looked to the invasion of France itself. But
what of the British cavalry during the battle and what was their contribution to this massive victory? The fact is that Wellington's cavalry played
a very minor role in the battle, whereas they could and should have
played a far greater part, particularly in the pursuit of the French after the
battle. Had it not been for a breakdown in discipline by the Allied army
in general following the collapse of the French army, this is undoubtedly
what would have occurred. The first cavalry to get into action were almost
certainly the 15th Hussars, who supported Kempt when his brigade of the
Light Division made its bold crossing over the Zadorra at the unguarded
bridge at Tres Puentes. But once across, the hussars formed up behind the
infantry and moved forward only in support of what might be termed the
'front line' troops. The story was the same for the other cavalry regiments
who sat and watched, often under fire from enemy artillery, while the
infantry did the bulk of the fighting. It was not until late in the afternoon,
between five and six o'clock, that the French finally broke, leaving Reille's
Army of Portugal to hold back Graham and allow the beaten troops in the
centre and to the south of Vittoria to make good their escape until Reille
himself disengaged and made off in relatively good order, keeping to the
tracks to the north of the road heading east from Vittoria, and by so doing
avoiding much of the confusion that reigned to the east of the town.

With all order lost and with Joseph's defeated army streaming away from
the battlefield in total disarray, it was surely the moment for Wellington's
cavalry to be unleashed against the fugitives. And yet it appears that only
Grant's hussars got forward to actually engage the enemy whilst the other
brigades simply crossed the Zadorra, again in support of the infantry,
until they were ordered to halt and bivouac to the north-east of Vittoria.
In fact, our study of the British cavalry at Vittoria really involves only the
hussar brigade, whose conduct was both reckless and undisciplined, and
Anson's light dragoons, who engaged both French infantry and cavalry
during the closing stages of the battle. Anson's cavalry had been with
Graham's column during the battle and had not, therefore, been engaged
at all until they crossed the bridge over the Zadorra at Gamarra Mayor.
Two squadrons, one each from the 12th and 16th Light Dragoons, then
attacked Reille's rearguard near the village of Zurbano, just to the north-
east of Vittoria. Initially, the light dragoons were repulsed by enemy
dragoons and hussars, but they reformed and charged again, this time
driving off their adversaries. Their advance brought them upon a regiment of French infantry, the 36th Ligne, who formed square to meet them.

The light dragoons charged the square but could make no impression upon it and they withdrew, leaving the French infantry to continue their retreat. There would be no repetition at Vittoria of the disastrous attacks on enemy infantry squares that had dogged the cavalry earlier in the war. Elsewhere on the battlefield, the light dragoons busied themselves keeping the French on the move, rounding up prisoners and joining in the plundering of the wagons and carriages which had now begun.

The hussar brigade, on the other hand, had been launched against the retreating French infantry just after the collapse had started and, indeed, it was their arrival that sparked off much of the chaos amongst the fugitives when they charged into the rear of the fleeing mass, firing their pistols and carbines to create panic. Some Spanish accounts claim that General Alava, Wellington's liaison officer and a native of Vittoria, had managed to close the gates of Vittoria in order to save it from the sort of treatment Ciudad Rodrigo and Badajoz had suffered the previous year. However, it is almost certain that some British hussars managed to get into the town and, indeed, charged right through it, emerging on the other side in pursuit of the French. It was at this point that the 18th Hussars disgraced themselves when, instead of charging the fleeing French, groups of them stopped to plunder the town. Many got themselves drunk and were in this intoxicated state when Wellington himself came up, which did nothing for their reputation. Furthermore, Captain Kennedy's squadron of the same regiment came close to taking King Joseph himself and might have done so had not his men stopped to join in the plundering. Elsewhere, the other regiments of hussars, the 10th and 15th, charged some units of French infantry but were thrown back by enemy cavalry. It was always going to be difficult for Grant to maintain order given the mass of treasure accompanying the French, much of which had been abandoned, and it was this that continually proved to be the object of the hussars' attention. One squadron of the 10th Hussars, under Henry Wyndham, got in amongst the enemy's baggage and, after fighting off several determined attacks by the enemy to recover it, began emptying the wagons of their contents. The 10th actually came very close to taking King Joseph when Wyndham and Henry, Marquess of Worcester, a lieutenant in the 10th, took his carriage, throwing open one of the doors at the very moment that Joseph was jumping out of the other side. It was a very close call for Napoleon's brother. The Hussar brigade had by now dispersed to join in the plundering of the French treasure wagons, as did hundreds of other British, Portuguese, Spanish and, indeed, French troops, and it was this that allowed the French army to get away without the pursuit that should have taken place. It was not, therefore, a very creditable performance by the cavalry.

At the Battle of Vittoria the British cavalry numbered around 6,000 officers and men with a further 1,332 KGL and 893 Portuguese cavalry taking part also.[10] They had never before been present in such strength, nor would they ever be again in the Peninsula. Indeed, Wellington's British cavalry regiments at Waterloo numbered just 5,913, which gives us some idea of how strong the cavalry arm was at Vittoria. And yet, despite this, the cavalry suffered only 154 casualties, which reflects the small part played by them during the battle.[11] The French cavalry, also, played little part in the battle, losing only 472 men out of a strength of around 10,000.

It might be argued that the ground did not allow for widespread use of cavalry, and this may be argued with some validity, for the Zadorra river effectively divided the battlefield into two sections – the first, consisting of Wellington's staging areas, and the second of the actual fighting area itself. In his despatch to Earl Bathurst, Wellington himself mentioned the fact that the unfavourable ground did not allow the cavalry a good opportunity to act during the battle.[12] We need not trouble ourselves with Hill's column, as its allotted fighting ground was atop the lofty heights of Puebla, where no cavalry could operate at all. The cavalry attached to him, the brigades of Alten, Fane and Long, simply moved on along the valley floor in support of O'Callaghan's brigade once the remainder of Hill's infantry began to ascend the heights. Dalhousie, also, can be discounted, as no cavalry moved from the mountains with his column. The majority of Wellington's cavalry at Vittoria had to wait for the infantry to establish themselves on the French-held side of the Zadorra, the south bank, and until that moment they waited patiently in the rear. Furthermore, once the Allied infantry had fought their way across the bridges at the western end of the battlefield at Villodas, Tres Puentes and Mendoza, the cavalry still had to wait until the French were pushed back sufficiently for them to deploy. At Gamarra Mayor, the cavalry with Graham, being Bock's and Anson's brigades, would not get across the Zadorra until late in the day, by which time the French army was on the point of collapse.

It was the opportunities after the battle, lost by the cavalry, that so incensed Wellington. Although the ground to the east of Vittoria was very difficult for cavalry, there is little doubt that had even a couple of brigades been got forward in good order, the haul of French prisoners would have been far greater than it was,[13] One could, of course, speculate about the influence Stapleton Cotton might have had if he had been present at the battle. Bock, commanding the cavalry in Cotton's absence, appears to have had little influence on the performance of the cavalry as he was present with Graham throughout. It is almost certain that Wellington himself would have controlled the cavalry brigades he had with him, although once they had got in amongst the treasure there was little he could do to bring the men to their senses. But not all of the British cavalry regiments joined in the widespread plundering and looting that followed the battle and, indeed, many were unaware of the presence of the treasure, which is probably just as well. The majority of the cavalry retained their good order and camped to the north of the town afterwards as night fell over the battlefield.

Wellington's extreme annoyance at his men's failure to maintain order and conduct an effective pursuit led to two famous outbursts in his Despatches. In the first, written to Earl Bathurst on 29 June, he wrote:

> We started with the army in the highest order, and up to the day of the battle nothing could get on better; but that event has, as usual, totally annihilated all order and discipline. The soldiers of the army have got among them about a million sterling in money, with the exception of about 100,000 dollars, which were got for the military chest. The night of the battle, instead of being passed in getting rest and food to prepare them for the pursuit of the following day, was passed by the soldiers in looking for plunder. The consequence was, that they were incapable of marching in pursuit of the enemy, and were totally knocked up... This is the consequence of the state of discipline of the British Army. We may gain the greatest victories; but we shall do no good until we shall alter our system, as to force all ranks to perform their duty. The new regiments are, as usual, the worst of all. The 18th Hussars are a disgrace to the name of a soldier, in action as well as elsewhere; and I propose to draft their horses from them, and to send the men to England, if I cannot get the better of them in any other manner.[14]

It is interesting to note how Wellington himself was moved to lay the blame for the misconduct by the cavalry after the battle of Vittoria at the feet of the 'new' regiments, the hussar brigade. Woodberry, himself an officer with the 18th Hussars, wrote in his journal, 'The Hussars brigade will be broke up immediately by Lord Wellington, who is not at all pleased with Colonel Grant's manoeuvring at the Battle of Vittoria. They all allow the officer to be possessed of courage and resolution, but all say he wants judgement.'[15] It will be remembered that Woodberry had earlier described the hussars at Morales as being 'mad for action', and given their lengthy absence from the Peninsula, one wonders whether this had any bearing on their conduct. After all, the more experienced cavalry regiments appear to have had little share in the plundering of the French baggage train. The majority of the British cavalry benefited from much experience, having been in the Peninsula for many years and having endured both the highs and lows of years of hard campaigning. The hussar brigade, on the other hand, had come out to Spain when all was going well and when the defeat of the French seemed inevitable. They were, in other words, able to reap the benefits of many years' hard grafting by the light and heavy dragoons and seemed determined to make up for lost time.[16] True, they had proved their worth during the campaign of 1808–9 but much water had flowed under the bridge since the dark days of the retreat to Corunna and the hussars now found themselves in the midst of a very different war, with far greater numbers involved and with the Allies in the ascendancy. They did well at Morales but were fortunate that the French had no desire to turn and fight as Lallemand had done at Maguilla, whilst at Vittoria they were simply pursuing a beaten enemy. The victories at Sahagun, Mayorga and Benavente must have seemed a world away, and it is interesting to speculate on how they might have performed had they been present with Wellington's army during the hard years of the war in 1810 and 1811.[17]

An even greater – and more famous – condemnation of Wellington's troops at Vittoria came on 2 July, again in a despatch to Earl Bathurst. 'It is quite impossible for me or any other man to command a British army under the present system. We have in the service the scum of the earth as common soldiers; and of late years we have been doing every thing in our power, both by law and by publications, to relax the discipline by which alone such men can be kept in order... It is really a disgrace to have any thing to say to such men as some of our soldiers are.'[18] By the time Wellington sent this letter to Bathurst, he had already called in Colonel Grant to give him a thorough dressing-down over the conduct of his hussars, and the 18th in particular. Apparently, Wellington 'expressed himself in strong terms' against the 18th and told Grant to pass on his views to the officers of the regiment.[19] These sorts of rebukes were not to be taken lightly and one cannot help thinking that the 18th were lucky not to be sent home. After all, the army was about to enter the Pyrenees where there would be little for them to do and with his army now in great strength, unlike the earlier years of the war, they probably could have been spared if it meant avoiding the sort of scrapes into which some of the cavalry regiments had got themselves earlier in the war. In the event, the 18th Hussars remained in the Peninsula, albeit with the threat of an early return to England hanging over them.

With the Battle of Vittoria won, and the French pushed back over the Pyrenees, the war in Spain was effectively at an end. Only Pamplona and San Sebastian remained in French hands while Suchet, who had fought a relentless if somewhat anonymous war on Spain's eastern coast, pulled back to the borders of his own country. There was still the Battle of the Pyrenees to come, when Soult – who replaced Joseph as French commander – launched an offensive in late July, but the years of open warfare in Spain and Portugal were at an end and Wellington was finally able to turn his attention to the invasion of France. But before this could happen, Wellington needed to take both San Sebastian and Pamplona, and it was the relief of this latter town which led to the Battle of the Pyrenees between 25 July and 2 August. In the event, Soult was unsuccessful and his bid to relieve Pamplona came to a halt at Sorauren, a tantalising few miles north of the town, after two hard-fought battles on 28–30 July. The mountain terrain afforded hardly any opportunities for the cavalry to get into the action, although the 14th Light Dragoons did become involved at Beunza, whilst the 18th Hussars did good work at Sorauren on Wellington's right flank, engaging enemy cavalry in an extended exchange of carbine fire.

But overall, the role of the British cavalry in July 1813 was merely as support to the infantry. Indeed, whilst Wellington's field army advanced to the Bidassoa in preparation for the invasion of France – San Sebastian fell in August – the majority of the British cavalry returned south to the area around Logroño and Olite, where forage was relatively easy to obtain. Other than some of the light cavalry regiments who would be needed for piquet and intelligence work, there would be no further need for the cavalry until the early spring of 1814, by which time Wellington's army had firmly established itself in France.

Notes

1 For more on these Provisional Battalions, see *Sir Charles Oman's Wellington's Army, 1809–1814* (London, 1913), 186–8.
2 See *General Orders*, Freineda, 13 March and 25 April 1813.
3 The commanding officer of the 18th Hussars, this particular Colquhoun Grant is not to be confused with Colquhoun Grant, the famous intelligence officer.
4 Indeed, the Esla at Almendra was described as being as wide as the Thames at Windsor.
5 Lieutenant George Woodberry, *Manuscript Journal of the 1813 Campaign*.
6 Ibid.
7 Ibid. There are various accounts of the fight at Morales. Woodberry, a participant with the 18th Hussars, is pretty accurate, whilst other accounts introduce other incidents and units. Fortescue, for example, in his *History of the British Army* (London, 1899), IX: 142–3, relies upon Digeon's own report and ends up with an account of the fight which agrees largely with Woodberry. Oman, on the other hand calls Digeon's report 'unconvincing', and gives the action only a few lines. *History of the Peninsular War* (Oxford, 1902), VI: 331–2. Napier, *History of the War in the Peninsula* (London, 1828), V: 525, says very little whilst Grant's own report to Wellington (Wellington to Bathurst, 6 June 1813, *The Despatches of Field Marshal the Duke of Wellington, during his various campaigns* (London, 1834), X: 422) is similarly short. John Mollo, in his *Prince's Dolls: Scandals, Skirmishes and Splendours of the Hussars, 1793–1815* (London, 1997), assembles several good eyewitness reports but then makes a complete hash of pulling them together, citing two separate chases of two miles, followed by another for two miles. Indeed, he scatters Woodberry's account all over the place, and generally gets his account out of all synchronisation.
8 Fortescue, *History of the British Army*, IX: 143.
9 Woodberry, MSS.
10 Oman, *History of the Peninsular War*, VI: 750. The figures represent the strengths at the end of May 1813, so there almost certainly would have been reductions in these figures, although not many. Oman gives the strength of Victor Alten's brigade as 1,005, which includes the 1st Hussars KGL. There are no accurate figures for the strength of the 14th Light Dragoons, the other regiment in the brigade, although they numbered 380 in April 1813. The total figure arrived at, therefore, being around 6,000, is not too wide of the mark. At Waterloo, the

British cavalry numbered 5,913. See Weller, *Wellington at Waterloo* (London, 1967), 242. Weller arrived at his figure after a careful comparison of James, Fortescue, Siborne, Hooper, Ropes and Becke.

11 These casualties were nevertheless enough for 'Vittoria' to be awarded as a battle honour to the following regiments and their descendants: 3rd Dragoon Guards, 5th Dragoon Guards, 3rd Dragoons, 4th Dragoons, 10th and 15th Hussars, and the 13th, 14th and 16th Light Dragoons. David Ascoli, *A Companion to the British Army* (London, 1984), 233.

12 Wellington to Bathurst, 22 June 1813, *Despatches*, X: 452.

13 2,825 French prisoners were taken at Vittoria, which compares rather unfavourably with the number taken at Salamanca, for example, which was around the 7,000 mark. It says much for the ineffectiveness of the Allied pursuit that, considering the disarray of the French army after Vittoria, such a low number of prisoners were taken.

14 Wellington to Earl Bathurst, 29 June 1813. *Despatches*, X: 472-3. In the printed version of *Despatches*, the name of the newly-arrived cavalry regiment is omitted, one of the more irritating aspects of Gurwood's editorship. The blanked-out names are not difficult to discover in the original despatches, however.

15 Woodberry, MSS.

16 It is interesting to note that, unlike the 10th and 15th Hussars, the 18th Hussars were not awarded 'Vittoria' as a battle honour, despite – or rather because of – their showing during the battle.

17 Mollo makes the significant point that, unlike the 7th, 10th and 15th Hussars, all of which had been converted from light dragoon regiments, the 18th Hussars had not been present during the periods of training at Ipswich under Lord Paget and that being 'an Irish regiment, full of Irish hotheads, they had never been properly part of the Hussar Brigade'. *The Prince's Dolls*. 133–4.

18 Wellington to Earl Bathurst, 2 July 1813, *Despatches*, X: 495–6. This was the first time Wellington used his infamous 'scum of the earth' remark. He used it again some eighteen years later in a conversation with Earl Stanhope, although on the second occasion he added, 'and it really is wonderful that we should have made them the fine fellows they are.' Philip Henry, 5th Earl Stanhope, *Notes of Conversations with the Duke of Wellington, 1831–1851* (London, 1888), 18.

19 Mollo, *The Prince's Dolls*, 132. Mollo's book contains a good account of the plundering in which the hussar brigade indulged after the battle of Vittoria.

CHAPTER IX

France: From the Bidassoa
to Toulouse and Home

The winter of 1813–14 may have been a quiet one for the majority of Wellington's cavalry, but for the infantry the closing months of the year, from October to December, saw some of the hardest fighting of the war and in the most miserable conditions. On 7 October Wellington crossed the Bidassoa close to the sea, with Soult believing the invasion would come many miles inland. The following month, on 10 November, Wellington reversed the process and advanced inland, with Soult on this occasion massing his troops along the coast. The Battle of the Nivelle was one of Wellington's greatest achievements, with his army hitting the over-stretched French line in overwhelming strength along two thirds of its length. On 9 December Hill crossed the Nive river and by so doing brought the Allied army to the powerfully defended town of Bayonne, Soult's military base, on both left and right banks of the river. Bayonne was never besieged in the same way that Ciudad Rodrigo, Badajoz and San Sebastian were, but was blockaded, with the Allies firmly ensconced to the south and east of the town, which was itself protected not only by very strong walls and defences but by strong armed camps. The town itself lay on the Adour river, and so was protected to the north.

The Battle of the Nive is the collective name for a series of small actions fought to the south of Bayonne from 10–13 December, the largest of which took place on the final day at St Pierre. In fact, this latter action is often called the Battle of St Pierre although it officially forms part of the Battle of the Nive. It was all part of a French counter-attack which, despite some very hard fighting during which Soult made significant gains, was ultimately a failure. On 24 February the Allies crossed the Adour river and in doing so blockaded Bayonne from all sides, although by this time Soult and his field army had left the town and had marched to the north-east, leaving Bayonne with a strong garrison of around 14,000 troops. After leaving a blockading force around Bayonne, Wellington marched after Soult, and on 27 February the two armies clashed in the last major battle of the war to be fought in open country.

We may well ask what the cavalry was doing during this period. Well, Wellington's cavalry was doing very little as far as the main battles were concerned and, indeed, it can be said with a degree of certainty that what might be called the 'golden age' of the British cavalry in the Peninsula was firmly in the past. The 7th Hussars had arrived in the Peninsula in September, but otherwise there was little to lift the tedium of routine work. The cavalry collectively suffered just a handful of casualties during the Battles of the Nivelle and Nive, and during the operations crossing the Bidassoa and the invasion of France. This is not surprising given the nature of the ground. The Bidassoa flows inland beneath a series of towering heights which stand on the northern or French side of the river. Indeed, the ground was difficult enough for infantry to fight over, let alone mounted troops. Once across the Bidassoa, the army deployed in preparation for the attack on Soult's position along another line of hills on the Nivelle river. Here again the ground is unsuitable, although the hills are much lower and the ground to the south of the Nivelle did allow a small measure of room for cavalry to deploy, although only in support of the attacking infantry. All in all, Wellington's cavalry was virtually unemployed during the latter months of 1813, save for the usual routine such as patrols and piquet work. There was literally no room for them at the front.

Having flushed Soult from the forts and redoubts along the Nivelle, Wellington's men found themselves fighting across lush, green fields with high hedges, reminiscent of England. Many British officers mentioned the similarity between the English countryside and the area in which they found themselves at the end of 1813. This again restricted the movements of Wellington's cavalry, for they found themselves almost entirely confined to the country lanes and roads that lay to the east of Cambo and the Nive river.[1] It was yet another variation in the campaigning country in the Peninsula and was similar in many ways to the ruggedness of Portugal. Indeed, the wide open spaces of Andalucia and Castille and Leon must have seemed a world away to the men of the light cavalry regiments in southern France, whilst the heavy cavalry regiments were still confined to the areas around Logroño, Pamplona and Olite. This is not to say that the cavalry were not active, however. Indeed, the 18th Hussars in particular, who had enjoyed mixed fortunes since their arrival in the Peninsula, embroiled themselves in one or two notable scraps, as did other regiments. Although it would be tedious to mention every single skirmish it would, nevertheless, be of interest to take a look at two of these fights just to examine the nature of cavalry operations in this area.

The first of these two actions came on 12 December at Hasparren, a village on the right bank of the Nive river. With his offensive on the left bank of the Nive against Wellington and the main body of the Allied army having yielded few gains, Soult decided to try his hand on the right bank against Hill and his wing of the army. Soult accordingly advanced Pierre Soult's cavalry from the Bidouze river as well as General Paris's infantry who drove Vivian's cavalry, the 14th Light Dragoons, from Hasparren. Hill's force lay farther north towards the Adour, his only communication with Wellington being a pontoon bridge over the Nive at Villafranca and the fords and bridge at Ustaritz, farther south. Vivian, a relative new comer in the Peninsula,[2] decided to turn about and charge and immediately ordered Major Thomas Brotherton with the 14th Light Dragoons to charge back across the narrow bridge at the village, on the opposite side of which were drawn up the 13th Chasseurs and the 2nd Hussars. The task facing Brotherton was such a daunting one, and unlikely to be attended with any degree of success, that he himself called his small party a 'forlorn hope'.[3]

Brotherton's 'force' consisted of what he described as his own 'party' of hand-picked men supported by a further half squadron. The trumpeter sounded the charge and the 14th duly charged with Brotherton at their head. Unfortunately, his misgivings were well founded for the bridge was so narrow it allowed only three men to pass, one being Brotherton himself plus his orderly, and the third being Lieutenant Southwell. The ensuing fight was recalled later by Brotherton and paints so vivid a picture of cavalry combat that it is worthy of quotation at length.

> The enemy received us with a volley from their pistols and carbines when we were close upon them. Southwell's horse fell dead, and he under him. However, myself and orderly closed with the enemy. The orderly had his bridle-hand nearly chopped off, and was run through the body, and I was left alone amidst the enemy. I was belaboured with cuts and thrusts from all sides, defending myself as long as I could against such odds. However, after receiving eleven thrusts, three of which only wounded me (as I wore a buffalo leather cuirass which I had made at Madrid, after having been run through the body at Salamanca) I was wounded through the neck, in the right hip, or to speak more plainly, in the bottom, on the right side, and another stab in the thigh, which would have proved the worst of all, had it not been for a bunch of letters which I had put into one of the pockets which were then worn with pantaloons. The sword penetrated the letters, and went a quarter of an inch into the thigh, close to what is called, I believe, the femoral artery, which, had it touched, probably it would have proved fatal; but the blow which rendered it impossible to make further resistance was a sabre-cut, aimed at my head, which fell on the peak of my helmet with such force that it bent it on my nose, which flattened and nearly broke, and completely stunned me. As I said, this blow disabled me from further resistance, and, indeed, no signs of any assistance appearing, rendered it useless to resist any longer. Surrounded as I was by fellows cutting and thrusting at me in all directions, and so occupied was I in parrying, that I had not time for assaulting in my turn. It was my intention to surrender, but a little circumstance caused me to be much more roughly treated than I otherwise should probably have been.

I had, previously to advancing to the 'charge', twisted my silk sword-knot round and round my wrist, by way of securing my sword the more effectually; and when stunned by the cut on my helmet, which I have just before mentioned, and summoned on all sides by the vociferations to surrender (*rendez vous*), my sword was seized, but as it was so tightly fastened to my wrist, this was taken for an intention not to surrender it; and a fellow cocked his pistol, and put it to my head to blow out my brains, when I had just sufficiently recovered to articulate *Je me rends*! I was then secured, and tied on my horse, being too faint to sit on otherwise, and galloped off to the rear.[4]

Seeing the predicament in which Brotherton found himself, Vivian brought up the rest of the 14th Light Dragoons and charged but without any success.[5] They were beaten back and were forced to retire upon Morrillo's Spaniards at Urcuray, leaving Brotherton in enemy hands. The fight at Hasparren was typical of the many skirmishes in which the British cavalry became engaged whilst out on patrol during the winter and early spring of 1813–14. These were often what might be termed 'encounter' battles, as one side came across another amidst the hedgerows and fields of southern France. There is little to be learned from such fights, other than those examined in the chapter on piquet and patrol work in the Peninsula. There was never any danger of Wellington's cavalry ever getting out of hand owing to the restrictive nature of the ground. Hasparren bears some relation to Usagre, with the French waiting for the 14th Light Dragoons to come across the bridge, although there were so few of Brotherton's men that comparisons are negligible. However, Pierre Soult's ADC., Lemonnier-Delafosse, claimed in his memoirs that Vivian was led into a trap laid by the commanding officer of the 13th Chasseurs, which does throw up at least one comparison with Usagre.[6]

With Soult's counter-offensive in December at an end, and with his army retreating eastwards, we must leave the Bayonne area to follow the fortunes of the cavalry on their pursuit of Soult to Orthes, which was the last major battle in the Peninsula in open country. The area between the Nive and Orthes is divided by rivers and *gaves*, the latter being the local name for mountainous streams or rivers. These obstacles were, from west to east, the Joyeuse, the Bidouze, the Saison,[7] the Gave d'Oloron and the Gave de Pau. One can imagine, therefore, the difficulties faced not only by the cavalry but by the army in general in getting through this country, for in addition to these watercourses, the roads were bounded by hedges and ditches whilst the roads themselves were not particularly good given the bad weather in January and February 1814. Nevertheless, Wellington's army pushed forward in pursuit of Soult with each river and *gave* being duly passed with varying degrees of difficulty.

These operations naturally involved, the infantry in the majority of the fighting, although the 13th Light Dragoons saw action during the crossing of the Saison on 17 February.[8] The only other cavalry involvement during the river crossings came on 24 February during the crossing of the Gave d'Oloron. During this operation, Picton's 3rd Division was ordered to assemble near Osserain and Arriverete in order to make demonstrations again Villate's left flank, whilst other divisions crossed the Gave farther north. The division was to operate in conjunction with Cotton and the Hussar Brigade but, as was often the case with Picton, he exceeded his orders and tried to cross the river himself. Instead of confining himself to demonstrations, he ordered the light companies of Keane's brigade to ford the Gave d'Oloron at Monein whereupon the infantry duly began to wade out into the deep waters. The light companies reached the other side of the river only to find themselves charged by two battalions of the French 119th Regiment, positioned at the top of the ascent leading from the ford. The French sent Keane's men reeling back into the river and no fewer than ninety were either killed, wounded, taken prisoner or drowned. Cotton, seeing the infantry in difficulty, sent a squadron of the 7th Hussars to their assistance but, with the enemy in strength on the opposite bank, they were recalled. Apparently, 'high words' were exchanged between Picton and Cotton, with the former obviously feeling let down by the cavalry, who were nevertheless blameless.

Gradually, the rivers and *gaves* were passed and with the crossing of the Gave de Pau on 26 February Wellington brought his army face to face with Soult at Orthes. The battle was fought on 27 February amidst tall hedges and woods, and once again the ground ensured there would be very little for the British cavalry to do during the battle. Present at Orthes were Fane's brigade, comprising the 13th Light Dragoons and the 14th Light Dragoons, Vivian's brigade, of the 18th Hussars and the 1st Hussars KGL, and Somerset's brigade, being the 7th, 10th and 15th Hussars. It is a measure of how little work there was for these three brigades that, of 3,373 present, only thirty-seven became casualties, all of whom were British.

The battle involved Wellington's army in an attack on Soult's position which lay along the main Dax-Orthes road. Once again it was the infantry which did the overwhelming majority of the fighting as they struggled up the frosty slopes to get to grips with the French infantry in position along the road. It was a very hard-fought battle, with Wellington's army sustaining some 1,645 casualties, 699 of which were from Picton's 3rd Division. The day ended with Soult's army, fighting on home soil, retreating in the direction of Mont de Marsan, where Soult had established a large supply of stores.

Although the brunt of the fighting at Orthes fell upon the infantry, it is worth recording two incidents which involved the British cavalry. The first took place on the French left flank, where Hill was attacking with the 2nd Division. During the course of the morning French cavalry were observed moving in from the east towards Hill's left flank, whereupon

Sir William Stewart ordered the 13th Light Dragoons to move not only in order to protect the guns of Captain Bean's battery, but to meet the threat posed by the enemy cavalry. As the 13th advanced the French were seen, 'advancing in considerable force and at a brisk pace'.[9] For once, the road was wide enough for the 13th to form into column of divisions, being three abreast, whereupon Lieutenant-Colonel Doherty, commanding the regiment, ordered the charge with his two sons, Captain Doherty and Lieutenant Doherty at his side.[10] The French also charged and the two sides clashed with the 13th getting the better of their enemies. During the fight, Lieutenant Doherty was attacked by the French commanding officer, but he parried his thrust and gave him a cut 'between the bottom of his shako and his collar, instantly killing him'. The French quickly turned about and fled but, apparently, got themselves wedged into a bend in the road which allowed the 13th to get in amongst them with their sabres. The French finally managed to extricate themselves and were pursued for almost a mile before the halt was sounded, 'it not being deemed prudent to proceed farther without support'. These words from the regimental history show just how much the 13th Light Dragoons had learned during the war after having been let down at Campo Mayor at the outset of their campaign. If Long had realised he had no support on this latter occasion, these very words would probably have been used then. However, the comparison is only slight, as Doherty had a major battle in progress behind him at Orthes and was hardly likely to go galloping off in pursuit of a beaten enemy for too great a distance. Instead, he merely broke the French cavalry, again in a fair stand-up fight, chased them away and returned to his station having done another good job.

There was some considerable disorder within the French ranks elsewhere on the battlefield as they retreated, but there was never going to be any effective pursuit by the British cavalry as the ground prevented this. Despite the bad ground, the 7th Hussars, in their first real action, managed to catch up with the French rearguard before Sault-de-Navailles. In the ensuing charge they cut off two units of French infantry from Harispe's division and took hundreds of prisoners.[12] The mere presence of British cavalry was enough to spread panic throughout the retreating French army and create some confusion. It was just as well that the battlefield did not resemble some of those farther south in Spain, where pursuit of a broken enemy was never achieved through having an insufficient number of cavalry. At Orthes, as at Vittoria, British cavalry were present in great strength, but it was suitable ground that was lacking.[13]

After the Battle of Orthes Soult continued his north-easterly retreat with Wellington's cavalry following behind. There may not have been much action for the cavalry, but there was still plenty of work to keep them occupied, a task that was made easier by the arrival, on 10 March, of the various brigades of heavy cavalry – the Household Brigade, Arentschildt's KGL dragoons[14] and Ponsonby's and Clifton's dragoons – which had finally left their cantonments south of the Pyrenees and now joined the main army. Wellington's cavalry was now at full strength, numbering over 8,000 men. What would he have given for this number of cavalry during the lean years of the war between 1810 and 1812 when he was continually outnumbered by French cavalry? Now, with 8,000 cavalry under his command, the war was almost at an end and there would be little scope for his cavalry, save for routine work, such as patrolling, piquet and escort work.

On 20 March Hill came upon the French rearguard under Clausel at Tarbes. The ensuing fight involved the Light Division attacking uphill against two French divisions, those of Villatte and Harispe, who only broke and fled after some very hard fighting. Somerset's cavalry managed to get around the French right flank, but were once again prevented by the hedges, ditches and enclosures from cutting off the French, and consequently Clausel managed to get away and rejoin Soult's main force which was making its way east towards Toulouse. There were numerous small fights in February and March 1814 which involved mainly the British hussar brigade, but this is not to say that other light cavalry regiments were not active. Indeed, on 22 March the 13th Light Dragoons, veterans of countless battles in the Peninsula, demonstrated that the inactivity of the winter months had done little to take the edge off their fighting abilities when they came up against four squadrons of French cavalry at St Gaudens, a town about thirty-five miles east of Tarbes. Two squadrons of the 13th, under Colonel Doherty,[15] found four squadrons of the enemy drawn up in front of the town, whereupon Doherty formed his men and charged, breaking the French and driving them pell-mell through the streets. The French rallied on the far side of the town but were charged once again by the 13th, with the same result. This time the French were broken and pursued for a full two miles before the 13th halted, having taken over a hundred prisoners and inflicted many casualties.

It is rather fitting that one of the last cavalry actions of the war should have been fought out by the 13th Light Dragoons, a regiment which had seen much active service since first arriving in the Peninsula in February 1810. They had seen their fair share of controversies, none more so than at Campo Mayor, but had demonstrated their effectiveness during numerous other battles and skirmishes ever since. At St Gaudens the 13th broke their enemies as they had done at Campo Mayor almost three years to the day earlier, although on this occasion their pursuit was not attended with the same misfortune. There was no French reserve and although there was no British reserve either, there was no need for one as the 13th halted once their task had been accomplished, whereupon they returned to St Gaudens.

The end of March saw Wellington's army at the very gates of Toulouse, with Soult's army bottled up inside the town. With 49,000 men, Wellington outnumbered Soult by 7,000, although this meant very little given the fact that the Battle of Toulouse on 10 April was akin to an assault on a town, where numbers mattered little and the defenders held the advantage. Two days before the actual battle the British cavalry engaged their French counterparts on one of the last occasions in the Peninsula, at Croix d'Orade, north of Toulouse. With Wellington's army advancing upon Toulouse from the north in two columns on opposite sides of the Ers river it was absolutely vital for him to secure the bridge in order for the two wings of the army to concentrate. The French had not blown the bridge at Croix d'Orade but had left it defended by Vial's cavalry brigade who had drawn up in front of it.[16] At the head of the left wing of Wellington's army were the 18th Hussars, with Vivian at their head, who came up against Vial's piquets at the village of St Loup, driving them back and inflicting several casualties upon them. With Vial's cavalry dispersed, Vivian got the 18th Hussars forward to the bridge and found the 22nd Chasseurs defending it, with the 5th Chasseurs dismounted on the far side of the river, firing away at the 18th with their carbines. At this point Vivian was joined by Wellington and Beresford, who had come forward to reconnoitre this vital bridge themselves. Vivian knew what he had to do and, returning to the 18th Hussars, ordered them to form for the charge. As he did so he was struck in the arm by a carbine ball. At first there appeared to be no damage, but as he raised his arm to give the signal for the charge to begin, the bone of his arm snapped, whereupon he fainted and was led from the field. Major Hughes, of the 18th, assumed command of his regiment and led them forward against the French at the bridge. Their charge was so ferocious that the French 22nd Chasseurs at the bridge were thrown back and jammed in against it, much in the same manner that Bron's dragoons had been at Usagre in 1811. Pierre Soult, commanding the French cavalry, was there in person and narrowly escaped capture himself as the French broke and fled to the rear in the face of the 18th's charge. Others were not so lucky, however, and trapped on the bridge or in front of it were simply hacked down by the British hussars. Eventually, the French broke completely and streamed away to the rear with the 18th Hussars in pursuit, the British cavalry not halting until they came within range of the French guns at Toulouse itself. Here, they turned and rode back to the bridge which was secured by Ross's brigade of the 4th Division, having taken over 120 prisoners in addition to inflicting scores of killed and wounded.[17]

The 18th Hussars had enjoyed an unfavourable reputation with Wellington ever since their misadventures at Vittoria, and it was with some relief that they received his praise. 'Well done, the Eighteenth; by God, well done.'[18] It was indeed a fine achievement for the 18th. At a cost of just fifteen killed and wounded they had secured the vital bridge over the Ers river and thus allowed the two wings of Wellington's army to join together and move against Toulouse. Any delay would have allowed the

French to blow the bridge, which would have seriously compromised Wellington's plans.

It was the last cavalry combat of the Peninsular War and was a most satisfying one for the British cavalry. Fortescue calls it a 'brilliant little affair'.[19] In a repeat of Usagre they had acted swiftly in scattering Vial's piquets and had once again beaten their French counterparts in a stand-up fight, trapping them against a bridge which allowed the French no freedom to defend themselves. The pursuit was carried on for some distance and, although it brought the 18th within cannon shot of the defenders, casualties were slight and with no French counter-attack they were allowed to return to the bridge having successfully accomplished their task. It was a fine end to the cavalry's service in the Peninsula.

The Battle of Toulouse was once again an infantry affair, although Wellington's cavalry was present in support. The battle, fought on 10 April, involved Wellington's infantry attacking the defences around Toulouse at several different places. The city was not fortified in the same manner as Ciudad Rodrigo, Badajoz or San Sebastian, but it was protected by a series of earthworks and redoubts situated upon Mont Rave, to the east of the city, and was covered not only by the Garonne river but by the Languedoc canal which effectively isolates the city on the right bank of the river. The attacks were made difficult by the shortage of open frontage, and by the end of the day severe casualties had been sustained for no great gain. Wellington's cavalry spent the day supporting the infantry but there was no real role for them here. The day ended with Wellington losing 4,568 men, against French casualties of 3,236, a high price to pay for such small gains. Furthermore, unbeknown to Wellington, Napoleon had actually abdicated four days earlier, which meant that the assault need never have taken place at all. On 12 April Soult managed to extricate himself from Toulouse, leaving the city by the only open roads to the south-east of the city, between the Garonne and the Ariege stream.

Soult finally surrendered on 17 April, but it was to be a further ten days before Thouvenol, the governor of Bayonne, surrendered the town to the Allies. Indeed, on 14 April he had launched a sortie from the town against the British and KGL infantry blockading him to the north of the Adour. The end result of this mischievous act was over 1,500 casualties suffered by both sides. It was the final action of the war.

With the war at an end, it only remained for the army to return home. This was something which could not begin immediately, of course, and the cavalry did not begin their march home until the beginning of June. There were affecting scenes when the British and Portuguese regiments, which had fought side by side for so long, finally had to part. Many British soldiers had married Spanish or Portuguese women, many of whom had to return to their homes in Spain or Portugal, whilst hundreds of camp followers did likewise. The British soldiers had long since regarded the

Portuguese troops as their brothers-in-arms, and it was something of a wrench when it came to saying farewell to them. But it had to be, and before the end of May 1814, long columns of Portuguese infantry and cavalry were winding their way over the Pyrenees on the long march home. Thousands of muleteers, who had followed and served Wellington's army faithfully for years, did likewise. In fact, a great meeting took place at Almeida after the war when thousands of these muleteers gathered to settle their outstanding pay claims. It was a momentous occasion.

The British Army, meanwhile, assembled at Bordeaux to begin re-embarkation aboard the ships that would take them home to England or Ireland or, if they were unlucky, to some other foreign station. For the cavalry, however, it was quite a different story, for they would return home not aboard ships but would march through France to the ports of Calais and Boulogne from where they would finally sail home to England. The task of getting the cavalry home fell to the Quartermaster General's department, which organised all army movements. The cavalry marched home to England along with the Royal Horse Artillery batteries of Bean's Troop, Gardiner's Troop, Ross's Troop and the horses of the Waggon Train. Altogether there were some 11,300 horses, the overwhelming majority being from the cavalry regiments.

The entire mounted force was divided into two columns. The first or right column consisted of four separate units, each of which had staggered departure dates to avoid clogging the roads and to ease the burden of supply. The four units were A; the 7th, 10th and 15th Hussars, some 2,000 in all, B; the 5th Dragoon Guards, and the 3rd and 4th Dragoons, 1,400, C; the 3rd Dragoon Guards, 1st (Royal) Dragoons, and Bean's Troop RHA, 1,300, and D; the 1st and 2nd Life Guards, Royal Horse Guards, and Gardiner's Troop RHA, 1,600. The first of these units, A, would begin the long march north from Grizolles, starting on 1 June, with the three other units departing on each of the succeeding days. They would arrive at Calais between 14 and 17 July.

The second column, marching farther to the west, consisted of four more units. A; the 12th, 13th and 16th Light Dragoons, 1,500 in all, B; the 1st Hussars KGL, the 18th Hussars and Ross's Troop RHA, 1,500, C; the 1st and 2nd Dragoons KGL, and the horses of the 4th and 6th Divisions, 1,500, and D; being the 14th Light Dragoons and the horses of the Waggon Train, 500. Unit A of this column started north from Saint-André on 3 June, with the remaining three units setting out on the three succeeding days. They arrived at Boulogne between 5 and 8 July.[20]

The journey home appears to have been relatively free of incident. During the long march the various regiments almost certainly reflected on the past years of campaigning, particularly the light and heavy dragoon regiments that had been out in the Peninsula since 1809. The 13th Light Dragoons, for example, could reflect on the controversies and injustices of

Campo Mayor and on a whole host of successful actions in the Peninsula. The 1st (Royal) Dragoons probably cast their minds back to southern Spain, to Maguilla, and their period of service under the command of 'Black Jack' Slade. The 5th Dragoon Guards, on the other hand, could consider themselves as having done their duty, having fought in several actions including Salamanca, where they had charged under John Gaspard Le Marchant on that hot, dry, dusty summer's day. That particular field must have seemed a long way off to the men riding through the green fields of France on their homeward journey. What a pity Le Marchant himself wasn't coming home with them.

Once back in England, the cavalry regiments returned home to their respective stations to refit, recover and to re-adjust to home life after what was for some a period of five years' absence. But if Wellington's cavalry thought they had seen the last of the French army they were mistaken, for within a year they would be preparing for war once again following Napoleon's escape from exile on the tiny Mediterranean island of Elba. The Hundred Days campaign was about to begin.

Notes

1 Napier wrote, 'deep ditches and enclosures and small copses, villages and farmhouses, prevented the British cavalry from acting'. William Napier, *History of the War in the Peninsula* (London; 1828), VI: 618.

2 Colonel Hussey Vivian had served in the Corunna campaign of 1808–9 but had not been in the Peninsula since. He returned only in August 1813.

3 Brotherton, quoted in Colonel H.B. Hamilton's *History of the 14th Hussars, 1715–1900* (London, 1901), 130.

4 Ibid. 130.

5 Napier describes Vivian's order to Brotherton to pass the bridge as 'ill-judged', something which created much ill-will between the two in later years. Indeed, in 1846, the *United Service Journal* published an account of the fight which prompted Vivian, Brotherton and Southwell – who survived the action – to put pen to paper, each taking different sides.

6 Sir Charles Oman, *History of the Peninsular War* (Oxford, 1902), VII: 260–1.

7 The Saison river is often referred to as the Gave de Mauleon, a river which flows to the south of the Saison from somewhere around Nabas, Charre and Haute. This gives rise to some confusion as one often thinks of them as being two separate rivers whereas they are, in fact, one river. Weller, perhaps falling foul of some of this confusion, actually gives the crossing of the Saison as happening on 23 February, whereas this was the date of the crossing of the Gave d'Oloron. *Se Weller, Wellington in the Peninsula* (London, 1962), 344.

8 See CR.B. Barratt's *History of the 13th Hussars* (London, 1911), I: 232.

9 Ibid. 236.

10 Ibid. 237. Napier incorrectly says the incident took place at St Gaudens and, as usual, is followed by Oman.

11 Echoing Napier's description of the ground, Oman wrote, 'the French army had become a mere hurrying crowd. That it suffered no greater damage than it did from the British cavalry was due to the character of the country – cultivated fields surrounded by walls, and cut across by ditches. Though Vivian's, Fane's and Somerset's brigades were all to the front, they got few opportunities of dealing effective blows.' Oman, *Peninsular War*, VII: 371.

12 Thornhill, of the 7th Hussars, put the number of prisoners taken at 700, although Lord Somerset thought it to be lower, at around 500, still no mean achievement. See John Mollo, *Prince's Dolls* (London, 1997), 162. Thornhill also claims to have captured a halberd carried by one of the escorts to the prized Imperial Eagles, carried into battle by French infantry. See the Hon. C. Vivian (Ed), *Richard Hussey Vivian, 1st Baron Vivian, a Memoir* (London, 1897), 203. Mollo writes that the 7th must have been very close to capturing one of these eagles, a feat performed on just six occasions in the Peninsula, at Barrosa, Salamanca (twice), Foz d'Arouce and Madrid. These latter two eagles were merely found in a barracks, whilst that 'taken' at Foz d'Arouce was simply found in the river after the French dropped it during their retreat. The 50th came very close to taking an eagle at Vimeiro when they captured the pole and box upon which the bird was carried. The French had a crafty way of unscrewing the brass eagle from its pole in order to get it away in the event of its being in danger of capture.

13 Vivian, *Richard Hussey Vivian*, 203.

14 The KGL dragoons had previously been under the command of Bock but he had drowned, along with his son, during his return voyage to England in January 1814.

15 Napier, *War in the Peninsula*, VI: 619, incorrectly gives Doherty's rank as Major.

16 Oman claims the French were in the process of blowing the bridge but were caught unawares by the charge of the 18th Hussars. *Peninsular War*, VII: 463.

17 See Vivian, *Richard Hussey Vivian*, 240–4.

18 Col. Harold Malet, *The Historical Memoirs of the 18th Hussars (Prince of Wales's Own)* (London, 1907), 96.

19 J.W. Fortescue, History of the British Army (London, 1899), X: 76.

20 All of this comes from S.G.P. Ward's excellent article, 'The Quartermaster-General's Department in the Peninsula, 1809–1814,' *Journal for Army Historical Research* (London, 1945), XXIII: 133–54.

CHAPTER X

The Waterloo Campaign:
The Retreat from Quatre Bras

The Waterloo campaign has generated a massive amount of literature since 1815, and continues to do so even today. With so much of the current research concentrating on the relationships between the Allied army commanders, on Anglocentrism and on the political intrigues of the day, one might almost think the actual campaign and battle were of minor importance. This, of course, is not so, for it is what happened on the field of Waterloo itself that is important and not the various other theories. The end result of one of the greatest battles in history was the ending of a great era, the Napoleonic era, and no matter how many thousands of words we expend in analysing the various controversial theories and interpretations of the battle, however plausible, the end result is always the same; the Allied armies of Wellington and Blucher between them defeated the French army under Napoleon, and about this there can be no argument. It is not my intention, therefore, even to think of entering into any of the controversies surrounding the Waterloo campaign but to concentrate instead on the part played by the British cavalry during the campaign and to examine both their performance and subsequent reputation.

The British cavalry regiments arrived back in England in July 1814 after their long march through France. The war in the Peninsula was finally at an end, and the cavalry, as well as the rest of the British Army, no doubt anticipated a period of reflection, refit and rest after six long years of fighting during which many cavalry regiments, in particular the light dragoons, had seen a great deal of service. However, if they thought they were in for a return to their pre-war duties of acting as a secondary police force, or of long periods of inactivity in barracks, they were to be sadly mistaken.

The defeat and abdication of Napoleon in April 1814 had resulted in his exile to the tiny Mediterranean island of Elba, where he was to brood over the past years in the company of around a thousand of his most trusted followers. To the victorious powers of Europe the island seemed far enough away and the ideal place to send the great thief of Europe. The consequent Congress of Vienna, at which the future of the continent was to be discussed and frontiers redrawn, went ahead in November 1814 amidst an air of optimism. This optimism, however, was to prove sadly misplaced when, in March 1815, the Congress received the news of Napoleon's escape. Elba, it would seem, was not far enough away after all. His escape and subsequent return to France came at a critical moment for the Allied powers who, driven by various rivalries and ambitions, were on the brink of war themselves. The news galvanised them, and plans were hastily formed and put into action for a massive advance upon the borders of France. This time, they declared, there would be no way back for Bonaparte. They meant to rid themselves of him for good.

In Britain Wellington's victorious Peninsular army had sadly been broken up and scattered with several veteran infantry regiments being sent overseas to America and other outposts of the fledgling British Empire. Fortunately, the situation was not so bad for the cavalry although, as we shall see, many of Wellington's veteran Peninsular cavalry regiments played no part in the Waterloo campaign. The upshot of all of this was that the army which was to take on Napoleon's legions for one last time was a far cry from that which had driven them from the Iberian Peninsula. It was, as Wellington famously remarked, 'an infamous army', and the question will always remain; what might have happened if the great army that had crushed Joseph at Vittoria on 21 June 1813 had been present on top of the ridge at Mont St Jean two years later? It is one of the great 'what ifs' of British military history. However, this is not to say that the British contingent of Wellington's army at Waterloo was completely inexperienced. Far from it. Of twenty-seven British infantry battalions present on 18 June 1815, over twenty-six had seen action either in the Peninsula or in Holland during the campaign against Bergen-op-Zoom. Furthermore, many of the 2nd Battalions of regiments which had been present in the Peninsula were full of good, seasoned soldiers. Indeed, many officers in the 1st Battalions took promotions into the 2nd Battalions. The Coldstream Guards, for example, whose 2nd Battalion was present at Waterloo, could boast sixteen veteran Peninsular officers out of the thirty-five present at the battle whilst a further thirteen had seen action in Holland.[1] The rank and file also boasted scores of Peninsular veterans to which the various muster and medal rolls testify. The traditional view of the British contingent at Waterloo as 'green' and untried is, therefore, something of a myth.

It is not necessary to go too deeply into the causes of the Waterloo campaign. They are well enough known. But, basically, Napoleon, faced with a massive invasion of France by the Allied powers of Britain, Prussia, Russia and Austria, had one chance of remaining in power and that lay in the defeat of one or more of the Allied powers. If successful, Napoleon hoped that this would bring the other nations back to the negotiating table, whereupon he could begin once again to establish his authority in both France and Europe. It was a last throw of the dice and was one which, ultimately, was to end in disaster both for him and his army. This was still a few months off, however. In the meantime the Congress of Vienna broke up as the various commanders left to rejoin their respective armies to begin preparing for the campaign, a campaign which was to be one of the shortest but most decisive in modern history.

Even as Wellington rejoined his army in Brussels, Napoleon was laying plans for the coming action. He was gambling on one swift victory against one or more of the Allied armies, and it was the Anglo-Dutch army under Wellington and the Prussian army of Blucher which were to be the targets of his attack. His strategy for the campaign required the defeat of the Prussian army, after which he would turn his attention to Wellington and his inexperienced Anglo-Dutch army which, if he judged Wellington correctly, would fall back to the relative safety of the Channel ports. It was a fairly simple plan, but it did hinge very heavily upon the abilities of his men to be able to inflict a decisive defeat upon Blucher and the Prussians. It was vital that they were driven away from Wellington's army, and it was the failure to accomplish this which, ultimately, would prove the decisive factor.

When Wellington arrived in Brussels on 5 April 1815, he found just 14,000 British troops waiting for him, the bulk of which had been campaigning farther north under Sir Thomas Graham against Bergen-op-Zoom. The background to the assembling of the British Army in Brussels is long and very complicated for, although Napoleon was busy concentrating his own forces for the forthcoming campaign, Wellington was hamstrung by an Act of Parliament which resulted in the British government's reluctance or inability to call out the Militia. This they were only able to do lawfully in time of war and, since no war had actually been declared in April 1815, they could not do so. The upshot was, of course, that the duties which should have been taken over by the Militia were still being carried out by regular British Army units. The situation was particularly acute in Ireland, where a brigade of heavy cavalry and four infantry battalions were stationed. These troops could be sent immediately to Brussels once the Militia took over. The arguments were long and complex and, incredible as it seems, a Bill was passed by Parliament to call out the old Militia on 14 June, just four days before the Battle of Waterloo was fought, which is quite astonishing.[2] On reflection it seems a ludicrous situation, particularly when one considers that the Royal Navy was very busy taking French prizes at sea even before the end of March.

By the end of April 1815 Wellington's army numbered about 60,000 men, though only around a third of these were British, the rest a mixture of Dutch, Hanoverians, KGL and Belgians, the latter being of highly dubious quality having fought for Napoleon only the year before. In fact, the whole situation was not particularly good as regards the army, for as well as the questionable loyalties of some of his men, Wellington had under him senior officers too, who had earlier fought for Napoleon. One such senior officer was Lieutenant General Baron Chassé, who commanded the Third Dutch-Belgian Division. Chassé had commanded a French brigade in the Peninsula and had fought particularly well on 21 June 1813 at Vittoria where his men defended the villages of Santa Margarita and La Hermandad, the latter very fiercely. Fortunately, Chassé proved to be one of the heroes of the campaign when his men held Quatre Bras on 16 June against the initial French thrusts. There were others like him who fought well on the Allied side at Waterloo, but it is indicative of some of the problems Wellington faced during the campaign. Little wonder, therefore, that he was moved to remark, 'I have got an infamous army, very weak and ill-equipped, and a very inexperienced staff.'[3]

We need not concern ourselves with the various components of Wellington's Anglo-Dutch army, for it is the British cavalry contingent that interests us. There were just over 14,000 cavalry in Wellington's army, although 8,559 were KGL, Hanoverian, Dutch-Belgian and Brunswick.[4] The British contingent numbered 5,913, much larger than the majority of the Peninsular battles but still 300 or so below the number of British cavalry at Vittoria two years earlier.[5] On the face of it, 10,155 cavalry would appear to represent a strong contingent, but Napoleon had twice this number at his disposal. In the event, the disparity was not to prove crucial. The British cavalry regiments themselves had an average strength of 396 and were a mixture of Peninsular veterans and inexperienced 'Johnny Newcomers'. Among the former were the 1st (Royal) Dragoons, the 11th, 12th, 13th and 16th Light Dragoons, all very experienced regiments with much Peninsular service between them. Then there were the 7th, 10th, 15th and 18th Hussars, all of whom had seen a limited amount of service in the Peninsula at both the beginning and end of the war, whilst the Household Brigade, comprising the 1st and 2nd Life Guards and the Royal Horse Guards, had likewise seen only limited service from the end of 1812 to the end of the war, during which time they had rarely been involved in any action. Finally, there were the 23rd Light Dragoons, whose exploits at Talavera resulted in their recall to England, an exploit which we have examined in an earlier chapter. Other cavalry regiments with Peninsular experience included five regiments of KGL cavalry. The inexperienced troops included the 2nd Dragoons (Scots Greys), the 1st (King's) Dragoon Guards, and the 6th (Inniskilling) Dragoons. As we shall see, two of these last named regiments were to demonstrate the old failings that so bedevilled the British cavalry on certain occasions in the Peninsula, whilst the 1st (Royal) Dragoons also proved that old habits do indeed die hard.

From the above list it will be deduced that many of the cavalry regiments that had performed so well in the Peninsula, in particular the light dragoon regiments, were present at Waterloo. However, there were still some notable absentees, in particular the 14th Light Dragoons, who had been present throughout most of the Peninsular War. Three of the regiment's squadrons had sailed to North America to take part in the war there, although they returned in May 1815 and should have been available for service at Waterloo. The most obvious absentees, however, were the 3rd, 4th and 5th Dragoon Guards, and the 3rd and 4th Dragoons, all of whom had served with great distinction in the Peninsula. In fact, of the veteran British heavy cavalry that had served in the Peninsula, only the 1st (Royal) Dragoons were present at Waterloo. We cannot really include the Life Guards or Royal Horse Guards as they entered the Peninsular War rather belatedly when much of the hard work had been done, and at a time when, with the Pyrenees looming, there would be little scope for extensive cavalry operations. It is something of a mystery why these fine heavy cavalry regiments were not present at Waterloo. Their 'replacements', the Scots Greys, Inniskillings and King's Dragoon Guards, had seen no service in the Peninsula and, indeed, the Scots Greys had not even left Britain's shores for twenty years prior to the Waterloo campaign. They were, therefore, very inexperienced cavalry.

As well as these regimental omissions there were also some notable absentees amongst the senior staff officers, none more so than Sir George Murray, who had proved to be one of Wellington's most trusted and reliable lieutenants in the Peninsula. Murray was still in America when the Waterloo campaign began, and his place as Quartermaster General was taken by Sir William de Lancey who, whilst not as gifted as Murray, was nevertheless far more suitable than the original choice for the position, Sir Hudson Lowe.[6] The most important change of personnel as far as we are concerned, however, was the return of Henry, Lord Paget, by now the Earl of Uxbridge, as commander of the Allied cavalry. Wellington himself was hopeful that he would have the services of both Uxbridge and Sir Stapleton Cotton, his cavalry chief in the Peninsula. Cotton, by now Lord Combermere, had twice written to Wellington offering his services once again but, for whatever reason, both the Prince Regent and the Duke of York preferred to see Uxbridge in command.[7] Wellington could certainly consider himself fortunate to have two such fine cavalry commanders at his disposal, and it is a pity that both the royal personages saw otherwise. As Wellington himself pointed out, the body of cavalry under his command would not only be very numerous, but would also consist of many different nations. Uxbridge and Combermere, side by side, would have been wonderful to see, but it was not to be. Uxbridge duly left for Brussels while Combermere remained at home. It will be remembered that Uxbridge had not served in the Peninsula under Wellington and, in fact, had not been in Spain or Portugal since the end of the Corunna campaign. After his return to England he had eloped with Wellington's sister-in-law and thus effectively ruled himself out of any service under him, although it should not be forgotten either that Uxbridge, when still Lord Paget, was actually senior to Wellington. When Wellington was made field marshal in 1813 this latter barrier was removed, whilst Uxbridge's elopement, although not forgotten, does not appear to have worried Wellington.[8]

Uxbridge's cavalry concentrated around Ninove, about fifteen miles west of Brussels. There was much to do during the period leading up to the campaign, with equipment, arms and ammunition all being attended to. The usual business of procuring forage for the horses was made much easier than in Spain owing to abundance, not forgetting the fact that, with England so close, supplies were far easier to obtain from across the Channel. It was a busy time for the cavalry and, in fact, the army in general, but it did not stop the officers from engaging in a variety of pastimes, from playing cricket and football to sightseeing. Nor did it stop the endless drilling and reviews, the largest and most famous of which occurred on 29 May near Grammont, on the Dender river, when the entire British cavalry contingent as well as eight batteries of Royal Horse Artillery and five regiments of KGL cavalry were reviewed by Wellington, Blucher and an 'immense cortege' of some of the most distinguished officers in Europe. It must have been a truly spectacular sight with over 6,000 cavalry present, both Peninsular veterans and 'Johnny Newcomers', fresh from England. It was probably the last time that such a gathering ever took place during this period as many of those who took part in the review were soon to fall on the field of Waterloo. Captain Mercer, whose journal provides one of the best accounts of the Waterloo campaign, wrote:

The Dender, flowing through a broad tract of rich meadow-land perfectly flat, makes a bend from Grammont to the village of Jedgeghem, the ground on its left bank rising in a gentle slope, whilst on the right the meadows extend back for about half a mile, and then terminate at the foot of an abrupt wooded height, which forms, as it were, a chord of the arc described by the river. This was the arena chosen for the review, and a more favourable one could scarcely have been chosen. We were formed in three lines. The first, near the banks of the river, was composed of hussars in squadrons, with wide intervals between them, and a battery of horse artillery (6-pounders) on either flank. Opposite the centre of this line was a bridge (temporary, I believe) by which the cortege was to arrive on the ground, descending from the village of Schendelbeke. The second line – compact, or with only the usual squadron intervals – was composed entirely of heavy dragoons, having two batteries – the one of 24-pounder howitzers, the other of 9-pounders – in front of the centre, and a battery of 9-pounders on either flank. The third was a compact line like the second, but entirely of light dragoons, supported also on either flank by a battery of 9-pounders.

It was a splendid spectacle. The scattered line of hussars in their fanciful yet picturesque costume; the more sober, but far more imposing line of heavy dragoons, like a wall of red brick; and again the serviceable and active appearance of the third line in their blue uniforms, with broad lapels of white, buff, red, yellow, and orange – the whole backed by the dark wood of the declivity already mentioned – formed, indeed, a fine picture. There were, I understood, about 6,000 men on the field; and as I looked and admired their fine appearance, complete equipment, and excellent horses, I wondered how any troops could withstand their attacks, and wished Napoleon and his chiefs could but see them as they stood.[9]

The campaign country across which the Waterloo campaign was fought was not entirely dissimilar to that in southern France in 1814. It is marked by fields and hedges, whilst the main road to Brussels, along which the French were advancing, was crossed by a series of ridges of varying heights. There is nothing like the sort of ridge which Wellington's men had used to great advantage at Busaco or Sorauren, for example. The battlefields of Quatre Bras and Waterloo itself were almost flat in comparison. However, most of these ridges between the French border and Brussels did afford Wellington the sort of defensive characteristics which had become such a hallmark of his tactics in the Peninsula, in particular a good reverse slope, behind which he was able to shield his troops from both enemy fire and observation. Aside from the hedgerows and ditches, the rolling fields on which the campaign was fought afforded Wellington's cavalry suitable space to deploy and the battlefield itself, whilst not being the largest he had ever fought on – Waterloo is about three and a half miles wide compared with over twelve miles at Fuentes de Oñoro – did allow for good cavalry deployment. The omens were good, therefore; Uxbridge was back in command of the cavalry, they were present in strength, and the ground was good.

The campaign got underway on 15 June when Napoleon's troops crossed the Sambre river close to Charleroi and attacked the forward positions of Blucher's army. In the ensuing skirmishing the Prussians were pushed back a few miles and they adopted a line along the villages of St Amand, Ligny and Sombreffe. Meanwhile Wellington, taken by surprise by both the direction and speed of the French advance, was still in Brussels where, on the night of 15 June, he spent a few hours at the now famous Duchess of Richmond's ball. When news of the French attack reached him, he issued a series of orders which moved his army closer towards the right flank of the Prussians. Now, as I have already stated, it is not my intention to enter into discussion of any of the controversies surrounding this phase of the campaign. Suffice it to say that Wellington had indeed been surprised and the speed of the French advance had almost severed communications between the two Allied armies. Napoleon's assessment of the characters of both Wellington and Blucher proved absolutely correct. If he attacked Blucher he was quite certain that Wellington would not march to the

Prussians' assistance, whereas Blucher, on the other hand, if Wellington was attacked, would march to help his ally. Therefore, if the two Allied armies were to be kept apart, Blucher would have to be attacked first. And so it proved. Napoleon duly attacked the Prussians whilst Wellington struggled to concentrate his army. Fortunately, Dutch-Belgian troops holding the vital road between the crossroads at Quatre Bras and the village of Brye, where Blucher had taken up his command post, had disregarded Wellington's orders to concentrate farther west and in doing so effectively thwarted Napoleon's plan to isolate Blucher totally from Wellington.

On 16 June the first two battles of the Waterloo campaign were fought. Napoleon did battle with Blucher's Prussians at Ligny whilst Wellington, whose army arrived piecemeal throughout the day, took on Ney at Quatre Bras. The two battles have naturally tended to be overshadowed by the battle at Waterloo two days later, but they were major actions in their own right, particularly that at Ligny where the Prussians took a real mauling, sustaining nearly 20,000 casualties. To their immense credit, however, they refused to simply pack up and march in the direction of Namur and Germany, but instead marched north towards Wavre, and in doing so maintained a vital communication with Wellington's army. Wellington, meanwhile, held on grimly at Quatre Bras, where his army took over 4,500 casualties in the desperate struggle at the crossroads and thus prevented Ney's wing of the French army from falling upon the Prussian right, although by the same token it prevented Wellington from coming to the Prussians' assistance. The first stage of Napoleon's plan, therefore, which, if successful, might have given him the victory he so needed, floundered, largely as a result of Ney not being able to separate Wellington from Blucher, and the credit for this has to go to the redoubtable British infantry. Indeed, writing of the battle, Jac Weller wrote, 'If Waterloo had not occurred forty-eight hours later, Quatre Bras would be remembered as one of the great days of the British Army.'[10]

But what of the British cavalry throughout the day? Well, Uxbridge's cavalry played no part whatsoever in the Battle of Quatre Bras as they had been concentrating around Ninove. In fact, only the 11th Light Dragoons saw the fighting at Quatre Bras and even they only arrived on the battlefield late in the day, too late to contribute anything to Wellington's victory. Where the cavalry did begin to make their presence felt was during the retreat from the Quatre Bras position on 17 June. After the desperate fighting both at Ligny and Quatre Bras, Wellington naturally expected a vigorous pursuit the following morning. However, Ney, paralysed by indecision, simply had his men cook their breakfasts and see to their morning ablutions. He seems to have been oblivious to the fact that a renewal of the hostilities on the morning of 17 June would have made it impossible for Wellington to disengage his forces, and with Napoleon, free from any Prussian interference in his front, sitting on Wellington's left flank, the consequences can well be imagined. In the event, Wellington was able to draw off his infantry along the road to Brussels, covered by both his cavalry and horse artillery, owing to Ney's inactivity. It can be argued that this was possibly the most crucial moment of the campaign, for all that Napoleon had planned for, being the separation of the Anglo-Dutch and Prussian armies, could have been achieved had Ney shown the sort of vigour that had earned him the sobriquet 'the bravest of the brave' from Napoleon himself. But it was not to be, and with the Prussians retreating north instead of east, the two Allied armies maintained some sort of contact with each other and Napoleon's one great chance went begging.[11]

Other than the 11th Light Dragoons, Uxbridge's British cavalry had played little part in the fighting at Quatre Bras on 16 June. However, by the morning of 17 June all but one regiment out of the six cavalry brigades had arrived on the field and were preparing to cover the retreat of Wellington's infantry. Wellington, who had spent the night of 16 June at the Roi d'Espagne Inn at Genappe, returned to Quatre Bras the next morning and immediately sent out a patrol to ascertain what had happened at Ligny. Uxbridge, meanwhile, busied himself positioning the cavalry piquets in anticipation of a renewal of the action. However, at 10am Wellington, having received news of Blucher's withdrawal towards Wavre, and with the French obviously in no position to attack, gave the order for his infantry to withdrawal to Mont St Jean with the horse artillery, cavalry and two battalions of light infantry.[12] The French did not get themselves into order until well past mid-day which, given the need for a swift resumption of the attack upon Wellington, is astonishing. In fact, it was not until about 2pm that Ney's cavalry finally stirred them selves from their lethargy, by which time the Allied infantry were well and truly off along the road north to Mont St Jean. The focus of attention now fell upon Uxbridge and his rearguard of cavalry and horse artillery.

The Allied retreat to Mont St Jean is one of the great episodes of the Waterloo campaign, marked by a series of sharp exchanges between Uxbridge's cavalry and horse artillery and the pursuing French cavalry. It was, as Captain Mercer of the Royal Horse Artillery described it, 'a fox chase'.[13] Wellington could ill afford to lose either guns or good men during the retreat and ordered Uxbridge not to engage in any serious fight. However, given the close nature of the French pursuit, this was always going to be difficult to avoid. And so it proved. Fortunately, both Uxbridge and the rearguard were up to the challenge and the retreat was conducted with great skill and daring.

June 17th was a very hot, still and sultry day, with dark, grey clouds gathering overhead. It was almost like the conditions at Albuera four years earlier, although this time the weather was to be even hotter. Whilst the storm clouds gathered above him, Uxbridge formed his cavalry for the retreat and divided his force into three columns. The right or western column, consisting of Dörnberg's brigade, was ordered to cross first the Dyle and then the Fonteny rivers to the west of Genappe. To the east of Genappe the left or eastern column, consisting of Vivian's and Vandeleur's brigades, was to fall back and cross the Dyle at the tiny hamlet of Thy. The bulk of Uxbridge's cavalry, consisting of the heavy brigades of both Somerset and Ponsonby, as well as the 23rd Light Dragoons and the 7th Hussars, passed through the centre of Genappe itself, crossing the Dyle by way of the bridge which is situated at the southern end of the town. The main Charleroi to Brussels road passed through Genappe and it was this route that this latter column took during the retreat.

Napoleon's massed ranks of cavalry were seen to be moving forward at around 2pm, at which Uxbridge began to pull steadily back from Quatre Bras. The cavalry had gone barely a few hundred yards before the flanking columns peeled off right and left, according to orders, with the guns of the Royal Horse Artillery unlimbering now and then to let loose a few shots before limbering up again and continuing north. The bulk of the French cavalry marched north directly along the main road to Brussels, whilst to the east other squadrons shadowed Vivian and Vandeleur towards Thy. To the west, Dörnberg's passage of the Dyle and Fonteny rivers was relatively free of incident as he was farthest away from the French cavalry. In the centre, meanwhile, the two British heavy cavalry brigades, along with the 23rd Light Dragoons and 7th Hussars, made their way through the narrow streets of Genappe, before Uxbridge drew them up on the northern side of the town astride the main road. With the enemy coming on in strength, he sent the two battalions of light infantry to the rear along with a few men of the 11th Light Dragoons who had remained with the centre column, whilst the remainder of their regiment marched farther to the east with Vandeleur. By now, the rain which had been threatening all day finally came down in torrents, soaking the ground and turning many of the minor roads into quagmires.[14] Whilst the rain came down, Uxbridge deployed his men to the north of Genappe. Somerset's Household Brigade drew up about 600 yards from the town on the main road, whilst Ponsonby's Union Brigade were deployed to their right in an open field. In front of the heavies were the 7th Hussars, about 200 yards from Genappe, with the 23rd Light Dragoons in support.

With his cavalry in position on the rising ground to the north of Genappe, Uxbridge turned and waited for the French cavalry to come on. He did not have to wait too long, for after about twenty minutes scores of French lancers were observed pushing through the streets of the town. Uxbridge, the rain dripping from his fur cap, turned to the 7th Hussars and ordered them to charge before the enemy had time to form. The 7th duly charged the French lancers, described by Standish O'Grady as being about eighteen squadrons strong, 'all very young men, mounted on very small horses, and commanded by a fine-looking and a very brave officer'.

The flanks of the enemy lancers were protected by the houses, but this in turn prevented the French from deploying in any great strength, as well as preventing those at the head of their column from escaping from the 7th Hussars. Indeed, many of the lancers to the rear turned about and tried to find another way through the town. The 7th Hussars, meanwhile, charged straight into the lancers, but could make little impression on them. This was not due to any superiority of the French cavalry but merely to the fact that the enemy's lances prevented the hussars from getting too close. It was the one great advantage the lance had over the sabre, namely the ability to inflict wounds upon an opponent without too much danger to oneself. This is not to say that the 7th Hussars were easily beaten back. Far from it. The 7th saw their commanding officer, Major Edward Hodge, cut down but in turn cut down the French commander in a fight described as being a see-saw, as first one side was pushed back and then the other.[15] Eventually the 7th were forced to withdraw from the fight and they galloped up the main road out of Genappe, passing through the 23rd Light Dragoons as they went, and formed in a field by the side of the road.

According to O'Grady, the French lancers did not pursue the 7th Hussars but regrouped, which allowed him and some of his men to turn and look to some of their wounded, and after a short while returned to join the remainder of the regiment. Uxbridge, meanwhile, rode up to the 23rd Light Dragoons and ordered them to charge but, as he himself later wrote, 'My address to these Light Dragoons not having been received with all the enthusiasm that I expected, I ordered them to clear the *chaussée*, and said, "The Life Guards shall have this honour", and instantly sending for them, two squadrons of the 1st Regiment, gallantly led by Major Kelly, came on *with right good will*.'[16] The Life Guards crashed into the leading ranks of French lancers, throwing them back upon those behind, and a furious fight developed during which the Life Guards got the better of the French, whose lances appear to have been of little use in the crush. Indeed, the Life Guards drove the lancers back through the town where 'they punished them severely'.[17] The weight of the British heavy cavalry was almost certainly the telling factor in the fight as it will be remembered that O'Grady, of the 7th Hussars, remarked upon the small size of the French lancers' horses. The Life Guards, on the other hand, would have been mounted on appreciably larger horses and this, coupled with the fact that they were charging downhill and had the momentum of their charge as an advantage, proved a major factor in their success. Once the French lancers had been thrown out of the town, the Life Guards returned to the main road north of Genappe and the retreat continued with the French following at a 'respectful distance'.[18] The charge was, as Dr Haddy James, Assistant-Surgeon of the 1st Life Guards, wrote in his journal, 'perhaps one of the most important charges of the battle, although but limited in its extent, for it checked the advance of the French cavalry. Had the Life

Guards joined the retreat of the other regiments, it is difficult to say where the thing would have stopped, and this was an event not at all unlikely to happen if young troops unused to action were to see two of the elite British regiments running away at full speed'.[19]

Away to the east of the main Brussels road, meanwhile, Vivian and Vandeleur had been falling back slowly towards the Dyle. Lieutenant Swabey, of the Royal Horse Artillery, had been sent ahead to reconnoitre the passage of this small but potentially troublesome river and returned to Vivian to tell him that he had found a bridge at the small hamlet of Thy. Swabey immediately set off along the narrow lane that led to it with his guns bounding behind him, whilst Thomas Dyneley, also of the Royal Horse Artillery, turned with two of his guns and opened fire on the French cavalry pursuing them. This artillery did little to dampen the French cavalry's ardour, however, and they continued to advance, 'with as much unconcern as if I had only been pointing my finger at them'.[20] By now the heavens had well and truly opened and the fields were turned into swamps. Indeed, the historian of the Waterloo campaign wrote, 'The concussion [of Dyneley's guns] seemed instantly to rebound through the still atmosphere, and communicate, as an electric spark, with the heavily charged mass above. A most awfully loud thunder-clap burst forth, imme-diately succeeded by a rain which has never, probably, been exceeded in violence even within the tropics. In a very few minutes the ground became perfectly saturated; so much so that it was quite impracticable for any rapid movement of the cavalry.'[21] The opening of the heavens was just as well, for the French lancers who were coming on after Vivian appeared to slow down in the muddy fields and, rather than maintain their vigorous pursuit, began skirmishing instead. Dyneley again: 'Vivian then told me to get away as fast as I could and join the other four guns, when we set at a gallop, and at that pace, with whip and spur, we were obliged to keep it up for 10 miles, the rain coming down the whole time in bucketfuls, and the water up to the axle-trees in many parts of the road; to make my own situation more uncomfortable, my horse had cast a fore-shoe.'[22] Whilst the guns galloped off across the small bridge over the Dyle, Vivian and Vandeleur faced about in order to confront the French cavalry.

The ground which they took up was on top of a plateau which sloped steadily down to Thy where two small stone bridges cross the Dyle, a river which, in places, is little more than a stream although its banks are somewhat steep here and there. The guns had already gone off down the narrow lane which leads to the bridge, a road which turns sharply to the right and then to the left before crossing the river itself. Vandeleur had already got his brigade into position a few hundred yards from the bridge when Vivian arrived. The latter fully expected Vandeleur to open and let him through, but when Vivian got within about sixty yards of him, Vandeleur turned his brigade around and headed for the bridge himself, leaving Vivian's men to take up the ground previously adopted by Vandeleur and skirmish with the ever-increasing number of French cavalry which came on in front of them. His own left flank, meanwhile, was covered by the very able 1st Hussars KGL. It is unlikely that too much skirmishing with carbines would have taken place owing to the torrential rain. However, the 18th Hussars were ordered by Vivian to charge in order to keep back the French. There is no evidence that such a charge ever took place although they continued to skirmish until, at length, the French pressed so hard that Vivian sent off an ADC to Vandeleur, whose brigade was still crowding around to the south of the Dyle, to tell him to get across the bridge, 'in order that I might have no interruption in my retreat in case I was hard pressed'.[23]

The 18th were then replaced as the rearguard by the 1st Hussars KGL, whilst the remainder of Vivian's brigade galloped down to the bridge. Soon, the French cavalry was forward in such strength that Vivian finally gave the order for the 18th Hussars to fall back across the bridge which Vandeleur had now cleared. The 10th Hussars had already done so, and these were followed by the 18th Hussars. The KGL cavalry, however, were very closely pressed and the French attempted to get in between the left-hand squadron and the remainder of the regiment, forcing the squadron to cross the Dyle a hundred yards or so to the east of the rest of Vivian's brigade by way of another small stone bridge.[24] Once the field was clear of British cavalry, the French came forward and galloped down to the Dyle and the small stone bridge there. However, they found their way barred by the 10th Hussars who had dismounted and, taking shelter behind a bank overlooking the bridge on the northern side of the river, opened fire with their Baker rifle carbines,[25] a fire which was evidently hot enough to discourage the French from getting too close. This, coupled with the downpour, was enough to allow Vivian's brigade to continue its retreat along a hollow lane without too much trouble, the French restricting themselves simply to sending forward a patrol to watch their movements.

Elsewhere, Uxbridge's cavalry continued their northerly retreat towards the position at Mont St Jean, to which the infantry had retired previously. 'The Royals, Inniskillings, and Greys manoeuvred beautifully,' wrote Uxbridge, 'retiring by alternate squadrons, and skirmished in the very best style; but finding that all the efforts of the enemy to get upon our right flank were vain, and that by manoeuvring upon the plain, which was amazingly deep and heavy from the violent storm of rain, it only uselessly exhausted the horses, I drew these regiments in upon the chaussée in one column, the guns falling back from position to position, and from these batteries, checking the advance of the enemy. We were received by the Duke of Wellington upon entering the position of Waterloo, having effected the retreat with very trifling loss. Thus ended the prettiest Field Day of Cavalry and Horse Artillery that I ever witnessed.'[26]

It had indeed been a triumph of skill for Uxbridge's cavalry during the retreat. At a cost of just twenty-two killed, forty-four wounded and twenty missing, Uxbridge's rearguard cavalry had covered the retreat of the Anglo-Dutch army with great skill and tenacity, never allowing the numerically superior French cavalry to interfere.[27] In his History of the Waterloo Campaign, Siborne called it 'exceedingly beautiful', and compared it more with a field-day than an operation conducted in the presence of a large enemy.[28] I would be inclined to agree with him, for while the British cavalry, and in particular the heavy dragoons, have attracted more than their fair share of criticism for their performance on the field of Waterloo on 18 June, their performance during the retreat is often overlooked. Considering the inexperience of the Union Brigade their performance is all the more creditable, particularly when we consider that their role during the retreat was that which was usually assigned to light cavalry. Heavy dragoons were by tradition shock troops, but here we find them engaging in a different role, taking on various kinds of enemy cavalry, lancers, hussars, dragoons and cuirassiers, and out-manoeuvring them with great success. Ultimately, the Union Brigade in particular is to be judged by its performance on 18 June, but its skilful part in the retreat should not be forgotten either.

Notes

1 See the Waterloo officer roll in Daniel Mackinnon's Origin and History of the Coldstream Guards (London, 1837) II: 220–1.

2 The situation is well documented in the Hon. J.W. Fortescue's History of the British Army (London, 1899), X: 232–5.

3 Wellington to Lord Stewart, 8 May 1815, The Despatches of Field Marshal the Duke of Wellington during his various campaigns (London, 1834), XII: 358.

4 These figures are from W. Siborne, History of the Waterloo Campaign (London, 1990), 534.

5 There were 8,317 Allied cavalry at Vittoria, of which around 2,000 were KGL and Portuguese.

6 Wellington is actually on record as calling Lowe, 'a damned fool'. T. Creevey, The Creevey Papers (London, 1903), I: 290. Lowe later achieved fame – or notoriety – as Napoleon's jailer on the island of St Helena.

7 According to Combermere's biography, the Prince Regent took the opportunity to exact revenge for Combermere's lack of discretion when, as General Cotton, he was the source of some gossip about the Prince Regent during the period when he was 'visiting' Mrs Fitzherbert at Brighton. Cotton apparently happened to mention an incident involving one of the Prince's nocturnal visits to Mrs Fitzherbert to Lady Liverpool, who in turn passed it on to the London gossips. Cotton was later found to be the source of this very harmful gossip and so, when Uxbridge was again available to command the cavalry, the Prince took the opportunity of seeing to it that Combermere was overlooked.

Combermere, *Memoirs and Correspondence of Field Marshal Viscount Combermere* (London, 1866), I: 91–2, & I: 321–6.

8 When Uxbridge was appointed to command the Allied cavalry at Waterloo, it was suggested that this might cause some considerable scandal in London. Indeed, Wellington was asked, 'Your Grace cannot have forgotten the affair with Lady Charlotte,' to which Wellington replied, 'Oh no! I have not forgotten that. I'll take good care he don't run away with me; I don't care about anybody else.' W. Fraser, *Words on Wellington* (London, 1902), 169–70. The definitive account of Uxbridge's appointment is dealt with in Anglesey, *One Leg* (London, 1961), 119-23.

9 Cavalie Mercer, *The Waterloo Campaign* (London, 1927), 117–8.

10 Jac Weller, *Wellington at Waterloo* (London, 1967), 70.

11 Accounts of the Waterloo campaign are numerous and are good, bad or plain ugly. No other campaign in history appears to have attracted such discussion and argument and, indeed, there are more Waterloo 'experts' than any other kind. It is not my intention, nor is it of any real importance in relation to the subject of this book, to enter deeply into any of the strategical theories of the campaign. It will, nevertheless, be necessary to give a brief strategical overview from time to time in order to give the reader a background to the campaign.

12 Anglesey, quoted in H.T. Siborne, *Waterloo Letters* (London, 1891), 4.

13 Mercer, *The Waterloo Campaign*, 151.

14 Joseph Thackwell, of the 7th Hussars, described the fields as being 'perfect swamps', J. Thackwell, *Military Memoirs of Lt Gen Sir Joseph Thackwell* (London, 1908), 70, whilst Standish O'Grady, of the same regiment, wrote that the ploughed fields were 'so soft that the horses were sunk up to their knees always, and sometime to their girths'. Siborne, *Waterloo Letters*, 132.

15 Siborne, *Waterloo Letters*, 6.

16 Ibid. 6.

17 Ibid. 6.

18 Ibid. 6.

19 J. Vansittart (Ed), *Surgeon James's Journal* (London, 1964), 25.

20 Thomas Dyneley, *Letters written whilst on Active Service* (Cambridge, 1984), 64.

21 Siborne, *Waterloo Campaign*, 165.

22 Ibid. 64.

23 Siborne, *Waterloo Letters*, 156.

24 Both of the small stone bridges at Thy remain today. Indeed, the lane along which both Vivian and Vandeleur and the single squadron of the 1st Hussars KGL then called, are still largely cobbled. The ground upon which the cavalry skirmished to the south of the Dyle is unspoilt, and with a little imagination it is easy to visualise the fight on 17 June during the retreat. The bank and hollow way to the north of the bridge also remain, and it is a most satisfying place to visit when following the events of the campaign. The main road to Brussels is visible from the plateau where the skirmishing took place.

25 Vivian himself wrote that some of his men were armed with Baker carbines. And if proof were needed, a photograph in Weller's *Wellington at Waterloo*

shows a local farmer holding a Baker carbine with regimental markings to the 10th Hussars.

26 Siborne ,*Waterloo Letters*, 7.
27 These casualty figures are compiled by adding up the respective regimental losses as shown in Siborne's *Waterloo Campaign*, 558. His own figures simply do not add up correctly.
28 Siborne, *Waterloo Campaign*, 174.

CHAPTER XI

Waterloo: The Heavy Cavalry

Wellington's Anglo-Dutch army began taking up its position along the rain-soaked ridge of Mont St Jean on the evening of 17 June. It was a thoroughly unpleasant night for the men on both sides who found little to shelter them from the incessant rain that turned the ground into a muddy bog. There was nothing to sleep on, and fires were almost impossible to light or to keep burning. Nevertheless, the men made the best of it and, in fact, Wellington's Peninsular veterans even took some comfort from the tempestuous conditions, considering them an omen of victory. It had rained on the eve of Salamanca, Vittoria and Sorauren, three of Wellington's great victories in the Peninsula. For two-thirds of Wellington's army, however, this was small comfort, the coming battle being the first for many a soldier in his hotch-potch army.

The position at Waterloo lay, in fact, a few miles south of the village of the same name, but, as was his habit, Wellington named his victories after the location of his headquarters. Thus it was to be Waterloo, an English-sounding name, and not Mont St Jean, that gave its name to one of the greatest battles in history. Wellington's army lay astride the main Brussels road, along a ridge which ran east-west for barely three miles. On Wellington's left flank lay the hamlets and farm buildings of Papelotte, Smohain and La Haye, whilst farther east lay the woods from where Blucher's Prussians would, hopefully, begin to arrive at some point during the afternoon. To the west, on Wellington's right flank, lay the strongly fortified Château of Hougoumont, held by several companies of the British Foot Guards, ably supported by Nassauers and Hanoverians. Along the top of the ridge ran the Nivelles-Ohain road which was bisected by the main Brussels road. About 250 yards south of the crossroads lay the farmhouse of La Haye Sainte, a crucial outpost held by Major Baring and the 2nd Light Battalion KGL. The Waterloo position was nothing like the sort of ridge which Wellington's men had occupied at battles such as Busaco or Sorauren. Indeed, the use of the word 'ridge' is often misleading to those who have never visited any of Wellington's battlefields. In comparison with these two battlefields, Waterloo is as flat as a bowling green.

However, in spite of the shallowness of the ridge it was of sufficient depth to afford Wellington those characteristics which had become such a vital ingredient for his Peninsular successes. The reverse slope of the ridge was steep enough to shield his men from the prying eyes of the French and to protect them to a certain extent from enemy artillery fire. It was on this reverse slope that the majority of Wellington's men were to spend the day, either under enemy artillery fire or under attack from French cavalry.

Wellington's cavalry were initially scattered in their respective brigades along the ridge behind or alongside the infantry. Wellington's extreme left flank was secured by the light cavalry brigades of Vivian and Vandeleur, both of whom had enjoyed a relatively trouble-free retreat once they had crossed the Dyle at Thy. Vivian's brigade, consisting of the 10th and 18th Hussars, and the 1st Hussars KGL, were the most easterly Allied troops on the battlefield, about 1,000 yards north of La Haye and Papelotte, and were thus in contact with Blucher's Prussians thought the day until they were ordered into the centre. The 10th and 18th Hussars took post in front with the KGL hussars behind them. On Vivian's right was Vandeleur's brigade, consisting of the 11th, 12th and 16th Light Dragoons. These were about 750 yards north of Papelotte. Between these two brigades and Pack's British infantry brigade were Best's and Vinke's Hanoverian brigades. On Pack's right was Bylandt's Dutch-Belgians, and then came more veteran British infantry under Kempt. Sitting in a hollow behind Kempt's brigade was Ponsonby's heavy cavalry, the Union Brigade, so named apparently because its three regiments were English, Scottish and Irish, being the 1st (Royal) Dragoons, the 2nd (Scots Greys) Dragoons and the 6th (Inniskilling) Dragoons. On the other side of the Brussels road, immediately on Ponsonby's right, were Somerset and the Household Brigade, consisting of the 1st and 2nd Life Guards, the Royal Horse Guards and the 1st (King's) Dragoon Guards. Behind these two brigades were the Dutch-Belgian cavalry brigades of Tripp, Ghingy and Van Marlen. About 300 yards to Somerset's right was Frederick Arentschildt's brigade, consisting of the 3rd Hussars KGL, and the 13th Light Dragoons. On the south side of the road to Braine l'Alleud was Dörnberg's brigade, being the 1st and 2nd Light Dragoons KGL and the 23rd Light Dragoons (this being the regiment's first battle since Talavera). Finally, there was Grant's Hussar brigade, consisting of the 7th and 15th Hussars and the 1st Hussars KGL. Grant had his men positioned in front of Dörnberg's right, about 750 yards north of Hougoumont, although one squadron of the 15th Hussars started the day to the west of the Nivelles road, about 750 yards to the north-west of Hougoumont. In all, Wellington could call upon around 14,000 Allied cavalry, although only 5,913 were British. The KGL contingent numbered 2,560 and these could be relied upon in battle, but of the remaining cavalry he was simply not sure. Our story concerns the British cavalry at Waterloo, although it is worth pointing out that the Dutch-Belgian and Hanoverian cavalry performed with varying degrees of success. Indeed, one particular Hanoverian regiment simply fled from the field after just a short time.

The story of the Battle of Waterloo is well enough known and countless histories have since disected and analysed it. It is certainly not my intention to go too deeply into the dramatic events of the day, other than to touch upon them when and as they occur. Our real interest lies in the performance of the British cavalry, and it is a story which does not always attract full and accurate coverage. Indeed, once the charge of the heavy brigade is got out of the way, many histories would have us believe that the rest of the British and Allied cavalry simply did nothing for the remainder of the day. There are many myths concerning the cavalry, particularly the heavy brigades, which need to be addressed, whilst the role of the light cavalry at Waterloo has long been overlooked.[1]

June 18th began with thousands of French and Allied troops warming their bones after a particularly unpleasant night of almost incessant rain. However, uncomfortable as the conditions were for Wellington's men, he himself must have taken some comfort from the fact that Napoleon chose not to attack immediately, but waited instead for a crucial two hours or so in order to give the muddy ground time to dry. These two hours would allow the Prussians time to get forward and make their own vital contribution to what was to be an Allied victory, whereas an early morning assault by Napoleon might or might not have proved decisive. We will never know.

When Wellington said after the battle that Napoleon came on in the old style and was driven off in the old style he was not wrong, for he had beaten successive French marshals in the Peninsula, each of whom at some point in the campaign had attacked in their dense columns of infantry. Soult, Marmont, Masséna, Ney and Victor had all come to grief attacking in this way, whilst Mortier and Jourdan had been brushed aside by Wellington's offensive operations. Seven marshals had, therefore, been sent to deal with Wellington and all had failed. Now it was Napoleon himself who would try, although Bonapartists would like to put the blame for the French catastrophe on to Marshal Ney, who appears to have run a great part of the French show at Waterloo. As it turned out, Napoleon ultimately fared little better than his marshals, although he came mightily close to inflicting a first major defeat on Wellington.

The battle began at around 11.30[2], and although accounts vary as to the actual time, this is generally accepted to be correct. Napoleon's plan involved a diversionary attack on Wellington's right, at the Château of Hougoumont, an attack which he hoped would draw off Allied troops from the centre. If this went to plan he would be able to send forward his infantry against Wellington's left centre, to the east of the main Brussels road, before punching through to victory. The theory was good, if a little unimaginative, and it came close to succeeding. Indeed, as one British

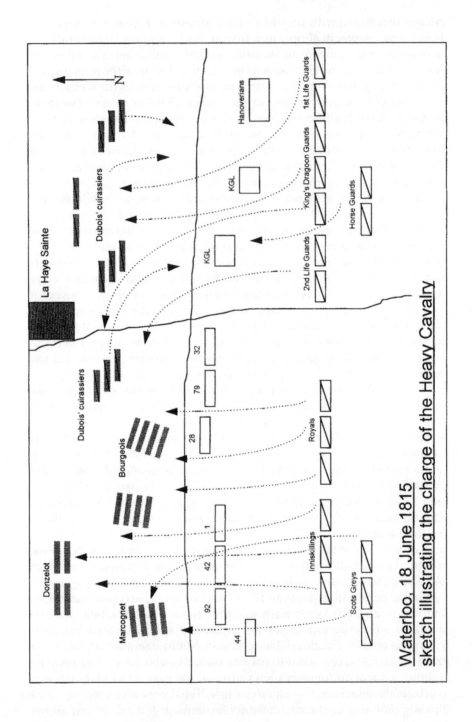

Waterloo, 18 June 1815
sketch illustrating the charge of the Heavy Cavalry

cavalry officer claimed afterwards, the difference between victory and defeat was, as we shall see, just two or three minutes.[3] The attack on Hougoumont developed into a battle within a battle and the failure of the French to take the château was certainly a crucial factor in the Allied victory.[4] The garrison held out against repeated attacks throughout the day, blissfully unaware of most of the other events happening elsewhere on the battlefield, whilst the French, in their efforts to take the château, committed thousands of troops to the assault and in so doing deprived other divisions of much-needed manpower. This, of course, was later in the day, but the first assaults on the château were merely a prelude to the great French infantry assault on Wellington's left centre.

The attack on Picton's sector of Wellington's line came at 1.30pm and was made by some 18,000 veteran French infantry from D'Erlon's corps, himself a Peninsular veteran. When we consider that the greatest single infantry assault of the Peninsular War, at Albuera, was made by 8,000 French troops,[5] we may well imagine the thoughts of Picton's veterans as they watched D'Erlon's men approaching. The Allied line had already been softened up by around eighty guns which had come forward to a spur just south of La Haye Sainte and opened up at a range of about 600 yards. Fortunately for Picton's men, Wellington had positioned them on the reverse slope of the ridge on the northern side of the Ohain road. The ridge was not exactly the sort which they had enjoyed on some of the Peninsular battlefields, being far less pronounced, but it did afford them a good measure of protection from enemy artillery fire, particularly when the men were ordered to lie down. Nevertheless, the fire from the French guns soon began to take its toll as round shot after round shot came bounding over the ridge to tear great gaps in the ranks of Allied troops on the reverse slope.

The French commanders in the Peninsula have been criticised for not altering their tactics on the battlefield, their dense columns meeting with little success against the British line. Their inability to respond to these setbacks is a bit of a mystery, but at Waterloo D'Erlon, no stranger to the defeats in the Peninsula, rather belatedly decided to attack using a formation which Wellington's men had yet to face.[6] Instead of attacking in columns formed of battalions on a double or single company frontage, D'Erlon deployed his corps in divisional columns of battalions, each formed in three lines, with the battalions placed behind one another at intervals of about ten feet. Each of the columns was, therefore, 180-200 files wide by twenty-four ranks deep, assuming each of the two brigades had four battalions in three-deep lines. Including the intervals between each battalion and brigade the width of each column was about 150 yards and the depth about seventy yards.[7] The whole point of the exercise was to enable the attacking French columns to fight on an equal footing with Picton's infantry, deployed in their usual two-line. D'Erlon's frontage certainly allowed for this, for between them the four attacking columns, those of Quiot,[8] Donzelot, Marcognet and Durutte, covered a frontage of over 600 yards, possibly even more. Admittedly, part of Quiot's division marched to the west of the Brussels road, but the massive bulk of the French attacking force came on square against the sector of the Allied line occupied by Picton's division. The attacking columns came forward in echelon by the left, with Quiot leading, tailing back to Durutte on the right. The French artillery fired whenever the columns disappeared into the dead ground between the rolling spurs to the east of the main road, and soon the Allied skirmishers were being steadily driven back towards the Ohain road.

Meanwhile the green-clad riflemen of the 95th, armed with the beautiful Baker rifle, began to take a toll of Bourgeois' men from the sanctuary of the sandpit, just to the north-east of La Haye Sainte, but even they were forced out as the French approached. Quiot's own brigade advanced to the west of the main road, and was protected by French cavalry, the dense ranks of steel-clad cuirassiers at their head.[9] The 1st Light Battalion KGL, defending the orchard of La Haye Sainte, was thrust back to the farm buildings as the French infantry advanced. It was at this point that a battalion of Hanoverians, the Luneberg battalion, was ordered forward to support the defenders of the farm. They duly marched down the forward slope but, apparently, were disordered when they fell in with Baring's skirmishers at the farmhouse. They were still in their disorderly line when a mass of cuirassiers, coming up on the left of Quiot's brigade, swept into them, and the end result was a severe mauling for the battalion which was forced to flee to the relative safety of La Haye Sainte to escape further punishment from the enemy cavalry.[10]

Meanwhile Wellington's artillery came into play. He was never given to counter-battery fire and, indeed, only once, at Vittoria, did he ever engage seriously in the practice. No, he invariably perceived the attacking infantry as the threat and ordered his guns to remain silent until the enemy came into range. D'Erlon's infantry duly presented a wonderful target, and the Allied gunners opened up first with round shot and then with canister as the range decreased. But there was still no sign of the French wavering, and soon enough their skirmishers were firing into the British battalions lining the hedge at the top of the crest along the Ohain road. Once again accounts vary as to the actual timing and sequence of events at this point. What we can be certain of is that the French, able to bring more than their usual firepower against the British line, made good headway and gradually began to drive both the British skirmishers and, indeed, the main firing line, back beyond the hedge. Sir Thomas Picton, the fiery veteran of countless Peninsular actions, had his own glorious career terminated by a French musket ball which struck him in the right temple, whilst elsewhere his Peninsula veterans began to reel under the pressure of the

French onslaught. Bourgeois' brigade struck home first, opening fire along their long frontage against Kempt's brigade, consisting of the 28th, 32nd and 79th Regiments, all Peninsular veterans. Bourgeois' men had actually gained the hedge which lined the road when Kempt's men met them with a volley and charged, 'in line', wrote Kempt afterwards, 'and completely repulsed the enemy's column, driving it in a state of the greatest confusion down the slope of the position'.[11] Kempt was later quite adamant that his defeat of Bourgeois' column was accomplished without the aid of a single cavalryman. Indeed, he stated quite forcibly that, 'Not one single cavalry soldier co-operated with this brigade throughout the whole day.'[12] This was a view shared by Cruikshank, of the 79th Highlanders, and Mounsteven and Shelton, of the 28th. We can assume, therefore, that both brigades of Quiot's division, being his own and that of Bourgeois, were not directly charged by either the Household or Union Brigade until after they had been repulsed by Kempt or had fallen back after their unsuccessful assault on La Haye Sainte. As we shall see, one of Bourgeois' regiments, the 105th, lost an 'eagle' to the 1st (Royal) Dragoons, confirming the fact that Kempt repulsed the French brigade only a short time before the Union Brigade launched its charge.

It was a different story to Kempt's left, however, where Donzelot's and Marcognet's divisions came up against Pack's division and Bylandt's shaken Dutch-Belgian brigade. Up on the crest at the Ohain road the attacking French troops had begun to cross the road and were actually passing through the hedge which partially ran along it. For those who had fought in the Peninsula it must have made a change to have got this far for, apart from Sorauren, attacking French units rarely got within smelling distance of the British line before being driven back. But here, on the field of Waterloo, they had begun to drive the long, red lines back and for a few minutes were actually established on 'the plateau'. Clark-Kennedy, who captured one of the French 'eagles', later wrote:

> The heads of the French columns, which appeared to me to be nearly close together, had no appearance of having been repulsed or seriously checked. On the contrary... they had forced their way through our line – the heads of the columns were on the Brussels side of the double hedge. There was no British infantry in the immediate front that I saw, and the line that had been, I presume, behind the hedges was wheeled by sections or divisions to the left, and was firing on the left flank of the left column as it advanced. In fact, the crest of the height had been gained, and the charge of cavalry at the critical moment recovered it. Had the charge been delayed two or three minutes, I feel satisfied it would probably have failed.[14]

It was the first major French attack of the battle and for a while it looked as if it might succeed. Indeed, the French were on the brink of achieving a major breakthrough, but any French thoughts of victory were soon to be quickly and ruthlessly dispelled when they suddenly became the unwilling victims of one of the most famous cavalry charges in history.

The Earl of Uxbridge, returning from behind Hougoumont, where he had been supervising the positioning of some of his cavalry, looked towards La Haye Sainte and saw the dark masses of French infantry passing the farm both to its left and right, supported to the west of the main road by Dubois' cuirassiers. He would have also seen the remnants of Bourgeois' brigade retiring after being defeated by Kempt's brigade. Quick to appreciate the situation, he immediately galloped over to Somerset and ordered the Household Brigade, sitting at the foot of the reverse slope, to form line and prepare to charge, with the Life Guards and King's Dragoon Guards in the first line with the Horse Guards in support. He then galloped across to the east of the road where he found Ponsonby, patiently waiting whilst Pack struggled at the crest above him. Uxbridge told Ponsonby to wheel the Union Brigade into line also, the 1st (Royals) and Inniskillings in the first line and the Scots Greys in support. He then returned to join Somerset before, in his own words, he 'put the whole in motion'.[15]

It is necessary, for the sake of clarity, to deal with the charges of the Household and Union Brigades separately. First of all, it should be remembered that, when Uxbridge initially gave the order for both brigades to form into line, the men themselves would have had no knowledge of what they would be facing, placed as they were at the foot of the reverse slope. Indeed, it was only when the French gained the top of the crest at the Ohain road that French troops would have been visible to them. Therefore, when they charged they would not have known what they would be attacking until they themselves reached the crest. Having issued his orders for the charge, Uxbridge took up a position just to the west of the main Brussels road and just in front of the left-hand squadron of the Household Brigade, that of the 1st Life Guards. Somerset's field trumpeter, the 16-year-old John Edwards[16] then sounded the charge and the Household Brigade trotted forward.

The Household Brigade quickly gained the top of the ridge and charged down the slope to meet Dubois' cuirassiers who were just to the west of La Haye Sainte. The 1st Life Guards were on the right of the line with the King's Dragoon Guards in the centre. On the left came the 2nd Life Guards with the Horse Guards in reserve. The heavy British cavalry came thundering down the slope and crashed into the ranks of Dubois' men, apparently sending them flying in all directions. Lieutenant Waymouth, of the 2nd Life Guards, who was taken prisoner during the charge, wrote that the Household Brigade and the cuirassiers, 'came to the shock like two walls, in the most perfect manner', and added, 'Having once penetrated their line, we rode over everything opposed to us.'[17] It was indeed an almighty crash as these two bodies of heavy cavalry collided with each other.

Waymouth went on to say that he thought the French had an advantage in having swords six inches longer than the British swords, and added that the position in which the British cavalry held their swords during the charge, i.e. straight ahead, was far more tiring than the French method. In the event, it mattered little, for the Household Brigade sent the French flying in all directions, the majority of them having to hack their way out and flee south along the main road as far as a cutting a few hundred yards south of La Haye Sainte where, through sheer weight of numbers, they became jammed in and found themselves at the mercy of the Life Guards and King's Dragoon Guards who set about their business with a deadly efficiency, cutting and hacking in all directions. The British themselves did not get off lightly, however, as a regiment of French chasseurs came to the top of the cutting and fired down into their tightly packed ranks, killing and wounding scores of them.[18] Elsewhere, the 2nd Life Guards and the left-hand squadron of the King's Dragoon Guards crossed to the east of the main road, north of La Haye Sainte, in pursuit of other cuirassiers, and in doing so found themselves in amongst the Union Brigade.

Ponsonby's Union Brigade had charged shortly after the Household Brigade. The brigade formed with the 1st (Royals) on the right and the Inniskillings on the left with the Scots Greys in support, although some eyewitnesses claim that all three regiments were in line together at the moment the charge was made. It matters little, however, for what is important is the effect of the charge and its consequences. On the extreme French right, Durutte's division made good progress towards the main Allied line to the west of Papelotte, La Haye and Smohain, whilst on their left Marcognet and Donzelot headed straight for that part of the line held by Pack's brigade and Bylandt's Dutch-Belgians. It is clear from eye witness accounts that the attacking French troops had passed through the hedge lining the Ohain road and that the 92nd Highlanders were both 'recoiling' and 'in confusion'. In fact, Ponsonby's men charged at the precise moment that the French infantry had gained the crest, and as they went up the slope towards it, the Union Brigade met the infantry of Pack's and Kempt's brigades wheeling back to let them through,[20] although the 92nd Highlanders apparently advanced after them and, indeed, are supposed to have gripped hold of the stirrups of their countrymen of the Scots Greys crying, 'Scotland for Ever!'

The signal for the Union Brigade to charge was given by De Lacy Evans, Ponsonby's aide-de-camp, who waved his hat in the air to set the brigade moving. In fact, the Scots Greys had already begun to move slowly forward for their commanding officer, Colonel Hamilton, observing the 92nd in difficulty, ordered them to do so. This is possibly how the Greys became level with both the Inniskillings and Royals who had originally been in front of them, although it is possible they moved forward, and a little to their left, in order to avoid the round shot which was continually bounding over the crest. It is of little consequence, however, for all three of these heavy cavalry regiments moved up the muddy slope towards the crest where the French were by now having thoughts of victory. The first they knew of the charge was when scores of French infantry suddenly began dropping in the midst of their columns. Colonel Duthilt, fighting in the front rank of Marcognet's division, later wrote:

> Just as I was pushing one of my men back into the ranks I saw him fall at my feet from a sabre slash. I turned round instantly to see English cavalry forcing their way into our midst and hacking us to pieces. Just as it is difficult, if not impossible, for the best cavalry to break into infantry who are formed into squares and who defend themselves with coolness and daring, so it is true that once the ranks have been penetrated, then resistance is useless and nothing remains for the cavalry to do but to slaughter at almost no risk to themselves. This is what happened, in vain our poor fellows stood up and stretched out their arms; they could not reach far enough to bayonet these cavalrymen mounted on powerful horses, and the few shots fired in the chaotic mêlée were just as fatal to our own men as to the English. And so we found ourselves defenceless against a relentless enemy who, in the intoxication of battle, sabred even our drummers and fifers without mercy.[21]

There were well over 10,000 French infantrymen piling up against the crest of the Ohain road when the Union Brigade charged into them, and it says much for the power and devastation of their charge that it was achieved by barely 1,100 horsemen. The Greys and Inniskillings had seen no action at all in the Peninsula and, indeed, the Greys had not even been overseas for twenty-five years. Only the 1st (Royals) had any experience of war, having served with distinction in the Peninsula, as we have seen in earlier chapters of this book. Therefore, it was a combination of the Royals' experience and the Greys' and Inniskillings' thirst for action which accounted for much of the havoc being wreaked amongst the French ranks. As Duthilt wrote, there was little an infantryman could do to combat the power of the charge once the cavalry got in amongst them. The British cavalrymen were big men mounted on big horses, and one officer of the 92nd, Lieutenant Winchester, actually described the Greys as having 'walked over' the French column.[22] This was probably what really happened, the huge grey horses simply knocking down those unfortunate enough to find themselves in the way of the charge. Those who did manage to offer resistance were easily cut down. The 1796-pattern heavy cavalry sword may not have possessed the finesse or length of the Klingenthals being wielded by the French heavy cavalry but, in the hands of the British heavy dragoons, it yielded a totally different power of its own which accounted for hundreds of French soldiers. Scores were cut and hacked to death whilst others were led from the field with fearsome slashing wounds. Many more suffered broken limbs as the result of a slash which, whilst not drawing blood, would have been powerful enough to fracture a bone. Sergeant Major Dickson, of the Greys, wrote:

> A young officer of Fusiliers made a slash at me with his sword, but I parried it and broke his arm... The French were fighting like tigers. Some of the wounded were firing at us as we passed; and poor Kinchant, who had spared one of these rascals, was himself shot by the officer he had spared. As we were sweeping down a steep slope on the top of them, they had to give way. Then those in front began to cry out for 'quarter', throwing down their muskets and taking off their belts. The Gordons at this point rushed in and drove the French to the rear. I was now in the front rank, for many of ours had fallen... We now came to an open space covered with bushes, and then I saw Ewart, with five or six infantrymen about him, slashing right and left at them.[23]

What Dickson saw happening in front of him was destined to become one of the most famous incidents of the battle. Sergeant Charles Ewart, six feet four inches tall, presented an imposing sight on foot, let alone in the saddle of a huge grey beast of a horse. Moreover, in the early 19th century, when the average height of a man was much shorter than it is today, a man like Ewart would have been considered a giant. Put a 1796 heavy cavalry sword in his hands and you have a perfect killer. Such was Charles Ewart as he tore into the ranks of Grenier's brigade, one regiment of which was the 45th Line. 'It was in the charge I took the eagle from the enemy,' wrote Ewart afterwards. 'He and I had a hard contest for it; he made a thrust at my groin, I parried it off and cut him down through the head. After this a lancer came at me; I threw the lance off by my right side, and cut him through the chin upwards through the teeth. Next, a foot soldier fired at me, and then charged me with his bayonet, which I also had the good luck to parry, and then I cut him down through the head; thus ended the contest. As I was about to follow my regiment, the general said, "My brave fellow, take that to the rear; you have done enough till you get quit of it." I took the eagle to the ridge, and afterwards to Brussels.'[24]

Although it has little bearing upon the performance of the Scots Greys at Waterloo, it is interesting nevertheless to consider the timing of Ewart's capture of the eagle of the 45th Regiment. Tradition has it that he captured it during the charge into the ranks of Marcognet's infantry. However, there is no evidence to suggest that the infantry attack was supported by lancers. Therefore, where did Ewart's lancer, whom he cut down, come from? The fact that Ewart had to fight off an enemy lancer indicates that his capture of the eagle almost certainly occurred during the latter phase of the charge, when the fugitives of Marcognet's column were fleeing to the relative safety of the main French position. After all, are we to doubt

Ewart's own word? The enemy lancer was either an invention or, if not, he must have taken the eagle after Jacquinot's lancers made their intervention, which we will deal with shortly. It is not particularly relevant but it is, nevertheless, an interesting point to consider. Away to Ewart's right, meanwhile, the other two regiments of the Union Brigade had also swept forward, riding down both Marcognet's and Donzelot's men as they charged across the Ohain road and down the slope beyond. Once again, the French could offer little resistance to the charge. Colonel Joseph Muter, commanding the Inniskillings, wrote:

> The Inniskillings came in contact with the French columns of infantry almost immediately after clearing the hedge and (I should call it) *chemin creux*. We all agree in thinking that the French columns had nearly gained the crest, perhaps twenty to thirty yards down the slope. We think there were three French columns. The French column did not attempt to form square, nor was it, so far as we could judge, well prepared to repel an attack of cavalry. Our impression is that, from the formation of the ground, the cavalry was not aware what they were to attack, nor the infantry aware of what was coming upon them.[25]

It is interesting to note that Muter thought the French had not, in fact, gained the crest, a view not shared by Clark-Kennedy of the Royals who, as we have already seen, claimed the French had passed the hedge and had gained the crest. This simply bears out the fact that two men, though within a few hundred yards of each other, often saw, or thought they saw, totally different events unfolding before them. Even allowing for the inequality of the ground and the fact that they may have been looking at different columns, it is difficult to see how one man saw the French on the crest and another did not. Add to this the smoke of battle and we see just how difficult it often was for participants to see what was really happening around them. It is also interesting to note that Muter thought there were only three French columns opposed to the Union Brigade. He would undoubtedly have seen Marcognet and Donzelot, but what was the third column? Was it Durutte or Bourgeois? I suspect it was the latter, for Durutte's was so far to the east that it escaped most of the carnage on the slopes of the crest, the Greys passing by Durutte's left flank.

On the right of the Inniskillings the 1st (Royals) had charged into Donzelot's division. Just to emphasise the inconsistencies of the eye-witness accounts, in his version of the charge Clark-Kennedy wrote that the French had actually crossed the Ohain road, had passed through the hedge and had even passed several of the British guns which had been placed behind the hedge and which had been abandoned by their gunners.[26] When we consider that Muter, commanding the Inniskillings, and not a great distance to Clark-Kennedy's left, thought the French had not reached the crest, we may well understand the difficulties under which historians must labour. However, as I have already stated, it is of no real importance in analysing the performance of the cavalry at Waterloo. What we can be sure of is that, between them, the three regiments of Ponsonby's Union Brigade completely devastated the first great French infantry attack at Waterloo. Whilst the Greys and Inniskillings savaged Marcognet, the 1st (Royals) hacked their way into the ranks of Donzelot's division. Clark-Kennedy again:

> From the nature of the ground we did not see each other until we were very close, perhaps eighty or ninety yards. The head of the column appeared to be seized with a panic, gave us a fire which brought down about twenty men, went instantly about and endeavoured to regain the opposite side of the hedges; but we were upon them before this could be effected, the whole column getting into one dense mass, the men between the advancing and retiring parts getting so jammed together that the men could not bring down their arms, or use them effectively, and we had nothing to do but to continue to press them down the slope, the right squadron of the Royals naturally outflanking them as the centre one (which I commanded) also did to a certain degree.[27]

We may well imagine the Royals 'pressing' the French back down the slope in much the same way that a police horse controls a mob of demonstrators, or a large crowd. We may also hark back to the fight at Usagre when, having got the French jammed in against the bridge at the village, Lumley's heavy cavalry simply 'pressed' the French back and jammed them against it, cutting and hacking down the French cavalry who were unable to defend themselves owing to the crush. And here too at Waterloo, the French infantry, particularly those at the front, were unable to offer any resistance whatsoever in their tightly packed crowd. After the first few volleys it is almost certain that no French infantry would have been able to get enough room to go through the process of loading and firing his musket. Probably only those towards the rear had time and, more importantly, room to fire back at their assailants. It is also worth noting that Clark-Kennedy states that he outflanked the French along with the right squadron of the Royals. This would have taken him past Donzelot's left flank, and would almost certainly have brought him into contact with the retreating men of Bourgeois' brigade which had been driven off by Kempt's infantry. This is corroborated by the fact that Clark-Kennedy took the eagle of the 105th Regiment, one of Bourgeois' regiments. We have already heard Ewart's story of how he captured the eagle of the 45th Line. The story of the taking of the eagle of the 105th Line is far more controversial. Once again, it is of little significance who actually took it, but it is, nevertheless, worth recording how it was taken. Recalling the episode years afterwards, Clark-Kennedy wrote:

I did not see the eagle or colour (for there were two colours, but only one with an eagle) until we had been probably five or six minutes engaged. It must, I should think, have been originally about the centre of the column, and got uncovered from the change of direction. When I first saw it, it was perhaps about forty yards to my left, and a little in my front: The Officer who carried it and his companions were moving... with their backs towards me, and endeavouring to force their way into the crowd. I gave the order to my Squadron, 'Right shoulders forward, attack the colour', leading direct on the point myself. On reaching it, I ran my sword into the Officer's right side a little above the hip joint. He was a little to my left side, and he fell to that side with the eagle across my horse's head. I tried to catch it with my left hand, but could only touch the fringe of the flag, and it is probable it would have fallen to the ground, had it not been prevented by the neck of Corporal Styles' horse, who came up on my left at that instant, and against which it fell. . . on running the Officer through the body I called out twice together, 'Secure the Colour, secure the Colour, it belongs to me.' This order was addressed to some men close to me, of whom Corporal Styles was one. On taking up the eagle, I endeavoured to break the eagle from off the pole with the intention of putting it into the breast of my coat, but I could not break it. Corporal Syles said, 'Pray, sir, do not break it', on which I replied, 'Very well, carry it to the rear as fast as you can, it belongs to me.'[28]

Unfortunately, when Styles carried the eagle from the field to deliver it to Lieutenant Bridges, an officer of the Royals who was absent from the field, the latter placed Styles' own name against it and thus was set in motion a dispute which was to last for over twenty years. It may seem churlish for these men, and Clark-Kennedy in particular, to drag out the issue over such a long period, but it should be remembered that the taking of a French Imperial eagle was not a particularly common occurrence. Indeed, during the six years of war in the Peninsula, only six eagles had ever been taken, of which two were found in the barracks in Madrid in August 1812 after the French had abandoned the place, one was found at Foz d'Arouce in a river, and a third taken from a French officer at Salamanca whose regiment had already begun to surrender to Leith's 5th Division. Thus, only two eagles can really be said to have been taken in battle, at Barrosa and at Salamanca. Therefore, two eagles in one cavalry charge was quite an achievement. There was talk of a third eagle being taken at Waterloo by a private of the Inniskillings named Penfold. Apparently, he took hold of an eagle during the charge, but the officer carrying it would not let it got. Penfold had to drag it away for some distance before the pole broke, upon which he rode off with it. However, Penfold went to the assistance of another officer of the Inniskillings, being engaged by some French soldiers, after first giving the eagle to another private of the same regiment for safe-keeping. At this point a Corporal of the Royals persuaded the young private to let him have it, whereupon he carried it off. The eagle with the broken pole was then seen in Brussels a few days later.[28] It seems a very unlikely story and the reference to a Corporal of the Royals is a little mischievous. Perhaps the story of Corporal Styles of the Royals having 'taken' an eagle was well known and in circulation at the time. Another story, and a very similar one, has a private of the Inniskillings taking an eagle but dropping it when going to the assistance of one of his comrades. All highly entertaining stuff but the fact remains that just two eagles were, at the end of the day, sitting in the hands of their new owners.

Thus, the first phase of the charge of the Union and Household Brigades can be said to have come to a dramatic and very successful conclusion. Between them the two brigades, numbering no more than 2,300 sabres, had scattered around 15,000 of D'Erlon's infantry, inflicting severe casualties, the precise number of which is unknown, and taking around 3,000 prisoners, with scores more apparently escaping in the turmoil afterwards. Two eagles were also taken. It was, in other words, a quite devastating attack, and the French would not try any other serious infantry attacks on Wellington's left centre for the rest of the day. However, it was now that Uxbridge cavalry needed to show restraint. They had reached the bottom of the muddy valley floor and, having over thrown D'Erlon's column, set about securing prisoners who were escorted back to the Allied lines and then on to Brussels by both British infantry and cavalry. Indeed, the Inniskillings, who had a strength of only 396, having been so reduced during the charge, were further reduced in numbers when a squadron was sent to the rear in charge of French prisoners. But, not content with the success of the initial charge, the two brigades demonstrated that the old failings of the British cavalry, first revealed at Vimeiro and Talavera, were still latent in 1815.

The Scots Greys, Inniskillings and King's Dragoon Guards can be forgiven – perhaps – for charging too far. They had not seen action overseas for years. The Royals, on the other hand, and the Life Guards and Horse Guards had been present in the Peninsula, although these last three regiments had seen little real fighting, having entered the war late on. Many commanding officers had already been either killed or wounded, whilst Uxbridge himself, by his own admission, was in no position to control his cavalry having gone forward with the Household Brigade. With the Union Brigade pouring down the slope on the east of the Brussels road, along with the 2nd Life Guards and the left-hand squadron of the King's Dragoon Guards, and the Household Brigade galloping in pursuit of Dubois' beaten cuirassiers, all order became lost and the moment that every fighting cavalryman dreamt of – and every good cavalry officer dreaded – had arrived.

The British heavy cavalrymen's blood was well and truly up and, having inflicted so much slaughter on the hapless French infantry, who fled across the valley 'like a flock of sheep',[30] they were not about to stop now. After all, sitting about 300 yards or so farther on, on a ridge just south of La Haye Sainte, was Napoleon's grand battery of over seventy guns. The two heavy cavalry brigades were now formed in a very rough line with the Scots Greys on the far left, the Inniskillings on their right and the 1st (Royals) beyond these. The 2nd Life Guards and the left-hand squadron of the King's Dragoon Guards completed the 'line' to the east of the Brussels road. To the west of the road were, from left to right, looking south, the two remaining squadrons of the King's Dragoon Guards and the two squadrons of the 1st Life Guards. These were supported by the two squadrons of Horse Guards. Both brigades now pressed on up the muddy slopes to the grand battery where they began slaughtering the gunners and drivers. Away to the east, the Scots Greys rallied before attacking the guns. Sergeant Major Dickson again:

> We now reached the bottom of the slope. There the ground was slippery with deep mud. Urging each other on, we dashed towards the batteries on the ridge above, which had worked such havoc on our ranks. The ground was very difficult, and especially where we crossed the edge of a ploughed field, so that our horses sank to the knees as we struggled on. My brave Rattler [his horse] was becoming quite exhausted, but we dashed ever onwards. At this moment Colonel Hamilton rode up to us crying, 'Charge! charge the guns!' and went off like the wind up the hill towards the terrible battery that had made such deadly work among the Highlanders. It was the last we saw of our colonel, poor fellow! His body was found with both arms cut off. His pockets had been rifled. I once heard Major Clarke tell how he saw him wounded among the guns of the great battery, going at full speed, with the bridle-reins between his teeth, after he had lost his hands. Then we got among the guns, and we had our revenge. Such slaughtering! We sabred the gunners, lamed the horses, and cut their traces and harness. I can hear the Frenchmen yet crying 'Diable!' when I struck at them, and the long-drawn hiss through their teeth as my sword went home. Fifteen of their guns could not be fired again that day. The artillery drivers sat on their horses weeping aloud as we went among them; they were mere boys, we thought.[31]

Uxbridge himself thought that as many as forty guns were put out of action, having been informed of the fact by a French artillery officer whom he later met in Paris. However, they could not be brought off because of the counter-attack by Napoleon's cavalry. The British cavalry rode in and out of the guns for quite some time within just 300 yards or so of La Belle Alliance, from where Napoleon watched with horror. Meanwhile thousands of retreating French infantry who had been overtaken by the cavalry now came up and passed through the guns, apparently oblivious to the slaughtering going on there. Uxbridge tried desperately to get his men to heed the trumpets sounding the recall, but to little avail. The heavy cavalry continued to enjoy themselves until, exhausted by their efforts, they finally turned and looked back across the valley towards their own lines. It was at this point that they really appreciated the extremely dangerous position they had got themselves into for, as they gazed back across the valley and over the carnage they had left in their wake, they saw hundreds of enemy cavalrymen riding in from both left and right, cavalry they would now have to fight if they were going to make it back to their own lines. Dickson wrote:

> I never saw horses become so ferocious, and woe betide the blue coats that came in their way! But the noble beasts were now exhausted and quite blown, so that I began to think it was time to get clear away to our own lines again. But you can imagine my astonishment when down below, on the very ground we had crossed, appeared at full gallop a couple of regiments of cuirassiers on the right, and away to the left a regiment of lancers. I shall never forget the sight. The cuirassiers, in their sparkling steel breastplates and helmets, mounted on strong black horses, with great blue rugs across the croups, were galloping towards me, tearing up the earth as they went, the trumpets blowing wild notes in the midst of the discharges of grape and cannister shot from the heights. Around me there was one continuous noise of clashing arms, shouting of men, neighing and moaning of horses. What were we to do?[32]

What Dickson and the two brigades of cavalry had to do was to run the gauntlet of both infantry and cavalry in order to fight their way home. Scores would never make it. The enemy cavalry approaching were Gobrecht's Brigade from Jacquinot's Division, being the 3rd and 4th Lancers, whilst from the direction of La Belle Alliance came two regiments of cuirassiers, the 5th and 10th. The British cavalry regiments, or what was left of them, gathered themselves together for the return home, but had not gone far when the enemy cavalry struck. Scores of isolated British cavalrymen were cut down or speared by enemy lancers who now took their revenge for the devastation the British had wreaked earlier. The two British brigades were scattered in isolated little groups who were easy prey for the French. The lancers were by no means invincible, as Ewart had demonstrated, but they had the very distinct advantage of having a nine-feet long lance with which to inflict their suffering on their adversaries who would, generally, not have been able to get within even striking distance of them. It was a formidable weapon, demonstrated with terrible efficiency upon Colborne's brigade at Albuera some four years earlier, and the lancers went to work with equal venom at Waterloo. Scores of wounded British cavalrymen were killed by the lancers who showed no mercy, a testament to which is the fact that the Greys, for example, suffered more dead than wounded, which is rather unusual. John Hibbert, of the King's Dragoon Guards, wrote, 'No sooner had they [the British cavalry] got about five hundred yards from the French infantry than they were met by an immense body of Lancers who were sent for the purpose of attacking them in this way. Our men were rendered desperate by their situation. They were resolved either to get out of the scrape or die, rather be taken prisoners, so they attacked them, and three troops cut their way through them; about a troop were killed or taken prisoner.'[33]

The situation of the two heavy brigades was desperate. Sir William Ponsonby, leading the Union Brigade, was killed by enemy lancers, as was the commanding officer of the Scots Greys. In fact, only eight out of twenty-three officers of the Scots Greys were unwounded. The commanding officers of the 1st (Kings) Dragoon Guards and the 1st Life Guards were killed also. It was during this phase of the charge that the majority of the British heavy cavalry casualties probably occurred, which is backed up by De Lacy Evans who wrote, 'It was at this part of the transaction that almost the whole of the loss of the Brigade took place.' There was no support for the Union Brigade as the Greys, who should have been in the second line, were up front in the thick of the fight. To the west of the Brussels road, however, the Horse Guards had maintained some semblance of order and were able to support and bring off the Household Brigade without too much damage to themselves. On the whole, however, the fight for survival for the two British heavy cavalry brigades was not a particularly successful one. It is interesting at this point to consider again the timing of Ewart's capture of the eagle of the 45th Line. Jacquinot's lancers came into action during the retreat of the heavy cavalry from the grand battery, but Ewart cut down an enemy lancer when he took the eagle. Was it actually during this latter phase of the episode that he took the eagle or were enemy lancers present in support during D'Erlon's attack? It is not a particularly important point but it is interesting nevertheless. Another point relating to the Scots Greys arises, being the alleged 'decimation' of the Greys as having taken place, not up at the grand battery and during the retreat back to their lines, but from the fire, apparently from Durutte's column. It is, of course, quite possible that the Greys received some fire from the left flank of Durutte's column, but to say that they were decimated as a result is quite ridiculous.[35] To imply that the Greys were decimated here is to say that they lost few casualties in their attack on the grand battery and during their retreat to the Allied lines.

But to return to our story. Jacquinot's lancers were causing severe problems for the isolated men of the two British heavy cavalry brigades. Individuals were easily speared whilst even small groups found it difficult to ward off their attackers. There was simply no support for the shattered remnants of the brigades to the east of the main road. De Lacy Evans again:

The French lancers continued to advance on our left in good order. If we could have formed a hundred men we could have made a respectable retreat, and saved many; but we could effect no formation, and were as helpless against their attack as their infantry had been against ours. Everyone saw what must happen. Those whose horses were best or least blown, got away. Some attempted to escape back to our position by going round the left of the French lancers. Sir William Ponsonby was of that number. All these fell into the hands of the enemy. Others went straight back – among whom myself – receiving a little fire from some French infantry towards the road on our left as we retired. It was in this part of the transaction that almost the whole of the loss of the brigade took place.[36]

To the west of the main road things were only just showing signs of improvement. The Royal Horse Guards, dressed in their blue tunics, had gone into action numbering just over 200 sabres, but this small number of troops was enough to help bring off the remains of the Household Brigade. Of the seven regiments of heavy cavalry which took part in Uxbridge's charge, only the Royal Horse Guards managed to maintain some semblance of order. They had formed the reserve of the Household Brigade and, although they suffered just under fifty per cent casualties for the day, the majority of which almost certainly occurred during the charge, they stuck to their task and were able to protect the survivors of the charge to the west of the main road as they made their way back to the Allied lines. In fact, theirs was a timely intervention because, like the Union Brigade, the regiments of the Household Brigade had been enjoying themselves at the grand battery, cutting down the gunners and generally doing much mischief. However, these too quickly became exhausted by their efforts and, when Travers' cuirassiers counter-attacked, they were in no condition to offer serious resistance. The Household Brigade also suffered heavy losses from the fire of Reille's divisions which lined the track from Hougoumont to La Belle Alliance, just beyond the grand battery. Uxbridge himself, having led the Household Brigade, was in no position to control affairs, and found himself in a similar situation to Long's at Campo Mayor four years earlier. Despite attempts to call his men to order Uxbridge found he had lost all control of them.

After the overthrow of the cuirassiers [he wrote] I had in vain attempted to stop my people by sounding the Rally, but neither voice nor trumpet availed; so I went back to seek the support of the 2nd line, which unhappily had not followed the movements of the heavy cavalry. Had I, when I sounded the Rally, found only four well-formed squadrons coming steadily along at an easy trot, I feel certain that the loss the first line suffered when they were finally forced back would have been avoided, and most of these guns might have been secured, for it was obvious the effect of that charge had been prodigious, and for the rest of the day, although the cuirassiers frequently attempted to break into our lines, they always did it *mollement* and as if they expected something more behind the curtain.[37]

It is curious that Uxbridge says that the second line, assuming this to be the Royal Horse Guards, 'unhappily had not followed the movements of the heavy cavalry'. The implication is that they should have been close on the heels of the first line, whereas surely by remaining a good distance to the rear they were able to maintain some order and be there to come to their comrades' aid when required. The Greys, to the east of the main road, had followed the movements of the Union Brigade but had been so close, probably in the first line, that they could not hold back once the charge got underway. Furthermore, from the casualties sustained by the Royal Horse Guards, it would appear that they had, after all, followed their comrades, or perhaps they were simply brought up afterwards and suffered their casualties in covering the retreat. In any case, I would suggest that this was just the sort of operation which was sadly lacking on occasion in the Peninsula, particularly at Maguilla. The heavy cavalry also received assistance from the infantry during the retreat when Kempt advanced some of his infantry down the slope to the east of La Haye Sainte, partly to secure the many French prisoners and partly to cover the retreat of the remnants of the Union Brigade. In fact, so effective was this covering fire that Clark-Kennedy thought it played a vital part in the retreat.

> Our infantry [he wrote] which we had passed at the hedge, now proved of essential service to us. They had formed small bodies or squares following in the rear of the charge, and not only checked the pursuit, but without their support and assistance I am satisfied we should not have got back so well as we did, and certainly we could not have secured one-half of the prisoners taken in the charge. Many who had surrendered effected their escape, yet above 2,000 were secured and sent to the rear.[38]

But the most effective support for the beleagured heavy brigades, and in particular the Union Brigade, came in the shape of Vandeleur's brigade which had sat, along with Vivian's brigade, on the ridge above Papelotte. The two brigade commanders had watched in awe as they saw the Union Brigade first break up the French attacking columns and then charge on to the grand battery, where they came under attack from Jacquinot's lancers. Earlier in the day both Vivian and Vandeleur had been given discretionary orders by Uxbridge to attack if conditions were favourable. 'About the time of commencing the action,' wrote Vandeleur, 'an order arrived from Lord Anglesey [Lord Uxbridge] to Generals Vandeleur and Vivian to engage the enemy whenever they could do so with advantage without waiting for orders, and subsequently an order came from the

Duke or Lord Anglesey to close to the infantry, which had left a vacancy by closing to its right. These two orders were the only orders received previous to the first charge made by Vendeleur's brigade.' Wellington had given Cotton similar orders at Salamanca, 'to charge at the first favourable opportunity', but both Vivian and Vandeleur, perhaps mindful of a series of episodes involving the arrest or censure of officers who had acted without Wellington's orders, refused to move without direct orders from the Duke.[40] The episode was recorded by General Muffling, the Prussian liaison officer at Wellington's headquarters. When Muffling suggested that they ride to the assistance of the heavy cavalry they replied, 'Both agreed with me fully but shrugging their shoulders answered, "Alas! We dare not! The Duke of Wellington is very strict in enforcing obedience to prescribed regulations on this point." Muffling later took up the point with Wellington himself who answered, 'The two generals were perfectly correct in their answer, for had they made such an onslaught without my permission, even though the greatest success had crowned their attempt, I must have brought them to a court-martial.'[41]

However, the sight of scores of British dragoons, struggling to fend off Napoleon's lancers and cuirassiers, was more than Vandeleur could bear and, in spite of the possibility of repercussions by way of a censure from the commander-in-chief, and presumably with Uxbridge's discretionary orders in mind, he ordered his brigade, consisting of three squadrons each of the 11th, 12th and 16th Light Dragoons, to move in support of the Union Brigade, the remains of which was floundering in the mud away to his right. Vandeleur's brigade was positioned directly north of Papelotte, close to the Papelotte-Verd-Cocu road, more of a track which ran north across the eastern end of the reverse slope to the latter hamlet. However, the ground in his immediate front presented him with two problems. First, a deep sunken lane, leading down to the east of the farm of La Haye, barred his way. Second, any move to his right and slightly to the south in order to cross the Wavre road at an easier point would bring him within range of Durutte's skirmishers, at that point attacking Papelotte. Therefore, he had his brigade wheel to the right and move along the reverse slope before turning to their left and passing through the Hanoverians of Best and Vincke. Even so, they still came under fire from Pack's brigade who, peering through the smoke of battle, found it difficult to distinguish friend from foe.[42] In fact, it was not only British cavalry who suffered at the hands of what might be termed today 'friendly fire', for the French artillery, still blazing away at the Union Brigade, caused many casualties to Jacquinot's lancers who were swarming around in the valley attacking small groups of Scots Greys and Inniskillings. Eventually, Vandeleur's brigade crossed the Wavre road and, presumably, the Ohain road, before charging Jacquinot's lancers and the units of D'Erlon's corps still remaining in front of the Allied position and in the valley. William

Tomkinson, author of one of the finest Peninsular and Waterloo diaries, charged with the 16th Light Dragoons. Writing of the charge, he said:

> On moving to support them [the Union Brigade], we had to cross a deep lane, which broke us, and occasioned some confusion; we, however, got forward as quickly as possible, charged, and repulsed a body of lancers in pursuit of a party of Scots Greys... The 12th on our left attacked and dispersed a considerable body of the enemy, and by being on our left, and not so much delayed with the lane, got in advance. We supported them, having formed immediately after our charge, and by forming line (with the 11th), presented a front which enabled the 12th to retire with safety, as likewise all the men of the 2nd Brigade that had retreated on this point. We had some difficulty in preventing the men of the 16th from attacking in small bodies, after the charge, those parties of the enemy which had pursued the 2nd Brigade. Had they done this, we should have got into the same scrape; at least, we could not have covered the retreat of the others, but must have retired to form ourselves.[43]

The charge by Vandeleur's light cavalry brigade, supported by de Ghingy's Dutch light cavalry brigade, spared the Union Brigade from almost total destruction, for without them there is little doubt that Jacquinot's lancers would have been able to inflict far heavier casualties than those which they had already done. The 12th Light Dragoons actually broke the French 46th Regiment from Marcognet's division before attacking the lancers. Unfortunately, the regiment went too far and, like the Union Brigade, suffered heavy casualties during their disordered return to the Allied position.

Captain Barton, of the 12th Light Dragoons, wrote:

> We advanced unperceived by the enemy, and on passing the hedgerow, occupied by the Highlanders, immediately made a flank attack on the French column. This attack was successful, and threw the enemy into disorder, who retreated in the greatest confusion followed by the regiment till we were stopped by their standing columns of reserve on the opposite side of a ravine. During the whole of this time an indiscriminate fire was kept up by the French artillery on the regiment as well as on their own retreating battalions. We were in considerable confusion, being mixed up with the enemy's broken infantry, suffering at the same time from a heavy cannonade, and before we could regain the position for formation, we were charged by the 3rd and 4th French lancers, who advanced from behind their own columns of reserve. From this charge and the heavy fire to which we had been before exposed we suffered great loss, having nearly one hundred killed and wounded; amongst the latter was our gallant Lieut.-Colonel, who at the time was reported killed.[44]

Frederick Ponsonby, commanding the 12th Light Dragoons was a veteran of the Peninsula, whom we have already met at Talavera and Villagarcia. His account of how he lay on the battlefield throughout the night with several serious wounds is one of the great Waterloo stories. He later wrote of the charge and aftermath of the Union Brigade:

> I have said that a good many men fell on the crest of the French position. I know we ought not to have been there, and that we fell into the same error which we went down to correct, but I believe that this is an error almost inevitable after a successful charge, and it must always depend upon the steadiness of a good support to prevent serious consequences. In a great battle the support was at hand, and I am therefore firmly of the opinion that although we sustained a greater loss than we should have done if our squadrons had remained compact, the enemy suffered a greater loss, was thrown into more confusion, and required more time to re-establish order, than if greater regularity had been preserved.[45]

The charge by Vandeleur's brigade had the desired effect of extricating the Union Brigade from the confusion at the bottom of the valley and beyond. That it was carried out with complete success is open to question, however, as the 12th Light Dragoons demonstrated the tendency to get out of hand and, as a consequence, suffered heavy casualties during the charge. Indeed, the regiment almost found itself on the verge of requiring rescue. The 16th Light Dragoons, on the other hand, adopted a far more professional approach and, as Tomkinson says, the regiment's officers managed to hold their men in check and prevent them from getting out of hand. The 11th Light Dragoons remained at the top of the ridge as a reserve and thus avoided becoming embroiled in the fight. In spite of the 12th charging farther than they should have done, Vandeleur's three veteran Peninsular regiments did their job well in supporting the Union Brigade at the moment of the latter's greatest danger. Losses within the ranks of the 12th Light Dragoons were fairly severe, but the entire losses for Vandeleur's brigade as a whole throughout the day totalled fewer than those of any of the individual regiments of the Union Brigade, which is, perhaps, a reflection of the difference in experience between the two brigades and in the way in which they were handled.

As for the Union and Household brigades, they suffered severe casualties during their charges. The Union Brigade lost 525 killed, wounded and missing, a large proportion of the latter being later returned dead. This was out of a total strength of 1,181, which represents a loss of just under 44.5%. It is difficult to establish just how many of these 525 casualties were sustained during the charge itself, for it should be remembered that, although the brigade was in no fit state to repeat the exercise, it did, nevertheless, remain on the battlefield for the rest of the day, during which time it would have taken further casualties. However, it is a fairly safe bet that the majority of the brigade's casualties occurred during the charge against D'Erlon's corps and the grand battery afterwards. It is also interesting to note regimental casualty figures. For example, the figures quoted in Siborne's *History of the Waterloo Campaign* show that the Scots Greys suffered more dead than wounded, 102 against ninety-seven, which probably reflects the ferocity of the attack by Jacquinot's lancers who apparently thought little of finishing off any wounded enemy cavalryman. The 1st (Royal) Dragoons showed a similarly high ratio of dead to wounded, eighty-nine against ninety-seven, whilst the Inniskillings returned seventy-three dead against 116 wounded. It is very unusual to note also that the Scots Greys posted not a single officer or private as missing. In fact, the entire Union Brigade returned just thirty-eight men missing, which again is probably accounted for by the merciless conduct shown towards wounded and dismounted cavalrymen by some of the French cavalry. The Household Brigade, which showed a strength of 1,226 at the beginning of the day, suffered 533 casualties, of which 250 were missing. The casualty rate of about 43.5% is about the same as for the Union Brigade and is still very high, although again, it is difficult to establish how many of the casualties were sustained during the great charge. The Household Brigade suffered to a lesser extent in killed and wounded due to the fact that the Royal Horse Guards were held slightly in rear as a reserve and were able to do for the brigade what Vandeleur had done for the Union Brigade, It appears, also, that the Household Brigade suffered less from Jacquinot's lancers and thus the high proportion of missing, presumably including a large percentage of prisoners, is probably due to the fact that Travers' cuirassiers were more disposed towards taking prisoners than were their pike-wielding comrades.[46]

So, having looked at the end result – in terms of casualties – of the British heavy cavalry charge, what did it actually achieve? Well, I believe it achieved a great deal. At a cost of just over 1,000 casualties Uxbridge's cavalry had completely destroyed the first great attack by Napoleon's infantry at Waterloo.[47] In fact, such was the effect of the charge that the French would not attack in any great strength to the east of the main Brussels road for the rest of the day. This left Wellington free to concentrate on the assaults on his right and centre. The struggle here was so intense that one cannot believe that Wellington would have been able to hang on had the French been able to launch further attacks against his left. True, the Prussian intervention occupied Napoleon's right flank during the late afternoon, but any further French attacks on the scale of D'Erlon's before the Prussian arrival would probably have tested even Wellington's resolve.

As for the conduct of the charge, it almost certainly gave Wellington a sense of *deja vu*, as he harked back, no doubt, to Vimeiro and Talavera. In fact, he is reputed to have turned to Uxbridge and said, somewhat sarcastically, 'Well, Paget, I hope you are satisfied with your cavalry now.'[48] Much has been written about Uxbridge's absence from the Peninsula and there is little doubt that he was indeed sorely missed. However, when it came to the final test at Waterloo even he was found wanting. His command of the rearguard during the retreat from Quatre Bras was exemplary, but on 18 June he allowed the heavy cavalry to charge too far, primarily because, like Long at Campo Mayor, he had taken up a position from where he was unable to control the charge, as he himself pointed out later. 'I committed a great mistake in having myself led the attack. The carrière once begun, the leader is no better than any other man; whereas, if I had placed myself at the head of the 2nd line, there is no saying what great advantages might not have accrued from it. I am the less pardonable in having deviated from a principle I had laid down for myself, that I had already suffered from a similar error in an affair at Irtragau, where my reserve, instead of steadily following as I had ordered, chose to join in the attack, and at the end of it I had no formed body to take advantage with.'[49]

It was, in fact, the old story, that had bedevilled the British cavalry in the Peninsula, the absence of a formed reserve, ready to act in support of the first line either to follow up a success or to cover a retreat. This, however, brings into question not Uxbridge but Lieutenant Colonel James Hamilton, commanding the Scots Greys who, according to Uxbridge, had been ordered to support the Royals and Inniskillings. We have seen how the Greys moved forward, probably to avoid enemy artillery fire, a movement which brought them into line with the other two regiments of the brigade. Perhaps this was the fatal move, for it deprived the Union Brigade of a much-needed reserve after the brigade had defeated the attacking French infantry, Vandeleur's brigade acting in its place upon the latter's own initiative. Should Uxbridge take the blame, as cavalry commander, or should Hamilton, for apparently disobeying his commander's order. And what of Ponsonby? He, of course, could not give his version of events afterwards, for he was killed, as was Hamilton, but when Uxbridge returned to lead the Household Brigade, should Ponsonby, as an experienced Peninsular veteran, have known better than to order his brigade to charge without first having reiterated Uxbridge's order for the Greys to act as support?

It is also worth considering whether Uxbridge or indeed Wellington underestimated the French infantry or perhaps even overestimated their own. Had they become complacent after years of success in the Peninsula? After all, Wellington had grown used to seeing the French driven off on countless battlefields in Portugal and Spain, which Uxbridge would have been well aware of, and perhaps they thought the outcome of D'Erlon's attack a foregone conclusion. Did the relative initial success of the French assault take Uxbridge and Wellington by surprise, forcing them to make rather hasty preparations for the heavy cavalry charge? There is certainly evidence to support this, with Uxbridge making a hurried dash from one side of the main road to the other, leaving some with the impression that the Scots Greys were to act as a reserve whilst others obviously thought otherwise. Then, without a moment to lose, the charge was launched, with the ensuing result examined above. With more time and due care and attention, I would suggest that more precise preparations could have been made, with the individual brigade and regimental commanders being made aware of just exactly what their role would be in the coming charge. The circumstances were different at Salamanca, but good planning by Cotton and execution by Le Marchant ensured that the charge of the heavy cavalry there was incredibly successful, as we have seen in an earlier chapter in this book. On that occasion, however, there was time enough for plans to be put into motion, whereas at Waterloo split-second timing was required and, as we have already seen, at least one British officer thought that the charge would have failed had it been delayed by just two or three minutes.[50] Ultimately, Uxbridge blamed himself for the error in not adequately organising a reserve and in his biography of his illustrious ancestor, the Marquis of Anglesey wrote that Uxbridge 'was haunted by this error' for the rest of his life.[51] However, this is to detract from the more significant and wider achievement of the Union and Household Brigades at Waterloo, which Anglesey quite perfectly summed up:

> Whatever blame must attach to Uxbridge for leading the charge himself, it cannot be denied that by choosing exactly the right moment to launch it he had so completely smashed an infantry corps and a large portion of its artillery that it was virtually out of action until late in the day and then so reduced in numbers and enthusiasm as to have no major effect on the battle.[52]

Notes

1 Symptomatic of these myths was a lecture I once heard, given by a re-enactor of a French regiment, whose 'account' of the charge of the Scots Greys ended with hundreds of them lying dead and wounded on the battlefield. This, of course, is sadly typical of many popular myths concerning the battle and is pure fantasy. Indeed, there were only 391 of the regiment present at Waterloo.

2 Wellington himself, using Belgian solar time, claimed the battle began at 10am. See *Wellington's Despatches*, XII: 481.

3 Captain Clark-Kennedy, who took an 'eagle' at Waterloo with the 1st (Royal) Dragoons, thought that Ponsonby's attack would have failed had it been delayed by two or three minutes. Siborne, *Waterloo Letters* (London, 1891), 72.

4 Wellington later claimed that the outcome of the Battle of Waterloo depended upon the closing of the gates at Hougoumont, a dramatic episode which

involved the Foot Guards who managed to close the gates after they had been forced open by about thirty to forty French infantry who were subsequently cut down, except for one small drummer boy. The fight at Hougoumont has even spawned books on the episode, including *Hougoumont: The Key to Victory at Waterloo* by Julian Paget and Derek Saunders (London, 1992).

5 Jac Weller, *Wellington in the Peninsula* (London, 1962), 175.

6 Historians have often criticised D'Erlon for employing such an unwieldy formation, but for once in his career he appears to have given a great deal of thought to it and, presumably tired of successive defeats in the Peninsula at the hands of British infantry in line, decided to try and meet fire with fire. The formation may have appeared clumsy, but it came much closer to achieving a breakthrough than any other formation employed during the six years of the Peninsular War.

7 All of this is explained in Jac Weller, *Wellington at Waterloo* (London, 1967), 98.

8 Quiot was commanding the division in the absence of Allix, whose division it initially was.

9 Weller, in *Wellington at Waterloo*, 99, incorrectly claims that the brigade which attacked La Haye Sainte was Quiot's left-hand brigade under the command of Bourgeois, whereas the latter commander actually drove the 95th from the sandpit and continued on against Kempt's brigade. It was Quiot himself who attacked the farmhouse.

10 The Lüneberg Battalion, part of Kielmansegge's Hanoverian Brigade, went into action 595-strong and suffered casualties of 205. Although the vast majority of these were probably sustained during the tragedy of the early afternoon, it is questionable whether this really was the kind of disaster that historians have often claimed it to be. After all, the 205 casualties represent just over a third of the battalion's strength, a high but not unusual casualty rate, and if we assume it includes casualties sustained throughout the remainder of the day, the total sustained during the incident was possibly not as high as imagined, and is certainly not of the sort that warrants such phrases as 'wiped out' or 'annihilated'. For example, Weller writes, 'the cuirassiers broke them completely and inflicted terrible casualties'. (Weller, *Wellington at Waterloo*, 100) and adds on the next page that they were 'destroyed', whilst Chandler, in his *The Hundred Days* (London, 1980), 142, says they were 'butchered'. With a casualty toll for the day of thirty per cent, I would suggest that this was not really the case. Some accounts claim that it was the Prince of Orange who gave the order for the Lünebergers to advance, although I have not seen any hard evidence to support this. Amongst those who claim it was the Prince are Weller (*Wellington at Waterloo*, 99–100). That the Prince was a brave man has never been in question, but it is quite evident that he never quite grasped the realities of war. He had seen active service in the Peninsula where he had seen Wellington's infantry fighting in line and, at Waterloo, he appears to have considered this as the only formation in which infantry could fight successfully. The fact that he had already sent the 69th Regiment to destruction at Quatre Bras two days earlier, by ordering them into line when it was patently clear to everybody else that French cavalry were hovering close by, did little to dissuade him from this view, as Christian von Ompteda discovered later

in the day. Chandler, Wood and Siborne all claim that it was Wellington himself who ordered the Lünebergers forward. Hamilton-Williams, in his *New Perspectives* (London, 1993), 292, writes that it was Kielmansegge who gave the order. Ultimately, it is of no great significance to us, although it is yet another example of the myths and inaccuracies that surround the battle.

11 Siborne, *Waterloo Letters*, 347.

12 Ibid.

13 Ibid. 349, 351 & 361.

14 Ibid. 72.

15 Ibid.8.

16 Michael Mann, *And They Rode On* (London, 1984), 36.

17 Siborne, *Waterloo Letters*, 44.

18 Ibid. 38. Waymouth, in Siborne's *Waterloo Letters*, 44, quotes Major Kelly, of the Life Guards, as claiming that the Life Guards, 'made great slaughter amongst the flying cuirassiers who had choked the hollow way... and that this road was quite blocked up by dead'.

19 Siborne, Waterloo Letters, 78, 81 & 198.

20 Ibid. 61. De Lacy Evans, who actually gave the signal for the attack to begin by waving his hat in the air, said that the Union Brigade waited for a few minutes at the foot of the reverse slope in order to let the infantry wheel back and pass around the flanks of their squadrons and also to ensure that the French were a little 'deranged' at having to pass both the hedge and the road.

21 Duthilt, quoted in Hamilton-Williams, *Waterloo: New Perspectives*, 299–300.

22 Siborne, *Waterloo Letters*, 383.

23 E.B. Low, *With Napoleon at Waterloo* (London, 1911), 143.

24 Cotton, *A Voice from Waterloo*, 60–1.

25 Siborne, *Waterloo Letters*, 85.

26 Ibid. 68. It is recorded that a sergeant of Royal Artillery from Rogers' battery, went so far as to spike one of his guns in the face of the French advance. Given the fact that Wellington did not lose a single gun in the entire Peninsular War it demonstrates just how close the French must have come to achieving success.

27 Ibid. 70–1.

28 Ibid. 75–6. According to Clark-Kennedy the eagle was taken about 300 yards east of La Haye Sainte and 270 yards south of the Wavre (Ohain) road.

29 The story is related in Siborne by Lieutenant Colonel Miller of the Inniskillings. Siborne, *Waterloo Letters*, 87–8.

30 Ibid. 61.

31 Low, *With Napoleon at Waterloo*, 144–5.

32 Ibid. 145–6.

33 Mann, *And They Rode On*, 50.

34 Siborne, *Waterloo Letters*, 62.

35 The claim is made in Hamilton-Williams' *New Perspectives*, 301. The author misquotes Wyndham, of the Greys, who says, 'In descending the hill, about three or four hundred yards from the hedge, the Greys came in contact with a 2nd French column or square, regularly formed, the fire from which they received did great execution. The loss at this moment in men and horses was most severe. This column was nearly destroyed, and the remainder of it were

taken prisoners.' First of all, Hamilton-Williams quotes Wyndham as saying that the Greys came upon *the* second column, and not a column (my italics), which was what Wyndham actually wrote. Then, he fails to quote Wyndham as saying that the French column was 'nearly destroyed, and the remainder taken prisoners', which is certainly not what happened to Durutte, or if it did it was certainly not the Greys who did it. Durutte's division was able to continue fighting late on, both in the vicinity of Papelotte and Smohain and farther west on the battlefield later in the day. I would suggest that, after they had cut their way through the first French formation they encountered, the Greys probably came up against simply a second formation which emptied a few saddles before the Greys continued on towards the grand battery. Most accounts agree that the Union Brigade sustained the vast majority of its casualties at the battery and on its return, when assailed by enemy lancers. His claim, made on page 302 of *New Perspectives*, that the Royal Dragoons broke a French square is also very dubious, and appears to be based upon no other authority than two watching infantry officers of the 28th, Shelton and Mounsteven, whose letters were printed in Siborne's *Waterloo Letters*, 349 & 351. Shelton, in fact, wrote that the broken 'column' was part of the division which had already been beaten, i.e. Marcognet's or Donzelot's, whereas Mounsteven could not remember whether it was a column or square which was broken. I would suggest that it was a column and that it was again part of either Marcognet's or Donzelot's. There is no mention of such an incident in either Ainslie's or Atkinson's histories of the regiment, nor in Clark-Kennedy's *Attack the Colour!* The breaking of an infantry square was such a very rare occurrence that, had it occurred, it would surely have found a place in the pages of the regiment's histories. Atkinson, in his *History of the Royal Dragoons*, says that Radclyffe, who commanded the 3rd or left-hand squadron, struck the left flank of Donzelot's column. Durutte was forced to fall back only because of the failure of the attack by the other three divisions of D'Erlon's corps and by his own failure to take Papelotte, and nice as it would be to think that the Royals broke a French square I think it unlikely that it ever happened. Durutte, in fact, suffered more from the charge of Vandeleur's light cavalry than it did from the Union Brigade.

36 Siborne, *Waterloo Letters*, 62.
37 Ibid. 9.
38 Ibid.71.
39 Ibid. 105.
40 Notable figures who had felt the full force of Wellington's wrath included Norman Ramsay (arrested after Vittoria), James McGrigor (berated very harshly in front of Goya), Charles Stewart (reduced to tears!), Charles Bevan (commanding officer of the 4th Foot, who committed suicide after being partly blamed for the escape of the French garrison from Almeida), and Henry Sturgeon (got himself shot by French piquets after being blamed for fouling up the postal system after the battle of Orthes).
41 Carl von Muffling, *Passages from my Life* (London, 1853), 245.
42 Sir Evelyn Wood, *Cavalry in the Waterloo Campaign* (London, 1895), 149.
43 James Tomkinson (Ed), *Diary of a Cavalry Officer in the Peninsular and Waterloo Campaigns, 1809–1815* (London, 1895), 301. Interestingly enough, Tomkinson,

who had witnessed many of the highs and lows of the cavalry in the Peninsula, thought the charge by the British heavy cavalry at Waterloo to be, 'one of the finest charges ever seen', Ibid. 300.

44 Siborne, *Waterloo Letters*, 114–15.
45 Ibid.113–4.
46 See Evelyn Wood, for example, with two anecdotes involving cuirassiers sparing the lives of British cavalrymen. *Cavalry in the Waterloo Campaign*, 150–1.
47 I do not include the French assaults on Hougoumont as these were, by definition, intended to be only diversionary attacks as a prelude to the great assault on Wellington's left and centre.
48 Anglesey, *One Leg*, 135.
49 Siborne, *Waterloo Letters*, 9–10.
50 Ibid. 72.
51 Anglesey, *One Leg*, 141.
52 Ibid. 142.

CHAPTER XII

Waterloo: The Light Cavalry

Thus far we have examined the charge of the two heavy brigades of British cavalry at Waterloo. However, the role of the British light cavalry is invariably overlooked by historians who fail to look beyond the great charge by the heavies. Indeed, many accounts fail even to mention the role of Vandeleur's light cavalry during that particular episode, a vital saving role which we have already seen in the previous chapter. It is only natural that interest should focus upon the great charge by the Union and Household Brigades not least because of its dramatic consequences, being the virtual destruction of both assailed and assailant. It is also an episode which has attracted much romanticism, as borne out by the numerous paintings of the charge, some of which have since become among the most famous military paintings of all time. A less glamorous but equally vital task was that which was carried out by the light cavalry at Waterloo, a task which they accomplished with a minimum of fuss, with great success and without any real recognition.

Apart from the brigades of Vivian and Vandeleur, the British light cavalry had remained fairly inactive throughout the day, taking the occasional casualty through French artillery fire. At around 4pm, however, it became clear that this inactivity was not to last for much longer when, to the astonishment of all those who could see from the top of Wellington's ridge, thousands of French cavalry began to muster for the first of a series of massed cavalry charges against the Allied line.

The French cavalry charges have been the subject of much discussion and study over the years. The overwhelming opinion is that such attacks against infantry which had yet to be assaulted by French infantry were doomed to failure. The attacks were delivered against a relatively narrow front – given the numbers involved – of about 700 yards between Hougoumont and La Haye Sainte. Furthermore, they would be delivered uphill over ground which became increasingly boggy as thousands of horses ploughed it up time and time again. Also, the attacks were unsupported by either infantry or artillery, a major factor in their ultimate failure. In fact, the French cavalry charges came as a welcome relief to

Wellington's infantry who had begun to wilt under the intense pressure of the French artillery bombardment. As long as they remained steady, there would be little prospect of any enemy cavalry breaking their squares, bristling as they were with four ranks of fixed bayonets. And so it proved.

While Wellington's infantry played the part of the rocks against which the sea of French cavalry crashed time and time again, the Allied cavalry remained at the bottom of the reverse slope. There were, altogether, around 5,000 Allied cavalry at hand, although many of the non-British contingent could not be made to charge at all. Indeed, the Duke of Cumberland's Hussars, a Hanoverian regiment, simply turned and fled from the field in disgrace, leaving their allies to fight on without them. The British cavalry to the west of the main Brussels road consisted of Grant's brigade, being the 7th Hussars, 15th Hussars and the 13th Light Dragoons. Originally, this brigade had included the 2nd Hussars KGL, but as this regiment was still on the Belgian border, it was replaced by the 13th Light Dragoons, an experienced regiment of Peninsular veterans. There was also Major General Domberg's brigade, consisting of the 1st and 2nd Light Dragoons KGL, and the 23rd Light Dragoons, who had not seen action since their exploits at Talavera, some six years earlier. In addition to these two brigades, there were the remains of the two heavy brigades, the Household and Union, the survivors of which, some 400 in all, had been moved to their right in order to bolster the line.

Just prior to the attack by Ney's cavalry, Grant had moved the 13th Light Dragoons and the 15th Hussars to the west, just north of Hougoumont, in order to counter a threat by Piré's lancers. Writing of this in Siborne's *Waterloo Letters*, Joseph Thackwell said:

> I beg to state that it [his brigade] was under the crest of the position, in rear of the angle at Hougoumont, until about three p.m. when the 15th Hussars and 13th Light Dragoons were moved to the ravine between the Nivelles road and Braine-la-Leud [sic] for the purpose of attacking 10 squadrons of lancers in two lines... Whilst dispositions were making for the attack the Lancers began cheering, and on looking towards the position we had quitted, the cause of cheering was discovered to be an impetous attack by the French cavalry upon our Infantry and Guns, the limbers of which were going rapidly towards the Nivelles road.[2]

The shouting by Piré's lancers heralded the beginning of the mass French cavalry attacks. Piré, in fact, retired upon Grant's approach, leaving the latter to return to his original position which lay at the northern end of the track which runs north-west from La Belle Alliance and terminates upon the Allied ridge north-east of Hougoumont. On their return to their original position, the 13th Light Dragoons formed into line and made a charge against a body of cuirassiers, driving them back about 300 yards until being forced to retire at the sight of dense columns of enemy cavalry preparing for another charge. The 15th Hussars had charged on their left and these too retired in good order to the Allied ridge. 'The steadiness of the two regiments,' wrote Thackwell, 'had the effect of checking further serious attacks upon this point for some time; but the skirmishers of the 15th were employed against the cuirassiers and other cavalry in front, who were kept at some distance.'[3]

As Grant's men rode back to this position, they witnessed the French cavalry passing between the Allied infantry squares before being driven back by Domberg's cavalry in the first of what was to be a series of very successful counter-attacks by Wellington's cavalry. It was this series of counter-attacks which proved the light cavalry's most valuable contribution to the Battle of Waterloo, a series of controlled charges which drove back the French cavalry time after time without any of them ever going too far or running into the same sort of problems which the Household and Union Brigades had got themselves into earlier in the day. Sadly, this vital role has long since been overshadowed by the exploits of the heavy cavalry at Waterloo and thus, the image of the British cavalry has become firmly that of the heavy brigades and in turn has resulted in a further slight on their reputation.

Unlike the well-documented charges made by the heavy cavalry, the exploits of the light cavalry at Waterloo are much harder to follow in terms of timings and individual charges. Siborne's *Waterloo Letters* contains several accounts by officers in Grant's, Dörnberg's, and Vivian's and Vandeleur's brigades, describing charges made against the French cavalry during the late afternoon. Unfortunately, it is difficult to separate them. What becomes clear, however, is that the British light cavalry was employed in different ways against Ney's cavalry. The first was in the manner of the 13th Light Dragoons, attacking the French cavalry as the latter made their way up to the Allied position. By charging down the slope in front of them, the British cavalry had the advantage of momentum which broke up the French attacks before they reached the Allied infantry squares. The charges were controlled and purposeful and, after having taken the sting out of the French charges, the British cavalry simply returned to the Allied ridge. Obviously, these sorts of charges could only take place against smaller bodies of enemy cavalry, for there is no way that even Uxbridge would have launched his cavalry against any of the main French massed attacks. The second way in which the British cavalry were used was in the counter-attacking mode, being launched against the French once the latter had passed through the infantry squares. This, of course, meant that the French cavalry would have already suffered much disorganisation from both the effects of the long charge uphill to the ridge and from the musketry and artillery fire from the Allied troops. Once through the squares, the French cavalry were then faced by relatively fresh

British and other Allied cavalry units who literally swept them away from the ridge. The third way in which the light cavalry appears to have been employed during the day was in charging French cavalry as it reached the crest of the ridge or plateau as some called it. Once again, the French cavalry had suffered the effects of the long gallop up to the Allied position, and once there faced charging British cavalry who had come forward to meet them. All three of these methods were successful in their own way and, whilst never having the same dramatic consequences of the charge by the two heavy brigades, were very effective in clearing the Allied position of enemy cavalry. The charges made by the British light cavalry regiments at Waterloo gradually took their toll, with the 7th Hussars in particular suffering severe casualties.[4]

I suspect that we shall never really know what the French cavalry charges looked like. Certainly, we know the ground over which they attacked and what it must have looked like after the first few charges had churned it up. But, contrary to popular belief, the charges did not come on at full pelt, as some artists in particular would have us believe, at least not after the first charge. In fact, much credit has to go to the French cavalry for having both the stamina and gallantry to persist in the attacks long after it must have become clear to all present that little advantage was ever to be gained other than to the Allies. The French had to negotiate a ride of almost one mile from their starting positions before they swept over the Allied ridge. Then, after having endured both the ride up to the ridge and through the infantry squares, always under fire, they had to wheel round and make their way back before trying again. All this meant that each charge was made over a distance of about three miles or so. It is reckoned that about sixteen such charges were made, which represents an enormous amount of ground covered by those cavalrymen who took part in all of them.

Needless to say these attacks, when delivered, were nothing like those seen at Garcia Hemandez, for example. 'None of your furious galloping,' wrote Captain Mercer in his journal, 'but a deliberate advance, at a deliberate pace, as of men resolved to carry their point.'[5] It is a measure of the success of Wellington's cavalry that the vast majority of work to the west of the main Brussels road during this phase of the battle was done by light cavalry and this was against all kinds of enemy cavalry, including cuirassiers, carabiniers and horse grenadiers, some of the heaviest cavalry in Europe. For the 13th Light Dragoons to be able to scatter, on more than one occasion, cuirassiers protected by heavy steel breastplates was no mean achievement. We are left, therefore, wondering what might have been, had the Household and Union Brigades been present in strength to act at this point. In fact, the survivors of the Household Brigade were gathered together by Uxbridge and launched on more than one occasion against French cavalry but, their numbers having dwindled as a result of their earlier charge, they were never going to play anything other than a cameo performance during the latter stages of the battle. Both brigades of heavy cavalry were combined during the evening to form one single brigade. It was then brought into the line to bolster the Allied position and played a vital, if unusual, role by literally plugging the gap in the line following the fall of La Haye Sainte, so short of men was Wellington.

It will be remembered that the brigades of Vivian and Vandeleur had been relatively inactive throughout most of the afternoon owing to their positioning to the east of the Brussels road which, consequently, took them out of the cavalry actions going on around the Allied infantry squares to the west of the road. Vivian had taken part in supporting the Union Brigade during the latter's retirement but, other than this, had watched and waited while events unfolded elsewhere on the battlefield. However, with the arrival of the Prussians to the east of the battlefield, Uxbridge decided that the time was right to move them to their left to help shore up the defences in the centre of the Allied line. Lord Greenock, who was Assistant Quartermaster General to the Cavalry, wrote, 'Lord Anglesey... gave orders for the better concentration of his Corps by removing the brigades from the left of La Haye Sainte towards the right of the position, as soon as their presence in that quarter became no longer necessary in consequence of the arrival of the Prussians on that flank.'[6] The move came at a crucial time, for with the French troops now in possession of La Haye Sainte, Wellington's centre came under intense pressure. Vivian wrote, 'These brigades [Vivian and Vandeleur], then, were moved to the right, and arrived at a most opportune moment. The effect of their formation, immediately in the rear of the line of infantry on the position, was to give confidence to the troops almost worn out with the protracted and murderous combat.'[7]

With the arrival in the centre of Vivian and Vandeleur we can be said to have reached at the final phase of the battle. The mass French cavalry attacks had ended, and what might be termed more 'conventional' cavalry charges took place by individual regiments. These were met in style by the British, and indeed the Allied light cavalry regiments who demonstrated the sort of control which had been lacking in the earlier charges by the two heavy brigades, although Uxbridge did manage to make a satisfactory counter-attack with the remains of the Household Brigade against some French cuirassiers. The 23rd Light Dragoons in particular were very effective and showed none of the rashness that had so marred their performance at Talavera. At one point they charged a body of cuirassiers and threw them back for a considerable distance before being brought up by French infantry. The 23rd fell back after coming under fire from the enemy square but, unfortunately, suffered a similar fate from their own troops when they returned to the Allied line, Hence, they drew off to their right and fell in with Vivian's brigade.

With La Haye Sainte in his hands and with the Prussians making an ever-increasing impression on the course of the battle, Napoleon decided the time had come to launch his Imperial Guard against Wellington. It was his last throw of the dice and, as we know, it failed, but only after a very stiff firefight at the top of the Allied ridge. The Guard took the route taken by Ney's cavalry earlier in the afternoon and, like the cavalry, met with similarly scant success. When the Imperial Guard fell back Wellington, raising himself in his saddle for all to see, waved his hat in the air as the signal for a general advance and, after hours enveloped in dense smoke, the tired and weary Allied infantry advanced to discover that it was, in fact, a very pleasant evening with the setting sun lighting up what must have been an awesome sight. As the Imperial Guard fell back Wellington ordered Vivian to advance whilst Vandeleur followed behind him, slightly to his right along the eastern edge of the wood outside Hougoumont. Despite the fact that the French were clearly beaten, the task confronting both Vivian and Vandeleur and, in fact, the rest of the British cavalry, was not an easy one. It was difficult to determine whether the retreating infantry were ripe for the sort of charge which Le Marchant had executed at Salamanca and which was sorely missing after Vittoria, or whether the French infantry were capable of putting up the sort of resistance which might leave the British with another Villar de Puerco on their hands. In other words, they were to proceed with caution which, as we have seen, was not always an easy thing for British cavalry to do. At the bottom of the valley into which Vivian was moving, crowds of French fugitives were in retreat, but opinions differ as to whether they were completely broken they were moving off in relatively good order. Vivian was apparently ordered not to charge any infantry squares unless he felt sure of breaking them,[8] something which was a rarity on the field of battle.

At length, Vivian led the 10th Hussars against a regiment of French lancers who appeared to pose a threat to British infantry. The lancers were duly scattered and then, despite the intervention of a squadron of cuirassiers who tried, in vain, to halt the 10th Hussars, the British hussars galloped into several bodies of enemy cavalry which were making their way from the field. Vivian then ordered the 10th to halt before galloping back to the 18th Hussars to order them forward. As he rode back to the 18th Vivian was attacked by a cuirassier. It will be remembered that Vivian had lost the use of his right arm as a result of a wound received at the Croix d'Orade before Toulouse, but despite this disadvantage, he managed to deal with his would-be assailant. 'As soon as we were well into the enemy and mixed up, the French making off,' he wrote later, 'I gave the word "halt", and galloped off to the 18th. En route I was attacked by one of the cuirassiers whom we had passed. I was fortunate enough to give him a thrust in the neck with my left hand (for my right was in a sling, and I was just capable of holding the reins with it only), and at that moment I was joined by my little German orderly, who cut the fellow off his horse.'[9] Given that Vivian said he gave the Frenchman a thrust in the neck, one wonders what sort of sabre he was using, as the 1796 light cavalry sabre was more of a cutting than a thrusting sword. It also says much for Vivian's prowess both as a horseman and a swordsman that he was able to control his horse with his right arm in a sling and still manage to fend off and wound his assailant with his left hand.

As far as the infantry were concerned, the job had been virtually completed, but for the cavalry there was the task of following up their work and continuing with the pursuit, and it was during this phase of the battle that several notable casualties occurred. As the Allied army rolled down from the ridge, Uxbridge found himself riding alongside Wellington. As they rode passed the west of the orchard of La Haye Sainte a grape shot passed over the top of Wellington's horse and struck Uxbridge in the knee. The exchange between the two men is well known and is one of the most oft-quoted incidents of the battle. Apparently, Uxbridge, upon realising the consequences of his wound, exclaimed, 'By God, sir, I've lost my leg!' To which Wellington replied, 'By God, sir, so you have!'[10] While Uxbridge was carried from the field – he later had his right leg amputated – his cavalry carried on driving the French from the field. With Uxbridge wounded, Vandeleur assumed command of the cavalry with Colonel Sleigh taking over in command of Vandeleur's brigade.

Vivian, meanwhile, had reached the 18th Hussars and called out to them, '18th, will you follow me?', to which Sergeant-Major Jeffs replied, 'Yes, General, to hell if you will lead us.'[11] Well, it may not have been hell into which Vivian was leading the 18th Hussars, but there was certainly much danger at the foot of the ridge, for, despite the fact they were in retreat, the French were still capable of defending themselves and giving a bloody nose to all those who got too close. The 18th duly charged and scattered some squadrons of enemy cavalry which were covering the retreat of the French infantry. Whilst the 18th reformed, Vivian rode back and brought up the 1st Hussars KGL and a weak squadron of the 10th Hussars under Major Howard, whilst around them Howard's men began to fall from the fire of an enemy square close by. Upon seeing that a British battalion was approaching, apparently with the intention of attacking the square, Howard led his men against it, but as he reached the bayonets of the front rank he fell dead, shot through the body. His men continued riding round the square as the British infantry battalion passed by. The French square, meanwhile, continued to pull back and, in spite of the efforts of the 10th Hussars to break in, fell back slowly but steadily along the main road in the direction of Genappe. Captain Taylor, of the 10th Hussars, later wrote of the attack on the square:

Sir H. Vivian had directed Major Howard to co-operate with some infantry that were coming along the road in attacking this square; that he, Major

Howard, sent to the officer of infantry to say so, who for some reason declined; that Major Howard asked this officer of the Regiment what he thought of it, who said that without the co-operation of the infantry it was better not as the square was well formed, but other troops coming up and surrounding them, they must surrender. Major Howard said that having been ordered to attack he thought it a ticklish thing not to do it, and gave the order accordingly and did it with effect, though the enemy stood well the officers being wounded close to the bayonets, and Major Howard falling so that a man in the ranks struck him with the butt end of his musket.[12]

Whilst Vivian was in the act of driving the French from the valley, Vandeleur was advancing on right. His men came up against a square of French infantry and, apparently, broke it, taking many prisoners. The 16th Light Dragoons also came across a French square and likewise dispersed it, whilst farther west, the 11th Light Dragoons captured a battery of guns which had remained in position to the last. George Farmer was with the 11th as they charged down the slope towards the end of the battle, and he later described the excitement and confusion of the final moments of the battle.

How can I pretend to describe what followed! On we went at a gallop, dashing past the weary yet gallant footmen, and, shouting as we went, drove fiercely and without check up to the very muzzles of a hostile battery. A furious discharge of grape met us, and thinned our ranks. Before it man and horse went down; but the survivors, never pulling bridle or pausing to look back, scattered the gunners to the winds, and the cannon were our own. Just at this moment, Sergeant Emmet of the 11th, whom I covered, received a shot in the groin, which made him reel in the saddle, from which he would have fallen, had I not caught him; while at the same time a ball struck me on the knee, the bone of which was saved by the interposition of my unrolled cloak. For in the morning I had not found time to pack it in its place; and it hung before me in loose folds, through most of which the bullet made its way, terribly bruising, yet not disabling the limb. I was glad to save my sergeant, for he was a good and a brave man. Yet I own that I felt bitter mortification when the tide of war swept past us, and I felt myself cut off from sharing in the general triumph. Accordingly, perceiving a corporal near, I called to him to lend his assistance, and no sooner saw him seize the sergeant by the other arm, than I loosed my hold. 'One whole man,' thought I, 'is enough to take care of a wounded one;' and then I plied my spurs into my horse's sides, and flew to the front. But by this time it was too dark to distinguish one corps from another. I therefore attached myself to the first body of horse which I overtook, and in three minutes found myself in the middle of the enemy. There was a momentary check, during which the men demanded one of another, what regiment this was. I do not know how the discovery of their own absolute intermingling might have operated, had not an officer called aloud, 'Never mind your regiments, men, but follow me.' In an instant I sprang to his side, and, seeing a mass of infantry close upon us, who, by the blaze of musketry, we at one recognised to be French, he shouted out, 'Charge!' and nobly led the way. We rushed on; the enemy fired, and eight of our number fell, among whom was our gallant leader. A musket-ball pierced his heart; he sprang out of his saddle and fell dead to the ground. Another check was the consequence, and almost instinctively we recoiled; neither, indeed, was the movement opportune, for the impetuosity of a mere handful of men had carried them into the middle of a retreating column, and their destruction, had they lingered there, must have been inevitable. For myself, having gazed hastily round, and noticed that the field was thickly studded with dung heaps, I scoured off in search of my own regiment, with which, when it had halted, a good way off, I succeeded in coming up.[13]

Lieutenant Colonel Sleigh, of the 11th Light Dragoons, now in command of Vandeleur's brigade, was another who witnessed the confusion.

We took the last battery and received their last fire, which was given when the brigade, then under my command, was so close that I saw the artillery-men fire their guns; fortunately the ground was undulating, and we only lost by the fire Lieutenant Phillips of the 11th [Light] Dragoons, and Hay of the 16th [Light] Dragoons. It was after this, when continuing our advance, that the 1st Hussars came up in the rear of our brigade, and from its being nearly dark were all but in collision with the 11th and 16th, which regiments, knowing there was a brigade of French cavalry on our right, went threes about, and were in the act of charging, when they recognised the 1st Hussars by knowing their cheer; it was very dark, and the men knew of the French brigade being behind them.[14]

The confusion was indeed so great that many British soldiers were killed or wounded by Prussians who by now had emerged from the carnage at Plancenoit to join up with their Allies who had reached the French staging areas. Many Prussians became casualties also.

The Battle of Waterloo, the last great battle of the Napoleonic Wars, ended at around 9.30pm. Napoleon's last throw of the dice had yielded nothing but thousands of killed and wounded men from the various combatant nations. British and KGL casualties are estimated to have been around 8,500, whilst their allies suffered a further 5,500 casualties. The Prussians lost around 8,000 casualties whilst French casualties are almost impossible to determine, with estimates ranging between 30,000 and 47,000. By 26 June Wellington had taken Peronne, the last of the three lines of defence north of Paris, and on 6 July the capital itself surrendered. Nine days later Napoleon himself surrendered and was soon aboard HMS

Bellerophon, bound for Torbay. His fate is well-known, being his final exile to the lonely island of St Helena, where he died in May 1821.

The performance of the two heavy brigades of British cavalry has already been analysed, and it remains only to examine that of the light cavalry which, as I have already stated, has often been overlooked owing to the attention given to their much heavier comrades. The part played by the British light cavalry at Waterloo may not have been as dramatic as that of the heavy cavalry but if was, nevertheless, an extremely vital one, Vandeleur's brigade saved many of the Union Brigade from being either killed, wounded or taken during their great charge in the early afternoon, but the real contribution to the Allied victory was made during the afternoon and evening, during the mass French cavalry charges and afterwards, when, as we have seen, a series of steady and controlled charges prevented the French cavalry from making a bigger impact by either breaking up the attacks before they reached the ridge or by simply clearing them away once they had passed through the Allied infantry squares. Indeed, the presence of the British light cavalry during this phase of the battle was a crucial one, and was one which made it extremely dangerous for the French cavalry to linger for any length of time between the Allied squares. It was dangerous enough as a result of Allied infantry fire, but with British and other Allied cavalry units charging at the same time, the reverse slope of Wellington's position was a particularly unhealthy place to be for a French cavalryman. The brigades of both Vivian and Vandeleur also helped plug the gap in the Allied line during the early evening at the crisis of the battle, and along with the remains of the heavy cavalry, they actually acted like infantry by forming in line and sitting there, taking punishment from the enemy and providing an unusual but effective solution to the problem of filling the gap in the line when things became desperate for Wellington.

It was during the French cavalry charges and, in fact, following the defeat of Napoleon's Guard, that the British light cavalry proved they were capable of maintaining discipline even in the most trying of circumstances. After all, the confusion during this latter stage of the battle was extremely great and, with the onset of night, it was difficult at times to distinguish friend from foe. Furthermore, they had to proceed with caution, lest any French unit – and there were plenty of formed enemy units still loose on the battlefield – attack them. In the event, they performed their duty well, attacking successive enemy units, both infantry and cavalry and, as the 11th Light Dragoons demonstrated, they were still capable of charging and taking an enemy gun battery. Not all was sweetness and light, however, for the light cavalry still found it difficult to resist charging formed squares of French infantry. Indeed, the majority of Napoleon's army may well have been fleeing south in panic but there were still many regiments, particularly those of the Imperial Guard, which were capable of maintaining discipline in the most trying of circumstances, and they did not come more trying than on the evening of 18 June.

Some of these experienced French regiments formed square and made their way smartly from the battlefield and, as the 10th Hussars found to their cost, were still capable of seeing off British and other Allied cavalry units during the retreat south. The British cavalry units can, however, be forgiven for being under the impression that the infantry were easy game, particularly given the fact that the majority of French soldiers were simply running scared. There are shades of Villar de Puerco in the attack by the 10th Hussars on one of the French squares, and for Talbot we must read Howard, the commanding officer of the 10th who, like Talbot, commanding the 14th Light Dragoons at Villar de Puerco, lost his life leading the attack on a French square.[15] Despite this late setback, which had little effect on the outcome of the battle, the performance of the British light cavalry at Waterloo was a very creditable one, and whilst not as brilliant or as controversial as the charge of the heavy brigade was, in its own way, every bit as important by providing crucial support for Wellington's infantry in the afternoon during the French cavalry attacks and in the evening by making a series of important charges to consolidate the gains made after the defeat of Napoleon's Guard. All this was achieved with a minimum of fuss and, more importantly, with far fewer casualties than those sustained by the Union and Household Brigades.

The Battle of Waterloo was the most decisive battle of the Napoleonic Wars. Napoleon had been defeated before, notably at Leipzig, but he had returned to haunt Europe afterwards. After Waterloo, however, there was no going back. The Allies' victory at Waterloo was a crushing one, and with the subsequent three-year occupation of Paris, there was little prospect of Napoleon ever returning as Emperor. The battle marked the end of an era and, save for a few comparatively minor and more distant conflicts, was to ensure peace in Europe for a further ninety-nine years before a much more horrific war began.

Notes

1   This ravine is referred to as ravine D in the *Waterloo Letters*, as there was a map which accompanied the letter. The ravine can be found today in the middle of a housing estate which covers most of the battlefield to the north of the motor-way, which in turn follows the course of what was once the Nivelles road. The ravine is now called, somewhat inappropriately, the Rue de Lefevbre-Desnouettes.

2   J. Thackwell, *Military Memoirs of Lt Gen Sir Joseph Thackwell* (London, 1908), 77.

3   Ibid. 78. Also quoted in Siborne, *Waterloo Letters* (London, 1891), 126.

4   The regiment suffered fifty-six killed and ninety-nine wounded at Waterloo. Siborne, *Waterloo Letters*, 564.

5 Cavalie Mercer, *Journal of the Waterloo Campaign* (London, 1927), 174. Mercer, in fact, has left probably the best description of the French cavalry charges and of the effects of it both on his own men in his battery of Royal Horse Artillery and on the Allied army in general.

6 Siborne, *Waterloo Letters*, 14.

7 Ibid. 159. According to Siborne's *Waterloo Campaign*, Vivian, upon arrival at his new position, asked Lord Edward Somerset, 'Where is your brigade?' to which Somerset replied, 'Here', and pointed to a group of cavalrymen numbering no more than a squadron which represented all that was left of the two brigades of British heavy cavalry which, at the beginning of the battle, had numbered over 2,000. Siborne, *Waterloo Campaign*. (London, 1990), 334. There is some confusion as to who actually ordered Vivian and Vandeleur to move, with Evelyn Wood suggesting that the move was made on their own initiative. 'He [Vivian] hearing of the stress in the centre of Wellington's position, suggested to Vandeleur, his senior officer, that the two brigades should move westwards. Vandeleur declined to stir without orders; so Vivian decided to take his own brigade to the centre of the position, and had got near the Brussels-Genappe road, when he met Lord Uxbridge, who was coming to bring both brigades to support the infantry near La Haye Sainte.' Sir Evelyn Wood, *Cavalry in the Waterloo Campaign* (London, 1894), 176. In fact, this is exactly what did happen, with Vivian meeting Uxbridge on his way towards the centre. Vandeleur, however, would not move without orders and waited for Uxbridge to fetch him. Marquess of Anglesey, *One Leg* (London, 1961), 147.

8 Wood, Cavalry in the *Waterloo Campaign*, 179. It is quite possible that this order came from Sir Cohn Campbell, who brought an order from Wellington to halt. Siborne, *Waterloo Letters*, 163.

9 Ibid. 163–4.

10 Anglesey, *One Leg*, 149.

11 Wood, *Cavalry* in the *Waterloo Campaign*, 179–80.

12 Siborne, *Waterloo Letters*, 176.

13 Gleig, *The Light Dragoon* (London, 1844), 81–5.

14 Siborne, *Waterloo Letters*, 108. Tomkinson, of the 16th Light Dragoons, also mentions this close shave. 'The men were ordered to stop, not knowing in that light what force the enemy might have, and the brigade being scattered we halted and formed... On forming, we were told that a regiment of French cavalry was coming up in our rear, and that the men had a general inclination to charge them. We were moving for that purpose, but on approaching we found them to be one of our own regiments – the 1st Hussars KGL, the old regiment with which the 16th had for such a length of time been brigaded in Spain. Each happy to discover its error.' *Diary of a Cavalry Officer*, 313–4.

15 See Part Two, Chapter III, 'Wellington and his Cavalry: The Early Years', for an account of the Villar de Puerco fight.

CHAPTER XIII

Conclusion

Ninety-nine years were to pass before the British Army fought another battle on mainland Europe, with the first shots fired at Mons, coincidentally just a few miles from Waterloo. There were several campaigns fought in India, during which British cavalry, many of whom were armed with lances, served with distinction. However, in terms of the sort of battles which we have been studying in this book, there were no more. Many of the lessons learned between 1808 and 1815 were forgotten, and the British cavalry regiments simply returned to their bad old habits. 'On our return to English duty,' wrote William Tomkinson, 'we continue the old system, each regiment estimating its merit by the celerity of movement. I do not think one idea has been suggested since our return from service by the experience we there gained, and in five years we shall have all to commence again on going abroad.'[1] It is indeed sad that no lessons were heeded.

Although it did not fight again on mainland Europe until 1914, the British Army did, nevertheless, journey to the Crimea to take part in the ill-fated war against Russia where not only were the failings of the old British Army system exposed, but also those of the cavalry, its tactics and, in fact, its entire system. The purchase system certainly did not work here, and when the Light Brigade charged to glory and disaster at Balaclava, it did so with Lord Cardigan, one of the great examples of a flawed system, at its head. However, all of this was in the future, and the problems concerning the army in the Crimea are dealt with by many other works.

When the British Army returned home from its part in the occupation of Paris in 1818, the cavalry could reflect on some wonderful achievements during the war. What started out as a relatively inexperienced and very small cavalry force blossomed into a very accomplished one. But this was only achieved after the sorts of setbacks and victories featured in this book. As a fighting force the British cavalry was certainly one to be reckoned with, particularly after Campo Mayor, a pivotal action which set the tone of future battles between British and French cavalry. The cavalry also developed its skills at piquet, patrol and reconnaissance work, with

299

scores of anonymous cavalry officers carrying out the sort of work usually attributed only to the famous exploring officers like Grant, Cocks and Waters. Even on the field of battle, the British cavalry demonstrated its effectiveness and, despite the errors committed at Vimeiro and Talavera, neither of which proved to be crucial errors, battles such as Salamanca and Waterloo saw the cavalry in its most devastating mode, destroying huge elements of the enemy armies and making a massive contribution to these most vital victories. The one disappointing aspect of the cavalry's performance on the battlefield was its effectiveness in pursuit afterwards, with Vittoria and Orthes in particular standing out as prime examples. However, whilst the cavalry did fail to follow up Wellington's victory at Vittoria it should, nevertheless, be pointed out that here and at Orthes, the nature of the ground prevented effective pursuit. It is a point which is argued in the relevant chapters in this book. Furthermore, at the risk of seeming to be repetitive, the British cavalry suffered from a lack of an experienced, consistent commander, from poor cavalry country and from a lack of numbers. It is little wonder, therefore, that it did not achieve more between 1808 and 1815.

The reputation acquired by the British cavalry is well known and is best summed up by the sort of damning comments made by Wellington at various times both during the wars and after they had finally ended. I have already stressed and, hopefully, shown how, by various mis-adventures experienced first hand by Wellington, he grew to distrust his cavalry. However, this mistrust certainly appears to have had an adverse effect on the cavalry which can, perhaps, be demonstrated by the fact that many of the fine victories gained by the British cavalry were achieved in Wellington's absence. Many cavalry, and indeed, infantry, officers were often intimidated by his overpowering presence to the extent that Vandeleur, for example, at Waterloo, would not move without orders for fear of being placed under arrest. Little wonder, therefore, that cavalry officers in the presence of Wellington were frequently unable to execute such successful moves as those at Sahagun, Benavente, Usagre and Villagarcia. It would appear that, when the great man was absent, his subordinates were able to act without feeling as though somebody was breathing down their necks. This may seem to be a little harsh but it is certainly not wide of the mark. Successful cavalry actions achieved in Wellington's presence were very few and far between. Indeed, of Wellington's major battles, only Fuentes de Oñoro, Salamanca and Waterloo witnessed effective use of his cavalry, and even here we find the cavalry acting on Wellington's orders, at Salamanca, for example. Indeed, instances of Wellington's cavalry commanders acting in the sort of improvised manner, whilst under his personal command, that Colborne's infantry did at Waterloo, are very few and far between. They were simply paralysed by his presence and any unauthorised moves usually met with either arrest or a thunderous rebuke. Even such notables as Ramsay, McGrigor and Stewart were to feel his rasping tongue.

The cavalry's reputation has not been helped by the accounts of historians who, ever since 1815, have frequently damned them for their misadventures, drawing on such episodes as Campo Mayor, Maguilla, Vimeiro, Talavera and even Waterloo. It is hoped that this book, itself as much a reappraisal of the treatment of the cavalry as of their own actions, has demonstrated the failings of much of their research and the dangerous influence of Oman in particular, whose great work on the Peninsular War is unlikely to be surpassed but which work has proved highly damaging to the cavalry's reputation. Of all the great historians, only Sir John Fortescue would appear to have emerged with anything like an accurate assessment of their performance and, sadly, Fortescue is frequently overlooked as being a more general work on the British Army, rather than a specialised study of the Peninsular and Waterloo campaigns in the way that Oman, Napier and Siborne, for example, are. However, this is not the case. Indeed, Fortescue's version of the Peninsular War forms the very core of his monumental work and should be essential reading for all students and historians of the campaign. Sadly, Fortescue's conclusions have not become anywhere near as influential as those of either Oman or Napier.

Ultimately, I suspect that many of the arguments put forward in this book will fall upon deaf ears. It is often very difficult to fly in the face of history, and in this case it is not so much the bare facts that represent history but the manner in which these facts have been interpreted. We have seen how the respective views of two great historians, Oman and Fortescue, differed immensely on occasion, none more so than in their verdicts on Campo Mayor. As we have already seen, Oman's view damned the cavalry, following Wellington's remarks, whilst Fortescue followed up the commander-in-chief's words and his subsequent 'retraction'. Unfortunately for the British cavalry, it has been the views of Oman, the perceived historian of the Peninsular War, that have been followed and, after nearly a century of having had successive historians follow him, it is difficult to shake a belief so firmly held by so many. Nevertheless, Oman was writing a century after the Peninsular War had been fought and his views are, after all, only those of a historian, interpreting events as he saw them. It is almost a hundred years since his first volume was published, during which scores of eyewitness accounts have come to light, most of which he never read and many of which contain important accounts of the cavalry's actions. Hopefully, we are more informed today and if we can shake off the complacency of merely dipping into Oman whenever and wherever we seek information on the Peninsular War, we may be able to take a far more balanced view not only of the British cavalry but of the campaign in general.

Note

James Tomkinson (Ed), *The Diary of a Cavalry Officer in the Peninsular War and Waterloo Campaign, 1809–1815* (London, 1894).

Bibliography

The Peninsular and Waterloo campaigns produced a rich vein of memoirs and journals into which historians have been able to tap over the years. It is unfortunate, however, in terms of this particular book, that the vast majority of these memoirs have come from the infantry regiments. Indeed, published accounts by cavalrymen are by comparison very few and far between. There are, of course, several good unpublished accounts by cavalrymen but, again, there is an even greater number by infantrymen. Given the ratio of infantry to cavalry, however, we should not be too unduly surprised by the anomaly. Many of the factors examined in this book go some way to explaining the situation, e.g. far fewer cavalry than infantry and less exposure to action, particularly in the period towards the end of 1813 and the beginning of 1814, when the war in the Peninsula was predominantly an infantry one. The situation improves a great deal when we come to study the Waterloo campaign, largely due to the efforts of William Siborne and his son, Herbert, who between them gathered and published the now famous *Waterloo Letters*, a collection of letters written by surviving officers of the British Army who had served in the campaign. The letters have since attracted criticism from some historians, not for their accuracy but for the fact that there are no letters by any of the officers who served with a non-British regiment. However, as long as we appreciate this and the fact that the British Army formed only a third of the Allied army at Waterloo, then I see no problem. In the study of British cavalry, which is the purpose of my own use of the *Waterloo Letters*, this poses no problem whatsoever. In fact it is a benefit, for we have no real need for any letters by Dutch, Belgian or Hanoverian cavalrymen. Instead, we are able to draw on the experiences of officers from every single regiment that fought at Waterloo.

In spite of the relative lack of cavalry memoirs, the Peninsular War is well documented in the pages of some very good memoirs and journals. The most famous, and probably the best, is almost certainly Tomkinson's *Diary of a Cavalry Officer*, which covers the period 1809 to 1815. Tomkinson served in the 16th Light Dragoons and witnessed the majority of the great events of the war and, later on, the Waterloo camp The 16th were one of the most consistent and best cavalry regiments in the army and as a result we have the benefit of many vivid descriptions and astute observations. Other good memoirs include Gordon's *The Cavalry in the Corunna Campaign*, Bragge's *Peninsular Portrait*, Hawker's *Journal of the Campaign of 1809*, Vivian's *Memoir and Letters*, Hay's *Reminiscences under Wellington* and Tale's *Jotting's from my Sabretache*. This rare last volume affords a wonderful insight into the life of a cavalry regiment at home and abroad. Unfortunately, none of these memoirs covers the entire period of the war, which highlights the problem of too few cavalry memoirs. Instead, we must piece them all together like a puzzle until we have a complete documentation of the years between 1808 and 1814. There have been numerous letters and diaries published in the Journal for Army Historical Research, including Verner's *Reminiscences* and Carnock's *Cavalry in the Corunna Campaign*, whilst Hall's *Letters* and Madden's *Diary* have been likewise published in the Royal United Services Institute Journal.

There are other good cavalry memoirs, including two works by Gleig. The first, *The Light Dragoon*, is an account of the service of George Farmer, of the 11th Light Dragoons. Farmer was taken prisoner during the capture of Captain Lutyens' piquet at Jeromenha in 1811. Although devoid of good action, until the Waterloo campaign, it provides useful background information and illustrates some of the problems faced by the light cavalry in the Peninsula. Gleig's other work, *The Hussar*, recalls the service of Norbeit Landsheit, of the 20th Light Dragoons. This two-volume work includes a good account of the infamous charge of the 20th Light Dragoons at Vimeiro. Maxwell's *Peninsular Sketches* includes a superb little chapter entitled 'The British Cavalry on the Peninsula'. Recently reprinted as a stand-alone book, the account was written by an officer of the 1st (Royal) Dragoons. It is a mine of information and includes several important comments on the performance of the cavalry. Amongst other memoirs are James' *Journal*, Luard's *Scarlet Lancer*, and Thackwell's *Memoirs*, whilst Julia Page's *Intelligence Officer in the Peninsula* covers the life, letters and diaries of Edward Charles Cocks, one of Wellington's so-called 'exploring officers', whose potentially great career came to an untimely end at Burgos in 1812. Cocks left extensive notes on the duties of cavalry in respect of patrol and piquet work and is a valuable addition to Peninsular War literature and to the study of Wellington's cavalry. There are many memoirs written by infantrymen containing pertinent observations on the British cavalry, but there are far too many to mention here. Certainly, Siborne's *Waterloo Letters* contains letters by infantry officers who saw the great charge of the heavy cavalry at Waterloo.

One of the most important sources for study of the cavalry in the Peninsula is the two-volume set, *Memoirs and Correspondence of Field Marshal Viscount Combermere*, published in 1866. Combermere, or Sir Stapleton Cotton as he was during the Peninsular War, commanded the cavalry for the greater part of the war and these two volumes are in many ways as vital as Wellington's own *Despatches* and *Supplementary Despatches*, which are of equal importance and which contain many letters and reports relative to the conduct and organisation of the British cavalry both in the Peninsula and at Waterloo. As you would expect, senior cavalry commanders have left their own accounts of the war and these include Henry, Lord Paget, whose exploits are recalled in the Marquess of Anglesey's *One Leg*, and John Gaspard Le Marchant's *Memoirs*. Le Marchant, in fact, is the subject of another biography, *Scientific Soldier*, by Thoumine. Other important volumes include *Peninsular Cavalry General*, which contains the letters of Robert Ballard Long, one of the more colourful characters in the Peninsula, as we have already seen. The correspondence between himself and Beresford and, subsequently, his nephew and Beresford, formed the basis of the infamous *Strictures* and *Further Strictures*, being the various arguments and counter-arguments relating to the conduct of Beresford's campaign in Estremadura. The background to the pamphlet war is very tiresome and is too long to examine here. Suffice it to say that, fuelled by Napier's *History of the War in the Peninsula*, another important work, the various disputants got stuck into each other with a ferocity the likes of which was only bettered on the field of battle. The letters and various volumes of *Strictures*, which first appeared in the 1830s, have since been reprinted and are essential for any study of the war in the south.

The two great histories of the Peninsular War are Oman's *History of the Peninsular War* and Napier's *History of the War in the Peninsula*. The former work, which is unlikely to be surpassed, is the source of a great deal of mythology relating to the performance of the British cavalry in the Peninsula. Indeed, many instances of Oman's ill-founded analysis have been highlighted in this volume, particularly of the events at Campo Mayor. Contrasting with this is Fortescue's *History of the British Army*, at the core of which are several volumes which deal with the war in Spain and Portugal. Fortescue, perhaps enjoying the benefit of much wider research into the army, comes to a far more balanced view of the cavalry. In fact, his analysis of several cavalry actions in the Peninsula differs so radically from Oman's that, at times, one is left wondering whether the two great historians are in fact writing about the same action. My own view, of course, takes the Fortescue line rather than Oman's, whose analysis is often flawed, as demonstrated with Campo Mayor where he goes no further than Wellington's censure to the 13th Light Dragoons. Fortescue, on the other hand, takes the story a step further and ends with Wellington's remark that he would not have issued the censure had he been aware of the full facts, this after having received a full account of the action from the 13th's officers. Sadly, Oman's account invariably finds favour with historians and thus the reputation of the cavalry is further blackened. In fact, it was on the basis of much ill-founded analysis that I was moved to write this account of the cavalry between 1808 and 1815. Of course, the performance of the British cavalry is not the only area in which Fortescue and Oman differed, but it is the one which has had the greatest effect on any particular aspect of the army.

The work and performance of the British light cavalry between 1808 and 1815 is the subject of a marvellous little book by the late John Pirnlott. Published in 1977, *British Light Cavalry* examines the role of the light cavalry including their tactics, the problems they faced, and their performance on piquet duties, reconnaissance work and as skirmishers. The book is sadly all too short and, at forty-eight pages, of which ten are colour illustrations, is a long essay rather than a serious study. However, as a short and accurate view of Wellington's light cavalry it is an excellent introduction to the subject. It is a pity the author chose not to examine the heavy cavalry, but in spite of this it is a book well worth reading. Other shorter works on the British cavalry include Bryan Fosten's *Wellington's Heavy Cavalry* and *Wellington's Light Cavalry*, Philip Haythornthwaite's *British Cavalryman, 1793-1815*, and John Mollo's *Waterloo Uniforms: British Cavalry*. John Mollo is also the author of *The Prince's Dolls*, a book which captures the flavour of the British hussar regiments during the Regency period. Another, much larger book, covering the equipment of Wellington's cavalry, is Tylden's *Horses and Saddlery*, an excellent work on the types of horses and saddles used by the British Army, not only in the Peninsula but in many other campaigns.

The two most important official cavalry manuals were the *Instructions and Regulations for the Formations and Movements of the Cavalry* and *The Rules and Regulations for the Sword Exercise of the Cavalry*, both of which appeared in 1796 with subsequent revised editions. It was laid down that every cavalry officer in the army should avail himself of these most important works. There were many more private publications which dealt with the theory of cavalry formations, most of which were based either upon the respective author's own experience or on the official regulations with suitable additions and 'improvements', again usually born out of experience. Wellington's

Despatches and *Supplementary Despatches* have already been mentioned, but one further work is of great use when dealing with the army, being the *General Orders*, which were compiled between 1809 and 1815. These orders contain numerous references to the cavalry in relation to organisation, equipment and operational matters.

Finally, we have the various regimental histories. Fortunately, the histories of the British cavalry regiments are among the finest of all regimental histories. When one considers just how much information and detail is contained within them they certainly make up for the apparent lack of cavalry memoirs. In fact, many of the regimental histories contain extensive passages from the letters and diaries of cavalry officers and men who served either in the Peninsula or at Waterloo. Among the finest are those by Atkinson, Barrett, Wylly and Hamilton.

I have not made a great effort to seek out the numerous unpublished accounts written by British cavalrymen, which I know exist in various institutions and in private hands, as this book is not intended to be a blow-by-blow account of the cavalry's doings between 1808 and 1815. I must stress that this is a reappraisal and, therefore, much use is made of secondary sources, such as Oman and Fortescue, as this book is as much a reappraisal of their respective treatment of the British cavalry as is of the cavalry themselves. After all, I believe it is largely from such secondary sources that the reputation of the cavalry has emanated.

Anglesey, Marquess of, *One Leg: The Life and Letters of Henry William Paget, First Marquess of Anglesey* (London, 1961).

Atkinson, C.T. History of the Royal Dragoons, 1661–1934 (Glasgow, 1935).

Barnett, Correlli. *Britain and Her Army*, 1509–1970 (London, 1970).

Barratt, C.R.B. *History of the 13th Hussars* (London, 1911).

Beamish, N Ludlow. *The King's German Legion* (London, 1832).

Bisset, Sir John. *Memoranda and Observations regarding The Duties of the Commnissariat on Field Service Abroad* (London, 1846).

Brett-James, Anthony. *Life in Wellington's Army* (London, 1972).

Cassels, S.A.C (Ed). *Peninsular Portrait, 1811-1814: the letters of Captain William Bragge, Third (King's Own) Dragoons* (London, 1963).

Chandler, David. *The Hundred Days* (London, 1980).

Combermere, Mary, Countess, and Capt. W.W. Knollys. *Memoirs and Correspondence of Field Marshal Viscount Combermere* (London, 1866).

Coss, Ed. 'The Misadventures of Wellington's Cavalry from the Peninsula to Waterloo', *A.F.W.C. Journal*, X, No.1, April 1988.

Cotton, Edward, *A Voice from Waterloo* (6th Edition, London, 1862.).

The Courier, 20th April 1811.

Curling, Henry (Ed), *Recollections of Rifleman Harris* (London, 1929); 53–4. Jonathan Leach, author *of Rough Sketches of the Life of an Old Soldier* (London, 1831).

Dickson, Alexander. *The Dickson Manuscripts* (Woolwich, 1905).

Dyneley, Thomas. *Letters written whilst on Active Service* (Cambridge, 1984).

Eliot-Wright. 'British and French Cavalry 1808–1814 in *Age of Napoleon*, Nos 11 and 12.

Fletcher, Ian. *Gentlemen's Sons: The Foot Guards in the Peninsula and at Waterloo, 1808-1815* (Tunbridge Wells, 1992).

Fletcher, Ian. *In Hell Before Daylight: The Siege and Storming of the Castle of Badajoz*

(Staplehurst, 1994, 2nd edition).

Fletcher, Jan (Ed). *For King and Country: The Letters and Diaries of John Mills, Coldstream Guards, 1811-14* (Staplehurst, 1995).

Fortescue, Hon. J.W. *History of the British Army* (London, 1899).

Fosten, Bryan. *Wellington's Heavy Cavalry* (London, 1982)

Fosten, Bryan. *Wellington's Light Cavalry* (London, 1982).

Fraser, W. *Words on Wellington* (London, 1902).

Further Strictures which relate to Colonel Napier's History of the War in the Peninsula (London, 1832).

Fytzwygram, Lt. Col. *Lectures on Horses and Stabling* (London, 1862).

Gleig, George. *The Light Dragoon* (London, 1844).

Gleig, George. *The Hussar* (London, 1837).

Glover, Michael. *Wellington as Military Commander* (London, 1968).

Glover, Michael. *Wellington's Army in the Peninsula, 1808–1814* (Newton Abbot, 1977).

Glover, Richard. *Peninsular Preparation: The Reform of the British Army, 1795-1809* (Cambridge, 1988).

Gordon, Captain A. *A Cavalry Officer in the Corunna Campaign* (London, 1913).

Gray, Ernest *The Trumpet of Glory: The Military career of John Shipp, first veterinary surgeon to join the British Army* (London, 1985).

Gurwood, J. *The Despatches of Field Marshal the Duke of Wellington during his various campaigns* (London, 1832).

Gurwood, J. *The General Orders of Field Marshal the Duke of Wellington in Portugal, Spain and France, from 1809 to 1814, in the Low Countries and France, in 1815, and in France, Army of Occupation, from 1816 to 1818* (London, 1837).

Hamilton, Col. H.B. *Historical Record of the 14th (King's) Hussars* (London, 1901).

Hamilton-Williams, D. *Waterloo: New Perspectives* (London, 1993). Hartley, Corporal Andrew. MSS Journal.

Haswell, Jock. *The First Respectable Spy: the life and times of Colquhoun Grant, Wellington's head of intelligence*, (London, 1969).

Hawker, Col. P. *Journal of a Regimental Officer* (London, 1811).

Haythornthwajte, Philip. *British Cavalryman, 1792–1815* (London, 1994).

Haythornthwajte, Philip. *The Armies of Wellington* (London, 1996).

Instructions and Regulations for the Formations and Movements of the Cavalry (London, 1796).

Jones, Sir J.T. *Journal of the Sieges carried on by the Army under the Duke of Wellington in Spain between the Years 1811 and 1814, etc* (London, 1846).

Journal of the Royal United Services Institution, 'The Diary of Lieutenant Charles Dudley Madden, 4th Dragoons, 1809–1811', 1914, LVIII.

Larpent, Sir George (Ed). *The Private Journal of F. Seymour Larpent, Judge-Advocate General attached to the Headquarters of Lord Wellington during the Peninsular War, from 1812 to its close* (London, 1853).

Le Marchartt, Denis. *Memoirs of the late Major General Le Marchant* (London, 1841).

Longford, Elizabeth. The Years of the Sword (London, 1969).

Low, E.B. *With Napoleon at Waterloo* (London, 1911).

Ludovici, Anthony (Ed), *On the Road with Wellington: The Diary of a war commissary in the Peninsular Campaigns*, by August Ludolf Friedrich Schaumann (London, 1924).

McGuffie, T.H (Ed). *Peninsular Cavalry General (1811–13): The Correspondence of Lieutenant-General Robert Ballard Long* (London,1951).

Mackinnon, Daniel. *Origin and History of the Coldstream Guards* (London, 1837).

Malet, Col. Harold. *The Historical Memoirs of the 18th Hussars (Prince of Wales's Own)* (London, 1907).

Mann, Michael. *And They Rode On* (London, 1984).

Maxwell, Sir Herbert. *The Life of Wellington, The Restoration of the Martial Power of Great Britain* (London, 1899).

Maxwell, H. *The Creevey Papers* (London, 1903).

Mercer, Cavalie. *Journal of the Waterloo Campaign* (London, 1927).

Mollo, John. *Prince's Dolls: Scandals, Skirmishes and Splendours of the Hussars, 1793-1815* (London, 1997).

Moore-Smith, G.C. *The Life of John Colborne, Field Marshal Lord Seaton* (London, 1903).

Muir, Rory. *Tactics and the Experience in the Age of Napoleon* (London, 1998).

Müffling, Carl von. *Passages from my Life* (London, 1853).

Napier, William *History of the War in the Peninsula* (London, 1828)

Neale, Dr Adam. *Letters from Portugal and Spain* (London, 1809).

Nosworthy, Brent. *Battle Tactics of Napoleon and his Enemies* (London, 1995).

Oman, Sir Charles. *History of the Peninsular War* (Oxford, 1902).

Oman, Sir Charles. *Wellington's Army, 1809–14* (London, 1913).

Page, Julia (Ed). *An Intelligence Officer in the Peninsula: the letters and Diaries of Major the Hon. Edward Charles Cocks, 1786–1812* (Tunbridge Wells, 1984).

Pimlott, John. *British Light Cavalry* (London, 1977).

Rathbone, Julian. *Wellington's War* (London, 1984).

Robson, Brian. *Swords of the British Army: The Regulation Patterns 1788 to 1914* (London, 1996).

Rogers, H.C.B. *Wellington's Army* (London, 1979).

Rousseau, I.J. (Ed), *The Peninsular Journal of Major-General Sir Benjamin D'Urban, 1808-1817* (London, 1930).

The Royal Military Chronicle, 'British Cavalry', October 1811.

Rules and Regulations for the Sword Exercise of the Cavalry (London, 1796).

Saunders, D. and Paget, J. *Hougoumont: The Key to Victory at Waterloo* (London, 1992).

Shipp, John. *Cases in Farriery, in which the Diseases of Horses are treated on the principles of the Veterinary School of Medicine* (Leeds, 1808).

Siborne, H.T. *Waterloo Letters* (London, 1891

Siborne, W. *History of the Waterloo Campaign* (London, 1990).

Standing Orders as given out and enforced by the late Major General Robert Craufurd for the use of the Light Division during the years 1809, 1810 and 1811 (Corfu, 1837, and various subsequent editions).

Stanhope, Philip Henry, 5th Earl. *Notes of Conversations with the Duke of Wellington, 1831–1851* (London, 1888).

Stewart, P.F. *History of the 12th Lancers* (London, 1950).

Sulivan, George James. *The Peninsular War Memoirs of Lieutenant George James Sulivan, lst Regiment of Life Guards, 1812–14*, MSS, Private Collection.

Tale, William. *Jottings from My Sabretache* (London, 1847).

Thackwell, J. *The Military Memoirs of Lieut.-General Sir Joseph Thackwell* (London, 1908).

The Trial of Colonel Quentin, of the Tenth or Prince of Wales's Own Regiment of Hussars (London, 1814).

The Trial at Large of Lieut. Gen. Whitelocke, late commander of the Forces in South America

(London, 1808).

Tomkinson, James (Ed). *The Diary of a Cavalry Officer in the Peninsular War and Waterloo Campaign, 1809–1815* (London, 1895).

Tylden's, Major G. *Horses and Saddlery: An account of the animals used by the British and Commonwealth Armies from the Seventeenth Century to the Present Day with a description of their Equipment* (London, 1965).

The United Service Journal, 'A Hussar's Life on Service' (London, 1829).

Vansittart, J (Ed). *Surgeon James's Journal* (London, 1964).

Verner, Ruth (Ed). 'Reminiscences of William Verner, 7th Hussars', *Journal of the Society for Army Historical Research*, Special Publication No.8 (London, 1965).

Vivian, The Hon. C. (Ed). *Richard Hussey Vivian, 1st Baron Vivian, a Memoir* (London, 1897).

Ward, S.G.P. 'The Quartermaster-General's Department in the Peninsula, 1809–1814', *Journal for Army Historical Research* (London, 1945), XXIII.

Warre, Reverend Edmund. *Letters from the Peninsula, 1808-1812* (Staplehurst, 1999).

Weller, Jack. *Wellington in the Peninsula* (London, 1962).

Weller, Jack. *Wellington at Waterloo* (London, 1967).

Wellington, 2nd Duke of (Ed). *Supplementary Despatches, Correspondence and Memoranda of Field Marshal the Duke of Wellington* (London, 1860).

Williams, Captain G.T. *The Historical Records of the Eleventh Hussars Prince Albert's Own* (London, 1908).

Woodberry, Lieutenant George. Manuscript Journal of the 1813 Campaign

Wood, Sir Evelyn. *Cavalry in the Waterloo Campaign* (London, 1895).

Wrottesley, G. *Life and Correspondence of Field Marshal Sir John Burgoyne* (London, 1873).

APPENDIX

Cavalry Organisation in the Peninsula

The following appendix, save for the 1808 segment, was written by C.T. Atkinson and appeared in Oman's *Wellington's Army, 2809–14*. It is reproduced with kind permission of Lionel Leventhal and Greenhill Books.

1808

When Sir Arthur Wellesley landed in Portugal in August 1808 he had under his command just the 240-strong contingent of the 20th Light Dragoons which, for obvious reasons, does not constitute any serious cavalry force. However, when Sir John Moore embarked upon his Corunna campaign his force consisted of the Hussar brigade under Henry, Lord Paget, consisting of the 7th Hussars, 10th Hussars, 15th Hussars and 18th Hussars, plus the 3rd Hussars KGL.

1809
G.O.C. Cotton

14th Light Dragoons, 16th Light Dragoons, 2 squadrons 20th Light Dragoons, detachment 3rd Hussars KGL.
Fane's Brigade; 3rd Dragoon Guards, 4th Dragoons.

Order as of June 18th
G.O.C. Payne

A [*Fane*] Dragoon Guards, 4th Dragoons.
B [*Cotton*] 14th Light Dragoons, 16th Light Dragoons.
Unattached: 2 squadrons 20th Light Dragoons, 23rd Light Dragoons, 1st Hussars KGL, detachment of 3rd Hussars KGL.

Subsequent changes;
20th Light Dragoons and the detachment of the 3rd Hussars KGL left the Peninsula before the end of July. By June 21st a new brigade C was added, under G Anson, composed of 23rd Light Dragoons and 1st Hussars KGL. On November 1st the 1st (Royal) Dragoons (who arrived at Lisbon in October) replaced the 16th Light Dragoons in B, now under Slade, as Cotton was assisting Payne in command of the division. 16th

311

Light Dragoons were transferred to C vice 23rd Light Dragoons who were ordered home after their losses at Talavera.

1810
G.O.C. Payne; Cotton 2nd in command

A [*Fane*] 3rd Dragoon Guards, 4th Dragoons.
B [*Slade*] 1st (Royal) Dragoons, 14th Light Dragoons.
C [*G Anson*]; 16th Light Dragoons, 1st Hussars KGL.

Subsequent changes;
Payne went home before June 1st, Cotton obtaining sole command from June 3rd. On April 1st the 13th Light Dragoons arrived at Lisbon, joining the army in May, and being attached to Hill's division, along with four regiments of Portuguese cavalry, the whole under Fane, who gave over his brigade to De Grey from May 13th. Two troops of the regiment went to Cadiz, but rejoined the regiment in September. Before the end of the year Fane seems to have gone home ill.

1811
G.O.C. Cotton

A [*De Grey*]; 3rd Dragoon Guards, 4th Dragoons.
B [*Slade*] 1st (Royal) Dragoons, 14th Light Dragoons.
C [*G Anson*]; 16th Light Dragoons, 1st Hussars KGL.
Unbrigaded; 13th Light Dragoons

Subsequent changes;
Cotton went home on January 15th, returning on April 22nd. Slade commanded in his absence until March 7th, when Erskine seems to have been placed in command of both the cavalry and the Light Division. While Slade had command of the cavalry division, his brigade was apparently under the command of Hawker, of the 14th Light Dragoons, and from March 1st to May 15th, G. Anson, being absent, Arentschildt, of the 1st Hussars KGL, commanded C. On March 19th, Long was posted to command Hill's cavalry, although Beresford commanded the whole in Hill's absence. At Albuera, Lumley was given command of Beresford's cavalry. (Long's conduct not having been given satisfaction to the Marshal.) On May 11th Erskine was appointed to command 'the cavalry south of the Tagus.' On June 13th, a new brigade, D, was formed under Long, composed of the 13th Light Dragoons and 2nd Hussars KGL, two squadrons of which had landed on April 8th. On June 18th the 11th Light Dragoons (who had arrived on June 1st) replaced the 13th, transferred to Slade's brigade. On June 19th a reorganisation of the cavalry in two divisions was ordered;

1st Cavalry Division G.O.C. Cotton
B [*Slade*] 1st (Royal) Dragoons, 13th Light Dragoons, 14th Light Dragoons.
C [*Anson*] 16th Light Dragoons, 1st Hussars KGL.
unbrigaded; Madden's Portuguese.

2nd Cavalry Division G.O.C. Erskine
A [*de Grey*]; 3rd Dragoon Guards, 4th Dragoons.
D [*Long*] 11th Light Dragoons, 1st Hussars KGL.

On July 19th another reorganisation took place, the final result being;

1st Cavalry Division G.O.C. Cotton
B [*Slade*] 1st (Royal) Dragoons, 12th Light Dragoons (arrived July 1st), *vice* 13th (to C) and 14th (to D)
C [*G Anson*]; 13th Light Dragoons, 16th Light Dragoons.
E [*7 Alten, a new brigade*]; 11th Light Dragoons (from D) 1st Hussars KGL (from C). unbrigaded; Madden's Portuguese

2nd Cavalry Division
A [*De Grey*]; 3rd Dragoon Guards, 4th Dragoons.
D [*Long*] 14th Light Dragoons, 2nd Hussars KGL.

On August 1st, the 9th Light Dragoons (newly arrived) were posted to Long's brigade, together with the 13th Light Dragoons, which exchanged from C with the 14th. On August 30th a new brigade, F, was added, comprising the 4th Dragoon Guards (arrived August 15th), and the 3rd Dragoons (arrived before August 20th), its commander being Le Marchant. By October 1st, the 5th Dragoon Guards had been added to this brigade. On October 5th, De Grey's brigade was transferred to the 1st Cavalry Division, to which Le Marchant's was attached by Orders of November 8th, the Portuguese brigade being struck off from that division. From December 8th onwards, the Morning States do not give any G.O.C. for the 2nd Cavalry Division.

1812
1st Cavalry Division G.O.C. Cotton

B [*Slade*] 1st (Royal) Dragoons, 12th Light Dragoons.
C [*no G.O.C., G Anson absent*]; 14th Light Dragoons, 16th Light Dragoons.
E [*Cuming 11th Light Dragoons, in V Alten's absence*]; 11th Light Dragoons, 1st Hussars KGL.
A [*no G.O.C., D Grey absent*]; 3rd Dragoon Guards, 4th Dragoons.
F [*Le Marchant*]; 5th Dragoon Guards, 3rd Dragoons.

2nd Cavalry Division [No G.O.C.]

D [*Long*] 9th Light Dragoons, 13th Light Dragoons, 2nd Hussars KGL.

Subsequent changes;
On January 1st the 1st and 2nd Dragoons KGL, under Bock, arrived at Lisbon. They remained near there until March 12th, joining the army at Estremoz on March 23rd, and were designated as the 2nd Brigade (G) of the 2nd Cavalry Division. By January 8th Victor Alten was again in command of his brigade. Several changes took place under

orders issued January 29th; the 3rd Dragoon Guards and 4th Dragoon Guards were posted to Slade's brigade, from which the 12th Light Dragoons were removed to G. Anson's brigade, the 4th Dragoons replaced the 4th Dragoon Guards in Le Marchant's brigade, and De Grey's brigade disappeared. F. Ponsonby of the 12th Light Dragoons took command of C in Anson's absence. By April 8th Erskine had resumed command of the 2nd Cavalry Division, to which Slade's brigade was transferred on April 14th, Bock's joining the 1st Cavalry Division. On July 1st, an exchange was ordered between the 11th Light Dragoons and the 14th Light Dragoons. G. Anson, who had resumed command of his brigade, having the 11th Light Dragoons, 12th Light Dragoons and 16th Light Dragoons, Victor Alten the 14th Light Dragoons and 1st Hussars KGL. At Salamanca, Cotton was wounded and Le Marchant killed. While Cotton was disabled, Bock commanded the cavalry, de Jonquieres having his brigade. W. Ponsonby, of the 5th Dragoon Guards, succeeded to Le Marchant's brigade (by orders of July 23rd). Cotton rejoined before October 15th, but had to go home again in December invalided. From August 1st Victor Alten was absent, but rejoined by the middle of September. Bu orders of September 17th, the 2nd Hussars KGL were transferred to Victor Alten's brigade.

1813
1st Cavalry Division. No G.O.C. (Cotton absent)

F [*F. Ponsonby*]; 5th Dragoon Guards, 3rd and 4th Dragoon.
C [*G Anson*]; 11th Light Dragoons, 12th Light Dragoons, 16th Light Dragoons.
E [*V Alten*]; 14th Light Dragoons, 1st Hussars KGL, 2nd Hussars KGL.
G [*Bock*] 1st Dragoons KGL, 2nd Dragoons KGL.

2nd Cavalry Division No G.O.C.

B [*Slade*] *3rd Dragoon Guards, 4th Dragoon Guards, 1st (Royal) Dragoons.*
D [*Long*] 9th Light Dragoons, 13th Light Dragoons.

Subsequent changes;
By January 25th a new brigade (H) was added composed of two squadrons each of the 1st Life Guards, 2nd Life Guards and Royal Horse Guards. O'Loghlin had apparently been appointed to command it, but by orders of November 28th 1812, F.S. Rebow was appointed to command it in his place. It ranked as 3rd Brigade, 2nd Cavalry Division, but was transferred to the 1st Cavalry Division on February 5th. In March it was under the command of Sir R. Hill, Rebow having gone home. Orders of March 13th directed the distribution among the regiments remaining in the Peninsula of the horses of the 4th Dragoon Guards, the 9th Light Dragoons, the 11th Light Dragoons and the 2nd Hussars KGL, these regiments returning home. Their place was taken by a new brigade (I), under Colquhoun Grant, of the 15th Hussars, composed of the 10th, 15th and 18th Hussars. This first appears in the States on April 15th. Orders were issued on April 21st for the amalgamation of the two cavalry divisions, under the command of Cotton. However, he did not rejoin until June 25th and in his absence Bock appears to have commanded the cavalry, his brigade being under Bülow. On May 20th, Fane,

appointed a major-general on the staff on April 24th, was given command of B *vice* Slade, who had been ordered home on April 23rd. On July 2nd, orders were issued to transfer the horses of the 18th Hussars to V. Alten's brigade, *vice* the 14th Light Dragoons who moved to Long's brigade, which had been reduced to one regiment by the departure of the 9th Light Dragoons (out of the States by April 4th). Lord E. Somerset at the same time was given command of the Hussar brigade *vice* Grant, and Vandeleur command of C *vice* G. Anson, who was removed to the Home Staff. On September 6th Grant was appointed to take over Long's brigade, Long having apparently gone home before the battles of the Pyrenees, as his name was not among the commanders of cavalry brigades thanked by Parliament on November 8th for those operations. On November 24th Hussey Vivian was appointed to take Grant's place. The 7th Hussars arrived in Spain in September, and were added to the Hussar brigade. They would seem to have been with the brigade by October 21st but were not in Orders until November 24th. In October O'Loghlin seems to have taken over the Household Brigade, he had been placed on the Staff on June 17th.

1814
Cavalry G.O.C. Cotton

I [*O'Loghlin*] 1st Life Guards, 2nd Life Guards, Royal Horse Guards.
F [*F Ponsonby*]; 5th Dragoon Guards, 3rd Dragoons, 4th Dragoons.
C [*Vandeleur*]; 12th Light Dragoons, 16th Light Dragoons.
D [*Vivian*] 13th Light Dragoons, 14th Light Dragoons.
E [*V. Alten*] ; 18th Hussars, 1st Hussars KGL.
C [*Bock*] 1st Dragoons KGL, 2nd Dragoons KGL.
B [*Fane*] 3rd Dragoon Guards, 1st (Royal) Dragoons.
H [*Somerset*]; 7th Hussars, 10th Hussars, 15th Hussars.

Subsequent changes;

By January 16th several changes had taken place. Victor Alien had gone and Vivian had been transferred to his brigade, Fane having been transferred from B to D (late Vivian's). Bock also went (he was drowned off the coast of Brittany in February) about the same time. From January 25th W. Ponsonby was absent, Lord C. Manners of the 3rd Dragoons commanding his brigade. By March 25th Arentschildt (of 1st Hussars KGL) had been given Bock's old brigade, On Vivian being wounded (April 8th) Arentschildt was transferred to E, and Bülow got the 'German Heavy Brigade.' Fane's name appears in the States both as commanding B and D. According to Hamilton's Regimental History of the 14th Hussars, he commanded both, working them practically as a division, the brigades being respectively commanded by Clifton of the Royals (B) and Doherty of the 13th Light Dragoons (D).

Index